# Many Faces of the Caucasus

Studies of the Caucasus in the West have been dominated by issues of security and ethnic conflict based on Eurocentric theoretical paradigms. By contrast, this volume offers contributions from researchers working within a range of disciplines, including history, social anthropology, sociology and cultural studies as well as international relations and security studies. Some of the contributions demonstrate in-depth knowledge of the region from 'inside', while others explore the issues within a wider Eurasian and global perspective. The volume examines the politically-defined division of the region into the North and South Caucasus, the evolution of national identity and citizenship, and the role of the NGOs in the development of civil society in the post-Soviet period. Its content demonstrates the advantages of an area studies inter-disciplinary approach to the study of the region and the importance of collaboration between Western and local researchers. It highlights the importance of the Caucasus as a geographical, political and civilisational entity and examines the historical, cultural, political, religious and psychological factors behind the region's particular susceptibility to territorial and ethno-religious conflict. The book will be of benefit to scholars and students researching the Caucasus, Russia and the post-Soviet space. It will also appeal to policy-makers, NGO activists, journalists and a wider audience interested in this fascinating region.

This book was published as a special issue of *Europe-Asia Studies*.

**Nino Kemoklidze** is a PhD candidate at the University of Birmingham. Her dissertation topic concerns problems of nationalism and ethnic violence in Georgia.

**Cerwyn Moore** is a Senior Lecturer in International Relations at the University of Birmingham. He works on interpretive IR theory and conflict in the Caucasus and Central Asia.

**Jeremy Smith** is Professor of Russian History and Politics at the Karelian Institute, University of Eastern Finland. He has recently completed projects on the Khrushchev era and on Georgian nationalism and Soviet power in the 1950s.

**Galina Yemelianova** is a Senior Lecturer in Eurasian Studies at the University of Birmingham. She heads the University of Birmingham Research Group on the Caucasus and Central Asia and teaches an MSc Pathway on the Caucasus and Central Asia.

# Routledge Europe-Asia Studies Series
*A series edited by Terry Cox*
*University of Glasgow*

The **Routledge Europe-Asia Studies Series** focuses on the history and current political, social and economic affairs of the countries of the former 'communist bloc' of the Soviet Union, Eastern Europe and Asia. As well as providing contemporary analyses it explores the economic, political and social transformation of these countries and the changing character of their relationships with the rest of Europe and Asia.

**Challenging Communism in Eastern Europe**
1956 and its Legacy
*Edited by Terry Cox*

**Globalisation, Freedom and the Media after Communism**
The Past as Future
*Edited by Birgit Beumers, Stephen Hutchings and Natalia Rulyova*

**Power and Policy in Putin's Russia**
*Edited by Richard Sakwa*

**1948 and 1968 – Dramatic Milestones in Czech and Slovak History**
*Edited by Laura Cashman*

**Perceptions of the European Union in New Member States**
A Comparative Perspective
*Edited by Gabriella Ilonszki*

**Symbolism and Power in Central Asia**
Politics of the Spectacular
*Edited by Sally N. Cummings*

**The European Union, Russia and the Shared Neighbourhood**
*Edited by Jackie Gower and Graham Timmins*

**Russian Regional Politics under Putin and Medvedev**
*Edited by Cameron Ross*

**Russia's Authoritarian Elections**
*Edited by Stephen White*

**Elites and Identities in Post-Soviet Space**
*Edited by David Lane*

**EU Conditionality in the Western Balkans**
*Edited by Florian Bieber*

**Reflections on 1989 in Eastern Europe**
*Edited by Terry Cox*

**Russia and the World**
The Internal-External Nexus
*Edited by Natasha Kuhrt*

**Civil Society and Social Capital in Post-Communist Eastern Europe**
*Edited by Terry Cox*

**New Media in New Europe-Asia**
*Edited by Vlad Strukov, Jeremy Morris and Natalya Rulyova*

**Many Faces of the Caucasus**
*Edited by Nino Nino Kemoklidze, Cerwyn Moore, Jeremy Smith and Galina Yemelianova*

**Explaining Policy Change in the European Union's Eastern Neighbourhood**
*Edited by Julia Langbein and Tanja A. Börzel*

**Transition Economies after 2008**
Responses to the Crisis in Russia and Eastern Europe
*Edited by Martin Myant and Jan Drahokoupil*

# Many Faces of the Caucasus

*Edited by*
Nino Kemoklidze, Cerwyn Moore,
Jeremy Smith and Galina Yemelianova

LONDON AND NEW YORK

First published 2014
by Routledge

2 Park Square, Milton Park, Abingdon, Oxfordshire OX14 4RN
711 Third Avenue, New York, NY 10017

*Routledge is an imprint of the Taylor & Francis Group, an informa business*

First issued in paperback 2018

Copyright © 2014 Taylor & Francis

All rights reserved. No part of this book may be reprinted or reproduced or utilised in any form or by any electronic, mechanical, or other means, now known or hereafter invented, including photocopying and recording, or in any information storage or retrieval system, without permission in writing from the publishers.

Notice:
Product or corporate names may be trademarks or registered trademarks, and are used only for identification and explanation without intent to infringe.

*British Library Cataloguing in Publication Data*
A catalogue record for this book is available from the British Library

ISBN 13: 978-0-415-73967-2 (hbk)
ISBN 13: 978-1-138-37759-2 (pbk)

Typeset in Times New Roman
by Taylor & Francis Books

**Publisher's Note**
The publisher accepts responsibility for any inconsistencies that may have arisen during the conversion of this book from journal articles to book chapters, namely the possible inclusion of journal terminology.

**Disclaimer**
Every effort has been made to contact copyright holders for their permission to reprint material in this book. The publishers would be grateful to hear from any copyright holder who is not here acknowledged and will undertake to rectify any errors or omissions in future editions of this book.

# Contents

| | |
|---|---|
| *Citation Information* | ix |
| 1. Many Faces of the Caucasus<br>*Nino Kemoklidze, Cerwyn Moore, Jeremy Smith &*<br>*Galina Yemelianova* | 1 |
| 2. The Origins and Trajectory of the Caucasian Conflicts<br>*Vicken Cheterian* | 15 |
| 3. Securing the South Caucasus: Military Aspects of Russian<br>Policy towards the Region since 2008<br>*Tracey German* | 40 |
| 4. Young Soldiers' Tales of War in Nagorno-Karabakh<br>*Nona Shahnazarian & Ulrike Ziemer* | 57 |
| 5. Co-optation or Empowerment? The Fate of Pro-Democracy<br>NGOs after the Rose Revolution<br>*Brian Grodsky* | 74 |
| 6. A Broken Region: The Persistent Failure of Integration Projects<br>in the South Caucasus<br>*Thomas de Waal* | 99 |
| 7. Re-thinking Citizenship in the South Caucasus<br>*Lale Yalçin-Heckmann* | 114 |
| 8. Re-making a Frontier Community or Defending Ethnic Boundaries?<br>The Caucasus in Cossack Identity<br>*Anton Popov* | 129 |
| 9. Post-Soviet Ethnic Relations in Stavropol'skii *Krai*, Russia: 'A Melting<br>Pot or Boiling Shaft'?<br>*Andrew Foxall* | 148 |
| 10. Suicide Bombing: Chechnya, the North Caucasus and Martyrdom<br>*Cerwyn Moore* | 170 |
| *List of Contributors* | 198 |
| *Index* | 201 |

# Citation Information

The chapters in this book were originally published in *Europe-Asia Studies*, volume 64, issue 9 (November 2012). When citing this material, please use the original page numbering for each article, as follows:

**Chapter 1**
*Many Faces of the Caucasus*
Nino Kemoklidze, Cerwyn Moore, Jeremy Smith &
Galina Yemelianova
*Europe-Asia Studies*, volume 64, issue 9 (November 2012)
pp. 1611–1624

**Chapter 2**
*The Origins and Trajectory of the Caucasian Conflicts*
Vicken Cheterian
*Europe-Asia Studies*, volume 64, issue 9 (November 2012)
pp. 1625–1649

**Chapter 3**
*Securing the South Caucasus: Military Aspects of Russian Policy towards the Region since 2008*
Tracey German
*Europe-Asia Studies*, volume 64, issue 9 (November 2012)
pp. 1650–1666

**Chapter 4**
*Young Soldiers' Tales of War in Nagorno-Karabakh*
Nona Shahnazarian & Ulrike Ziemer
*Europe-Asia Studies*, volume 64, issue 9 (November 2012)
pp. 1667–1683

**Chapter 5**
*Co-optation or Empowerment? The Fate of Pro-Democracy NGOs after the Rose Revolution*
Brian Grodsky
*Europe-Asia Studies*, volume 64, issue 9 (November 2012)
pp. 1684–1708

CITATION INFORMATION

**Chapter 6**
*A Broken Region: The Persistent Failure of Integration Projects in the South Caucasus*
Thomas de Waal
*Europe-Asia Studies*, volume 64, issue 9 (November 2012)
pp. 1709–1723

**Chapter 7**
*Re-thinking Citizenship in the South Caucasus*
Lale Yalçin-Heckmann
*Europe-Asia Studies*, volume 64, issue 9 (November 2012)
pp. 1724–1738

**Chapter 8**
*Re-making a Frontier Community or Defending Ethnic Boundaries? The Caucasus in Cossack Identity*
Anton Popov
*Europe-Asia Studies*, volume 64, issue 9 (November 2012)
pp. 1739–1757

**Chapter 9**
*Post-Soviet Ethnic Relations in Stavropol'skii* Krai, *Russia: 'A Melting Pot or Boiling Shaft'?*
Andrew Foxall
*Europe-Asia Studies*, volume 64, issue 9 (November 2012)
pp. 1758–1779

**Chapter 10**
*Suicide Bombing: Chechnya, the North Caucasus and Martyrdom*
Cerwyn Moore
*Europe-Asia Studies*, volume 64, issue 9 (November 2012)
pp. 1780–1807

Please direct any queries you may have about the citations to clsuk.permissions@cengage.com

# Many Faces of the Caucasus

## NINO KEMOKLIDZE, CERWYN MOORE, JEREMY SMITH & GALINA YEMELIANOVA

THIS COLLECTION ADDRESSES SOME OF THE MAJOR challenges facing scholars and practitioners who are dealing with the Caucasus, as well as with ethnic and ethno-religious relations in Eurasia and the wider world. The collection is one of the outcomes of a two-day international multi-disciplinary conference entitled 'The Caucasus and Central Asia: Theoretical, Cultural and Political Challenges', held at the University of Birmingham on 3–4 July 2009.[1]

The conference was the largest event to date organised by the University of Birmingham Caucasus and Central Asia Research Group which was created in July 2008 by over 20 academics and PhD students specialising in the Caucasus and Central Asia at the University of Birmingham. The core of the group consists of researchers from the Centre for Russian and East European Studies (CREES), the Department of Political Science and International Studies (POLSIS), as well as academics from the Centre of Byzantine and Ottoman Studies, the Institute of Archaeology and Antiquity and the Department of Theology. The *raison d'être* behind the creation of the research group was an acute awareness of considerable gaps in British studies on the region. Most existing work has been grouped under the heading of security studies and has been directly related to policy making. Without undervaluing this research, it has suffered from the relative dearth of independent research into the cultural, social, historical, ethnic and religious complexion of the region. The intention of the Birmingham research group therefore has been to generate a more balanced and multi-faceted research into this culturally fascinating and geopolitically central region of the world.[2]

---

[1] The conference was organised with financial support from CEELBAS (Centre for East European Language Based Area Studies), ASSC Seed Corn Fund and the Department of Political Science and International Studies, both at the University of Birmingham. The editors and contributors would like to express their thanks to those organisations for their financial support and to the editorial team at *Europe-Asia Studies*, and to numerous anonymous reviewers for help and assistance.

[2] The Birmingham research group aims to contribute to filling the existing academic shortcomings in British studies of both the Caucasus and Central Asia by generating comprehensive, in-depth and language-based research into the region. The research group emphasises its genuinely multi-disciplinary nature reflected in its members' affiliation to a range of disciplines (area studies, political sciences, security studies, history, geography, archaeology, anthropology and theology).

## Why does the Caucasus matter?

There are a number of factors which necessitate deeper research into the Caucasus. The region is a cradle of ancient civilisations and has centuries-long traditions of statehood. In the middle ages, the region was part of the world's most powerful empires, including the Abbasid Caliphate, the Gengizid, Ottoman and Safawid empires, and was characterised by a highly developed urban and spiritual culture, rooted in Zoroastrianism, early Christianity (Georgia and Armenia), Islam (the Northern Caucasus and Azerbaijan) and Judaism (the North Caucasus). The region is unique in its ethnic and linguistic diversity. It is inhabited by over 30 million people of Caucasian, Slavic, Iranian and Turkic ethnic origins speaking over 100 different languages.

The region is of immense geopolitical and strategic significance due to its frontier location between Europe and Asia. In the nineteenth century, the Caucasus, alongside Central Asia, was at the centre of the Great Game between the British and Russian empires. In the twentieth century, the region became a constituent part of the Soviet Union. Following the end of communism and the break-up of the USSR, the region witnessed political fragmentation with the emergence of the independent states of Georgia, Armenia and Azerbaijan while the North Caucasus remained within the Russian Federation. In administrative terms, it was divided between the autonomous republics of Chechnya, Ingushetia, Dagestan, Kabardino-Balkaria, Karachaevo-Cherkessia, North Ossetia, Adyghea and the Russian regions (*oblasti*) of Krasnodar, Stavropol', and Rostov. Despite 70 years of Soviet atheism, peoples of the Caucasus preserved their distinctive religious identities. Thus, over 80% of the population in the North Caucasus are Sunni Muslims. The majority of Dagestanis, Chechens and Ingush adhere to mystical Islam–Sufism. By comparison, the bulk of the population of Azerbaijan are Shi'a Muslims. Armenians and Georgians adhere to different variants of Eastern Christianity—the Georgian Orthodox Christian Church and the Apostolic Orthodox Armenian Church.

The collapse of the Soviet centralised system and communist ideology triggered the rise of ethnic and religious nationalisms in the region. Since the late 1980s, the Caucasus has been fraught with ethnic and ethno-religious conflicts and territorial disputes. The most protracted and devastating among the latter have been the Azerbaijani–Armenian conflict over Nagorno (Mountainous) Karabakh; the conflicts between Georgia, on the one side, and Abkhazia and South Ossetia on the other, which culminated in the full blown Russian–Georgian war of August 2008; the Ingush-Ossetian conflict and Russo-Chechen conflict which culminated in two Russo-Chechen wars of 1994–1996 and 1999–2000.[3] An important feature of the region's post-communist transition has been the rise of Islam and Christianity. The North Caucasus has also witnessed the resurgence of radical Islam, including *jihadi*sm. It is significant that the second Russo-Chechen war was characterised by the involvement of a notable number of foreign Islamist fighters, as well as ideologues and financiers, particularly when turning to the study of external actors and their influence on local

---

[3]Albiet somewhat dated, for a primer on the Russian military responses to the conflicts in Chechnya, see Kramer (2005).

insurgencies. Although small in number, many Islamist volunteers came from Arab states; others were from the diaspora communities, while the most numerous came from the region, and the surrounding environs which border the North and South Caucasus (Moore & Tumelty 2008, pp. 412–33; Sagramoso 2012, pp. 561–95).

The end of tight Soviet political and military control over the region was accompanied by the return of major global and regional powers—the USA, the EU, Turkey and Iran—to the region. A major factor behind increasing Western interest in the region has been the large oil and gas reserves of the Caspian basin. Since the early 1990s, the region has been at the centre of a new edition of the 'Great Game' between major global energy companies over their respective involvement in the Caspian oil and gas extraction and transportation process. The pivotal events of 9/11 and the ensuing US-led global war on terror have provided justification for the US and Western Europe to strengthen its political and military engagement in the region. Meanwhile, the newly independent states of the Southern Caucasus have become the focus for the European Neighbourhood Policy. Georgia has established close ties with the West and NATO, in particular.

Rapid political and ideological reorganisation of the Caucasus since the end of the Soviet Union has highlighted the problematic nature, or even the validity of the very notion of the Caucasus. As is shown in Thomas de Waal's contribution in the present collection, the existing notions of the Caucasus, the South Caucasus, the Greater Caucasus and the more fragmented Western, Eastern, Central and North-Western Caucasus reflect not only geographical but dated political realities.[4] Geographically, the Caucasus is referred to as the territory between the Black, Azov and Caspian Seas, extending from the Kuma-Manych depression in the north to Georgia's and Armenia's borders with Turkey, and Azerbaijan's borders with Iran in the south. Politically, various notions of the Caucasus are largely constructs of the late Russian and Soviet supremacy in the region and therefore reflect St Petersburg's, or Moscow's perceptions of it.[5] It was Russia's arrival in the region in the eighteenth and nineteenth centuries which introduced the notions of the 'Caucasus', the 'Transcaucasus' and the 'North Caucasus'. This terminology persisted into the Soviet period. Thus, the 'Transcaucasus' related to the three union republics of Georgia, Armenia and Azerbaijan, and the autonomous republics of Abkhazia, Ajaria and South Ossetia within Georgia, and the Nakhichevan autonomous republic and the area of Nagorno-Karabakh within Azerbaijan. The 'North Caucasus' referred to Russia's autonomous republics of Dagestan, Checheno-Ingushetia, North Ossetia, Kabardino-Balkaria, the Krasnodar and Stavropol' provinces (*krai*), which included Adyghea and Karachaevo-Cherkessia autonomous regions (*oblasti*), respectively, and the Rostov region (*oblast'*).

Following the break-up of the USSR and the decline of Russia's political influence and military presence in the region, the 'Transcaucasus' was transformed into the 'South

---

[4]It is worth noting that some researchers and commentators stretch the notion of the Caucasus even further to include the north-eastern part of Turkey and north-western part of Azerbaijan because for many centuries these areas were part of a single socio-economic and ethno-cultural entity (Akkieva 2008, p. 270).

[5]For a detailed discussion of notions of the Caucasus see Akkieva (2008, pp. 253–73). The Russo-centric view of the Caucasus has also affected Western scholarship. For example, King (2008) effectively begins with the Russian Empire's annexation of Kartl-Kakheti in 1801.

Caucasus', or even dissolved into a larger Black Sea region, a zone where the geopolitical and economic interests of major world and regional powers and transnational companies collide. As for the 'North Caucasus', it was reduced to the seven autonomous republics of Russia: Dagestan, Chechnya, Ingushetia, Kabardino-Balkaria, Karachaevo-Cherkessia, North Ossetia and Adyghea (Akkieva 2008, p. 255).

One of the consequences of this new politically-driven fragmentation of the Caucasus has been an advance in the region of integrationist Caucasian academic and cultural discourses. At its core lies an idea of the Caucasus as a specific Caucasian civilisation, defined by certain historical commonalities in socio-economic patterns, traditions, mentalities, cuisine and dress code which constitute 'Caucasianness' (*Kavkazkost'*).

## Caucasus studies in the West

Despite the great political relevance and scholarly importance of the study of the Caucasus, the region has received very limited attention among Western academics. In the late nineteenth and early twentieth centuries, the British diplomat Oliver Wardrop and his sister Marjory, both Georgiaphiles, were part-time scholars whose treatment of the region as something which existed apart from Russian interests was the exception that proved the general rule of scholarly neglect. For much of the twentieth century, the region fell under Soviet studies, while the major academic contributions came from *émigrés*, or scholars with ethnic roots in the region such as the historians Richard Hovanissian and Hélène Carrère d'Encausse. In the post-Soviet period, scholarship, with a few exceptions,[6] has been dominated by studies of the security implications of the Nagorno-Karabakh, Russo-Chechen, Russo-Georgian and some other recent ethno-political conflicts in the region. There are a number of factors behind the relative lack of research on the Caucasus, and the difficulties associated with researching the region. One reason may well be the difficulty in acquiring translations or getting access to relevant archives, particularly in Iran. The influence of the Middle East, especially Persia/Iran, both historically and in more recent times, is a case in point. Little historical research exists in the West which flags up the role that Persia played in the Caucasus. Furthermore, the influence of other regional powers, most notably Turkey, is recognised by many, but also simultaneously neglected in some studies.[7] Likewise, research on the Caucasus has also been complicated by the influence of the Soviet bureaucracy. The creation of an official, centralised nationalities policy, as well as the atheism of the communist regime not only forced religion underground, but it also led to the wholesale movement of different ethnic and sub-ethnic groups throughout the Soviet Union. The corollary of this was that much of the history of the region in the Soviet period became sanitised.[8] In short, from a

---

[6]Thus, social and cultural changes in post-Soviet Muslim Caucasus and their political implications are addressed in Ware (2010); Gammer (2008); Sagramoso (2007); Dannreuther and March (2010); Pilkington and Yemelianova (2003); and Yemelianova (2010). The historical development of Circassian, Abaza, Abkhaz and Ubykh languages and myths is examined in Colarusso (2002) and Richmond (2008).

[7]Notable exceptions would include the likes of Allen and Muratoff (2011) and Gammer (2006).

[8]Some works have made headway in addressing this problem since the opening of the region and its archives to scholars. See: Ro'i (2000) and Zelkina (2000).

historical perspective, much of the local history was neither publicly available, nor accessible, beyond official Cold War statements.

Although very different from the Cold War, another problem affects a considerable portion of the contemporary work on the Caucasus, which is that it takes Russian studies as a starting point. This often generates a discursive lens through which the region is analysed: after all, the Caucasus is on Russia's southern security flank; the Caucasus is in Russia's sphere of influence, neighbourhood, or near abroad; and many of the people speak Russian across the region. But is it possible to examine, assess and interpret the region from the local perspective? Can research draw on Russian studies, while also reflecting the complex local and regional dynamics which have done much to shape the recent history of the Caucasus? Can researchers who study the region adopt approaches which are not shaped by popular themes, or orthodox discourses? And can studies of the region draw on inter-disciplinary approaches, or at least prompt a conversation between disciplines?

In the post-Soviet period, it is possible to read swathes of work on the Caucasus, with little mention of regions beyond Chechnya. It is also possible to read swathes of work on the instability in Chechnya, with little reference to contemporary works by writers who work on the insurgency. This is not to say that work on the South Caucasus does not exist, or that some of this work is not insightful. But it is to recognise, rather unfortunately, that the reader can be left without any straightforward local perspective or any understanding of the politics of the region due to the focus on Russian area studies. The importance of other themes is further diminished by a diet of popular and orthodox accounts of violence in the region. Of course human rights organisations have taken the presidential administrations of the Putin and Medvedev eras to task for initiating a campaign of repression in the North Caucasus and the centralisation of power in the Kremlin, while others have focused on a ready-made reading of the violence, and the influence of political Islam, since the end of the Cold War. However, these popular readings and general overviews need to be challenged, assessed and, where feasible, criticised. The danger arises when these approaches act as key points of reference and become viewed as coherent or all encompassing reflections of the Caucasus.

Similarly, it may be possible to arrive at general conclusions and quantitative readings of political, social, and economic relations without travelling to a region. But this entails lack of engagement with grass-roots movements, local voices and the complex inter-relations between groups which have done much to shape the recent history of the region. The aim of qualitative research involves establishing and exploring not only explanations and opinions, but also advancing an understanding shaped by alternative opinions and counter-argument.[9] All too often the mainstream research that does exist—be it in the Russian, British or US academy—is not born of understanding or dialogue.

The in-depth analysis of Russia's Caucasus has been hampered, somewhat, by the disengagement of local scholars, who possess unique factual data, from Moscow-centred Russian, as well as Western, academics who work on the region. In part then, this is a plea for further dialogue with the local writers, academics and researchers; a plea for further dialogue which we recognise may be challenging, but which,

---

[9]See, for instance, the seminal work by Derluguian (2005). See also: Dunlop (1998).

nonetheless, would do much to enrich analysis of the local narratives about social, political, economic and cultural life in the Caucasus.

Instead, the Caucasus is often used to make theoretical and political capital, to reify explanations held by academics in important positions, or to reaffirm entrenched popular and commonplace beliefs, especially since 9/11. There are, of course, notable exceptions to these general points—but the more broad argument remains—that the Caucasus is treated as a periphery often viewed through a core, and this leads to a set of attendant problems.[10] To have dialogue—a conversation even—requires a move beyond the orthodox narratives which have dominated research on the region. That is to say, to recover local voices is difficult, but not necessarily impossible.

This brings us to a series of starting points for further research, which we hope this collection will play a role in. The first may well be to take into consideration that the study of the region originated from the metropolitan centre of Russia and the Soviet Union; a position which is, self-evidently, not risk free. However, this approach would serve to recognise the influence of Russian studies as one of many ways to read the Caucasus. Another starting point could well be to reconcile the inherently inter-disciplinary approach and associated qualitative research techniques with area studies.[11] This is not so much a Gordian Knot, but is rather, a necessary precondition of dialogue; identifying a theoretical starting point, unpacking the benefits of area studies, while also retaining an awareness of the need to bridge the two. Of these, it is perhaps research in the field which is fraught with the most practical difficulties, but again, that does not make it impossible. After all, journalists, travel writers and documentary makers have long since travelled to the region, and photographed, documented and represented the peoples in stories, travelogues and novella. What is needed then is old-fashioned research in the field, research in archives, research in social anthropology and auto-ethnography so as to start dialogue, to enrich theoretical debate and unpack the realities of a fascinating region and peoples.

### *Understanding and conceptualising ethnic conflict in the Caucasus*

As already noted, in the West the Caucasus has been largely associated with violent ethnic conflicts. Thus, the Caucasus first came to the attention of Western journalists, policy makers and the wider public in 1988 with the outbreak of conflict between Armenians and Azerbaijanis, fuelled by a series of claims and counter-claims over the status of the autonomous region (*oblast'*) of Nagorno-Karabakh. As this conflict developed into all-out war between the republics of Armenia and Azerbaijan, further conflicts erupted over the status of Abkhazia and South Ossetia in relation to Georgia, between Ingush and Ossetians over the Prigorodny district (*raion*) of North Ossetia, and finally Chechnya under the leadership of Dzhokhar Dudayev rebelled and declared its independence from the Russian Federation, leading to the two Russo-

---

[10] An example of a notable exception would be the work of Marie Bennigsen-Broxup (1996).

[11] Examples of the ways forward for research can be found in the two edited collections on Islam and the state in the Caucasus and wider Eurasia by Moshe Gammer (2008) and Galina Yemelianova (2010).

Chechen wars of the 1990s.[12] Azerbaijan and Georgia also experienced bloody internal civil wars in the early 1990s. However, the Armenia–Azerbaijan war over Nagorno-Karabakh has remained the only example of open warfare between independent post-Soviet states of the Caucasus. In August 2008, unresolved Georgia–Abkhaz and Georgia–South Ossetia ethno-territorial disputes were aggravated by a direct Russian involvement, culminating in a Russo-Georgian war. On the basis of this evidence, the region by some way could be described as the most conflict-torn part of the former USSR. Civil war in Tajikistan and conflicts between Kyrgyz and Uzbeks in the Osh region of Central Asia, as well as the war of 1992 between the Russia-backed breakaway territory of Transnistria and Moldova were the only other exceptions to the predominantly peaceful dissolution of the world's second superpower.

Given this turbulent recent history, it is little surprise that, at least as far as Western scholarship and policy is concerned, the Caucasus has been treated primarily as a security concern. The opening of new gas and oil fields off the coast off Azerbaijan, followed by the construction of the Baku–Tbilisi–Ceyhan pipeline at a time when Europe's dependence on energy supplies from Russia appeared to make it vulnerable, added a further security dimension to the study of the region.

Curiously, the Caucasus has not figured very highly in most general studies of ethnic conflict, which tend to base their models on experience from Yugoslavia, Africa and the Far East. Theoretical understandings of ethnic conflict have progressed considerably over the past two decades through large-scale comparative studies made possible in great part by large databases such as the Minorities at Risk (MAR) database started by Ted Gurr in 1986 and maintained at the University of Maryland,[13] and the Correlates of War Project started by J. David Singer in 1963 at the University of Michigan and now continued at Penn State University.[14] Before coming on to the findings of such studies, it is worth asking why relatively few attempts have been made to apply such theories to the Caucasus. One factor is that the issues have become muddied by the earlier contributions of scholars from the region itself, whose efforts have generally been politicised to an extent which is rare even for the former Soviet Union. As long ago as the 1860s, after the Russian Imperial authorities had obligingly removed most of the Abkhaz population from the Caucasus, Georgian intellectuals set out to demonstrate that the Abkhaz lands had originally been inhabited by Georgians in any case (Shnirelman 2001, pp. 240–41; Cheterian 2008, pp. 49–70). A hundred years later historians, anthropologists, archaeologists and other Soviet scholars from Georgia, Abkhazia, South Ossetia, Armenia and Azerbaijan renewed the debate about original settlement and political authority over the contended territories. The results were often fascinating but usually untestable and effectively meaningless.[15] This tradition of scholarship has continued in the post-Soviet period and buttresses popular

---

[12]Some authors point to the role of war-torn Abkhazia as a breeding ground for armed resistance of many hues. They highlight the fact that a considerable portion of the volunteers in the Abkhaz conflict were from Chechnya. In 1994, they went back to Chechnya and played a pivotal part in the Russo-Chechen wars. See, for example, Moore and Tumelty (2009) and Derluguian (2007).

[13]For more on this, see for instance, Gurr (1993, 2000).

[14]For one of the earlier publications on this project see Singer and Small (1972).

[15]For an example in English of the incompatibility of such accounts, see Alijarly (1995) and Walker (1995).

belief in the validity of territorial claims on all sides. And in spite of the fact that claims based on ancient history have no status in international law or practice, they are not without influence internationally.

Underpinning and complementing these scholarly Soviet and post-Soviet approaches has been an adherence to a primordial view of nationality, which became hegemonic in the Soviet Union (Tishkov 1997, pp. 1–7). As well as giving credence to the relevance of distant history, primordialism chimes with popular notions of ethnic conflict being based on ancient hatreds which are ultimately insurmountable, an approach which is often echoed in journalistic accounts and which has had some impact in international circles. With a disparaging turn of phrase, David Laitin and Ronald Suny have criticised such notions with the characterisation of the origins of the Karabakh conflict as 'lost in the mists of the twentieth century' (Laitin & Suny 1999, p. 146). Constructivist understandings of nations pioneered by the likes of Ernest Gellner and Benedict Anderson have done much to undermine the appeal of primordialism at least in Western academic circles, but equally have not succeeded in finding an explanation for conflicts which in no way serve the purposes for which, under these accounts, nations were constructed.

A further barrier to applying theories of ethnic conflict is that in important ways they do not look like typical ethnic conflicts. With important exceptions (Sumgait, Khojaly), the conflicts of the Caucasus were generally not marked by the deliberate and systematic slaughter of civilians for the crime of belonging to the wrong group which has characterised some of the twentieth century's worst ethnic conflicts. Most of the casualties have been military, and while there has been widespread ethnic cleansing in Nagorno-Karabakh and Abkhazia, these followed, or accompanied military operations and were relatively orderly and free of bloodshed. In Chechnya, the taking of innocent hostages by one side and brutality against captured combatants and some civilians by the other have also characterised inter-state wars, but at no time did the authorities of the republic seek to expel, or massacre Russians, or *vice versa*. What has mostly been at stake has not been the survival, or subjugation of a particular ethnic group but the status and political order of territories the borders of which were well marked out in the Soviet period. This leads to the question of whether we are really talking about ethnic conflicts at all, or territorial wars which have more in common with wars between states. A further response is to blame the conflicts entirely on the territorial structures of the Soviet Union which, whatever they were designed for, served only to promote conflict once the overarching structure collapsed (Cornell 2002). Such approaches are, however, based on assumptions about Soviet nationalities' policy which have largely been discredited by historians and which, if accepted, can only encourage us to ignore the specificities of the local situation.

A book by Christoph Zürcher does seek to apply mainstream theories of ethnic conflict to the Caucasus (Zürcher 2007). Zürcher outlines six factors which comparative research has identified as related to the likelihood of ethnic conflict breaking out: levels of economic development; regime strength, type and change; available finances; previous wars; ethnic diversity and inequality; and terrain. The presence of at least some of these factors in the Caucasus is evident: while economic development was not particularly low or uneven, the collapse of Soviet power clearly left a political and military vacuum; finances from *émigrés*, co-religionists and Russia played a part in escalating conflicts; there existed a history of conflict between Armenians and Azerbaijanis, Abkhaz and Georgians, as well as Ossetians and Georgians, Chechens and the Russian state; the ethnic diversity of the region was addressed, in some cases perversely, by Soviet policies producing political imbalances; and mountainous terrain certainly aided the Chechen rebels once they had been ousted from Grozny (Zürcher 2007, pp. 45–57). As is evident from Zürcher's account, however, these factors emphasise opportunity rather than motive: Karabakh Armenians may have been able to draw on support from the Republic of Armenia and from wealthy émigrés, but this does not tell us why they chose to draw on this support or, indeed, why that support was offered. One response, pursued by Valery Tishkov, is to focus on elites who stood to gain materially or in terms of power and status either from the process of rebellion itself or from the state formations that it was hoped would result from those rebellions.[16] However, Tishkov notes that 'Rank-and-file participants in the drama tended to follow a logic of collective behaviour rather than rational individual strategy' (Tishkov 1997, p. 155). It is this logic which is harder to unravel. More nuanced models may hold some clues. For example, James Fearon's statement of the 'commitment problem', developed with Croatia in mind, might equally be applied to Abkhazia (Fearon 1998), where Georgian politicians and their international backers have frequently expressed puzzlement at the Abkhaz' refusal to accept the goodwill of the government and promises of prosperity and protection of their rights as a minority.[17]

Theories of ethnic conflict do provide useful insights into the conditions under which ethnic conflicts might occur but, by the admission of most of their authors, they fall short of actually predicting when conflicts will occur. In establishing frameworks in which ethnic conflict can be understood comparatively, social scientists have helped both to understand the causes of conflict in the Caucasus, and to allow lessons from the Caucasus to be applied elsewhere (Souleimanov 2007). Yet, every framework or theory is subject to exceptions, and whichever case we look at cries out for closer examination of local conditions.[18] The four main conflict regions of the Caucasus share common background factors in the collapse of the Soviet Union and the uncompromising (at least until 2007) stance of the international community on territorial integrity, but beyond that they differ from each other in origins, scale, nature and consequences. At times the tendency to treat the Caucasus as a single conflict zone, together with a fear of setting precedents, has hampered international agencies in their pursuit of solutions.

All those theoretical, political and cultural complexities surrounding the Caucasus were at the centre of discussion at the Birmingham conference. The conference brought together 63 participants specialising in the Caucasus and Central Asia from across the

---

[16] See for example the discussion on the Ingush–Ossetian conflict in Tishkov (1997, pp. 155–56).

[17] See for example the article by Georgia's then Minister for Reintegration Temur Yakobashvili (2010).

[18] Of interest in this respect is a book by Cerwyn Moore (2010) on *Contemporary Violence: Postmodern War in Kosovo and Chechnya* which challenges the orthodox accounts of ethnic conflict and the transformation of armed resistance movements by using hermeneutics and theories of narrative identity to analyse Kosovo and Chechnya.

University of Birmingham, and from other UK universities within the CEELBAS[19] network (academics and PhD students), leading international scholars, policy makers, representatives of NGOs and journalists who work on this region. Its speakers included historians, anthropologists, linguists, political scientists and theologians researching the region and academics and practitioners with expertise in Russia, Iran and Turkey. This mix enabled the conference to examine both internal and external factors shaping the cultural, socio-economic and political dynamics of individual countries, as well as wider regional trajectories, and to analyse the region's positioning *vis-à-vis* the major regional powers (Russia, Turkey, Iran and China), as well as the US and Western Europe.

*The case studies*

As the August war between Russia and Georgia in 2008 demonstrated, even more than two decades after the break-up of the Soviet Union, the Caucasus remains one of the most turbulent regions in the former USSR. It is no surprise, therefore, that most essays in this collection are concerned with the conflicts that have characterised the region. However, they do so from a variety of perspectives which are themselves under-researched.[20] While none provides the final word on the topics they address, they do suggest a broader research agenda is needed if we are to fully understand the conflicts, their origins and possible solutions.[21]

Conflicts in the Caucasus are the main topic of the essay by Vicken Cheterian who examines the violence that erupted in the region in the late 1980s and early 1990s. Cheterian addresses the origins of the Caucasian conflicts and the trajectories they have taken since their first outbreak. His central argument is that while beginning mainly as a result of the weakening of the institutions of the Soviet Union, conflicts in Abkhazia, South Ossetia, Nagorno-Karabakh and Chechnya have gone through some major transformations since then. The author identifies three main phases that these conflicts have gone through transforming from 'triangular conflicts' into bilateral 'total wars'. According to him, the third wave in these conflicts that we see since the events of August 2008 is the 'internationalisation of the conflicts'.

Another essay that deals with conflicts in the South Caucasus is Tracy German's 'Securing the South Caucasus'. Unlike other contributors to this collection, German's essay takes a more traditional security studies approach and is more policy oriented in nature than others. The essay's main focus is on Russian policy towards Abkhazia and

---

[19]CEELBAS is a partnership of University College London, the University of Oxford and the University of Birmingham with a network of partners at the Universities of Bath, Cambridge, Kent, Manchester, Sheffield, Warwick and the School of Oriental and African Studies (SOAS).

[20]The essays are based on six papers (out of a total of 21), which were presented at the conference's seven panels. Those panels covered 'Language, Narration and State-Building in the Caucasus; 'Ethno-Nationalism and Politics in the South Caucasus'; 'History of the Caucasus'; 'Central Asia and Caucasus and the Outside World'; 'Traditionalism *versus* Reformism in Islam'; 'Domestic and Foreign Policies of the Central Asian and Caucasian States' and 'Culture and Society in the Caucasus.' The essays by Andrew Foxall, Brian Grodsky and Cerwyn Moore were added to the collection at a later stage.

[21]Or, to be more accurate, in the short term at least scholarship may reveal why certain solutions can be ruled out.

South Ossetia after the August 2008 war and what impact it had on the region. German provides a detailed overview of the Russian military presence in the Caucasus and argues that far from providing a security guarantor in Abkhazia and South Ossetia, Russia has effectively turned them into Russian satellites, dependent on continuous Russian support. By doing this, Russia has undermined security not only in these regions but outside Georgia as well.

The conflict over Nagorno-Karabakh is dealt with in the essay 'Young Soldiers' Tales of War in Nagorno-Karabakh', co-authored by Nona Shahnazarian and Ulrike Ziemer. The authors examine the effects of war on soldiers and especially on young, teenage soldiers—a topic which is largely neglected by existing scholarship on the region. The essay draws on intensive ethnographical work and biographical interviews and provides insightful analysis of young male soldiers' experiences of war and how it has shaped these young peoples' identities.

Georgia is a case study in Brian Grodsky's essay where he explores the fate of pro-democracy NGOs since the 'Rose Revolution' of 2003. The essay is based on the author's elite interviews with former and present members of NGOs. Grodsky reveals that many of the former leaders of the NGO community took up later important government posts. The author seeks to answer the question whether their inclusion into government structures has further enhanced or, in fact, inhibited democratic institution-building in the country. The essay concludes that Georgia has not benefited much from this practice and that inclusion of the members of pro-democracy organisations has weakened the NGO community who face their one-time allies now occupying high government posts and with very different agendas.

Regional integration in the South Caucasus is the main theme of de Waal's essay. The author poses an interesting question of whether in such a troubled region like the Caucasus, with blurred boundaries and so many multiple identities it makes sense to talk about the Caucasus as a 'region' at all. de Waal engages in a concise overview of the history of the regional integration of the South Caucasus identifying different elements that bind the region together (such as geography, shared culture, economics and trade) and also talks about why at different points in history, the three republics of the South Caucasus have failed to work together as a region. However, the conclusion that de Waal reaches is that despite persistent failures regional integration in the South Caucasus is not a utopian project and without any doubt should be encouraged.

Lale Yalçin-Heckmann's essay investigates the issue of citizenship in the South Caucasus. It goes beyond the widely accepted frameworks of conflictology which are limited to studying the relationship between the state and its citizens through the prism of ethno-national principles. Instead, it studies citizenship from 'below' 'by looking at how the state–citizen relations are conceptualised, perceived and how these are embedded in common people's everyday lives'. Yalçin-Heckmann's essay is based on research findings by the Caucasus Research Group in Halle, Germany, with different researchers located in the three South Caucasus republics of Georgia, Armenia and Azerbaijan.

Anton Popov's essay shifts focus from the South Caucasus to the Russian North Caucasus. It offers an anthropological and ethnographical investigation into the role of the Caucasus in the ethno-national identity of Cossacks in Krasnodar *Krai* (province) in southern Russia.[22] The author provides insightful details on how young Cossacks engage in the imagining, making and re-making of their socially, ethnically and frontier defined identities. Popov also examines in some depth how the Caucasus as a geographically and culturally defined region is used in the construction of neo-Cossack identity.

Andrew Foxall's essay also focuses on Southern Russia, exploring 'violent geographies' of post-Soviet ethnic relations in Stavropol' *Krai* (province). According to the author, Stavropol' *Krai* has traditionally occupied a rather significant place in Russian politics. Unlike other territories within the North Caucasus Federal District, ethnic Russians constitute the majority of the population here and historically it has played an important role in Russian control over the North Caucasus. Based on rich ethnographic interviews, Foxall's essay examines in some depth how ordinary people experience and negotiate ethnic relations in their day-to-day lives. In the author's words, the 'essay explores (rather than assumes) the importance of ethnicity in everyday life' and aims to contribute to a better understanding of inter-ethnic relations in the region.

Last but not least, Cerwyn Moore's essay goes back to the theme of suicide attacks and analyses two waves of Chechen-related suicide operations taking place during the period of 2000–2004. While the history and the local social and cultural dynamics of the Russo-Chechen conflicts have been explored in many previous studies, as the author indicates, the rationales behind the use of violence and terrorism in Chechnya have been largely overlooked. Moore tries to move away from the traditional analyses of terrorism in the North Caucasus, mainly done through quantitative approaches or through the disciplinary prism of Russian studies. He argues that the Chechen-related suicide attacks in 2000–2002 and 2002–2004, in fact, constitute two distinct waves that need to be 'contextualised in a shifting historical setting' in order to be understood properly.

The editors hope that the essays included in this collection will enhance a better understanding of what Zürcher admits are 'highly idiosyncratic social and cultural constellations' (Zürcher 2007, p. 230) and will contribute to the development of Caucasian studies in the West. Beyond this, it is hoped that the essays, and this collection as a whole, will contribute to ensuing dialogue between scholars who study the region from within, and those who view the Caucasus from afar. Indeed, each contribution and the collection a whole are designed to elicit and enable scholarly conversation, to infuse much needed background history into the realm of policy studies, and to enrich academic analyses, and further study, of the many faces of the Caucasus.

*University of Birmingham*
*University of Eastern Finland*

---

[22]Krasnodar *Krai* and the Republic of Adyghea are the only places in the North Caucasus that administratively belong to the Southern Federal District—one of eight federal districts of the Russian Federation. The other territories in the region constitute part of the North Caucasus Federal District, created in January 2010.

## References

Akkieva, S. (2008) 'The Caucasus: One, or Many? A View from the Region', *Nationalities Papers*, 36, 2, May.
Alijarly, S. (1995) 'The Republic of Azerbaijan: Notes on the State Borders in the Past and the Present', in Wright, J. F. R., Goldberg, S. & Schofield, R. N. (eds) (1995).
Allen, W. E. D. & Muratoff, P. (2011) *Caucasian Battlefields: A History of the Wars on the Turco-Caucasian Border, 1828–1921* (Cambridge, Cambridge University Press).
Bennigsen-Broxup, M. (ed.) (1996) *The North Caucasus Barrier: The Russian Advance towards the Muslim World* (London, Hurst and Co.).
Cheterian, V. (2008) *War and Peace in the Caucasus: Ethnic Conflict and the New Geopolitics* (New York, Columbia University Press).
Colarusso, J. (2002) *Nart Sagas from the Caucasus: Myths and Legends from Circassians, Abazas, Abkhaz and Ubykhs* (Princeton, Princeton University Press).
Cornell, S. E. (2002) 'Autonomy as a Source of Conflict: Caucasian Conflicts in Theoretical Perspective', *World Politics*, 54, 2.
Dannreuther, R. & March, L. (eds) (2010) *Russia and Islam: State, Society and Radicalism* (London, Routledge).
Derluguian, G. (2005) *Bourdieu's Secret Admirer in the Caucasus* (Chicago, University of Chicago Press).
Derluguian, G. (2007) 'Abkhazia: A Summary of Ethnic Conflict', in Jenkins, C. & Gottlieb, E. (eds) (2007) *Identity Conflicts: Can Violence be Regulated?* (New Brunswick, NJ, Transaction Publishers, 2007).
Dunlop, J. (1998) *Russia Confronts Chechnya: The Roots of a Separatist Conflict* (Cambridge, Cambridge University Press).
Fearon, J. D. (1998) 'Commitment Problems and the Spread of Ethnic Conflict', in Lake, D.A. & Rothchild, D. (eds) (1998) *The International Spread of Ethnic Conflict: Fear, Diffusion, and Escalation* (Princeton, Princeton University Press).
Gammer, M. (2006) *The Lone Wolf and the Bear: Three Centuries of Chechen Defiance of Russian Rule* (London, Hurst and Co.).
Gammer, M. (ed.) (2008) *Ethno-Nationalism, Islam and the State in the Caucasus: Post-Soviet Disorder* (London, Routledge).
Gurr, T. (1993) *Minorities at Risk: A Global View of Ethnopolitical Conflicts* (Washington, D.C., US Institute of Peace Press).
Gurr, T. (2000) *People Versus States: Minorities at Risk in the New Century* (Washington, D.C., US Institute of Peace Press).
King, C. (2008) *The Ghost of Freedom: A History of the Caucasus* (Oxford, Oxford University Press).
Kramer, M. (2005) 'Guerrilla Warfare, Counterinsurgency, and Terrorism in the North Caucasus: The Military Dimension of the Russian–Chechen Conflict', *Europe–Asia Studies*, 57, 2, March.
Laitin, D. & Suny, R. G. (1999). 'Armenia and Azerbaijan: Thinking a Way Out', *Middle East Policy*, 7, 1, October.
Moore, C. (2010) *Contemporary Violence: Postmodern War in Kosovo and Chechnya* (Manchester, Manchester University Press).
Moore, C. & Tumelty, P. (2008) 'Foreign Fighters and the Case of Chechnya', *Studies in Conflict and Terrorism*, 31, 5.
Moore, C. & Tumelty, P. (2009) 'Assessing Unholy Alliances in Chechnya: From Communism and Nationalism to Islamism and Salafism', *Journal of Communist Studies and Transition Politics*, 25, 1.
Pilkington, H. & Yemelianova, G. (eds) (2003) *Islam in Post-Russia: Public and Private Faces* (London, Routledge).
Richmond, W. (2008) *The Northwest Caucasus* (London, Routledge).
Ro'i, Y. (2000) *Islam in the Soviet Union* (London, Hurst and Co.).
Sagramoso, D. (2007) 'Violence and Conflict in the Russian North Caucasus', *International Affairs*, 83, 4.
Sagramoso, D. (2012) 'The Radicalisation of Islamic Salafi Jamaats in the North Caucasus: Moving Closer to the Global Jihadist Movements?', *Europe-Asia Studies*, 64, 3, pp. 561–95.
Shnirelman, V. A. (2001) *The Value of the Past: Myths, Identity and Politics in Transcaucasia*, Senri Ethnological Studies, 57 (Osaka, National Museum of Ethnology).
Singer, J. D. & Small, M. (1972) *The Wages of War, 1816–1965: A Statistical Handbook* (New York, John Wiley and Sons).
Souleimanov, E. (2007) *An Endless War: The Russian–Chechen Conflict in Perspective* (Oxford, Peter Lang).

Tishkov, V. (1997) *Ethnicity, Nationalism and Conflict in and after the Soviet Union: The Mind Aflame* (London, Sage Publications).

Walker, C. J. (1995) 'The Armenian Presence in Mountainous Karabagh', in Wright, J. F. R., Goldberg, S. & Schofield, R. N. (eds) (1995).

Ware, R. (2010) *Dagestan: Russia Hegemony and Islamic Resistance in the North Caucasus* (Armonk, NY, M. E. Sharpe).

Wright, J. F. R., Goldberg, S. & Schofield, R. N. (eds) (1995) *Transcaucasian Boundaries* (London, St Martin's Press).

Yakobashvili, T. (2010) 'Georgian Overtures to Abkhazia and Tskhinvali', 30 April, available at: http://www.opendemocracy.net/od-russia/temur-yakobashvili/georgian-overtures-to-abkhazia-and-tskhinvali, accessed 14 February 2012.

Yemelianova, G. (ed.) (2010) *Radical Islam in the Former Soviet Union* (London, Routledge).

Zelkina, A. (2000) *In Quest for God and Freedom: Sufi Responses to the Russian Advance in the North Caucasus* (London, Hurst and Co.).

Zürcher, C. (2007) *The Post-Soviet Wars: Rebellion, Ethnic Conflict, and Nationhood in the Caucasus* (New York, New York University Press).

# The Origins and Trajectory of the Caucasian Conflicts

## VICKEN CHETERIAN

### Abstract

Conflicts in the Caucasus began as a result of the weakening of the institutions of the Soviet Union. Since then there have been some major transformations. Initially, there were 'triangular conflicts' with the centre (Moscow) on the one side and two competing national projects on the other side (a Union Republic and a minority group with an autonomous status within this republic). After the collapse of the Soviet Union, these conflicts evolved into bilateral ones between two popular-nationalist movements with competing territorial claims: newly independent nation states, on the one hand, and minority groups with autonomous status, on the other.

ON 26 AUGUST 2008, SHORTLY AFTER THE SIGNING of a ceasefire between the Georgian and Russian forces, the popular Georgian TV station Rustavi-2 aired a video clip by Zurab Doijashvili. The next day Georgian Ombudsman Sozar Subari called for the privately owned television station to stop broadcasting the video because the 'lyrics of the song are extremely insulting towards the Russian people.... It represents an alarming example of the expression of ethnic hatred and xenophobia, and broadcasting this product can be regarded as an obvious attempt at inciting ethnic hatred'.[1] Soon afterwards the video clip was taken off air, revealing how far both public opinion and political culture in Georgia had moved from the days of Zviad Gamsakhurdia, the first president of independent Georgia, when 'Georgia for Georgians' or 'Five percent to foreigners' were popular slogans used by the ruling elite.

Less than two years later, Russian Federal security forces killed two rebel leaders in the North Caucasus: on 2 March 2010, Alexander Tikhomirov, better known as 'Said Buryatski', was killed in a village in Ingushetia. Another rebel leader Anzor

---

The author would like to thank the four editors of this collection for their invitation to Birmingham in 2009 when the first outline of this essay was presented, and for their detailed remarks on an earlier draft. Also, thanks to the comments of two anonymous reviewers, and special thanks to Jeremy Smith for his additional work on the revised version of this essay, which helped upgrade the essay linguistically and in its content.

[1]'Stop Russophobic Music Video'—Ombudsman Tells Georgian TV', *Civil Georgia*, 27 August 2008, available at: http://www.civil.ge/eng/article.php?id=19315, accessed 14 May 2010.

Astemirov, known as 'Amir Sayfullah', was killed on 24 March in a shootout on the streets of Nalchik, the main town of Kabardino-Balkaria. Tikhomirov was an ethnic Buryat, while Astemirov was an ethnic Kabard. The twin suicide bombing of the Moscow metro on 29 March, attacks which probably aimed at avenging the killed rebel leaders, in their turn killed some 38 people and wounded over 60. The suicide bombings were carried out by two young women: Jennet Abdurrakhmanova a 17-year-old girl and Mariam Sharipova a 28-year-old schoolteacher, both from Dagestan. Curiously, none of these four personalities were from Chechnya or of Chechen descent (Abdullaev 2010). The conflict in the North Caucasus had ceased to be conditioned by the Chechen national drive for sovereignty and self-rule, departing from the sources of tension that have caused two destructive wars in the recent past in the North Caucasus.

These two examples serve to illustrate how the political culture and sources of rebellion and violence have shifted in the Caucasus over the last two decades. It is no more mass nationalist sentiments which are fuelling revolt against an established order, or clashes with neighbouring political entities. From the time the conflicts in the Caucasus erupted in the late 1980s, we have witnessed a contextual change in political institutions, grassroots mobilisation and patterns of foreign influence and intervention. Yet, in spite of those evolutions, the Caucasus remains an unstable region, where sporadic explosions of violence remind us about regional tensions, with serious risks of spill-over. This was already apparent in the August 2008 war in Georgia, which escalated from clashes between Georgian troops and Ossetian militias into Russia's first war in its 'Near Abroad', accompanied by fears of a larger confrontation between Russia on the one side, and Europe and the US on the other. The conflict in Chechnya had already changed course, with an increasing number of violent attacks carried out outside its frontiers, destabilising the rest of the North Caucasus, as well as terrorist attacks against civilian targets deep inside Russia proper. Lastly, tension on the line of contact between Armenian and Azerbaijani forces has continued to claim victims, accompanied by verbal threats of larger military operations, with risks of neighbouring powers becoming involved.

The aim of this essay is to trace the evolution of the Caucasus conflicts over two decades, from the eruption of the Karabakh conflict in 1988 to the 2008 Russo-Georgian war. The essay aims both to be comparative (covering Karabakh, Abkhazia, South Ossetia and Chechnya), as well as suggesting paths of evolution from the beginning of those conflicts in the late Soviet years to their contemporary state. It is legitimate to question whether such a wide subject matter can be treated appropriately within the limits of an essay. It can only be achieved through a strict selection of facts to support observations and arguments, and by avoiding exhaustive coverage of developments and discussions of the conflicts in order to develop the central theme and support it by relevant references to events and literature. The interest of such an approach is in contextualising individual conflicts within larger historical trends, and linking the outbreak of violence back to the time of the Soviet collapse and the then functions of the USSR, as well as by underlining both continuity and change in the role conflicts played over two decades.

I will divide the time frame into three periods: first, the eruption of conflicts in the last years of the Soviet Union, from 1988 until 1996, with the Khasavyurt Agreement putting an end to the first Chechnya war; second, the period of state building and diplomacy, from 1996 until 2003—a symbolic date referring to the Rose Revolution in

Georgia and the coming to power of Ilham Aliev in Azerbaijan and third, the period lasting from 2003 to 2008, with new forces challenging the *status quo* and with unsuccessful diplomatic efforts in conflict resolution. I will consider three conflicts due to their relevance: the Armenian–Azerbaijani conflict over Nagorno-Karabakh; conflicts in Georgia between central authorities in Tbilisi and the two secessionist regions of Abkhazia and South Ossetia and lastly, the conflict in Chechnya between nationalist-Islamist forces on the one side, and Russian authorities and pro-Moscow Chechen forces on the other. Finally, I will consider different 'forces' that have shaped the conflicts over two decades, and consider three dimensions in my analysis: elites in power, popular mobilisation challenging the established order and outside influences.

My basic argument is that the conflicts in the Caucasus started as a result of popular mobilisations challenging the established Soviet order and its legitimacy. Although the conflicts started over local issues—for example, the status of Karabakh within the Soviet system or debates on language policy in Georgia—they evolved rapidly to generate popular movements with nationalist discourses which challenged the Soviet system as a whole, propelled a new leadership emerging from the Soviet-era intelligentsia to positions of power,[2] and eventually led to genuine revolutions; in Armenia, Azerbaijan, Chechnya and Georgia at various periods, we witnessed revolutions overthrowing the existing order of the Soviet *nomenklatura*, leading to the overall weakening and later collapse of the Soviet Union. Twenty years later, we see the absence of popular mobilisation over territorial issues, and a complete elite takeover of the national question. In the absence of major foreign powers capable of dictating the terms of conflict resolution, that the conflicts themselves have become a resource for elites in power, and instruments to legitimise their newly established political institutions and to mould new political identities, without any popular participation in political choices.

Finally, I would like to underline that by overemphasising the conflicts as 'ethnic' and 'nationalistic', we have undermined the social processes and power struggles taking place parallel to the conflicts. The conflicts in the Caucasus cannot be understood without looking at those events as struggles between competing political entities, but also as fights within each political unit. The conflicts in the Caucasus were simultaneously ethnic or nationalist conflicts, and civil wars, with the aim to establish domination over territories and populations.

### *The origins of the conflicts: triangular struggle*

The violent conflicts in the Caucasus have been at the centre of a large number of studies in the last two decades. With good cause: the Caucasus emerged as the major battlefield in the larger issue of redefining a post-Soviet political space. Interpretations of the causes of the Caucasus conflicts have focused on the success of nationality policies of the USSR in solidifying national–territorial identities (Suny 1993), claims to sovereignty by ethnic groups (Lapidus 1998), of 'ethnic fears' (Kaufmann 1998), 'secessionist ethnic conflicts... intensified (or 'escalated') by foreign intervention'

---

[2]Intelligentsia here refers to the Soviet-era professionals working in education, and arts and culture who had developed sub-cultures occupying the space between the official party line and the dissident movement, often being rather close to the dissidents as in the case of Georgia.

(Horowitz 2002, p. 633), or as the outcome of territorial policies and specifically the autonomous status of national minorities (Cornell 2002). Other studies have looked at the intellectual constructions serving as ideologies of confrontation, including the role of intellectuals and specifically archaeology or ethnography (Tishkov 1997, p. 13), or historians (Shnirelman 2001) which later served as justifications for ethnic mobilisation and confrontation. A number of studies have examined—and overemphasised—the role played by outside powers not only in manipulating existing conflicts, but as a major interpretative discourse. Another major trend in the literature is to look at 'nationalism' as a basic cause of the Caucasus conflicts. Thus, the Soviet period is seen as a historic exception which during its existence suppressed pre-existing 'nationalist' conflicts, which resurfaced only after its demise (Goldenberg 1994; Croissant 1998).

Yet, there is a need to redefine our understanding of the conflicts in the Caucasus, or, rather, to analyse the causes of current instability in the region. In other words, the Caucasus continues to be a region of instability and war, yet the reason for this is different today from what it was in the late 1980s. 'As tides of nationalism recede', Mark Beissinger has remarked, 'the renormalisation of political order is accompanied by a shift away from mobilised contention toward institutionalised forms of nationalist politics' (Beissinger 2002, p. 32). Such a new reframing is needed in order to grapple with the ideological but also sociological transformations of conflict dynamics in the post-mass nationalism era, as illustrated by the spread of *jihadi* ideologies in the North Caucasus following the collapse of the Chechen national-independence movement, as well as the new conflict dynamism in the post-August 2008 war between Georgia and Russia.

A series of conflicts that started with the Armenian–Azerbaijani dispute over Nagorno-Karabakh led to a chain-reaction of ethno-territorial conflict at the moment of Soviet collapse, leading to the wars in Karabakh (Chorbajian *et al.* 1994; de Waal 2003), South Ossetia, Abkhazia (Ekedahl & Goodman 1997; Coppieters *et al.* 1998) and to the two wars in Chechnya (Lieven 1998; Smith 1998; Malashenko & Trenin 2004; Tishkov 2004). National mobilisation with large popular appeal suddenly surfaced in the Caucasus and overthrew the reign of the Soviet *nomenklatura*. Although one should be careful of drawing a causal relation between nationalist movements on the one hand, and conflict and war on the other (Van Evera 1994), what distinguished the Caucasus from the Balkans or Central Asia was that popular movements inspired by a nationalist discourse overthrew the existing order in an attempt to replace it with a new one, very often led by the Soviet-era intelligentsia. By contrast in the Balkans, it was the *nomenklatura* itself which appropriated the nationalist ideology and project (Lukic & Lynch 1996), while in Central Asia the local *nomenklatura* resisted and retained power, with Tajikistan the obvious exception (Rubin 1993/1994; Schatz 2004), which more closely resembled the evolution of the states of the South Caucasus.[3]

---

[3]The first Armenian President Levon Ter-Petrossian, and most of the leaders of the Karabakh Committee that came to power in 1989, were members of the Soviet–Armenian intelligentsia; Zviad Gamsakhurdia and Abulfaz Elchibey, respectively, the first presidents of Georgia and Azerbaijan, were Soviet-era intelligentsia members with long records of dissident activism. In the North Caucasus, the intelligentsia played a key role in the development of the post-Soviet political space in the North Caucasus with figures such as Zelimkhan Yandarbiyev, a writer, and vice-president under the first Chechen *de facto* President Djokhar Dudaev, and Musa Shanibov, leader of the Kabard national movement who also played a key role in the Caucasus Peoples Confederation.

Historically, it was not evident that a popular movement emerging to challenge the Soviet order had to carry the banner of nationalism. The dissident movement in the Soviet Union since the 1960s was largely led by human rights activists. The first wave of popular mobilisation was not led by national movements, but by environmentalists (Geukjian 2007; Cheterian 2008, pp. 159–61; Cheterian 2009b); in Armenia, Azerbaijan and Georgia the first street demonstrations mobilising between 3,000 and 5,000 people, which were broader than just the dissident movements, were concerned with environmental issues.[4] Soon after, the emerging national movements swept away all other political formations and dominated the political scene. As popular mobilisation reached the North Caucasus, it did not go through the initial timid environmental movement as nationalism was already becoming a dominant force. What needs to be remembered is that nationalist movements in the Caucasus were both mass movements and anti-systemic (Evangelista 2002, p. 15). In other words, the conflicts evolved as superimposed political processes. They comprised both socio-political conflict between an emerging mass movement coloured by nationalism struggling against the Soviet system (whether against the Soviet central authorities or against the corruption and political monopoly of the republican ruling cast), and simultaneously, conflicts to define a new political entity which therefore entered into collision with neighbouring ethno-territorial projects.[5] They succeeded in overthrowing the ruling elites in the republics, that is the national *nomenklatura* ruling the three republics of the South Caucasus, and the Russian–Chechen *nomenklatura* ruling in the Checheno-Ingush Autonomous Republic. In other words, the national movements produced both political and also social revolutions, replacing a ruling class with another one, and accelerating social and economic transformation.

The aim of national movements was to reformulate the power structures and the institutional hierarchy between the centre and the regions. Their demands were initially addressed to Moscow, identified as the only source of authority: when Karabakh Armenians formulated their demands to transfer their autonomy from Azerbaijan to Armenia, they addressed Moscow and not Baku, since the Soviet centre was perceived as the only sovereign power which could achieve such important changes. Soon, however, the nature of conflict transformed into 'triangular conflicts', that is between the centre on the one side, and two competing national projects on the other: a first national movement of the titular nation of the Soviet union republic and a second national movement belonging to a 'minority' nation with autonomy status in the Soviet system.[6] As Moscow revealed itself to be incapable of addressing territorial

---

[4]They included demands closing down the Nairit synthetic rubber factory in Yerevan and Medzamor nuclear power station not far from the capital (1987), protests against the Caucasus Mountain Railway project in Georgia (1988), and opposition to the cutting down of the Topkhana forest in Azerbaijan (November 1988).

[5]I should clarify here that not all national movements in the Caucasus emerged as anti-systemic. For example, both the Ossetian national movement in South Ossetia and the Abkhaz national movement were anti-Georgian in their essence and looked towards Moscow for protection.

[6]The 'triangular conflicts' as defined here differ from Rogers Brubaker's 'triadic relational nexus' which considers the nationalising state, a minority group and external national homelands (Brubaker 1999, p. 55), and which takes its historic references from Central and Eastern Europe, rather than cases emerging from Soviet experimentation.

questions—as in the case of Karabakh—two new dimensions appeared: first, a national resistance in Azerbaijan developed opposing the transfer of territory, leading to an evolution from a bilateral Karabakh–Moscow conflict,[7] into a triangular one—Karabakh–Baku–Moscow. Moreover, a popular mobilisation in Armenia to support their ethnic kin in Karabakh complicated the picture even further, introducing the spectre of conflict between two neighbouring Soviet republics. This complication spilled over in the era of independence, when Baku argued that the conflict was essentially between a sovereign state and its western neighbour Armenia claiming part of its territory, while Armenia argued that the conflict was essentially between Azerbaijan and the Armenians of Mountainous Karabakh with Armenia being an interested party.

We can see the emergence of 'triangular conflicts' equally in the case of Georgia. The Georgian National Movement became a real political force starting from 1988. Initially, under pressure from this emerging new force, the Soviet Georgian authorities adopted a number of measures to strengthen national identity, including the passing of a language law in November 1988 (Birch 1996, p. 161). This was intended as a reaction to perceived Soviet policies of Russification, and referred to a decades-long struggle for the defence of the Georgian language and cultural rights against top-down modernisation policies imposed by Moscow. Yet, the Georgian national mobilisation had an adverse impact on national minorities, especially on those that enjoyed special standing—such as autonomous republic or autonomous region status. As Georgia was struggling to upgrade its status from a Soviet republic to independent statehood, other entities were trying to do the same: Chechens demanded the status of a union republic, while the South Ossetian parliament demanded to be upgraded from an 'Autonomous Region' to an 'Autonomous Republic' (Saparov 2010, p.100). The Georgian national movement took a radical position against the Soviet state considering all Soviet institutions illegitimate, including the Soviet Georgian constitution of 1925. Although the thrust of the Georgian national movement was directed against the central authorities, it nevertheless disregarded the sentiments of national minorities. More than that, mainstream Georgian public opinion regarded the autonomous entities of Abkhazia, Ajaria and South Ossetia as the product of Russian and Soviet policies of 'divide and rule'. In November 1988, a demonstration calling for the end of 'discrimination against Georgians by Abkhaz, Azerbaijanis, Ajarians and Ossetians' attracted some 100,000 people in the capital Tbilisi (Suny 1994, p. 321). Later, on 9 April 1989, demonstrations protesting against events in Sukhumi were violently repressed by the Soviet army causing 20 people to be killed and up to 1,400 wounded, mainly as a result of poisonous gas. This violent event effectively put an end to the last vestiges of legitimacy of the Soviet order in the eyes of the Georgian people. Tensions between ethnic Abkhaz and ethnic Georgians were well recognised since the clashes in Sukhumi in 1978, and yet the surprise was the eruption of violence in South Ossetia in March 1989, leading to the first bloody confrontations in Georgia.

---

[7] Igor Nolyain sees the Karabakh conflict as a Moscow–Armenian national movement conflict (Nolyain 1994).

The conflicts of the Caucasus emerged in the conditions of weakening and rapid collapse of the Soviet order which left behind a political and security vacuum that needed to be filled. In these conditions, various political projects emerged around social formations competing with each other. Rival nationalist projects competed, and even fought against each other, but also strengthened each other (Zverev 1996, p. 14). Without the Armenian territorial demands, Azerbaijani nationalism would have taken a different form, and without the anti-Armenian pogroms in a series of Azerbaijani cities, Armenian nationalism would have taken a softer tone. Yet, it is wrong to see these conflicts as primordial antagonisms, as 'ancient hatreds' between nations. Rather, it was the specificity of Soviet political culture—which imposed centralised hierarchical order and did not develop horizontal institutional mechanisms—and its rapid disintegration that left behind a power vacuum, creating the conditions of national mobilisation and territorial competition (Cheterian 2008, pp. 26–8).

The withering away of the Soviet state transformed what was up to then internal conflicts within the Soviet borders into conflicts with an international dimension. First, it divided the Caucasus between four newly independent states—Armenia, Azerbaijan, Georgia and Russia. The South Caucasus witnessed the emergence of three internationally recognised, and three *de facto* states, while the North Caucasus remained under Russian sovereignty, although the Chechen rebellion posed a serious challenge. The conflict over Karabakh led to an undeclared war between two newly independent states, Armenia and Azerbaijan; the conflict between Georgians and Ossets in South Ossetia had repercussions across the Georgian–Russian border, as did the conflict in Abkhazia.

The collapse of the Soviet Union led to the intensification of conflicts, from skirmishes to total wars. In Karabakh, the withdrawal of 11,000 Soviet troops from November 1991 to February 1992 led to an all out war. The violence of confrontations together with the havoc it caused, population movements, and the near collapse of economic activities made many question whether the independence of the new states was really viable. At the time, people in the South Caucasus imagined that the newly gained independence from Moscow was provisional, and that once the former imperial centre reorganised itself it would return to the region to bring it under its wings, in a similar way to what happened in the 1918–1920 period.

History has a curious and complex manner of moving forward yet, very often, in the minds of many in the Caucasus, Russian omnipotence was to take new forms: many thought at the time, and continue to insist, that the wars of the early 1990s were instigated and conditioned by Russia, as an imperial policy of 'divide and rule'.[8] Even more, the conflicts are often described as being fought between centralist forces of the former empire, and national liberation forces, rather than between newly independent states against minority groups within their borders in their turn striving for sovereignty. The collapse of the USSR deeply transformed the conflicts from triangular (Moscow–union republic–autonomy) to bilateral ones between two nationalist movements competing over the heritage of the Soviet Union. Russian

---

[8]This was in spite of the fact that the power of Moscow was in the midst of an unprecedented retreat on all fronts: from Eastern Europe to the former republics of the Soviet Union, making the area under Russian rule even smaller than the area occupied by the Tsarist Empire of the nineteenth century.

interference was very much present, yet it played only a secondary role. However, many nationalist leaders continued to deploy discourses of Russia's 'hidden hand' for a double purpose: to reject any legitimacy of the political demands coming from ethnic minorities, attributing them to old revanchist forces; and to absolve themselves from their own responsibilities in initiating the armed conflicts by pointing fingers towards the Kremlin.[9] Such interpretations helped justify why larger nations such as Azerbaijan or Georgia militarily lost wars against minority groups in the conflicts of Karabakh or Abkhazia. The dominant discourse, therefore, is that the conflicts were not 'Georgian–Abkhaz' or 'Armenia–Azerbaijani' but rather between Azerbaijan and Georgia on the one side seeking independence, and Moscow trying to hinder their efforts through these little conflicts. Russia has a similar alibi, an external enemy responsible for its own Caucasian mess: the West, which according to popular narrative was behind the Chechen conflict with the aim of destroying the Russian Federation.[10]

However, there can be other interpretations that help us shed more light on the conflicts in the Caucasus. These conflicts ended their 'first round' in the early to mid-1990s, with similar, as well as surprising outcomes: the 'smaller' challengers inflicted defeats over larger nations. This was the case with Karabakh Armenians against Azerbaijan, Abkhazia against Georgia and Chechnya against Russia. The image of Russia the imperial power being behind the conflicts in Karabakh and Abkhazia is not consistent with Russia's disorganised military campaign in Chechnya and its defeat in 1996. Therefore, a different set of arguments are needed to shed light on the conflict mechanisms in the Caucasus in the aftermath of the Soviet collapse.

First, these conflicts were not between states on the one side and non-state actors on the other. The conflicts were between popular-nationalist movements on both sides; the legal recognition of Armenia, Azerbaijan, Georgia and Russia as sovereign states by international organisations in late 1991 and early 1992 did not change the facts on the ground, mainly that these new states lacked institutional capacity at the moment of outbreak of conflict, including the police, military and espionage necessary to run a successful military campaign.[11] Second, the notion of 'separatism' does not help understand the nature of the conflicts as they developed in the field. It was not Karabakh, Abkhazia or Chechnya 'separating' from central authorities. Rather, they were asserting their political sovereignty on the background of a new and rather sketchy political order taking shape in a distant metropolis. It was the new leaders in Baku, Tbilisi and Moscow that did not accept the emergence of new sovereignties on their fringes, or even the recognition of the autonomous character of some provinces that had existed under the Soviet order. Instead they sent newly formed and often

---

[9] Russian omnipotence and responsibility in igniting and managing the conflicts in the Caucasus also fitted some Western reports which still carried the hallmarks of Cold War influence. See Goltz (1993).

[10] 'The West Masterminded Chechen War to Destroy the USSR and Russia', *Pravda*, 11 December 2009, available at: http://english.pravda.ru/russia/history/111072-0/, accessed 29 June 2010.

[11] This argument partially fits the Russian Federation, which inherited the old Soviet state institutions including the military infrastructure, but its situation had degraded as a result of a lack of investment, the withdrawal of Soviet forces from Eastern Europe and former Soviet republics and demoralisation resulting from cataclysmic political changes, leading to the catastrophic military campaign in Chechnya especially in the early months of the war.

irregular military forces to bring these rebellious provinces, which were in the thrall of popular mobilisation, under their own authority. The military campaigns of Azerbaijan in Nagorno-Karabakh, of Georgia in South Ossetia or Abkhazia and of Russian Federal troops in Chechnya resembled conquests rather than repressing centrifugal forces. As a result, the military effort demanded from the minorities entrenched in their mountainous and far away provinces were much less than the military and logistic effort needed by the new states fighting a war in distant regions. Lastly, the minority groups revealed superior motivation, organisational skills and mobilisation than could be achieved under the political mobilisation capacity of the newly independent states. One of the reasons for this discrepancy is that for the ethnic minorities the wars were seen as existential ones, and in case of defeat they feared losing the political autonomy they enjoyed in the Soviet period, while for the political elites of the states these wars in far away provinces had only secondary importance in a period of intense power struggle and resource and property distribution in the capital (Cheterian 2008, pp. 285–318).

The leaders of the independent states failed in their military campaign to impose their authority on independence-minded former Soviet autonomies. The end result was not a total military defeat for any conflict party, but rather an equilibrium of forces leading to ceasefire agreements, opening a new phase of competition and friction. The radical nationalism that emerged after the Soviet collapse, and led to the violent conflicts, did not survive long, nor did it take institutional forms. In the words of Ronald Suny in Georgia, 'exclusivist nationalism gave way to a more pragmatic inclusive idea of the nation that opened discussion of the possible restructuring of the state along federalist lines' (Suny 1999/2000, p. 141). It took 'defeat and state collapse' for Georgia to move away from an exclusivist nationalist political culture and explore new possibilities. Once the military conflicts subsided the identity issue relaxed and instead of ethnic homogeneity differences over politics, class or ideology emerged. However, the unsolved status of the territorial questions still made the Caucasus a dangerous neighbourhood, and the resolution of the conflicts a necessity in order not to see a re-run of the former quarrels.

### *State-building and conflict resolution attempts*

The ethno-territorial conflicts were directly linked to inter-elite power struggles (Cheterian 2001, pp. 18–20). In fact, we can see a dialectical interplay between the military developments on the conflict frontlines and the deepening power struggles in the republican capitals. The Azerbaijani defeats in Nagorno-Karabakh in winter and spring 1992 led to a sharpening of the power struggle in Baku; the Soviet era *nomenklatura* in power was overthrown by the Azerbaijani Popular Front (*Azerbaijan Khalq Jabhasi*), opening the way to the 11-month rule of former dissident Abulfaz Elchibey. The new powers, once consolidated in Baku, launched the summer 1992 offensive with remarkable initial military successes, occupying nearly two-fifths of the territory of Nagorno-Karabakh Autonomous *Oblast'*. Later, it was once again the military defeats of Azerbaijani forces that destabilised the rule of Elchibey and opened the way for the return of the former leader of Soviet Azerbaijan and Soviet *politburo* member Heidar Aliev to power. The same is valid in the case of the Abkhazia war: the first freely elected president Zviad Gamsakhurdia was overthrown by a coalition of opposition forces. Former collaborators of Gamsakhurdia, elements of the Georgian *nomenklatura* which had recently lost power, and illegal armed groups such as the notorious *Mkhedrioni*, came together to overthrow the rule of Gamsakhurdia in January 1992. Two months later the leaders of the *coup d'état* invited Eduard Shevardnadze, the former leader of Soviet Georgia and Soviet foreign minister under Gorbachev, to return to Tbilisi and lead the country out of its crisis. A power struggle between (and within) the Shevardnadze administration and supporters of Zviad Gamsakhurdia provoked the war in Abkhazia, and played a key role in the weak performance of Georgian forces. With the defeat of Georgian forces in Abkhazia in September 1993, pro-Gamsakhurdia forces attempted a comeback, taking over Zugdidi, the traditional stronghold of Zviadist forces and advancing eastwards to Kutaisi only to be stopped and beaten back. In Armenia, which did not suffer military defeat, the intelligentsia remained in power longer, but eventually Levon Ter-Petrossian was overthrown in February 1998 as he was pushing for concessions on the Karabakh issue, and a group of former leaders of the Karabakh war led by a former *de facto* president of Karabakh, Robert Kocharian, took power. The intelligentsia succeeded in overthrowing the Soviet-era *nomenklatura* in the Caucasus by leading popular revolutions, but wars, refugees and collapsed economies did not permit them to consolidate their power. In the case of the Russian invasion of Chechnya in December 1994, we see a similar pattern, whereby the Russian administration attempted to boost Yel'tsin's popularity at a time when he was coming under pressure from various nationalist and leftist forces, by provoking a 'small victorious war' (Gall & de Wall 1997a).[12]

The end of the violent period of the conflicts began in 1992 in the case of the Ossetian–Georgian conflict, followed by the Abkhaz–Georgian conflict in 1993, the Karabakh conflict in 1994 and the first war in Chechnya in 1996. The conditions of the end of the military phase of the conflicts were also similar: the failure of centralist forces in bringing political unity through the use of military force, and the signing of ceasefire agreements, while postponing the political resolution to later periods.

In South Ossetia the Dagomys Agreement was signed on 27 July 1992, and Joint Peacekeeping Forces (JPKF) composed of Russian, Georgian, North Ossetian and South Ossetian soldiers, five soldiers each, were deployed. In spite of the lack of political agreement on the status of the former Soviet province and any serious process of negotiations between the conflict parties, the ceasefire agreement held well and succeeded in normalising relations in this ethnically mixed region until the Rose Revolution of 2003. In Abkhazia, the ethnic Abkhaz forces, with support from the Russian military, took complete control of Abkhazia up to the Inguri River during heavy fighting in September 1993, after which the two antagonists signed a ceasefire agreement in Moscow on 14 May 1994.[13] Russian peacekeeping forces under the flag of the Commonwealth of Independent States (CIS) separated the belligerents. In Karabakh, the massive Azerbaijani counter-attack of winter 1993–1994 on several

---

[12]See also Evangelista (2002, p. 37).

[13]The text of the ceasefire agreement between Abkhazia and Georgia is available at: http://www.c-r.org/our-work/accord/georgia-abkhazia/keytext3.php, accessed 24 July 2012.

portions of the war-front did not manage to pierce the Armenian defences. On 16 May 1994, representatives of the three sides (Armenia, Azerbaijan and Nagorno-Karabakh) met in Moscow and signed a ceasefire agreement. As the sides failed to agree on the modalities of peacekeeping forces, no foreign troops were introduced to the conflict zone. In Chechnya, the rebel forces launched a massive attack on three major cities including Grozny, Gudermes and Argun in August 1996, forcing the Russian leadership to agree to a ceasefire arrangement, and eventually sign the Khasavyurt Agreement on 31 August. Here, too, no outside peacekeeping forces were introduced.

The ceasefire agreements in the conflicts of South Ossetia, Abkhazia and Nagorno-Karabakh, were signed under Russian patronage, and in the absence of engagement of other major powers in the conflict settlement. Moscow saw the ceasefire agreements as a step to preserve its own influence over the South Caucasus, and as a first step to introduce mainly Russian—or exclusively Russian—peacekeeping troops. The hesitation of Western powers in the immediate aftermath of the Soviet collapse to engage their troops in post-Soviet territories, which they saw as regions remaining firmly under Russian influence, and at a time when their attention was tied to the ongoing conflicts in the Balkans, helped Russia to bring about ceasefire agreements under its own conditions. But Russia failed to profit from its favourable political–military position in the period immediately following the ceasefires. This was mainly because Russia lacked a model for modernisation (Markedonov 2009, p. 19) that it could offer to states emerging from Soviet collapse as it was facing similar challenges itself. Moscow also lacked the funds and technology to help reshape the economies of the region or to invest in export-oriented sectors such as oil and gas. Eventually, it had to cede its dominant position to Western or Middle Eastern competitors. Russian influence over Armenia increased, with a military treaty keeping the Gumri military base, as well as achieving an increasingly dominant position over strategic sectors of the Armenian economy including the Medzamor nuclear power plant, the Hrazdan power plant, the natural gas distribution network and the electricity grid. Russia also had a dominant position over Abkhazia and South Ossetia through its military presence under peacekeeping flags, as well as through economic leverages. But Russian influence over Azerbaijan and Georgia decreased, as those two countries came closer to the economic orbit of Western powers following oil projects and pipeline deals.

In the immediate aftermath of violent confrontations, the period following the ceasefire arrangements was rich in attempts at conflict settlement. The most important diplomatic activities concentrated around settling the Georgia–Abkhazia conflict and the Armenian–Azerbaijani conflict. The Georgian authorities did not invest much energy in the conflict in South Ossetia, the logic being to attempt and solve the major ethno-territorial conflict from the Georgian perspective, that of Abkhazia, which would later lead to an easy solution in the case of secondary conflicts like the one in South Ossetia.

The Abkhaz position radicalised following the brief May 1998 war. Now, the Abkhaz *de facto* authorities searched for federal solutions not with Georgia, but with Russia. This Abkhaz change in position coincided with important developments in Moscow. The Yel'tsin administration had imposed a blockade against Abkhazia forbidding male inhabitants of the region aged between 16- and 60-years-old from crossing the border. After 2000, Moscow dramatically changed its policy towards

Abkhazia, distributing large numbers of Russian passports (Serrano 2007, p. 110; Trier *et al*. 2010, p. 8). Following 1998, there were diplomatic activities to regulate the Abkhazia conflict, with suggestions on conflict resolution advanced by foreign diplomats, like Liviu Bota in 1999 and Dieter Boden in 2001, both personal representatives of the UN Secretary General.

Following the signing of the May 1994 ceasefire, intensive meetings between Armenian and Azerbaijani representatives tried to find a political solution to the conflict. Two periods witnessed intensive negotiations during which the negotiating parties came close to finding a common agreement. The first was in 1997–1998, following intensive mediation from the OSCE Minsk Group, which first proposed a 'package solution' and later a 'phased' solution to the conflict. The intensive negotiations led to internal frictions. In Armenia, President Levon Ter-Petrossian was increasingly isolated as strong opposition mounted among his close collaborators. He was forced to resign in February 1998, as his Prime Minister Robert Kocharyan, Minister of Defence Vazgen Sargsyan and Minister of National Security Serge Sargsyan opposed his policy on Karabakh and forced him to step down.

Robert Kocharyan, his successor, was reputed to be a hard liner, but soon after taking power he too engaged in an intense process of negotiations. More than 16 face-to-face discussions took place between 1999 and 2001 between the presidents of Armenia and Azerbaijan, discussing conflict resolution from all possible angles. These meetings culminated in the Key West summit hosted by US Secretary of State Collin Powell. Yet, the Florida meeting failed to seal a deal as the Azerbaijani leader was 'taken aback by the strength of feeling in the country' (Stern 2001).

Aliev, in turn, found himself isolated from his own political elite, many of whom resigned prior to or following the Key West summit.[14] The lesson of the resignation of Ter-Petrossian and the failure of Key West was that isolating two leaders in a negotiation process could help them to find a common understanding, yet it distanced them from their own public opinion and possibly their own political class. The 1997 and 1999–2001 Armeno-Azerbaijani negotiations were the most serious attempts at conflict resolution in the Caucasus conflicts, and the Key West meeting was the moment that came closest to achieving a peace treaty.

From the ceasefire arrangements in the early to mid-1990s, the south and the north of the Caucasus mountain chain witnessed separate developments. In the case of the Russo-Chechen conflict, there were no serious attempts at negotiations following the formal signing of a peace treaty between the newly elected Chechen President Aslan Maskhadov and Russian President Boris Yel'tsin on 12 May 1997, in Moscow. The Khasavyurt Agreement (August 1996) which was supposed to end armed confrontation between the Russian Federal troops and the Chechen fighters and open the stage for a political solution failed to stabilise the region. The new Chechen leadership headed by Aslan Maskhadov could not unify the powerful Chechen field commanders, transforming the country into a state of constant civil war between rival factions competing over the control of territory and resources (Stanley 1997). Permanent

---

[14]Among those who resigned were the Foreign Minister Toufiq Zulfugarov, and the presidential advisor on international affairs Vafa Guliuzade, who resigned at the beginning of the negotiations process in 1999, revealing deep splits among Azerbaijani foreign affairs decision-makers.

instability in Chechnya further degraded the economy which was already in a deplorable state as a result of the collapse of the Soviet Union and the war of 1994–1996. It was the failure of the Chechen resistance to build state institutions that further radicalised many of the fighters under the influence of *salafi-jihadi* ideology and led them to form an alliance with Khattab—a Saudi *mujahed* who had moved to the North Caucasus after fighting in Afghanistan and Tajikistan. They sought to form a North Caucasian *imamat* whose activities would spread beyond the borders of Chechnya (Moore & Tumelty 2009). Looking from a wider historic perspective Moshe Gammer sees a 'circle in the spiral' being completed: anti-Russian resistance starting as *jihad*, turning into Chechen nationalism in the late 1980s, and again in the late 1990s moving back to *jihadi*, or Islamist, positions (Gammer 2006, p. 218). This political failure of the Chechen national idea was the explosive essence that ignited the misconceived adventure of Chechen fighters led by Shamil Basayev and Khattab and led them to invade Dagestan, crossing over the boundaries of ethno-territorial division to establish the state of the imagined Umma. The continuation of the conflict in Chechnya radicalised Chechen resistance and put it into contact with *jihadi* volunteers from the Middle East and Central Asia (Wilhelmsen 2005). The misadventure of Basayev and Khattab gave a strong reason for the Russian military and the new rising star of Russian politics Vladimir Putin to relaunch a military campaign in 1999 in an attempt to retake Chechnya (Kramer 2005). After heavy fighting and huge losses the Russian military succeeded in pacifying rebellious Chechnya, although the entire region of the North Caucasus has been destabilised as a result of a decade of war.[15]

During this post-war period, the South Caucasus entered a stage of stabilisation and state building, with various degrees of success. On the one hand some states, such as Armenia and Azerbaijan, succeeded in building institutions and eliminating illegal military formations, while Georgia had weak state institutions and the continuous existence of illegal armed formations (such as the guerrilla forces active in western Georgia, the 'White Legion' (*tetri legioni*) and 'Forest Brothers' (*tqis dzmebi*), or the paramilitary forces under the control of Ajaria's ruler Aslan Abashidze). Similarly, *de facto* independent states emerged with various degrees of success in state building, with Abkhazia and Nagorno-Karabakh succeeding in creating military structures under the command of the *de facto* political leadership, while Chechnya under Aslan Maskhadov failed to do that. As a result, Chechnya between the two wars was in a state of permanent civil war.

The period following the violent conflicts also witnessed the emergence of new political systems, with the new elites increasingly monopolising the political as well as economic space, while the popular mobilisation that the region witnessed in the late 1980s had died down. The front lines of Karabakh were mainly calm. In South Ossetia, relations between ethnic Ossetians and Georgians were normalising, in spite of the absence of a formal political agreement that could put a definitive end to the conflict. In Abkhazia, tension continued between the Abkhaz *de facto* authorities and Georgian paramilitary fighters. In May 1998, these tensions erupted into the large-scale military operations known as the 'six days' war as Georgian paramilitary groups

---

[15]'160 000 Zhertv', *Izvestiya*, 16 August 2005, available at: http://www.izvestia.ru/russia/article2515033/, accessed 17 May 2010.

tried to take over regions of the southern Gali district, leading to violent reactions from Abkhazian armed forces. In October 2001 fighting erupted once again in Abkhazia when a military group composed of 400 mainly foreign fighters led by Chechen field commander Ruslan Gelayev, and around 100 Georgian Interior Ministry troops (Razoux 2009, p. 262), advanced from Kodori Valley in the direction of Sukhumi, but were beaten back by Abkhaz resistance. On several occasions, the region went through new waves of popular mobilisation, for example to protest against the results of presidential elections in Armenia in 1996, and against the results of parliamentary elections in Georgia in 2003 leading to the Rose Revolution. However, there was no popular mobilisation for or against a solution proposed to the ethno-territorial conflicts. The conflicts became the domain of narrow circles within the ruling elite. The attempts to resolve the Karabakh conflict in 1997 and in 2001 were not opposed by street demonstrations. Opposition came instead from within the elites in power.

*Internationalisation of the conflicts and a new arms race*

The intensive Armenian–Azerbaijani negotiations of the late 1990s took place during a period when Azerbaijan was going through yet another metamorphosis: entering global oil markets. In September 1994, a major oil deal was signed between the Azerbaijani leadership and a consortium of oil companies led by British Petroleum. Known as 'the deal of the century' the $8 billion agreement brought Azerbaijan to global attention and attracted major powers into the Caucasus and the Caspian region. The construction of a pipeline pumping oil from Baku through Georgia to the Turkish port of Ceyhan added to the strategic importance of the region in the eyes of European capitals in search of energy diversification. It is interesting that Azerbaijani President Heydar Aliev used the new prestige of his country to return to the negotiations table and sincerely seek a compromise solution. Yet, after the failure at Key West there were no more serious attempts at engagement in intense negotiations, in spite of ongoing sporadic meetings and declarations. Instead, Azerbaijan was occupied with internal political issues, mainly the power transfer from Heydar Aliev the father to Ilham Aliev the son, and the creation of the first post-Soviet dynastic rule (Rasizade 2004).

The oil contracts signed in the first half of the 1990s under Heydar Aliev brought Caspian oil to international markets and resulted in a fundamental change in Azerbaijani policy under the new leader Ilham Aliev. It also brought about another major shift in the forces playing a role in the regional conflicts, by introducing a series of new foreign actors into the region. Neither the US nor the EU had paid much attention to the Caucasus during the violent period of the conflicts, limiting their attention to providing humanitarian aid and bringing international organisations to the region to supervise ceasefire agreements brokered by Moscow: thus, the UN mission to Abkhazia (UNOMIG) had a basic mandate that was limited to investigating and reporting by 88 military observers.[16] But the signing of the Caspian

---

[16]On UNOMIG's mandate, see http://www.unomig.org/glance/mandate/ (accessed 4 October 2011).

oil deals and the investment of several billions of dollars in the oil sector created a new reality involving Western business interests. Oil interests, in their turn, invited governments to provide them with the necessary protection against the dual danger of hostile states and a multitude of non-state actors. Among the lobbyists, there were personalities that had occupied critical posts in former US administrations with contacts inside the Clinton administration, and these lobbyists had visions that surpassed the simple protection of investments.[17] The active lobbying of oil companies in Washington soon led to the awakening of geopolitical interests in the American capital as well as in a number of European capitals, where the central question was: who is going to supervise and dominate the Caspian oil resources flowing to international markets? This competition between major powers, often labelled as 'the new great game' (referring to the nineteenth century competition between the British and Russian empires for supremacy over Central Asia), brought new state actors and their interests, oil companies, diplomats, journalists and a series of other interests to the region. It also redrew the power relations between the old actors of the conflicts: oil interests strengthened some and marginalised others (Cheterian 1997).

Exports of Azerbaijani oil and gas had not only economic and financial, but also strategic dimensions. Between 1994 and 2009 Azerbaijan received nearly $30 billion in direct foreign investment exclusively in its energy domain (UPI 2009). Net revenues from oil and gas by 2024 are estimated to be $198 billion (World Bank 2009). In 2010, Azerbaijani Gross Domestic Product (GDP) was $52.1 billion, while that of its rival Armenia was a mere $8.8 billion (International Crisis Group 2011, p. 6). Azerbaijani military spending increased from $160 million in 2003 to 3.1 billion in 2011, exclusively financed by petrodollars; over 92% of its total exports are hydrocarbon products. With petrodollars, Azerbaijan possessed the means to challenge the ceasefire agreement of 1994.

Another incident from outside the context of the Caucasus region that came to further overload the situation was 9/11. In the new age of 'war against terror' *jihadi* elements present in and around Chechnya became unacceptable. What was tolerated in the past had to be eliminated. This was the immediate reason for accelerated military cooperation between the US military and Georgian armed forces. The first target was the Pankisi Valley which, with its native Chechen population, had provided sanctuary to Chechen fighters (including the field commander Ruslan Gelayev mentioned above), but also to Arab *jihadi* volunteers *en route* to Chechnya. This was at the height of the second war in Chechnya and *salafi-jihadi* militants from the Middle East were very active in Chechnya.[18] For this purpose, intense military cooperation was begun with Georgia under the name 'train and equip', aiming at the development of Georgian armed forces to police the northern borders of the country. Soon, the programme evolved into a major operation. At the same time, the Shevardnadze

---

[17]'Among the most prominent names are former Secretaries of State Henry A. Kissinger and James A. Baker, III, former Defense Secretary Dick Cheney, former Senator and Treasury Secretary Lloyd Bentsen, former White House chief of staff John H. Sununu, and two former national security advisers, Brent Scowcroft and Zbigniew Brzezinski'. See Kinzer (2007).

[18]At the time, Chechnya was high on the agenda of *salafi-jihadi* groups. Eleven out of 19 aeroplane hijackers of 9/11 had either fought in Chechnya or had left home declaring that they were leaving for *jihad* in Chechnya. See Murphey and Ottaway (2001, p. A12) and Van Natta Jr and Zernike (2001).

administration seemed to be obsolete and incongruent for the new tasks ahead of the Georgian state, seen from the angle of new international realities. A weak and corrupt administration could not efficiently handle the fight against terrorism as well as the fight against criminalised elements that made up part of the Georgian political equation under Shevardnadze.

More lastingly, the 'War on Terror' placed the Caucasus in the geographic centre of a major military confrontation: to its east, there was Central Asia and Afghanistan with the US campaign against *al-Qaeda* and the *Taliban*; to its south, there was the Middle East with Iraq invaded and occupied by US forces in March 2003, and Iran continued to be a major preoccupation for Western leaders with the question of a potential military operation surfacing from time to time. This made the Caucasus a potentially important region from a logistical point of view. Azerbaijan, for example, was regularly approached as to making its ports available, especially in the case of an eventual US attack against the Islamic Republic.[19] The importance of an Azerbaijani base grew in the eyes of US military planners as difficulties in supplying troops in Afghanistan increased with attacks on convoys in Pakistan, and the closing down of Khanabad airbase in Uzbekistan in July 2005. Speculation concerning a foreign, possibly NATO, military base increased as Azerbaijan revised its military doctrine to allow the setting-up of foreign military bases on Azerbaijani soil.[20]

In the first half of the 2000s signs emerged that both Azerbaijan and Georgia were ready to challenge the ceasefire agreements of the 1990s. This was most evident in Georgia where, following the Rose Revolution of 2003 a new political class came to power with the project of establishing a strong state in Georgia. During the mobilisation phase of the Rose Revolution, the ethno-territorial conflicts did not play any significant role. But Mikheil Saakashvili started making references to the conflicts from his first inauguration speech of January 2004, claiming a responsibility to reunify Georgian territories. The new leadership succeeded in reforming the administration, increasing the capacity of the state to raise taxes. This was translated in various forms, first of all in establishing an effective administration, strong law enforcement agencies and a strong army. Simultaneously, defence spending increased from around $50 million in 2003 up to $1 billion or 5.6% of GDP in 2008 (Fuller & Giragosian 2008). The Georgian authorities declared that the 20-fold increase in military spending was necessary to upgrade the military in view of the declared objective to join the NATO alliance. Yet, the choice of the armaments procured, and especially the building of two major military bases, one in Senaki near Abkhazia and the other in Gori at a short distance from South Ossetia, clearly revealed Georgia's intention to use military pressure over the two *de facto* entities.

The intense militarisation of Georgia was taking place while the Russian military presence in that country was winding down. The Russian military evacuated its former bases in Akhalkalaki in the south and Batumi on the Turkish border, fulfilling Russian

---

[19]'US plans to expand military presence in Azerbaijan close to Iran', *Alexander's Gas and Oil*, 13 April 2005, available at: http://www.gasandoil.com/news/middle_east/b6e5b7a43c36e4bc336f009785cb9b46, accessed 5 October 2011; Sanamyan (2011).

[20]'Azerbaijan Parliament Approves Military Doctrine', *News Az,* 9 June 2010, available at: http://news.az/articles/17123, accessed 5 October 2011.

obligations made at the OSCE Istanbul summit of 2000. At the same time, the Russian military strengthened its presence in South Ossetia and Abkhazia. In fact, South Ossetia came under the direct administration of the Russian power structures when career military or intelligence officers took over posts such as prime minister and defence minister and the intelligence services of the *de facto* administration. Russia also increased its influence over the two break-away republics by distributing Russian passports to the local population; now, Moscow could claim that any future military intervention was to protect its citizens in the two regions. In this context, the Georgian–US military cooperation took on a significant importance, with training programmes and equipment transfers continuing. Foreign and especially US military assistance to Georgia relative to the Georgian defence budget was 'not that large' (Tseluiko 2010, p. 29) and was geared to prepare Georgian troops for peacekeeping operations in places like Afghanistan, Iraq or Kosovo. By 2007, Georgia had made a major military contribution to the US-led occupation of Iraq with 2,000 soldiers, the third contingent in the international force after the US and the UK and a smaller contingent was sent to Afghanistan as part of the International Security Assistance Force (ISAF). More important than training and hardware transfer, Georgia felt itself in league with the only superpower of our times. Now, the revolutionary leaders of Georgia thought it was time to challenge both the post-conflict *status quo* and Russian influence in the South Caucasus.

Similarly, Azerbaijan increased both its military spending and its bellicose rhetoric. The military spending of Azerbaijan grew from $160 million in 2004 to $300 million in 2005 and $600 million in 2006—the equivalent of the entire Armenian state budget. The military spending of Baku was $1.3 billion in 2008 and $2.1 billion in 2010.[21] This explosion of military spending was conditioned by the massive export of Caspian oil, after the Baku–Ceyhan pipeline was completed in May 2005 and in 2008 Baku was pumping 1 million barrels of oil per day. The petrodollars and military spending hardened the official Azerbaijani discourse, saying that Baku would agree to no more than autonomy for Nagorno-Karabakh within the framework of territorial integrity of Azerbaijan, and in case the ongoing peace negotiations would not lead to this result Azerbaijan would use force and start a second Karabakh war.

In the North Caucasus, there was a radical shift away from the ethno-national paradigm that characterised the region in the early 1990s. The Chechen resistance was undermined by the heavy military campaigns of the Russian Federal forces, as well as by the creation of a local administration with strong military capabilities entrusted to the former Mufti of the Chechen republic Ahmad Kadyrov, and after his assassination to his son Ramzan. However, it was not just the Russian policy successes that led to the weakening of the Chechen resistance, but the internal contradiction of the resistance movement itself: the idea of Chechen national independence, the banner around which the Chechens had fought with success in 1994–1996, was discredited in the years of *de facto* independence of 1997–1999. In the second Chechnya war, the Chechens fought against the Russian invasion without knowing why they were fighting; Maskhadov's only demand was the withdrawal of the Russian troops after

---

[21]See Yevgrashina (2008); 'Aliyev: Azerbaijan's defense spending tops Armenia budget', *Azernews*, 26 June 2010, available at: http://www.azernews.az/azerbaijan/21743.html, accessed 24 July 2012.

which he was ready to negotiate, including over the forms which Chechen sovereignty was to take.

The Russian military victory against Chechen resistance came with a price tag. The Chechen resistance was weakened but also radicalised towards the *salafi-jihadi* positions, which had previously constituted a marginal force. The resistance increasingly became terrorist aiming at (easier) civilian targets, especially in the neighbouring North Caucasus and in the Russian capital, bloody operations leading to the Beslan school tragedy or the Moscow metro bombings. Islamic ideology has the advantage of overcoming tribal and ethnic cleavages, as a result of which anti-Russian resistance has spread across the North Caucasus with a strong presence in Dagestan and Ingushetia, two neighbours of Chechnya. While North Caucasian *jamaat* (or Islamic resistance groups) have a global dimension and gain inspiration from global *jihad*, they can be more dangerous when they become the expression of national grievances, and become the embodiment of national-resistance struggles, as is the case in Iraq, Afghanistan or Somalia.

The Caucasus entered the globalised world through its hydrocarbon exports, which, in turn, had a deep impact on its social, economic and political structures. The Caucasus, while itself an area of geopolitical competition, simultaneously became part of several political sub-regions where severe political competition existed, similar to those of the Middle East and Central Asia (Sakwa 2011). We can see the interaction between local conflicts and great power competition most clearly in the clash of August 2008.

*Some remarks on the August 2008 war*

The August 2008 war between the Georgian and Russian armies took place against the background of the degradation of political relations as well as military escalation. In April, tension was high around the administrative frontier separating Abkhazia from Georgia. A Georgian unmanned aerial vehicle (UAV) was shot down, probably by a Russian warplane,[22] and Russia sent some 3,000 troops to repair the railway. At the same time, Georgian troops organised exercises under the supervision of US military advisors. In July 2008, two military manoeuvres underlined the degree of tension: Russia massed 8,000 of its troops along the northern border of Georgia for Kavkaz-2008 military exercises. At the same time, the joint military exercise codenamed 'Immediate Response 2008' brought together 1,200 US military personnel and 800 Georgian troops at the former Soviet air base Vaziani, situated only 20 km from Tbilisi (Bessonov 2008). During the first seven days of August, clashes between Georgian forces and Ossetian paramilitaries made a major confrontation seem dangerously real. Then, in the late hours of 7 August a massive Georgian military attack was unleashed against the regional capital, Tskhinvali.[23] In the course of the next day, as world leaders attended the opening ceremony of the Olympic Games in

---

[22]C.W. Blandy reports that 'the Abkhaz downed two Georgian drones on 18 March and 20 April, with a further two more on 4 May and a fifth on 8 May' (Blandy 2009).

[23]'Georgia Controls Tskhinvali—Saakashvili Claims', *Civil Georgia*, 8 August 2008, available at: http://www.civil.ge/eng/article.php?id = 18975, accessed 24 June 2010.

Beijing, Russian military forces started their slow but massive move towards the Georgian positions.

Although the military outcome was decided some 48 hours after the engagement of hostile forces (Litovkin 2008) and a ceasefire was announced five days after the start of the confrontation, the political consequences were far-reaching. The August 2008 war created immediate tension between Russia and Western powers, but did not bring any radical shift in relations between Moscow and the West—as some political analysts have suggested—nor did it mark the start of a new 'Cold War'. The tension it caused between Russia and the West was short term, and these relations were back to normal after a while and especially after the Obama administration initiated the 'reset' policy towards the Kremlin (Kessler 2009). Yet, it caused much harm in the process of conflict resolution in the Caucasus itself, and specifically in the conflicts between Abkhaz and Ossetians on the one side and Georgia on the other. Up to the 2008 war, Russia was theoretically in favour of Georgian 'territorial integrity', while developing protectorates in South Ossetia and Abkhazia. The Russian recognition of Abkhazia and South Ossetia as independent sovereign states has put an end to diplomatic efforts over two-decades to find a compromise solution and conclude a peaceful agreement to end the conflicts between the *de facto* governments and the Georgian central authorities. It also ended the duality of the Russian position. The current situation is a dead-end, since it is difficult to imagine how the Russian position of recognising Abkhazia and South Ossetia as independent states, and the Georgian position considering them to be part of its sovereign territory, could be reconciled. There is a need for fundamental change in the geopolitical situation in the Caucasus before imagining constructive negotiations between the conflicting parties and the normalisation of relations.

Yet, the August 2008 war was a fundamentally different war from the ones fought in the late 1980s in South Ossetia or the August 1992 war in Abkhazia (Cheterian 2009a). The earlier conflicts took place in revolutionary circumstances, when there was no clear, legitimate authority in Georgia, and when the various competing militias did not follow any superior civil or military hierarchy. For example, the Georgian military intervention in Abkhazia remains shrouded with mystery, as Eduard Shevardnadze, who was the head of the Georgian state at the time, claims that his defence minister took the initiative by himself when he ordered his forces to enter the Abkhaz capital Sukhumi (McGriffert *et al.* 1997, p. 265). The conflicts were the result of chaos following the disintegration of the previously existing order, and the Georgian defeat in Abkhazia was followed by an internal power struggle between the supporters of the former President Zviad Gamsakhurdia, and the Georgian authorities headed by Eduard Shevardnadze. The situation in 2008 could not be further away from the picture of the early 1990s. This time, it was well structured armies[24] under a clear military hierarchy which in turn followed orders of their civilian leaderships, fighting for territory and influence. The year 2008 was an attempt to establish order, not the outcome of chaos. A military defeat in the 1990s led to regime change, but not in 2008: Georgian forces were overwhelmed in front of superior Russian pressure, but the Saakashvili administration survived defeat.

[24]This applies to the Abkhaz, Georgian and Russian armies, while the Ossetian forces resembled paramilitary organisations with loose coordination.

The August 2008 war revealed that Russia, the US and the EU can be competitors as well as partners in the same geopolitical space. During the crisis, French diplomacy played a key mediating role in brokering a ceasefire agreement and an end to hostilities, at the same time as the US administration put pressure on Moscow in order not to enlarge the level of hostilities, and not to seek 'regime change' in Georgia by advancing towards Tbilisi. After the war, Western powers tried to stabilise the Georgian economy by providing massive aid, to avoid an internal backlash against Saakashvili as a result of economic hardship caused by the war. On the other hand, France, Russia and the US, the co-chairs of the OSCE Minsk Group, continued their efforts to mediate between the sides in the Karabakh conflict. Immediately following the August 2008 war, Russian President Dmitrii Medvedev launched a new initiative to bring the presidents of Armenia and Azerbaijan to a series of face-to-face meetings under his personal patronage. The Medvedev initiative was an expression of the increase of Russian power over the region following Russian military advances in August 2008. At the same time, the Medvedev initiative revealed the limits of Russian power; three years after the Moscow meeting, and after a number of face-to-face meetings between Aliev and Sarkissian, the Russian leader was 'frustrated' to see no real progress towards the solution of the Karabakh conflict.[25]

## *Conclusion: new elites and old conflicts*

In this essay, I have analysed the eruption and evolution of the conflicts in the Caucasus over two decades (1988–2008) by looking at three actors: mass movements, elites in power and foreign powers. I argued that the conflicts erupted with the emergence of mass mobilisations which were anti-systemic by their nature. After attempts by environmentalists to gather several thousand people in the city centres of the republican capitals, nationalist issues succeeded in mobilising hundreds of thousands for longer periods of time. Nationalist mobilisation opposed both central Soviet authorities as well as the republican ruling casts: the local *nomenklatura*. These nationalist movements created fears and anti-mobilisation among competing national projects. Next, nationalist movements came into friction and clashed with each other. The popular movements succeeded in overthrowing the local Soviet order and replacing them with a new ruling elite originating from the republican intelligentsia, and entered a period of confrontation with each other. With the disappearance of the Soviet centre, the various national movements clashed with each other over control of territories and populations, and created a new political order based on ethno-national legitimacy.

During this initial period—that is up to December 1991—there was no outside intervention. The conflicts themselves were the internal affairs of the Soviet state, which did not tolerate the presence of international organisations or actors of foreign states on its soil. With the collapse of the USSR and the recognition of Armenia, Azerbaijan and Georgia as independent states, the Karabakh conflict took on the dimension of a war between two states, while in South Ossetia and Abkhazia the

[25]See 'Russia's Medvedev 'Frustrated' With Karabakh Impasse', *Radio Free Europe/Radio Liberty*, 27 June 2011, available at: http://www.rferl.org/content/russia_medvedev_frustrated_karabakh_impasse/24248417.html, accessed 8 September 2011.

situation was considered by the international community as internal conflicts. Similarly, as Russian armies marched on Chechnya in December 1994, international organisations considered this an internal Russian conflict. The only outside force interfering in the conflicts of Karabakh, South Ossetia and Abkhazia was Russia. The problem was that former Soviet-turned-Russian military bases existed in those conflict zones, and before even Russia could formulate a clear policy towards what was called by the Russian Foreign Minister Andrei Kozyrev the 'Near Abroad' the Russian military was already on the ground and taking action. Soon, Russian politicians would start to use the military leverage they had on the ground as a political instrument to press concessions on new political entities trying to break free from Moscow's influence. One such Russian demand at the time was to force Azerbaijan and Georgia to join the ill-defined CIS which was meant to replace the former Soviet Union as a loose confederation of sovereign states. During the height of the wars, Western states were hesitant to intervene in any direct manner in the Caucasus, still considering it a region of Russian traditional influence. Similarly Iran, the former empire which dominated over the South Caucasus before the arrival of Russian troops into the region in the early nineteenth century, refrained from intervening in the conflicts, especially that of Karabakh, bordering its northern frontiers. Turkey, on the other hand, showed active political interest as well as limited military support in favour of Azerbaijan in the Karabakh conflict.

With the eruption of the violent phase of the conflicts, mass mobilisation, which played such a key role in the initial phase, soon disappeared as a factor. The various mass mobilisation and political movements that took place in the Caucasus outside the new elites in power were formed around non-nationalist and non-territorial issues. The large-scale demonstrations in Yerevan in 1996 and 2008, in Georgia in 2003 and 2007 and in Azerbaijan in 2005 were around electoral fraud, political representation and corruption of ruling elites. They were led by sections of the former elite groups that were chased from power and had no more space within the political institutions, and sought the support of the populace to bring about political change. On the other hand, opposition to diplomatic solutions to conflicts did not come from the street, but from elite groups within the ruling circles, as the cases of Armenia in 1997–1998 and Azerbaijan in 2001 reveal. At the same time, and in spite of ongoing military clashes such as those between Georgia and Abkhazia in 1998 and 2001, Georgia and South Ossetia in 2004, and Georgia on the one hand, and South Ossetia, Abkhazia and Russia on the other in 2008, as well as minor sporadic clashes between Armenian and Azerbaijani troops on the Karabakh frontlines, we did not witness mass mobilisation on the streets of Baku, Tbilisi or Yerevan around national themes. The hydrocarbon contracts signed in Baku in September 1994, a few months after the signing of the Karabakh ceasefire, introduced globalisation into the Caucasus arena. Major oil companies made investments in the Azerbaijan oil sector which has tilted the balance of forces towards Baku in the Karabakh conflict. It also brought a number of new outside actors into the geopolitical game of the Caucasus. Moreover, it accelerated social stratification within the region, with wealth concentrating within certain social and geographical spaces. In the early 1990s, Western capitals and international organisations were timidly involved in mediation efforts to stop violent clashes and find political resolutions to the confrontations. After the oil contracts, the role of numerous foreign diplomats posted in Baku changed from that of simple diplomatic envoys to representatives of countries with billions of dollars in investments in Azerbaijani oil and gas sector. In the early 1990s, the conflicts of the Caucasus were by and large viewed as Moscow's problem. In 2008, the eruption of conflict threatened Western investments and the energy security of European economies. The multiplication of foreign actors, whether state agencies or multinationals, and their influence over the Caucasus further complicates the geopolitical situation of the region. Now, there is no single power broker that can force the conflict parties into an agreement, unlike, for example in the early 1920s or in the early 1990s in the case of the South Caucasus, when a single outside power (Moscow) had enough influence to impose peace under its conditions on the warring little nations of the Caucasus.

Currently, there is no visible popular movement which is agitating for the conflicts, and nor are there mobilised popular movements calling for peace and resolution of the conflicts. The small initiatives that come from non-governmental organisations (NGOs) are often of foreign inspiration and funding, and remain isolated from broader social developments. Most of those initiatives are hostile to social movements, and consider them to pose more of a risk to the peace process rather than being a force in favour of it. International diplomacy (which is the exclusive funding source of the NGO initiatives) has focused its efforts on power elites, hoping that an agreement between them will be the solution to the conflicts in the Caucasus. The negotiations which have continued for two decades are held in secret, away from public scrutiny. The lack of real democratic processes fits well with the secretive negotiations, as both processes exclude the citizen from participating in policy making.

The elites that came to power following independence, upon which all international hope for conflict resolution seems to be focalised, have limitations in the way that they can approach the conflict issue. The three South Caucasus republics seceded to independence as the conflicts erupted; as a result, the independence movements and the mobilisation around ethno-territorial issue became intermingled. In other words, the issue of the conflicts lies at the heart of the definition of the new political space and legitimation of its institutions. It was the Karabakh Movement in Armenia that led the country into independence; and similarly in Georgia, it was the National Movement which fought against Moscow and against centrifugal forces in Abkhazia and South Ossetia. The Azerbaijani Popular Front was simultaneously anti-Soviet and opposed to the ceding of Nagorno-Karabakh. The Azerbaijani national movement emerged as a reaction to the Armenian mobilisation for Karabakh, and this reactive position has left its fingerprint on the formation of the Azerbaijani national self-image since. After doing field studies on Azerbaijani elite perceptions on the Karabakh conflict in 2001 and in 2009, Ceylan Tokluoglu concludes that 'Azerbaijanis (re)construct Armenian identity by defining the Armenians, not themselves, as a "unique community".... They also attribute a "special mission" to them, which is to occupy the lands of other nations' (Tokluoglu 2011, p. 1225). The increasingly negative and stereotypical image of the 'other' is yet another and novel obstacle to conflict resolution. Yet, those images of the 'enemy' do serve a function for the young states of the Caucasus: to limit the boundaries of the community and provide legitimacy to state institutions with shallow historic roots.

The ideological and emotional weight of the conflict thematic and their symbolic representation makes any compromise on the issue look like a defeat. Therefore, elites prefer preserving the *status quo* and shield behind radical rhetoric (de Waal 2009). Elites in power have equally used the conflicts as a resource, as a political instrument reinforcing their position *vis-à-vis* competitors. The two Russian invasions of Chechnya (1994, 1999) were conditioned not only by security and political challenges posed by Chechen separatist and Islamist forces, but also were utilised to project an image of the powerful leadership of the Kremlin. Following the contested presidential elections of February 2008 in Armenia, the Karabakh front-line was activated with violent clashes unseen since the 1994 ceasefire agreement.[26] In Georgia, the Georgian offensive on Tskhinvali in August 2008 took place less than a year after the most severe internal crisis of the Saakashvili administration, when in November 2007 mass demonstrations organised by opposition formations called for the resignation of the Georgian president. The ruling elites in the Caucasus, as well as in Russia, refer to the electoral system as a source for legitimacy but also violate it by manipulating elections. This lack of electoral legitimacy makes the symbolic value of the conflicts even more important for the elites in power. The population can be invited to make sacrifices for the higher goal, for the liberation and defence of national territory. As leaders continuously utilise conflict thematics for internal political reasons, they are also widening the chasm between their own position and the possibility of conflict resolution.

*CIMERA*

## *References*

Abdullaev, N. (2010) 'Bombings Look Like the Revenge of "Black Widows"', *Moscow Times*, 30 March, available at: http://www.themoscowtimes.com/news/article/analysis-bombings-look-like-the-revenge-of-black-widows/402775.html, accessed 30 March 2010.
Beissinger, M. (2002) *Nationalist Mobilization and the Collapse of the Soviet State* (Cambridge, Cambridge University Press).
Bessonov, K. (2008) 'Russia, Georgia Hold Military Exercises Amidst Tension', *Moscow News*, 18 July, available at: http://www.mn.ru/news/20080718/55338376.html, accessed 12 June 2010.
Birch, J. (1996) 'The Georgian/South Ossetian Territorial and Boundary Dispute', in Wright, J.F.R., Goldenberg, S. & Schofield, R. (eds) (1996) *Transcaucasian Boundaries* (New York, St. Martin's Press).
Blandy, C.W. (2009) 'Provocation, Deception, Entrapment: The Russo-Georgian Five Day War', *Defence Academy of the United Kingdom*, March, available at: http://www.da.mod.uk/colleges/arag/document-listings/caucasus/09(02)CWB.pdf/view, accessed 10 October 2011.
Brubaker, R. (1999) *Nationalism Reframed, Nationhood and the National Question in the New Europe* (Cambridge, Cambridge University Press).
Cheterian, V. (1997) *Dialectics of the Ethnic Conflicts and Oil Projects in the Caucasus* (Geneva, Program for Strategic and International Security Studies).
Cheterian, V. (2001) *Little Wars and a Great Game, Local Conflicts and International Competition in the Caucasus* (Bern, Swiss Peace Foundation).
Cheterian, V. (2008) *War and Peace in the Caucasus: Russia's Troubled Frontier* (London, Hurst).
Cheterian, V. (2009a) 'The August 2008 War in Georgia: From Ethnic Conflict to Border Wars', *Central Asian Survey*, 28, 2.

---

[26]The clashes on the north-eastern portion of the line of contact started on 4 March 2008, exactly two days after opposition demonstrations in Yerevan which were repressed by force, causing the death of 10 people. The two sides dispute who initiated the military operations. See 'Armenia/Azerbaijan: Deadly Fighting Erupts in Nagorno-Karabakh', *Radio Free Europe/Radio Liberty*, 4 March 2011, available at: http://www.rferl.org/content/article/1079580.html, accessed 7 October 2011.

Cheterian, V. (2009b) 'Politics of Environment in the Caucasus Conflict Zone: From Nationalizing Politics to Conflict Resolution', in Brauch, H.G., Spring, U.O., Grin, J., Mesjasz, C., Kameri-Mbote, P., Behera, N.C., Chourou, B. & Krummenacher, H. (eds) (2009) *Facing Global Environmental Change* (Berlin, Springer).

Chorbajian, L., Donabedian, P. & Mutafian, C. (1994) *The Caucasian Knot: The History and Geo-Politics of Nagorno-Karabagh* (London, Z Books).

Coppieters, B., Nodia G. & Anchabadze Y. (eds.) (1998) *Georgians and Abkhazians, The Search for a Peace Settlement* (Koeln, Bundesinstitut fuer ostwissenschaftliche und internationalr Studien).

Cornell, S. (2002) 'Autonomy as a Source of Conflict, Caucasian Conflicts in Theoretical Perspective', *World Politics*, 54, 2.

Croissant, M. (1998) *The Armenian–Azerbaijani Conflict, Causes and Implications* (London, Praeger).

de Waal, T. (2003) *Black Garden: Armenia and Azerbaijan through Peace and War* (New York, New York University Press).

de Waal, T. (2009) *The Karabakh Trap: Dangers and Dilemmas of Nagorno-Karabakh Conflict* (London, Conciliation Resources), available at: http://www.c-r.org/our-work/caucasus/documents/Nagorny-Karabakh-report-AW.pdf, accessed 7 October 2011.

Ekedahl, C.M. & Goodman, M.A. (1997) *The Wars of Eduard Shevardnadze* (London, Hurst and Co.).

Evangelista, M. (2002) *The Chechen Wars: Will Russia Go the Way of the Soviet Union?* (Washington, DC, Brookings Institute).

Fuller, L. & Giragosian, R. (2008) 'Georgia Reverses Decision to Cut Defence Spending', *Radio Free Europe/Radio Liberty*, 26 June 2008, available at: http://www.rferl.org/content/georgia_reverses_decision_to_cut_defense_spending/1145557.html, accessed 3 June 2010.

Gall, C. & de Wall, T. (1997a) *Chechnya, A Small Victorious War* (London, Picador).

Gall, C. & de Wall, T. (1997b) *Chechnya, Calamity in the Caucasus* (New York, New York University Press).

Gammer, M. (2006) *The Lone Wolf and the Bear: Three Centuries of Chechen Defiance of Russian Rule* (London, Hurst).

Geukjian, O. (2007) 'The Politicization of Environmental Issues in Armenia and Nagorno-Karabakh's Nationalist Movement in the South Caucasus 1985–1991', *Nationalities Papers*, 35, 2.

Goldenberg, S. (1994) *Pride of Small Nations: The Caucasus and Post-Soviet Disorder* (London, Zed Books).

Goltz, T. (1993) 'Letter From Eurasia: The Hidden Russian Hand', *Foreign Policy*, 92, 3.

Horowitz, S. (2002) 'Explaining Post-Soviet Ethnic Conflicts: Using Regime Type to Discern the Impact and Relative Importance of Objective Antecedents', *Nationalities Papers*, 29, 4.

International Crisis Group. (2007) *Nagorno-Karabakh: Risking War*, Europe Report 187, Brussels, available at: http://www.crisisgroup.org/en/regions/europe/caucasus/azerbaijan/187-nagorno-karabakh-risking-war.aspx, accessed 14 September 2011.

International Crisis Group. (2011) *Armenia and Azerbaijan: Preventing War*, Europe Briefing 60, Brussels, available at: http://www.crisisgroup.org/en/regions/europe/caucasus/B60-armenia-and-azerbaijan-preventing-war.aspx, accessed 2 October 2011.

Kaufmann, S. (1998) 'Ethnic Fears and Ethnic War in Karabagh', *CSIS*, available at: http://csis.org/files/media/csis/pubs/ruseur_wp_008.pdf, accessed 25 June 2010.

Kessler, G. (2009) 'Clinton "Resets" Russian Ties—and language', *Washington Post*, 7 March, available at: http://www.washingtonpost.com/wp-dyn/content/story/2009/03/05/ST2009030501526.html, accessed 11 June 2010.

Kinzer, S. (2007) 'Azerbaijan Has Reason to Swagger: Oil Deposits', *New York Times*, 14 September, available at: http://www.nytimes.com/1997/09/14/world/azerbaijan-has-reason-to-swagger-oil-deposits.html, accessed 4 October 2011.

Kramer, M. (2005) 'Guerrilla Warfare, Counterinsurgency and Terrorism in the North Caucasus: The Military Dimension of the Russo-Chechen Conflict', *Europe-Asia Studies*, 57, 2.

Lapidus, G. (1998) 'Contested Sovereignty: The Tragedy of Chechnya', *International Security*, 23, 1.

Lieven, A. (1998) *Chechnya: Tombstone of Russian Power* (New Haven, Yale University Press).

Litovkin, V. (2008) 'Tbiliskii blitzkrieg, Generali podvotyat piervii itogui', *Nizavisimaya Gazeta*, 11 August, available at: http://www.ng.ru/politics/2008-08-11/1_blitskrig.html, accessed 24 June 2010.

Lukic, R. & Lynch, A. (1996) *Europe from the Balkans to the Urals: The Disintegration of Yugoslavia and the Soviet Union* (Oxford, Oxford University Press).

Malashenko, A. & Trenin, D. (2004) *Russia's Restless Frontier: The Chechnya Factor in Post-Soviet Russia* (Washington, DC, Carnegie Endowment for International Peace).

Markedonov, S. (2009) *The Big Caucasus, Consequences of the 'Five Day War': Threats and Political Prospects* (Athens, Xenophon Papers).

McGriffert Ekedahl, C. & Goodman, M. (1997) *The Wars of Eduard Shevardnadze* (London, Hurst and Co.).
Moore, C. & Tumelty, P. (2009) 'Assessing Unholy Alliances in Chechnya: From Communism and Nationalism to Islamism and Salafism', *Journal of Communist Studies and Transition Politics*, 25, 1.
Mouradian, C. (1990) *Arménie, de Staline à Gorbachev, histoire d'une république soviétique* (Paris, Ramsay).
Murphey, C. & Ottaway, D.B. (2001) 'Some Light Shed on Saudi Suspects', *Washington Post*, 25 September, p. A12.
Nolyain, I. (1994) 'Moscow's Initiation of the Azeri-Armenian Conflict', *Central Asian Survey*, 13, 4.
Rasizade, A. (2004) 'Azerbaijan after Heydar Aliev', *Nationalities Papers*, 32, 1.
Razoux, P. (2009) *Histoire de la Géorgie, La Clé du Caucase* (Paris, Perrin).
Ruben, B. (1993/1994) 'The Fragmantation of Tajikistan', *Survival*, 35, 4, Winter 1993/94.
Rubien B. (1993/1994), 'The Fragmantation of Tajikistan', *Survival*, 35, 4, Winter, pp. 71–91.
Sakwa, R. (2011) 'The Clash of Regionalisms and Caucasian Conflicts', *Europe-Asia Studies*, 63, 3.
Sanamyan, E. (2011) 'Wikileaks: US Lobbied Turkey for Help with Azeri Airbase Upgrade', *Armenian Reporter*, 31 January, available at: http://www.reporter.am/go/article/2011-01-31-wikileaks-u-s–lobbied-turkey-for-help-with-azeri-airbase-upgrade, accessed 5 October 2011.
Saparov, A. (2010) 'From Conflict to Autonomy: The Making of the South Ossetian Autonomous Region 1918–1922', *Europe-Asia Studies*, 62, 1.
Schatz, E. (2004) *Modern Clan Politics: The Power of 'Blood' in Kazakhstan and Beyond* (Seattle, University of Washington Press).
Serrano, S. (2007) *Géorgie, Sortie d'empire* (Paris, CNRS Editions).
Shnirelman, V. (2001) *The Value of the Past: Myths, Identity and Politics in Transcaucasia* (Osaka, National Museum of Ethnology).
Smith, S. (1998) *Allah's Mountain: The Battle for Chechnya* (London, I. B. Tauris).
Stanley, A. (1997) 'Yeltsin Signs Peace Treaty with Chechnya', *New York Times*, 13 May, available at: http://www.nytimes.com/1997/05/13/world/yeltsin-signs-peace-treaty-with-chechnya.html?pagewanted=all&src=pm, accessed 29 September 2011.
Stern, D. (2001) 'US Brokers Peace Talks on Disputed Armenian Enclave', *Financial Times*, 4 April.
Suny, R. (1993) *The Revenge of the Past, Nationalism, Revolution, and the Collapse of the Soviet Union* (Stanford, Stanford University Press).
Suny, R. (1994) *The Making of the Georgian Nation* (Bloomington, Indiana University Press).
Suny, R. (1999/2000) 'Provisional Stabilities: The Politics of Identities in Post-Soviet Eurasia', *International Security*, 24, 3.
Tishkov, V. (1997) *Ethnicity, Nationalism and Conflict in and After the Soviet Union: The Mind Aflame* (London, Sage).
Tishkov, V. (2004) *Chechnya: Life in a War-Torn Society* (Berkeley, University of California Press).
Tokluoglu, C. (2011) 'The Political Discourse of the Azerbaijani Elite on the Nagorno-Karabakh Conflict (1991–2009)', *Europe-Asia Studies*, 63, 7.
Trier, T., Lohm, H. & Szakonyi, D. (2010) *Under Siege: Inter-Ethnic Relations in Abkhazia* (London, Hurst).
Tseluiko, V. (2010) 'Georgian Army Reform Under Saakashvili Prior to 2008 Five Day War', in Pukhov, R. (ed.) (2010) *The Tanks of August* (Moscow, Centre for Analysis of Strategies and Technologies).
UPI. (2009) 'Azerbaijan Seeks $60 billion in New Oil Investment', 6 October, available at: http://www.upi.com/Business_News/Energy-Resources/2009/10/06/Azerbaijan-seeks-60-billion-in-new-oil-investment/UPI-36681254858974/, accessed 10 October 2011.
Van Evera, S. (1994) 'Hypothesis on Nationalism and War', *International Security*, 18, 4.
Van Natta Jr., D. & Zernike, K. (2001) 'Hijackers' Meticulous Strategy of Brains, Muscle and Practice', *New York Times*, 4 November, available at: http://www.nytimes.com/2001/11/04/national/04PLOT.html?scp=23&sq=&pagewanted=all, accessed 2 September 2011.
Wilhelmsen, J. (2005) 'Between a Rock and a Hard Place: The Islamisation of the Chechen Separatist Movement', *Europe-Asia Studies*, 57, 1.
World Bank. (2009) 'Azerbaijan—Country Economic Memorandum', 23 December, available at: http://siteresources.worldbank.org/AZERBAIJANEXTN/Resources/Azerbaijan_CEM_FINAL.pdf, accessed 6 October 2011.
Yevgrashina, L. (2008) 'Azerbaijan announces 53 pct rise in army spending', *Reuters*, 15 April, available at: http://www.reuters.com/article/idUSL1597375, accessed 29 June 2010.
Zverev, A. (1996) 'Ethnic Conflict in the Caucasus 1988–1994', in Coppieters, B. (ed) (1996) *Contested Borders in the Caucasus* (Brussels, VUB Press).

# Securing the South Caucasus: Military Aspects of Russian Policy towards the Region since 2008

## TRACEY GERMAN

### Abstract

In the wake of the 2008 conflict with Georgia, Russia has re-established itself as the dominant actor in the South Caucasus, consolidating its military presence in the region and reinforcing its already substantial diplomatic and economic levers. This essay examines recent Russian policy towards the region as Moscow attempts to counterbalance growing Western involvement within what it perceives to be its zone of 'privileged interest', focusing on military aspects of its policy towards Abkhazia and South Ossetia, and the implications for security across the South Caucasus.

THE RUSSIAN MILITARY INTERVENTION IN GEORGIA'S separatist regions of Abkhazia and South Ossetia in 2008 raised questions about Moscow's intentions towards its 'Near Abroad' and the future direction of its foreign policy. Russia's decision to assist Georgia's separatist regions and build up a strong military presence there, ostensibly to protect the local populations, reflects the Kremlin's wider efforts to retain its influence over former Soviet states. Moscow considers the South Caucasus to be a sphere of its exclusive influence, or, as former Russian President Dimitrii Medvedev has put it, Russia's 'zone of privileged interest'. Growing interest from external actors such as the US, European Union (EU) and NATO since 1991 means it has become an area where the interests of different states meet, and sometimes collide, with the regional powers of Russia, Turkey and Iran striving for influence in the face of growing Western involvement.

Since 2008, Moscow has consolidated its already dominant position in the South Caucasus, establishing military bases in Abkhazia and South Ossetia, extending its strategic military partnership with Armenia until 2044 and maintaining its economic dominance. Furthermore, the impact of the global financial crisis on Western states, together with the Obama administration's attempts to 'reset' its relations with Moscow, mean that US and European influence in the South Caucasus has waned. This essay will examine the military aspects of Russian policy towards the South

Caucasus since 2008, focusing on Georgia's two separatist regions,[1] Abkhazia and South Ossetia, and assess the implications of Russia's consolidation of its dominance for stability in the region, as well as Georgia's NATO membership aspirations. Georgia is the most pro-Western of the three South Caucasus states, and since independence in 1991 it has consistently sought to maintain an autonomous foreign policy that partially rids the country of Moscow's domination, whilst simultaneously becoming more Westward-looking. This policy appears to have backfired and Georgia's NATO accession ambitions are very much on the back-burner.

*The South Caucasus and Russian policy*

In order to assess Russia's role in the region, it is important to understand why Moscow still considers this area to be so significant. Constituting Russia's southern border and its so-called 'strategic backyard', the South Caucasus not only has close ties with its powerful northern neighbour as a result of historical legacy, but is also vital for Russia's own security, both in military, economic and political terms. Russia is the historic dominant power in the South Caucasus region and has been since incorporating it into the Russian Empire during the nineteenth century, facing little significant competition for influence until the disintegration of the USSR. In spite of the breakup of the Soviet Union, close ties remain between Russia and the three South Caucasus states, as a result of the legacies of migration and centrally planned economies. Russia remains the principal economic power in the region and the presence of Russians within the South Caucasus states, as well as South Caucasian peoples within Russia, is still considerable: there have been high levels of migration between the South Caucasus and the 'centre', both before, during and after the Soviet era. Given the important historical ties and continuing population links, it is understandable why Moscow considers the South Caucasus to be within its 'zone of privileged interest' and why it has been unhappy about the growing influence of other external actors, which has posed a direct challenge to Russian hegemony in the South Caucasus since 1991.

Russian policies *vis-à-vis* the South Caucasus are focused on maintaining influence and, in the wake of its conflict with Georgia in 2008, Moscow has reinforced its already dominant position in the South Caucasus. This reflects changes in wider Russian foreign-policy over the past decade, as the country has recovered from the chaos of the Yel'tsin years and developed a more coherent, coordinated foreign policy, perceived by many to be more assertive. During his first eight years in the Kremlin, Vladimir Putin presided over Russia's return to the international stage as a strong state capable of exerting global influence, as outlined in the 2009 National Security Strategy (NSS) of the Russian Federation: 'The transition in the international system from opposing blocs to principles of multivector diplomacy, together with Russia's

---

[1]The author recognises the problematic nature of referring to Abkhazia and South Ossetia as 'separatist regions'. Russia refers to the two as 'independent states', whilst Georgia calls them its 'occupied territories', both emotive terms. However, as the majority of the international community has not recognised the sovereignty of either Abkhazia or South Ossetia and continues to recognise Georgia's territorial integrity, the term 'separatist region' will be used throughout this essay.

resource potential and pragmatic policy for its use, have broadened the possibilities for the Russian Federation to reinforce its influence on the world stage' (NSS 2009, paragraph 9).

Russia is keen to reassert its influence, both within the South Caucasus and across the former Soviet space, to counter the perceived expansion of Western involvement, particularly NATO enlargement, within its 'sphere of influence'. The Kremlin had become increasingly concerned about growing US (and European) influence in areas traditionally perceived as Russia's 'strategic backyard', that is, in former Soviet states such as Georgia, Ukraine and the Central Asian republics, a concern that is reflected in key Russian strategic documents, including the Foreign Policy Concept (2008), NSS (2009) and Military Doctrine (2010). All three documents express unease about further NATO enlargement, which, according to the Foreign Policy Concept (2008) 'violates the principle of equal security, leads to new dividing lines in Europe and runs counter to the tasks of increasing the effectiveness of joint work in search for responses to real challenges of our time'. The National Security Strategy states that 'plans to extend the alliance's military infrastructure to Russia's borders, and attempts to endow NATO with global functions that go counter to norms of international law, are unacceptable to Russia' (NSS 2009, paragraph 17). The three strategic documents also emphasise the importance of a multipolar world, reflecting Moscow's unhappiness with US dominance of the international system, which it feels is destabilising. In an attempt to counterbalance Western influence in the post-Soviet space and retain its leverage, the Kremlin adopted a strategy of seeking to reassert its influence by political, economic and military means. The military aspect of this approach is vital, as it provides credibility to the potential to project influence: without an effective military capability, Russia's ability to influence events in the South Caucasus would be undermined. Thus, the efficacy of Russian efforts to preserve its influence has been underpinned by its considerable military footprint in the Caucasus region.

*Maintaining influence: military levers*

Moscow has maintained a constant military presence in the South Caucasus since 1991, retaining Soviet-era military bases on Georgian territory until late 2007, together with bases in neighbouring Armenia, a radar station in Azerbaijan[2] and a considerable presence across the border in the North Caucasus, as well as the establishment of two new bases in Abkhazia and South Ossetia post-2008 (see Table 1).

As mentioned above, Moscow retained military bases on Georgian territory until late 2007, a hangover from the Soviet era.[3] Only a matter of months after the last

---

[2]The Gabala radar station is strategically important for Russia as it has the capacity to detect missile launches in the Indian Ocean and can also survey the whole of the Middle East. A 2002 agreement between Moscow and Baku acknowledged that the station belonged to Azerbaijan, but granted Russia a 10-year lease.

[3]In 1999 former Russian President Boris Yel'tsin agreed to an OSCE-facilitated deal, which obligated Russia to hand back its four bases in Georgia before 1 July 2001. Only two bases were returned within this deadline: Gudauta in Abkhazia and the air base at Vaziani, near Tbilisi. A new framework was drawn up in 2006, according to which the remaining two bases at Akhalkalaki and Batumi were to be completely vacated by the end of 2008. Moscow completed its withdrawal ahead of

TABLE 1
RUSSIAN MILITARY INSTALLATIONS IN THE SOUTH CAUCASUS

| Country | Location | Base | Purpose | Personnel |
|---|---|---|---|---|
| Azerbaijan | Gabala | Dar'yal radar station | Radar monitoring; missile attack warning | Approximately 1,400 |
| Armenia | Gyumri | 102nd military base | Cover for Russia's southern flank; guarantee defence of Armenia as a member-state of CSTO | 3,200 |
| Georgia: Abkhazia | Gudauta | 7th military base including air base, parachute regiment | Secure the Abkhaz–Georgian border | Approximately 1,700 |
| Georgia: South Ossetia | Tskhinvali, Djava | 4th military base | Secure Russia's southern borders | Approximately 1,200 |

Source: 'Bazovaya Tsennost', *Izvestiya*, 20 August 2010, available at: www.izvestiya.ru, accessed 24 July 2011.

Russian servicemen and military equipment had been withdrawn from Georgia in late 2007, reducing Moscow's ability to exert significant pressure on Tbilisi, its support for Georgia's separatist regions increased dramatically. Angered by the declaration at NATO's Bucharest summit in April 2008 that Georgia and Ukraine were likely to become members of the military alliance at some unspecified point in the future, the Kremlin increased its cooperation with the two separatist territories and unilaterally bolstered the number of troops deployed in Abkhazia.[4] Efforts to restore central Georgian control over South Ossetia in August 2008 triggered a Russian military invasion. With the majority of the South Ossetian (and Abkhaz) population claiming Russian citizenship, Moscow was able to cite concerns for the security of its citizens as a motive for launching a military operation on Georgian territory.[5] Having secured

schedule, in November 2007. Furthermore, in addition to its military bases, until the conflict of August 2008 there were two further groups of Russian military forces on Georgian territory, operating under the aegis of Commonwealth of Independent States (CIS) peacekeeping operations in Abkhazia and South Ossetia. The presence of thousands of Russian peace-keepers, who were considered neither impartial nor neutral, exacerbated relations between Tbilisi, Moscow and the regional leaders. Saakashvili has described the Russian peacekeepers as 'piece-keepers' who, in his opinion, were there 'to keep the pieces of the old empire and not the actual peace' ('Russian Threats Alarm Georgia', *BBC News*, 14 September 2004, available at: http://news.bbc.co.uk, accessed 30 March 2006).

[4]In May 2008, 400 Russian Ministry of Defence Railway troops moved into Abkhazia without Georgian permission. At the same time, a battalion of nearly 500 soldiers of the mechanised brigade based in Maikop was redeployed to Abkhazia. 'Polish think-tank sees possible "local war" in Georgia's rebel region in autumn' *Text of Report in English by Warsaw Eastern Studies Centre 4 June*, BBC Monitoring Online, 4 June 2008, available at: http://my.monitor.bbc.co.uk, accessed 23 May 2009.

[5]This was to be expected. In July 2004, the Russian authorities had warned that Moscow 'will not remain indifferent towards the fate of its citizens, which comprise the absolute majority of South Ossetia', a stance affirmed in 2005 by Andrei Kokoshin, head of the *Duma* committee on CIS affairs, who said that Russia 'will not stay aloof' if Georgia resorts to force, stating that: 'Many residents of South Ossetia are citizens of Russia and Russia has the right to defend the life, freedom, property and health of its citizens

the two regions militarily, Moscow took its political support one step further, formally recognising the independence of Georgia's separatist regions at the end of August 2008. An article in Russian newspaper *Izvestiya* identified this action as the most important achievement of President Medvedev's presidency: 'by securing victory and consolidating it by recognising the independence of South Ossetia and Abkhazia, Russia resolutely returned to the table in the big geopolitical game, where it had not had a seat for two decades'.[6]

Medvedev himself has stated his belief that the events of 2008 were vital for Russia 'for it to feel strong and not disintegrate—irrespective of how those events may be interpreted in other countries. This was important, first and foremost, for ourselves'.[7] This reflects a determination to re-establish Russia's authority as a strong state that is capable of influencing events within the global arena and pursuing an independent stance on international issues.

In the wake of the 2008 conflict, the Russian Defence Ministry announced plans to base up to 4,000 troops in each region,[8] establishing the 7th Base of the Russian Armed Forces at Gudauta in Abkhazia and the 4th Base in South Ossetia (based near Djava and Tskhinvali), both of which are part of the North Caucasus Military District (NCMD). The Georgian government was furious about the development of permanent military bases in what it considers to be Georgian territory, stating that 'the fulfilment of Russia's expansionist plans poses a real threat not only to Georgia but also to the entire Caucasus and the Black Sea regions' (Ministry of Foreign Affairs of Georgia 2010). This sentiment is supported by a description of the changed military balance in the region depicted by Russian weekly paper *Argumenty nedeli*:

> The conditions for Georgia following the last war have only grown worse. In place of a handful of lightly-armed peacekeepers, they now face two fully-armed motorised rifle brigades equipped with modern weapons and dug in to reinforced positions. To the north, there are reinforcements in the form of fully-armed brigades with modern equipments that are ready to come to the aid of military bases in South Ossetia and Abkhazia within 24 hours.[9]

using all means available to a state in modern circumstances'. Statement from the Ministry of Foreign Affairs of the Russian Federation, 'V svyazi s obostreniem situatsii vokrug Yuzhnoi Osetii', 9 July 2004, available at: www.ln.mid.ru/brp_4.nsf/sps/3C8799FB6DC16167C3256ECC0045352E, accessed 14 July 2011. Again, in September 2007, there was a similar warning that 'in the case of aggravation of the situation around South Ossetia Russia will take all the necessary steps determined by its peacekeeping and mediation mission and by its responsibility for the security of Russian citizens'. Statement by Russia's Ministry of Foreign Affairs: 'On the Situation in the Georgian–Ossetian Zone of Conflict', 14 September 2007, available at: www.mid.ru/brp_4.nsf/e78a48070f128a7b43256999005bcbb3/fd30396df64db2c9c3257356005ad343?OpenDocument, accessed 6 June 2009.

[6]*Izvestiya*, 11 March 2011, available at: http://www.izvestia.ru/news/372280, accessed 16 June 2011.

[7]Rossiya 24 news channel, Moscow, 09:00 GMT, 18 May 2011, BBC Monitoring, available at: http://my.monitor.bbc.co.uk, accessed 10 June 2011.

[8]Each base has a military camp in Russia, which enables the number of personnel to be varied according to requirement: at the beginning of 2010, there were only 1,500 troops at the 7th Base (Itar-Tass news agency, Moscow, 10:36 GMT, 25 February 2010, BBC Monitoring, available at: http://my.monitor.bbc.co.uk, accessed 19 October 2010).

[9]*Argumenty nedeli*, 11, 201, 25 March 2010, available at: http://www.argumenti.ru/army/2010/03/54434/, accessed 23 May 2010.

The Kremlin emphasises that these permanent military bases have been set up at 'the invitation and with the consent of the authorities of the receiving states [Abkhazia and South Ossetia], as well as on the basis of the appropriate interstate agreements' in order to 'protect the local population and prevent terrorist acts'.[10] Moscow has spent vast sums of money strengthening the military infrastructure in the two regions. Russian Prime Minister Vladimir Putin declared in 2009 that Moscow intended to spend R15–16 billion during 2010 on the construction of military bases in Abkhazia, as well as the development of border infrastructure. A further R4 billion has been spent on implementing infrastructure projects that will develop transport and border crossings, whilst a similar sum is being spent on military facilities in South Ossetia.[11]

Basing agreements were signed with the regional leaders in February 2010, endorsing changes that had occurred since 2008. The lease for each base runs for a 49-year term, but can automatically be extended at 15-year intervals. Military cooperation agreements with the separatist territories include provision for the training of the two regions' 'armies' and the development of military-technical equipment, i.e. arms deliveries.[12] This was taken one step further in 2011, when a Russian officer was appointed chief of the general staff of the Abkhaz armed forces, leading to (unfounded) rumours that they were to be disbanded and replaced by the Russian armed forces.[13]

The 4th base in South Ossetia is home to the 693rd motor-rifle brigade (MRB), equipped with 41 T-72B tanks and 150 BMP-2 infantry fighting vehicles. The 7th base in Abkhazia is manned by the 131st MRB (the Maykop brigade, which took heavy losses in Chechnya in 1995), armed with 41 T-90A tanks and 150 BTR-80 armoured personnel carriers. According to a report in a regional Russian newspaper, both bases have two 2SZ self-propelled gun divisions each, a Grad multiple rocket launcher battalion each and air-defence systems.[14] There was anger in Georgia when it became clear during 2010 that Russia had also deployed the S-300PS missile defence system to Abkhazia two years earlier. Thus, it is evident that Moscow is investing a substantial amount of equipment, troops and financial resources in order to 'secure' each region. The extent of the Russian military involvement is clear from this description of the situation in Abkhazia published in *Nezavisimaya Gazeta*:

> the joint military base will comprise former peacekeeping facilities and the Bombora military airfield located in the Gudauta region, a military firing ground and part of the sea bay near Ochamchire, as well as joint Russian–Abkhaz military garrisons stationed in the north of the

---

[10] *Komsomolskaya Pravda*, 19 February 2010, available at: http://www.kp.ru/daily/24444/609760/, accessed 20 January 2011.

[11] *Nezavisimaya Gazeta*, 14 March 2010, available at: http://www.ng.ru/cis/2010-03-17/1_military.html, accessed 21 May 2010.

[12] 'Zashchishchat' 49 let', *Vedomosti*, 19 May 2009, available at: http://www.vedomosti.ru/newspaper/article.shtml?2009/05/19/196146, accessed 3 June 2009.

[13] Major General Vladimir Vasilchenko previously held the post of deputy chief of staff of the Siberian military district.

[14] 'Russia: Post-reform situation in North Caucasus Military District criticized', Text of report by Russia's Volgograd Region weekly sociopolitical newspaper *Volgogradskaya Tribuna*, Volgograd, BBC Monitoring, 19 February 2010, available at: http://my.monitor.bbc.co.uk, accessed 18 July 2011.

Kodori Gorge and near a hydropower plant on the Inguri river. In addition, military administrative and medical facilities will be located in Sukhumi, Gagry, Gudauta, Novyy Afon, Eshery and other population centres.[15]

The development of a naval base at Ochamchire and the expansion of Russia's Black Sea coastline to include Abkhazia has significantly increased Russia's maritime footprint and influence in the Black Sea, where the borders of Western security structures such as the EU and NATO converge with Russia's south-western borders. Russia now has naval bases in Sevastopol, Novorossiisk and Ochamchire, together with access to facilities at Sukhumi. Agreement has been reached with Ukraine on an extension of basing rights for the Russian Black Sea Fleet (BSF) in Sevastopol until 2042, which negates the need for Russia to find an alternative, but a former commander of the Black Sea fleet believes that the use of mooring facilities at Sukhumi and Ochamchire (which is currently only being used by the Russian coastguard) by the BSF is a 'major geopolitical victory' as it will 'now be more dispersed and, consequently, less vulnerable'.[16] Russia's intervention in Georgia has not only allowed Moscow to consolidate its hold on the Caucasus, it has also enabled it to boost its military presence and reach in the Black Sea region.

### Strengthening 'state' borders

In addition to the extensive military deployment, the Russian government's recognition of Abkhazia and South Ossetia as independent states has been supported by the arrival of Russian border guards. In April 2009, Moscow signed bilateral agreements with Abkhazia and South Ossetia on the joint protection of the 'state' border. Border-guard directorates were set up by the Russian FSB (*Federalnaya Sluzhba Bezopasnosti*) Border Guard Service in both regions and units deployed (so-called 'green berets') at the request of the respective leaderships. The following year Russia's Federation Council ratified the border agreements with South Ossetia and Abkhazia, which outline how the 'state borders' of these two regions will be 'defended'. Responsibility for defending the 'borders' has been delegated to Russia, although the agreements envisage responsibility for border defence being returned to the respective local authorities once they are able to protect them. In the case of South Ossetia, the Russian authorities will '[deploy] checkpoints and the FSB border guard directorate on the South Ossetian–Georgian border; [finance] the expenses of its servicemen and civilian personnel; [help] the state bodies of South Ossetia train specialists for the border guard agency'.[17] By 2011, there were 1,200 Russian border-guards serving in South Ossetia and only two of 19 planned border posts had been constructed, with the remaining 17 expected to be built over the course of the year.

[15] *Nezavisimaya Gazeta*, 18 February 2010, available at: http://www.ng.ru/nvo/2010-02-18/1_abhazia.html, accessed 18 May 2010.

[16] *Nezavisimaya Gazeta*, 18 February 2010, available at: http://www.ng.ru/nvo/2010-02-18/1_abhazia.html, accessed 18 May 2010.

[17] 'Russian parliament ratifies border guard agreements with South Ossetia, Abkhazia', Excerpt from report by Russian news agency Interfax, Moscow, 10:30 GMT, BBC Monitoring, 26 March 2010, available at: http://my.monitor.bbc.co.uk, accessed 18 July 2011.

Russian and Abkhaz representatives have drafted agreements on the development of infrastructure at the 'Russian–Abkhaz state border', including the establishment of border checkpoints and reconstruction of a road bridge over the River Psou, which links Russian and Abkhaz villages. Around 1,300 Russian and 200 Abkhaz troops protect 215-km of maritime border, a 98-km land border and 39-km river border. A coastguard division (part of the border guard directorate) has been assigned to patrol Abkhazia's maritime borders. Based at Ochamchire, the division has two *Sobol* and two *Mangust* class patrol boats, although this is expected to be doubled.[18]

The leadership of South Ossetia is happy to increase its reliance on Russia, reflecting an understanding that the region would be unable to survive as a truly independent state. In a letter to President Medvedev in 2009 the South Ossetian leader, Eduard Kokoity, assured the Russian leader that South Ossetia 'will always remember to whom it owes its salvation', emphasising that 'the people of South Ossetia can now live in freedom and safety in the land of their ancestors in an alliance with great Russia'.[19] This is in contrast to Abkhazia, which is less keen to remain so dependent upon Moscow's continuing patronage. Unlike South Ossetia, which, prior to 2008, had been seeking reunification with the Russian republic of North Ossetia, Abkhazia has always sought full independence, based on close political and economic integration with Russia.[20] There has been growing unease in Abkhazia about its increasing reliance on Moscow, demonstrated during the presidential elections there in 2009 when the opposition candidate Raul Khadzhimba stood on a platform that opposed perceived Russian 'colonisation'. A change in Abkhazia's property laws prompted even Russian media to caution about a growing level of disquiet amongst the Abkhaz:

> Sukhumi has made a difficult decision to introduce amendments to the law on property which will enable Russian citizens to buy land and buildings in Abkhazia ... Affordable housing is a big problem in the republic, and given that Russians have much more money to spend than the local population, the reaction of Abkhaz citizens is not difficult to predict.[21]

Local dissatisfaction has manifest itself in attacks on property thought to be owned by Russians, as well as a reluctance to return homes to Russians who left Abkhazia

---

[18] 'Russia to double number of coastguard ships in Georgian breakaway region', Excerpt from report by Russian military news agency Interfax-AVN website, Moscow, 14:26 GMT, 28 April 2010, BBC Monitoring, available at: http://my.monitor.bbc.co.uk, accessed 18 July 2011.

[19] 'Kremlin "walking tightrope" with Abkhazia, South Ossetia–Russian website', Text of report by Russian Gazeta.ru news website, 26 August 2009, BBC Monitoring, available at: http://my.monitor.bbc.co.uk, accessed 24 May 2010.

[20] Following his election to power at the beginning of 2005, the Abkhazian leader Sergei Bagapsh stated that integration with Russia was a priority for his government. He described Abkhazia as being tied to Russia 'by an umbilical cord' and said his administration would do 'everything we can to make the laws and the acts of legislation of the republic of Abkhazia dovetail with those of the Russian Federation' ('Favourite in Abkhazia presidential election aiming to join Russian Federation', Excerpt from report by Russian external TV service NTV Mir, Moscow, 10:00 GMT, BBC Monitoring, 11 January 2005, available at: http://my.monitor.bbc.co.uk, accessed 6 March 2009).

[21] *Kommersant*", 18 February 2010, available at: http://www.kommersant.ru/doc.aspx?DocsID=1324162, accessed 23 May 2010.

during the early 1990s, a problem acknowledged by Russian First Deputy Foreign Ministry Andrei Denisov during a *Duma* briefing in 2011. Following the death of Abkhazian leader Sergei Bagapsh in June 2011, the subsequent 'presidential' election campaign was dominated by the issue of how the candidates would deal with its northern neighbour: the two frontrunners, Prime Minister Sergei Shamba and vice president Aleksandr Ankvab, have both made their commitment to Abkhaz independence (as opposed to dependence) clear. Khadzhimba, the third candidate, has seen his position weakened by the perception that he is now too close to Russia and the security services.

The different attitudes of the two regions are reflected in their attitudes towards the Russian military deployments. South Ossetian leader, Eduard Kokoity, has described the 4th Russian base as a 'reliable shield and guarantor of security'.[22] The former Abkhaz leader Sergei Bagapsh insisted that Russian military facilities in the region will not operate independently, but will be joint Russian–Abkhaz facilities, while Russian President Medvedev has stated that the base creates the 'foundation for the development of Abkhazia as an independent state', an objective somewhat undermined by the appointment in 2011 of a Russian officer to head up the Abkhaz armed forces.[23] Neither Abkhazia nor South Ossetia can be truly independent, whilst they are so reliant, both economically and militarily, upon their powerful northern neighbour.

Russia claims that it recognised their sovereignty

> because in our judgement there was no other possibility to ensure not only the security, but also the very survival of the South Ossetian and Abkhaz peoples in the face of the policies pursued by the Georgian leadership over the past 20 years, even if we leave aside the pre-Soviet period.[24]

While Russia claims it is protecting its 'citizens',[25] many view their actions as little more than *de-facto* annexation. The Kremlin dismisses such claims, stating that it only wants to establish a 'clear and understandable order' in the border zones: 'This is about the struggle against drug trafficking, arms contraband and organised crime. It is about the overall strengthening of law and order and tidying-up of the border regime' (Karasin 2009). There is no doubt that during the years that Abkhazia and South Ossetia were *de facto* independent, they undermined regional stability, not just because of the threat of a renewal of fighting, but because they created security vacuums that were outside of government control, providing ideal conditions for

---

[22]*Komsomolskaya Pravda*, 8 April 2010, available at: http://www.kp.ru/daily/24470.4/629636/, accessed 21 January 2011.

[23]'Russian president praises cooperation with Georgia's breakaway Abkhazia', Rossiya 24 news channel, Moscow, in Russian 10:52 GMT, BBC Monitoring, 17 February 2010, available at: http://my.monitor.bbc.co.uk, accessed 23 July 2012.

[24]Ministry of Foreign Affairs of the Russian Federation, Press and Information Department, 1 February 2010. The Russian position is at odds with its stance over Chechnya, a self-proclaimed 'independent' republic that has been seeking independence from the Russian Federation, and Moscow's anger at other states which have engaged with Chechen separatists.

[25]The majority of the populations of the two regions hold Russian passports.

transnational security challenges such as organised crime and illegal trafficking to flourish.[26] Thus, it could be argued that the appearance of Russian military bases, border guards and tighter border controls could serve to stabilise the wider South Caucasus region.

However, there is also a significant risk from the increasing militarisation of the volatile South Caucasus. In the wake of the 2008 conflict, Georgia embarked upon a rapid rearmament programme in order to be able to defend itself against the perceived threat from Russia. Moscow has been very critical of the apparent remilitarisation of its southern neighbour, accusing Western countries of encouraging 'official Tbilisi to continue a bellicose course, a policy of threats and provocations against its neighbours, and to fan up tensions in the region' (Karasin 2009). Tensions between Russia and Georgia remain high, as demonstrated by the impact of the 'fake' invasion documentary shown in March 2010, and in April 2010, Georgia's Interior Minister Vano Merabishvili warned that 'the war is not over yet'.[27] Georgia perceives the establishment of permanent Russian military bases on the territory of its separatist territories to be a threat and has continued to demand guarantees of the non-use of force from Russia. For its part, Moscow denies that it is a party to the conflict and thus is not in a position to give any such guarantee, highlighting the Russian stance that its forces are only there to protect the peoples of Abkhazia and South Ossetia from the threat of further Georgian aggression.

The international community has consistently called on Russia to withdraw its troops from the separatist territories, stating that their presence violates the restrictions on military forces in the region stipulated in the Sarkozy–Medvedev ceasefire agreement. Furthermore, the lack of international observers on the ground really hampers the acquisition of a true picture. The EU Monitoring Mission is not permitted access to what Georgia refers to as its 'occupied territories' and can only monitor the periphery. Georgia claims that Russia's moves to eradicate monitoring missions (United Nations Observer Mission in Georgia (UNOMIG) and Organization for Security and Cooperation in Europe(OSCE)) is an attempt to hide what it is up to and prevent 'impartial and unbiased monitors' witnessing 'crimes they commit in violation of... international law and all agreements signed'.[28] Certainly, Moscow has deliberately sought to dismantle existing conflict resolution mechanisms in the region, refusing to back a continuation of either the OSCE or UNOMIG missions, despite this contravening the terms of the Sarkozy–Medvedev six-point peace plan. In 2011, Russian deputy foreign minister Grigory Karasin again dismissed calls for an international presence in Abkhazia and South

---

[26]South Ossetia's status as a *de facto* independent republic enabled it to exploit the lack of official borders between Russia and Georgia (i.e. between North and South Ossetia), facilitating a prolific smuggling operation predominantly of alcohol and fuel. For further details of the alleged contraband that travelled between North and South Ossetia, see *Novyie Izvestiya* (1 July 2004, pp. 1–4). For a detailed analysis of the economic impact of these unresolved conflicts, particularly the problem of smuggling and criminal activities, see Gotsiridze (2004).

[27]*Kommersant"*, 7 April 2010, available at: http://www.kommersant.ru/doc.aspx?DocsID = 1350011, accessed 19 May 2010.

[28]'Russia needs no "eyewitnesses" in rebel regions—Georgian foreign minister', Channel 1 TV, Tbilisi, 12:00 GMT, BBC Monitoring, 19 May 2009, available at: http://my.monitor.bbc.co.uk, accessed 12 June 2009.

Ossetia, stating 'it is not quite clear why this is necessary'.[29] The lack of any international presence within the two regions, even in an observer capacity, undermines Russia's argument that it is merely acting to guarantee the security of the Abkhaz and South Ossetian peoples from Georgian aggression. The absence of a neutral, multinational observer mission heightens the risk of further conflict with mistrust and misinterpretation replacing independent factual verification.

*Russia's 'southern underbelly'*

The strengthening of Russia's military position in Abkhazia and South Ossetia needs to be viewed within the broader context of a desire to preserve influence and leadership throughout the South Caucasus region. The Russian government has compared its bases in the South Caucasus to US military bases in Romania and Bulgaria, reflecting the view that the South Caucasus lies within Moscow's traditional sphere of exclusive influence, a belief reflected in broader Russian foreign-policy (Karasin 2009). An article in *Komsomoloskaya Pravda* questioned 'why is the US decision to open bases in Romania and Bulgaria fully legitimate, while it is not possible for Russia to do something similar?'[30] This reflects Moscow's unhappiness with US dominance of the international system, which it feels is destabilising, and its own desire to play a leading role. An article in Russian military journal *Voennaya Mysl'* in 2009 suggested that an important objective of Russian foreign-policy was the establishment of a multipolar world, an aim that could be achieved by securing the country's geopolitical interests in various 'vectors' including the 'southern geopolitical vector', which includes the South Caucasus: 'The southern direction is the most worrying in terms of ensuring the national security of the Russian Federation. It is on our southern flank that events occur which directly affect national security and require a clear definition of Russia's geopolitical interests, particularly *in the Caucasus region*' (Maruev & Karpenko 2009, p. 9, emphasis in the original).

The article went on to suggest that, as a result of its actions in 2008, Moscow had strengthened its influence throughout the South Caucasus region and that it was vital to hold the positions it had 'won' in Abkhazia and South Ossetia and use them as a 'springboard for the further diffusion of [Russian] influence' in the Caucasus (Maruev & Karpenko 2009, p. 9). Certainly, the establishment of two permanent military bases in Abkhazia and South Ossetia since 2008 has led to a significant change in terms of the Russian military presence in the South Caucasus, initiating a consolidation of its position. In 2010, relations between Russia and Armenia were strengthened, with the signing of an extension of their 1995 agreement on the 102nd Russian military base at Gyumri, prolonging the operation of the base until 2044. According to the *Voennaya Mysl'* article, the strengthening of relations with Armenia is one of Russia's 'key geopolitical interests in the southern vector' and the base at Gyrumi allows Moscow to continue to exert pressure on Turkey, Azerbaijan and Georgia (Maruev & Karpenko 2009, p. 10).

---

[29]'Russia sees no point in international presence in Georgia's breakaway regions', Text of report by Russian news agency Interfax, Moscow, 17:51 GMT, BBC Monitoring, 7 June 2011, available at: http://my.monitor.bbc.co.uk, accessed 23 July 2011.

[30]*Komsomolskaya Pravda*, 19 February 2010, available at: http://www.kp.ru/daily/24444/609760/, accessed 20 January 2011.

Of concern for Armenia's neighbours was the announcement that the new agreement with Moscow had not only extended the timeframe for Russian use of the base, it had also expanded the scope of its 'geographic and strategic responsibilities'. According to President Sargasyan, 'the base's operation was limited by the former Soviet Union's external borders, but this restriction has now been removed from the text of the agreement'.[31] Furthermore, it was announced at the end of 2010 that an anti-missile defence command centre had been opened in Armenia, the result of cooperation between the Armenian air force and Russia's 102nd military base in the country. According to the Armenian Ministry of Defence, the centre is capable of rapidly identifying airborne threats and coordinating and managing the destruction of such threats.[32] Commenting on the extension of the 1995 agreement, President Sargasyan stated his belief that effective sovereignty is beneficial for any state, but in the South Caucasus region sovereignty includes participation in effective international and regional security systems: 'I believe that today military bases are not symbols of hegemony, but effective cooperation'.[33] The base in Armenia is intended both to serve the interests of the Russian Federation and provide security for Armenia. To this end, Russia also supplies Armenia with modern weapons and military equipment. The strategic partnership, and in particular the Russian military presence is viewed as a key component of the country's national security, as emphasised in the National Security Strategy:

> Although Russia includes a part of the Caucasus, Armenian–Russian relations go far beyond the regional level. The importance of Russia's role for the security of Armenia, the traditional friendly links between the two nations, the level of trade and economic relations, Russia's role in the Nagorno–Karabakh mediation effort, as well as the presence of a significant Armenian community in Russia, all contribute to a strategic partnership.[34]

However, Russia's partnership with Armenia has suffered as a result of the poor state of relations between Moscow and Tbilisi. Since 2008, Russia has been unable to transport military equipment across Georgian territory into Armenia and in April 2011 Georgia officially suspended its 2006 military transport agreement with Russia. This leaves the Russian base in Armenia isolated, with only the expensive option of military aviation to equip and bring in manpower. In the event of a renewal of fighting between Armenia and Azerbaijan over Nagorno-Karabakh, Georgia could find itself caught between the warring parties.

## *Winners and losers*

Moscow has attracted considerable international censure for its actions in Georgia in 2008 that have undermined its relations with the West. What has the Kremlin gained

---

[31]'Joint news conference following Russian-Armenian talks', 20 August 2010, 13:30, Yerevan, *Official site of the President of Russia*, available at: http://eng.news.kremlin.ru/transcripts/810/print, accessed 8 June 2011.

[32]'Russia installs air defence command centre in Armenia', Text of report in English by private Armenian news agency Mediamax, Yerevan, 12:57 GMT, 20 December 2010, available at: http://my.monitor.bbc.co.uk, accessed 15 March 2011.

[33]*Krasnaya Zvezda*, 19 August 2010, available at: www.kz.ru, accessed 20 August 2010.

[34]*Krasnaya Zvezda*, 19 August 2010, available at: www.kz.ru, accessed 20 August 2010.

from this consolidation of its military position in the South Caucasus? First, the Russian leadership has demonstrated its willingness to take action in the face of strong condemnation from the international community in pursuit of an 'independent' foreign policy and the Russian national interest, as well as the establishment of a multipolar international system. The influence of the upcoming 2014 Winter Olympics on Russian strategic planning should also not be overlooked. The International Olympics Committee (IOC) awarded the games to Sochi in July 2007, less than a year before Moscow increased its support for Georgia's separatist territories. With the establishment of a permanent military base in Abkhazia, as well as a border guard directorate, Russia has undoubtedly boosted the security of Sochi, which is close to the volatile North Caucasus. The head of the FSB's Border Service Coast Guard, Colonel-General Viktor Trufanov, stated in September 2009 that the coastguard has been expanding its presence in the Black Sea region specifically in order to provide security for the Sochi Olympic Games.[35] During April 2011, Russian Ministry of Defence and FSB forces conducted joint exercises in Abkhazia in preparation for the 2014 Winter Olympics, following similar exercises held by Russian border guards in the Kodori Gorge. In addition to the potential danger to the Games from insurgents in the North Caucasus, Georgia is also being depicted as a possible threat, with President Medvedev stating in February 2011 that Georgia 'represents the greatest potential threat to the Olympic Games'.[36] Abkhazia thus provides a secure buffer zone.

There is a prevalent view amongst many Georgians that the Russian military intervention in South Ossetia in 2008 was intended to 'punish' Georgia for its Euro-Atlantic aspirations. Certainly, one of the most apparent impacts of the 2008 conflict has been the stalling of Georgia's push for NATO membership. Russia is unhappy with Georgia's pro-Western tendencies and, since 1991, Moscow has sought to exert pressure on the country and maintain its influence in the South Caucasus through a variety of means, culminating in the use of military force in 2008. In 2008 Sergei Lavrov, the Russian foreign minister, accused Washington of 'infiltrating the post-Soviet space ever more actively: Ukraine and Georgia are graphic examples' and warned that if either country becomes a NATO member-state there will be a 'substantial negative geopolitical shift'.[37] In his view, 'NATO's incomprehensible, unwarranted expansion' is dividing Europe. The country's military doctrine, approved by President Medvedev in February 2010, defined NATO's eastward enlargement as the main external military danger facing Russia, warning 'efforts to impart global functions, which are implemented in violation of the norms of international law, to the force potential of the North Atlantic Treaty Organisation (NATO) bring the military infrastructure of NATO member countries closer to the Russian borders, including by way of the bloc's enlargement'. The publication of NATO's new strategic concept in 2010 appears to have eased some of the Russian concerns about future possible enlargement of the alliance, with one diplomat

---

[35] 'Russian coast guard preparing for Sochi Olympics and Abkhazia coastal duty', Text of report by the website of Russian newspaper *Gazeta*, Moscow, BBC Monitoring, 16 September 2009, available at: http://my.monitor.bbc.co.uk, accessed 7 June 2010.

[36] *Nezavisimoye Voennoye Obozreniye*, 11 April 2011, available at: http://www.ng.ru/nvo/2011-04-11/1_abhazia.html, accessed 12 June 2011.

[37] *Izvestiya*, 31 March 2008, available at: http://www.izvestia.ru/person/article3114615/, accessed 10 October 2009.

noting its 'balanced approach': 'As the tragic events of August 2008 showed, attempts at an accelerated, let alone politicised, pulling of new countries into NATO are fraught with direct threats, and tear up the single security space'.[38]

By contrast, Georgia views NATO membership as key to its national security and Article V of the Washington Treaty is a key driver of this desire for membership. The country's National Military Strategy makes it clear that a shift from the principle of territorial defence to one of collective defence is a cornerstone of Georgian defence policy. Without security guarantees from a third-party, there is a fear that the state is not strong enough to survive in the face of an increasingly assertive Russia. According to the Strategic Defence Review, the 'need for collective defence is underscored by Georgia's inability to put significant resources against a variety of internal and external threats, some originating from significantly more powerful sources' (Strategic Defence Review 2007, p. 67).[39] Georgia's latest Threat Assessment Document for 2010–2013, approved by Saakashvili in 2010, noted that Russia's continued occupation of the separatist territories 'poses a direct threat to Georgia's sovereignty, statehood, and represents the most important factor of political, economic and social destabilisation', and stated that the conduct of foreign affairs based on the politics of force poses 'a threat to the fundamental principles and norms of the global community' (Melikishvili 2010).

At first glance, the events of August 2008 appear to have been successful for Moscow. Not only did it demonstrate the lengths it was prepared to go to in order to protect its 'citizens', the military action also acted as a warning shot to other former Soviet states, such as Ukraine, and also to the West, that it will not stand by and let countries in what it considers to be its strategic sphere of influence integrate more closely with Western security structures. Russia's permanent representative to NATO, Dmitry Rogozin, has expressed his belief that the alliance's eastward enlargement has 'broken down' in the wake of the war. Although he considers further enlargement inevitable, according to Rogozin 'such an outrageous demarche, such an outrageous offensive on Russia's borders will not occur anymore'.[40] NATO's new Strategic Concept, adopted in 2010, made it clear that the door to membership remains open for '"all European democracies" that share the values of our Alliance, which are willing and able to assume the responsibilities and obligations of membership, and whose inclusion can contribute to common security and stability'.[41] The alliance intends to

---

[38]'NATO provoked Georgian use of force in separatist region—Russian diplomat', Text of report by Russian news agency Interfax, Moscow, 10:38 GMT, BBC Monitoring, 14 February 2011, available at: http://my.monitor.bbc.co.uk, accessed 22 July 2011.

[39]There is very little domestic opposition to Georgia's Western alignment and referendums on the issue of NATO membership demonstrate consistently high levels of support for accession, even amongst opposition groups. A plebiscite on NATO membership held in early 2008 showed 77% in favour of seeking membership. Fried (2006) believes that there is a 'strong national consensus' for Georgia's Western and Euro-Atlantic direction, even amongst opposition groups.

[40]'Georgian leader's policy halted NATO's eastward expansion—Russian envoy', Vesti TV news channel, Moscow, 07:36 GMT, BBC Monitoring, 6 August 2009, available at: http://my.monitor.bbc.co.uk, accessed 10 June 2010.

[41]'Active Engagement, Modern Defence: Strategic Concept for the Defence and Security of The Members of the North Atlantic Treaty Organisation, adopted by Heads of State and Government in Lisbon', 19 November 2010, p. 8, available at: http://www.nato.int/cps/en/natolive/official_texts_68580.htm, accessed 8 June 2011.

develop its relationship with Georgia within the framework of the NATO–Georgia Commission, whilst the EU has also indicated that it intends to intensify its cooperation with former Soviet states, rather than reduce it. Nevertheless, Georgian membership of either organisation remains a distant dream in the wake of August 2008, possibly more remote now than at any time since the 2003 Rose Revolution. Whilst Tbilisi has ambitious aspirations regarding further integration into the Euro-Atlantic community, these ambitions have been dashed as Western European and US allies seek to safeguard their relationship with Russia.

*Conclusion*

Russia is reluctant to lose its dominance in the South Caucasus and, since 1991, Moscow has sought to maintain its influence in the region through a variety of means. With its military incursion into Georgia in 2008, Moscow successfully demonstrated its ability to exert its authority, as well as its determination to re-establish Russia's authority as a strong state that is capable of influencing events within the global arena and pursuing an independent stance on international issues. Russia's policies towards the South Caucasus and the wider former Soviet area remain focused on maintaining influence and reasserting leadership, with the military lever constituting a key aspect of this strategy. The South Caucasus is part of Russia's 'southern underbelly' (*yuzhnaya podbryush'ye*), a term that underscores the sense of vulnerability it feels along its southern border. The area is an unstable neighbourhood that is divided by several unresolved conflicts, including Georgia's separatist regions, Nagorno-Karabakh and the ongoing insurgency in the North Caucasus, as well as being a buffer between Russia and the wider Middle East. In the wake of its 2008 conflict with Georgia, Russia has undoubtedly secured its southern flank, consolidating its already dominant position with the establishment of permanent military bases in Abkhazia and South Ossetia, and the extension of its strategic military partnership with Armenia. Furthermore, Russian border guards are now present in a wide area outside the borders of the Russian Federation. These changes have enabled Moscow to secure Sochi prior to the 2014 Winter Olympics, destabilise the Georgian leadership and its foreign-policy direction and potentially stall further NATO enlargement. However, with the escalating insurgency in the North Caucasus threatening its domestic security, Moscow should perhaps be concentrating its efforts, both military and financial, on boosting security within its own borders, rather than consolidating its position across the mountains in the south.

There is a risk that Russian–Abkhaz relations will deteriorate, undermining security across the Caucasus. As discussed above, there is growing unease in Abkhazia about the region's reliance on Moscow and the lack of true independence. The appointment of a Russian officer to head up the Abkhaz armed forces is a demonstration of Moscow's concern about the potential for unrest, as well as its determination to secure the region and maintain tight control over events there: by placing a Russian in charge, Moscow has ensured that it will be able to control the region's armed forces and prevent any potential dissent that may occur in the future.

Russia's intervention in Georgia has not only allowed Moscow to consolidate its hold on the Caucasus, it has also enabled it to boost its military presence and reach in the Black Sea region. The development of a naval base at Ochamchire and the expansion of

Russia's Black Sea coastline to include Abkhazia has significantly increased Russia's maritime footprint and influence in the Black Sea, where the borders of Western security structures such as the EU and NATO converge with Russia's south-western borders. Having consistently expressed its unease about further NATO enlargement, Russia's actions re-established its dominance in an area of competing influences and undermined any future eastwards enlargement of the military alliance. Moscow demonstrated the lengths it was prepared to go to in order to support its allies and the military action also acted as a warning shot to other former Soviet states, such as Ukraine, that it will not stand by and let countries in what it considers to be its strategic sphere of influence integrate more closely with West. Although NATO has subsequently made it clear that it remains committed to its 'open door' policy and that Georgian membership is not off the table, Georgia's accession hopes remain a distant dream.

The Russian intervention also demonstrated that the apparent weakness of Western security organisations such as NATO, highlighting the alliance's fragile cohesion, as well as the divergence between the European and US approach. European memberstates are more likely to be directly affected by the negative impact of any decision to enlarge, as they are far more dependent upon Russia, particularly in terms of energy. There is concern that, contrary to aims of the alliance, further enlargement will actually undermine security in the Euro-Atlantic area rather than strengthen it. Furthermore, the impact of the global financial crisis on Western states, together with the Obama administration's attempts to 'reset' its relations with Moscow, mean that the US and European influence in the South Caucasus has waned, enabling Russia to further consolidate its position.

*Kings College London at the Joint Services Command and Staff College*

## *References*

Foreign Policy Concept (2008) *The Foreign Policy Concept of the Russian Federation*, approved by Dmitry Medvedev, President of the Russian Federation on 12 July, available at: http://www.mid.ru/ns-osndoc.nsf/1e5f0de28fe77fdcc32575d900298676/869c9d2b87ad8014c32575d9002b1c38?OpenDocument, accessed 24 July 2011.

Fried, D. (2006) *US-Georgian Relations*, Assistant Secretary of State for European and Eurasian Affairs, Press Conference following Meeting with Georgian President Saakashvili, Tbilisi, 18 October, available at: www.state.gov/p/eur/rls/rm/75098.htm, accessed 3 June 2009.

Gotsiridze, R. (2004) 'Georgia: Conflict Regions and the Economy', *Central Asia and the Caucasus*, 1, 25.

Karasin, G. (2009) *Address by Russian Deputy Minister of Foreign Affairs at the Session of the OSCE Permanent Council*, Vienna, 4 June, available at: http://www.mid.ru/brp_4.nsf/0/16778FF5CE8C6C6DC32575CB00500A87, accessed 3 June 2009.

Maruev, A.Y. & Karpenko, A.O. (2009) 'Voenno-politicheskie aspekty formirovaniya interesov Rossii na yuzhnom geopoliticheskom vektore" *Voennaya Mysl'*, 11, November.

Melikishvili, A. (2010) 'Georgia's New Threat Assessment Document Identifies Russia as a Main Threat', *Eurasia Daily Monitor*, 7, 192, 25 October, available at: www.jamestown.org/programs/edm/single/?tx_ttnews[tt_news]=37077&tx_ttnews[backPid]=484&no_cache=1, accessed 18 June 2011.

Military Doctrine (2010) *The Military Doctrine of the Russian Federation*, approved by decree of the President of the Russian Federation on 5 February, available at: http://www.scrf.gov.ru/documents/33.html, accessed 5 June 2010.

Ministry of Foreign Affairs of Georgia (2010) 'Statement on the Treaty on the Creation of a Joint Military Base in Gudauta Signed between Russia and the so-called "Republic of Abkhazia"', 18 February, available at: http://www.mfa.gov.ge/print.php?gg=1&sec_id=59&info_id=11613&lang_id=ENG, accessed 6 June 2011.

Ministry of Foreign Affairs of the Russian Federation, Press and Information Department (2010) *Transcript of Remarks and Response to Media Questions by Russian Foreign Minister Sergey Lavrov Following the Signing of an Agreement between the Government of the Russian Federation and the Government of the Republic of South Ossetia on Mutual Visa-Free Travel for Citizens of the Two Countries*, Moscow, 1 February, available at: http://www.mid.ru/brp_4.nsf/0/54CFF3FDC0B9F75CC32576BE00382FC0, accessed 23 May 2010.

NSS (2009) *National Security Strategy of the Russian Federation*, approved by decree of the President of the Russian Federation, 12 May 2009, http://www.scrf.gov.ru/documents/1/99.html, accessed 6 June 2009.

Strategic Defence Review (2007) *Strategic Defence Review*, Final Report (Tbilisi, Ministry of Defence of Georgia).

# Young Soldiers' Tales of War in Nagorno-Karabakh

## NONA SHAHNAZARIAN & ULRIKE ZIEMER

### Abstract

The active participation of children and young men in armed conflicts has not lost its significance as a global phenomenon in the twenty-first century. In Eurasia, where numerous regions are plagued by violent conflicts, many of the everyday realities these young soldiers experienced still remain unclear and continue to be under-researched. Through the use of biographical interviews, this essay retrospectively explores the ways in which war in Nagorno-Karabakh impinged on male teenagers' identities. A biographical approach not only reveals these former young soldiers' experiences which may have otherwise never been told but also allows them to reflect on their war experiences more than ten years later. In this way, we aim to complement existing research on the Nagorno-Karabakh conflict with new insights.

THE STUDY OF WARS AND MILITARY CONFLICTS HAS been central to political debates and international relations (Bull 1977; Kaldor 2001; Suganami 2002; Waltz 1959). For a long time, the study of identities and their transformation during war have been less central to these debates. Only in recent years, has the study of identity found its way back as an important element in understanding questions of peace and war (Bloom 1990; Neuman 1992; Suganami 2008; Williams & Neuman 2000). Academic scholarship began to focus on the culture-changing aspects of war and the ways culture might impact on wars, especially when it comes to new technologies and conflicts in the post-socialist space (Campell 1998, 2003; Wills & Moore 2008). As early as 1941, Malinowski wrote that war is not merely a military undertaking. Whether it is rooted in human nature or social calculation, war soon becomes a key factor in the cultural lives and institutionalised relationships of all societies as well as identity transformations. In this vein, war is considered as much a cultural endeavour as it is a military undertaking.

Young people's suffering from, and fighting in, armed conflicts continues to be an everyday reality in many parts of the world in the twenty-first century. More than 250,000 children between seven and 18 years of age are actively involved in conflicts in over 40 countries (Denov & Maclure 2007, pp. 244). In view of the international impact of armed conflicts and the consequent civilian suffering, there now exist considerable scholarly publications on young people and war in different parts of the world (Amone-P'Olak *et al.* 2007; Bonanno 2004; Hamilton & Man 1998). Most of this literature focuses on the individual in medical terms and researchers have measured the psychological impact of war with an assessment of depression, post-traumatic stress disorder, and abilities to engage in the ordinary routine of everyday life. While the influence of the trauma model and other psychopathological paradigms is beyond doubt, more recent research shows that a fuller consideration of the assumptions that underlie such models questions the relevance and validity of the key findings (Boyden & de Berry 2004, pp. xiv-vi). This type of research also highlights that during conflict a blurring of the boundaries between military and civilian life takes place (Feldman 2002). It has been shown that militarisation permeates all aspects of economic and social life (Enloe 2000). Accordingly, in recent years anthropologists and sociologists have begun to explore meaning-making and identities during conflict often by means of interviewing and providing ethnographic accounts of social practices and discourse (Denov & Maclure 2007; Honwana 2006; Swaine & Feeny 2004; West 2004).

Despite the growing interest in young people and their war participation, many of the realities these young people have experienced remain unclear and continue to be under-researched, especially when it comes to conflicts in Eurasia, where numerous regions have been plagued by politically induced violence. While the history and politics of these conflicts are widely debated and researched, an explicit focus on young people's experiences resulting from these conflicts has been almost absent from these debates.[1] Our essay explores how war and warfare encroached on the identities and actions of former young soldiers in Nagorno-Karabakh, complementing existing research with new insights. In this essay, we use testimonies of the now adult men to show the various pathways of entry for young people into child soldiering and explore their diverse roles and experiences during war. In this way, the identity transformations of these young soldiers are told in retrospect.

Ethnographic fieldwork was conducted in Martuni, a small town and administrative centre of one the five districts in Nagorno-Karabakh. In this essay, we draw on biographical interviews with former youth soldiers. Nona Shahnazarian started her research in 2000, and returned to Nagorno-Karabakh every year since then.[2] In addition, Nona Shahnazarian made a fieldwork trip to the region to conduct research focusing on the war experiences of these former young soldiers in 2008.[3] Ulrike Ziemer made a fieldwork trip to the region in 2009.[4] Both of us let the interview participants choose the location for the interview. Research participants chose the place where they

---

[1] The only exceptions are two scholarly publications, Sabirova (2008) and Shahnazarian (2008).

[2] Since 2000 Nona has conducted more than 80 interviews.

[3] Most of her fieldwork trips were self-financed. Nonetheless, Nona used her Fulbright Visiting Scholar Program at UCLA to conduct additional research specifically on the topic of young soldiers' war experiences. For our essay in particular we analysed 15 biographical interviews, which addressed the topic of war and fighting.

[4] This fieldwork trip was funded by The Centre for East European Language Based Area Studies (CEELBAS) and was conducted as part of a CEELBAS Postdoctoral Research Fellowship on Migration and Diasporic Citizenship. Ulrike conducted a total of nine biographical interviews.

felt most comfortable. In most cases, this was the respondents' home, but also parks, on street benches outside their homes or even cafés. While we both conducted our ethnographic fieldwork separately and our cultural backgrounds are different,[5] we soon noticed that we covered some similar themes in our interviews. In addition, during both trips (Nona in 2008 and Ulrike in 2009) we experienced great difficulties in conducting interviews on the specific topic of the war in Nagorno-Karabakh, or even just asking questions about the war.[6] While some interviews were conducted with a Dictaphone, other research participants refused and we had to take notes. On many occasions former soldiers refused to talk about the war and their experiences, showing that this memory is still alive and that there is a 'no war no peace' situation in Nagorno-Karabakh.

Biographical interviews not only encourage the individual to talk about his or her life 'as completely and honestly as possible' (Atkinson 1989, p. 8), but also illuminate the ways identities have been shaped by the interplay of individual practices and structural aspects of culture and society during childhood and adolescence. Biographical interviews provide a platform for the native voice and a valid source for insider knowledge (McBeth 1993). A biographical approach is particularly relevant to the study of these young men's war experience because now, more than 15 years after the end of the war in Nagorno-Karabakh, they reflect on their experience by retelling it, while during the war their experience was rendered voiceless.

*Theoretical framework: identity, belonging and conflict*

Identity itself is a slippery concept and the way we use identity in this essay is based on four theoretical assumptions. First, following Hall (1996), it is presumed that identities are not fixed, but rather processual and constantly changing in the process of making sense of experience. Second, identities are discursively constructed through difference, whereby they are established by a symbolic marking of representation in relation to others. Identity formation is part of a meaning-making process, where meanings are the symbolic identification by social actors of the purpose of their actions (Castells 1997, p. 7). In this way, identities involve a process of self-construction that takes place 'within' and 'not outside discourse', at times consciously and unconsciously (Hall 1996).

As for the concept of identification, Brubaker and Cooper (2000, p. 14) argue that the use of this concept stresses the importance of 'agents doing the identifying'. In addition, they contend that the process of identification takes place within wider historical, political and cultural contexts, where 'actors' are affected by practices and discourses external to them and that change over time. In the context of war and conflict, it is important to note that, following Tajfel and Turner (1986), it is assumed that people prefer to have a positive self-concept. They prefer to see their ingroup in a positive light, that is positively distinct from other groups. Positive distinctiveness can

---

[5]While Nona is an Armenian from Nagorno-Karabakh, Ulrike has no cultural connections to Armenians or Nagorno-Karabakh.

[6]Therefore, in the subsequent discussion, interview participants are referred to by pseudonyms to ensure complete anonymity.

be achieved by (biased) intergroup comparisons. In other words, social identity is 'that part of an individual's self-concept which derives from his knowledge of his membership of a social group ... together with the value and emotional significance attached to that membership' (Tajfel 1982, p. 63). In the context of this essay on war identities in Nagorno-Karabakh, it is presumed that membership and belonging has different levels, as the subsequent discussion shows. For example, individuals may belong to the Armenian nation, to Nagorno-Karabakh, to a specific group of fighters, as well as a family.

Third, identities are constructed through our daily narratives, which constitute the ways we experience social life (Somers & Gibson 1994). Such an approach stresses identity as a relational and situational category and presumes that 'social life is itself storied and that narrative is an ontological condition of social life' (Somers & Gibson 1994, p. 38). It is 'through narrativity that we come to know, understand and make sense of the social world' and can form our social identities (Somers & Gibson 1994, p. 59). Somers and Gibson (1994, p. 38) further argue that the stories we tell each other guide our actions and are 'a repertoire of emplotted stories' which people employ 'to make sense of what has happened and is happening to them'.

Finally, identities are performances that vary in different contexts. Following Butler (1993, 1999), this postulation presupposes that narratives are more than informative; they are also performative. This last assumption about identity is mainly considered with regard to these young soldiers' gender identity. Performing gender means that the presentation of self 'will tend to incorporate and exemplify accredited values of society' (Goffman 1959, p. 45). Individuals express themselves in order to affirm and reproduce societal values with their social performance.[7] Gender is, therefore, constituted in 'acts, gestures, and desire which produce the effect of an "internal core" or substance, but produce this on the surface of the body, through the play of signifying absences that suggest, but never reveal, the organising principle of identity as a cause' (Butler 1999, p. 173). In other words, the effect of acts, practices, behaviour and mannerisms bring gender performatively into embodied being. For Butler, gender attributes are not expressive but performative and thus constitute the identity they are said to express or reveal. Accordingly, gendered behaviour is produced by gender identity which is 'tenuously constituted in time, instituted in an exterior space through a stylised repetition of acts' (Butler 1999, p. 174).

*Drifting into violence*

The self-declared, internationally unrecognised republic has existed for almost two decades in a state of 'no war, no peace'. Since the ceasefire in 1994, Azerbaijan and Armenia have remained at stalemate over the Nagorno-Karabakh region. Armenia and the Armenians living in the mountainous Karabakh insist on sovereign self-determination for the republic, which was previously an autonomous unit within Soviet Azerbaijan. Azerbaijan, however, insists on territorial integrity within its Soviet-era boundaries. To date, the conflict is a central obstacle to the political development of Armenia and Azerbaijan and a key impediment to the development of

---

[7]In this way, it is not gender identity only that is performed, but also ethnic identity amongst others.

the South Caucasus region as a whole and its integration into the wider world. The complex social problems generated by its marginal status are almost physically tangible in a region still struggling to overcome the economic, social and psychological consequences of the tragic events of this conflict over Nagorno-Karabakh.

In 1988, inspired by Gorbachev's slogans about democratisation and promises of correcting mistakes made by previous Soviet leaders, Karabakh Armenians turned to Moscow with a petition for the re-establishment of Nagorno-Karabakh under the jurisdiction of Armenia. However, this movement provoked a sharp reaction amongst Azerbaijanis, who opposed a sovereign Nagorno-Karabakh. While Moscow quickly lost control, the Armenian–Azerbaijani confrontation grew considerably, changing from a verbal battle to a war between militarised youth, equipped with stones, sticks and knives; and then to persecution and pogroms driven by ethnic hatred.

Aram[8] was aged 14 in 1988 when the Karabakh movement started. Together with his friends he threw stones at Azerbaijani cars, which drove through Martuni, as he tells us in the interview:

> In 1988, the Karabakh movement started and the war against Azerbaijanis[9] began. They [Azerbaijanis] wanted to kick us out [of Nagorno-Karabakh], but we started to fight back and threw stones. We would hear, for example, that there in Aghdam,[10] they threw stones at our buses ... so why should they drive through Martuni? Then after Sumgait happened we again [threw stones] ... why should they [Azerbaijanis] stay here [in Martuni]? ... Well, we were kids ..., the truth is, that adults told us to throw stones or do something, they gave us the idea: 'You're kids, no one can punish you for it, you're just kids, just go and do it [throw stones]'.[11]

This interview excerpt with Aram highlights how these young men became drawn into political violence. First, Aram emphasises the power of ideological propaganda that took place after the first demonstrations had started. When the dispute broke out with demonstrations in 1988, teams of pamphleteers and propagandists on both sides conducted intensive ideological propaganda (de Waal 2003). One could say that at the beginning of the conflict, in Armenia and Azerbaijan only one issue, Nagorno-Karabakh, was able to raise passions and bring large numbers of people out on to the streets (de Waal 2003, p. 83). Armenian–Azerbaijani tensions had persisted and even intensified under socialism since 'ethnonationalism was in certain ways "built into" the organisation of socialism, manifesting itself differently in different countries but fully absent from none' (Verdery 1993, p. 174). Hence, it was no surprise that by 1988 when

---

[8]Aram was born in Martuni in 1974. His mother was a teacher in a kindergarten and his father was a *militsioner* (policeman). Aram's father died from a heart attack right on the battle field.

[9]As there is no agreed linguistic distinction between the ethnic group Azerbaijanis and the citizens of the state of Azerbaijan, we use the term 'Azerbaijani' for the ethnic group.

[10]Today, the ghost town of Aghdam lies in ruins. Aghdam was a town of 150,000 inhabitants in the south-western part of Azerbaijan, just outside Nagorno Karabakh. During the 1993 summer offensives, Aghdam was besieged and captured by Armenian forces. As the town fell, its entire population fled eastwards. In the immediate aftermath of the fighting, the Armenian forces destroyed much of Aghdam to prevent its recapture by Azerbaijan, resulting in condemnation by U.N. Security Council resolution 853 (July 29 1993) (Laitin & Suny 1999, pp. 160).

[11]Aram, aged 17 in 1991, Martuni, 28 July 2009.

socialism had vanished as a guiding principle, it led to a growth of Armenian and Azerbaijani nationalism.[12]

Second, Aram refers to the pogroms in Sumgait, which are crucial for popular memory and sparked communal actions and hatred amongst Armenians. Shortly after the peaceful demonstrations in February 1988, riots broke out in Sumgait, a drab industrial Azerbaijani city near the capital, and later in Baku itself. A total of 31 people were killed, many were injured and thousands fled in panic (Kurkchiyan 2005, pp. 153–54). For Armenians, the pogroms of Sumgait were proof that Armenians could never live under Azerbaijani rule and feel safe. Armenian accounts refer to these events as evidence of Azerbaijani ethnic hatred, of the genocidal tendency among 'Turks' that Armenians experienced in the Ottoman Empire in 1915, which Azerbaijani 'Turks' were now reviving (Laitin & Suny 1999, p. 152). As such, Sumgait activated the historical memory of the genocide as well as of the mass killings of 20,000 Armenians by Azerbaijanis in Shushi, Karabakh in 1918–1920.[13]

Although it was relatively easy to draw these young men into political violence, it does not mean that they acted without self-doubts. In the following interview excerpt, Artak,[14] aged 13 in 1988, feels the need to justify himself for not going to school but instead for participating in activities like 'throwing stones' at 'Azerbaijani' cars and buses. He even defends his action by emphasising the cultural tradition of younger people listening to their elders:

> When I was in the 9$^{th}$ form at school, the [Karabakh] movement began. I maybe went to schools once or twice. My parents thought that I went to school much more often than that. I remember that once U. Marat[15] approached us on our way to school and said: 'Don't go to school, everyone has gone to the demonstration'. You see, they say that the younger ones should listen to the older ones ... we were brought up like that. So, we went to the main square in Martuni. We stood there for more than 24 hours, with the eldest together. It was an interesting time, a very unusual time.[16]

In 1988, when the Karabakh movement began, 15-year-old Arsen[17] was not interested in politics. Nonetheless, right at the start of the whole conflict, he had a traumatic experience that made him want to be actively engaged. One day, his younger sister and his parents drove home to Martuni from a neighbouring settlement where they had been visiting relatives. The road was blockaded by two Azerbaijanis. His

---

[12]For a thorough account of the long history of Armenian–Azerbaijani tensions see Chorbajian, Donabedian and Mutafian (1994), Chorbajian (2001), de Waal (2003).

[13]It is important to note that although Azerbaijanis, are a different Turkic people than the Ottoman Turks, they are 'Turks' in Armenian popular understanding (Azeri is a Turkic language).

[14]Artak was born in 1975 and brought up in Martuni. His mother worked as a pharmacist and his father was a builder. He has one older sister and one younger brother. His family left Nagorno Karabakh when the war started. Ten years after the ceasefire he finally returned from Russia to Martuni with his wife and five children after the end of the war.

[15]Ulubabian Marat was the founder and initial activist of the Karabakh movement.

[16]Artak, aged 16 in 1991, 6 July 2009, Martuni.

[17]Arsen was born in 1973 and lived all his life in Martuni. His mother was a representative of the Soviet nomenclature, his father was a musician.

father tried to somehow get through the blockade but did not succeed. Instead, Arsen's father was stabbed several times and almost killed. Arsen's mother and sister ran to town to get emergency help for their father.

> To be fair, I was too much in love at that time to be really interested in politics and throwing stones ... But after what happened to my parents, I didn't have any choice, in fact, no one really had any choice, when the real war began ... except maybe to leave Karabakh and never come back ... but this [the decision to leave] would have been shameful in the eyes of other people ... .

As becomes clear from Arsen's interview excerpt, it is not that every young person was actively involved in the political violence spreading across Nagorno-Karabakh. Yet, the events took such an omnipresent character and communal pressure that there was no choice but to participate.

### War narratives

Although demonstrations started in February 1988, the actual war did not start until August 1991. The outbreak of the war in Nagorno-Karabakh was closely linked with Armenia's and Azerbaijan's declarations of independence, which raised their dispute to a new interstate level. Now Azerbaijan immediately felt it possessed an even stronger argument than before. Formally, the new states retained the borders of the old republics and so Nagorno-Karabakh was—and is—an internationally recognised part of Azerbaijan. However, Armenia ignored international conditions and declared Nagorno-Karabakh 'independent'. The regional Soviet in Stepanakert, the capital of Nagorno-Karabakh, declared independence for the new 'NKR' on 2 September 1991, three days after Azerbaijan had declared its own independence (de Waal 2003, p. 161). To date, the Nagorno-Karabakh Republic is a *de facto* independent state within the former territory of western Azerbaijan.

When war broke out the situation became chaotic. Both newly independent states were at war with each other but with no armies. As a result, weapons were being handed out to men who had displayed nothing more than a willingness to fight. There was almost no coordination or training available (de Waal 2003, pp. 163). In Martuni, the situation was no different from the rest of the region. There were only a few men who knew how to use weapons. Those who had served in Afghanistan passed on all the knowledge they had. Gagik,[18] for example, had served in the Soviet Army in Afghanistan and only returned to Karabakh in 1990, when he was 19 years old. Unable to overcome the horror of Afghanistan, he quickly threw himself into the war preparations in Karabakh, where his knowledge proved extremely useful.

---

[18]Gagik was born in Martuni but lived and went to school in Baku until the age of ten. However, his parents died and he returned to Martuni to live with one of his uncles. At the age of 16, he finished school and moved to Baku to study and work there but then was conscripted into the Soviet Army and was sent to Afghanistan.

> Well, I saw that they threw stones at buses ... and I thought it would be better to show these kids more useful stuff then just throwing stones. So, I formed a group and once a month I took them into the forest to train them properly ... .[19]

Gagik not only talks about another possible way how young people got involved in the war preparations, but also about different statuses amongst young people. Gagik, then 19 years old, literally a teenager, talks about 'kids', thus referring to those even younger them him, some of whom were only 12 years of age. All of them were young, including Gagik, but Gagik in his own way is mature and experienced enough to teach those younger inexperienced teenagers. On the whole, for many young soldiers, like Gagik, the war created a unique space and opportunities to acquire a high social status amongst their peers. They became equated with adults, their status and communal rights sometimes surpassing them.

He continues by reminding us that danger was everywhere and to become a proper man, like Gagik, these young lads had to endure some physical tests.

> Well, I ate frogs and snakes, but at first they [the other young men] couldn't do anything like that. It made them sick at first. But after two or three days in the forest, how can I say it, the bloody hunger taught them ... When I suggested frogs or snakes for the first time, they thought I was mad, but when they tried it, they discovered that it was actually tasty ... I trained these kids—they could live a month without food supply.[20]

However, despite ubiquitous dangers and physical tests, these young soldiers had to deal with death on an almost daily basis. For example, Manuk lost his Dad and his two brothers, Suren (17 years) and Vahe (10 years) when he was only 15 years old.[21] Even Gagik, who had experienced the horrors of the war in Afghanistan, did not find it easy to come to terms with the deaths of his close friends, as he talked about it in the interview with us.

> ... I trained them, yes, these kids, they were only kids. Suren [17 years], Varuzhan [19 years]—they were killed ... You know what, I had 21 kids in my group, and most of them were killed, 14 kids were killed in total ... (*he clears his throat loudly*). Everyone died in battle, everyone died with honour.[22]

The war suddenly took on an all-encompassing character, reaching the whole society in Nagorno-Karabakh, independent of gender, age and class. For example, during the bombardment of villages by the Azerbaijani army, Karabakh Armenians offered their precious stored food, like honey-comb or dried fruits, to the *fedai/azatamartik* (freedom fighters) (Shahnazarian 2010). A group of women baked bread around the clock for the soldiers on guard and in the trenches (de Waal 2003, p. 160).

---

[19]Gagik, aged 22 in 1991, 10 August 2009, Martuni.
[20]Gagik, 10 August 2009, Martuni.
[21]Manuk was born in Martuni in 1976. His mother was a housewife and his father worked as a construction engineer. Manuk's father became a member of an underground organisation when the Karabakh movement started.
[22]Gagik, 10 August 2009, Martuni.

Everyone was affected by the war and thus united by one shared aim—to protect themselves. The home front and war front became almost indistinguishable and often it was not possible to determine where it was more dangerous, at home or on the front line.

During the war there were only a few positions that could be taken up by these boys or young men for them to be directly involved in the war. There were special units (*spetsnaz*), who would sortie into the opponent's camp, usually with an intelligence aim or the seizure of weaponry or just participation in open confrontation. The most significant task during the war became the protection of Martuni. Guarding a post became the most sought after and symbolic act of 'serious' war for young men. In fact, many young soldiers were killed while performing guard-post duties.

> I was on guard in Guruchukh[23] ... this was a guard post ... you could throw a grenade with your eyes closed and it would land somewhere in Martuni, we took our responsibility seriously. Usually the Azerbaijanis either attacked early in the morning before dawn or before midnight ... once during guard change at 5pm ... the fight for the guard post started and there was an exchange of fire for about an hour. But Avo[24] got there in time with his tanks, four volunteers from Armenia also came with him and they [Azerbaijanis] retreated ... .[25]

For many children (10–14 years), guarding a guard post became an everyday activity: 'I slept right there on two chairs, and from the constant reloading of magazines my fingers became almost numb in this position (*he shows the position*)'.[26]

While they were still too inexperienced to fight, this task gave them a chance to be directly involved in the war. For example, they would carry cans of food under constant fire to the guard post of Guruchukh, located at the top of the mountain. Often these cans of food would weigh more than 10 kilograms.

> In 1991, I began to help the soldiers ... Everyone wanted to guard the post (*laughs*). As they [soldiers at the post] said: 'Even horses died [when carrying food up the mountain], but this 14-year-old lad [Sevak] can carry everything, he can bring everything to the post'. In general, I brought food to the post.[27]

Noteworthy here is that Martuni's defence was organised by the whole population. Men older than 45 were mobilised to dig trenches around the town. Four guard posts were built around Martuni: Orla, Guruchukh, Elektroset and Russkii Kvartal. Each of the posts was equipped with three hunting rifles and one improvised machine gun. In addition, the defenders had knives and other cold arms. Each of the four posts was guarded by adults as well as young soldiers like Artak and Sevak, who were 15 and 14 years old at the outbreak of the war in Karabakh in 1991. This act was dangerous, the

---

[23]This guard post was named after the mountain of Guruchukh.

[24]Avo is the nickname of Monte Melkonian, a representative of the US Armenian diaspora who became a hero of the Karabakh war. He was the leader and organiser of Martuni's defence.

[25]Artak, aged 16 in 1991, 6 July 2009, Martuni.

[26]Sevak, aged 14 in 1991, 21 June 2009, Martuni.

[27]Sevak, 21 June 2009, Martuni.

narrow path to the post was constantly under fire and children, like Artak or Sevak, who guarded the posts, were like targets for Azerbaijani snipers. Sometimes parents and relatives would not want their children to guard these posts, but these children would resist and do their duties:

> My Mum and Dad didn't want me to guard the post at Guruchukh, but I didn't listen and did it. No one wanted to bring food to this post, because they heavily bombarded Guruchukh—our near by mountain was a strategically important point.[28]

Despite encountering opposition from their parents and relatives, these boys and young men reassured us ever so often during our interviews that they never experienced any communal pressure to guard any post. Without exception all research participants maintained that it was their choice to participate in the war: 'Everything was voluntary, who could force whom!? If I'd said that I didn't want to go, they'd say: "Ok go home and relax. If you're scared, don't go"'.[29]

## *The politics of war identities*

Without question the war became a determining factor and cause for self-identification, dynamically transforming boys' and young men's identities. To date, life in Karabakh is divided into two periods—'before the war' (Soviet period) and 'after the war' (post-Soviet period). On the whole, research participants draw on five major identity narratives during the war in Nagorno-Karabakh: 'I am a patriot of my country'; 'It is my highest honour'; 'I am a real man because I fought'; 'I am a staunch friend'; and 'I am a killer'. Research participants draw on these five identities to different degrees to justify their actions to survive during the war.

The first identity narrative of 'being a patriot' of one's country simply meant that each of the research participants felt like a responsible member of a small community loyal to their small homeland. Overall, this narrative is a collective narrative, where everyone is there for each other. In war situations, this identity does not require words, but collective actions and solidarity. It is an identity that can provide comfort in extreme situations, like war and fighting. For example, Irina, the mother of Manuk (15 years old in 1991), lost her husband and two sons, aged 17 and 10 years, in close succession, and only Manuk survived. Commanders and other soldiers who fought together with Manuk considered it their duty to protect Manuk during fighting. None of them needed to tell her this, she just knew and this was her last comfort, as she knew they would not give him any dangerous tasks. Everyone of them understood that they 'should' protect the last remaining son of this widow. This was a special duty—a duty that was created by feelings and did not need any words to express. This example and many others like it were constructed by a communal unity and communal values, where all members not only know each other but also know details of their biographies, and their personal problems and difficulties.

---

[28]Sevak, 21 June 2009, Martuni. Sevak was born in 1977 in Groznii (Chechen Republic). His parents left the city for Martuni in 1980 when Sevak was only three years old.
[29]Arsen, 14 June 2009, Martuni.

Moreover, this identity narrative of being a patriot also includes the feeling of belonging to a great nation—the Armenian nation, giving Armenians around the globe the belief in a big homeland and respect for shared national history (Ziemer 2009, 2011). Evidence for this aspect of the identity triangle community–society–nation can be found in the thousands of Armenian volunteers from Armenia as well as from the diaspora who came to fight alongside Karabakh Armenians during the war. Representatives of the foreign Armenian diaspora came from the USA, European countries and from the Middle East, from countries like Lebanon and Iran (Shahnazarian 2010, p. 162). Thus, Karabakh became the centre for diverse groups of Armenian patriots, fighting together for the republic's independence. In other words, research participants' identity boundaries are drawn and cherished from the local (Martuni) to the regional (Nagorno-Karabakh) to the Armenian nation.

The second narrative is linked to one's 'honour'. It can also be seen as an element of imposed observation of communal rules and regulations of correct and normal behaviour. In some ways, it can be seen as a cultural, perhaps even Caucasian trait:

> Male dignity here [in Nagorno-Karabakh] is the most important thing [in a man's life] ... our men constantly think about it.[30]
>
> You see, it's a question of honour (*thasibi harts*). You do things so that they [the community] wouldn't say you're a coward. It's my dignity and honour to fight for my homeland.[31]

The narrative of honour also correlates to semantic categories of folk narratives about honour like 'in the name of', 'in the face of', about 'the corrupted, black face'. These concepts are widespread in the Caucasus and even beyond the Caucasus. Just as *Nuer* in East Africa have 100 different names for their cows (Evans-Pritchard 1940), the concept of honour in Nagorno-Karabakh and for the entire Caucasian region has a whole range of names. The most important aspect of the diversity of names relating to honour is its local context, as Gagik proclaimed proudly: 'I will give my life to the motherland, I will give my soul to the people, but I won't give honour to anybody!'[32]

This narrative of 'one's honour' is especially crucial for those research participants, who were too young and too inexperienced at the beginning of the war, but after intense training and endurance got to the stage where they became experienced enough to hold a gun. It was a great honour when a gun was given to them and they could fight in the war. At this point, there was pressure from older people to fight, now they were perceived to be 'adult enough'. Earlier we stated that they did not feel pressured to participate in the war, but now they did not have a choice, otherwise the community would have seen them as cowards. At this stage, it was as if society prescribed the boys' feelings, which they should experience, but no one asked them whether they actually experienced them. In this way, their actions were constructed according to societal 'norms'. Arsen told us an excellent example of this communal discourse. Arsen and his friend Serob were among the first to participate in the preparatory training camps in the forest and to be given a gun:

---

[30]Manuk, aged 15 in 1991, 17 July 2009, Martuni.
[31]Gagik, 10 August 2009, Martuni.
[32]Gagik, 10 August 2009, Martuni.

> Serob [aged 18 in 1991] and me [aged 18] were the first to get guns, the others envied us. We entered a special unit (*spetsnaz*). Two were already injured—Gagik and another lad—and we went instead of them. The lads were injured and they gave me one of the 30 machine guns. I also kind of got the gun through connections, as in, my father got injured by Azerbaijanis and my friends got injured and killed ... so really I should feel deep hatred and take revenge .... .[33]

Arsen continued our interview by talking about his friend and comrade's death. When they brought the dead body of Suren, who was only 17 years old, Suren's father took the machine gun from his dead body and put it around the neck of his middle son, Manuk. The father did not say anything but expected that his remaining son would avenge the death of his younger brother. In contrast to Suren's father, all other soldiers witnessing this incident talked about honour and the need for revenge. In the end, even Arsen at that point felt revenge and hatred as a result of his close friend's death. In short, in these situations, although there was no need to talk about honour, everyone talked about honour and honour was defined by male actions.

Similarly, after his older brother was injured, young Sevak, who was only 14 years old, when he started to use a gun, gradually began active service in the Nagorno-Karabakh army: 'When my brother was injured for the second time, I officially entered service in the army in Martuni'.[34]

Although research participants interpreted the act of getting a gun handed over by an older person as an honour and a special duty, this act can also be seen as a 'folk technique' for 'quick therapy', to stop these young soldiers from losing heart. Despite being terribly upset about the death of a close friend, comrade, cousin or brother, acquiring an active position in fighting served like a mechanism to overcome sadness accompanied by possible doubts about the worthiness of such big sacrifices.

The third identity narrative refers to 'masculinity'. The way these young men constructed their masculine identity is closely connected to the first two identity narratives, that of patriotism and honour, and is communicated as follows: 'I am a real man and therefore I have the honour to fight for my country. I cherish this honour and I am not afraid'.[35]

> If a man isn't a patriot of his motherland, he doesn't have the right to call himself a man. If he can't defend his family, his house and his country, he isn't a man. A patriot is someone, who can defend his home, his land and his family.[36]

Another important narrative which is also closely linked to the narratives of honour and being a real man is the narrative of being a 'staunch friend'. Male friendship during war times seems like a part of a whole complex of masculine traits. Research participants spoke about friendship, mutual help and support in many different contexts. In every culture, there are differences surrounding the means of friendship. Specifically, in the Karabakh community friendship is organised

---

[33] Arsen, 14 June 2009, Martuni.
[34] Sevak, 21 June 2009, Martuni..
[35] Gurgen, aged 17 in 1991, 3 August 2009, Martuni.
[36] Sevak, 21 June 2009, Martuni.

according to gender. In Karabakh culture, friendship is a quasi-intimate formation in contrast to other societies where friendships between people can be found in a loose union of people spending their spare time together. There are different discourses in respect to friendship, but some are more important than others. First, there is the discourse of trust and reliability (one can count on a friend); then there is the discourse of unconditional loyalty. A ritual for these aspects of friendship can be found in having a joint meal together, sharing the last remaining bits of food together in the forest or at the guard post. To share the very last thing—these are multiplied acts of support and solidarity; unselfish caring for each other which fulfils the imagination of an ideal way of life that once existed for these young soldiers before the war.

The final identity narrative and perhaps the most difficult to clearly define deals with the question of how to cope with 'being a killer'. All research participants thought of many reasons to justify and ease the killing they did. The strongest justifications for their actions was framed in terms of survival as well as self-preservation: 'If I wouldn't have killed him first, then he'd have killed me... it was all over in seconds'.[37]

The narrative of 'being a killer' is rich in verbs like: 'we—defended, protected, guarded the post, repelled the attack, survived'. This narrative is also full of nominations such as 'our defensive position, an army of self-defence, military liberators'. In this sense, killing during war is justified as a moral act since war creates a special moral universe with its own rules, including the understanding of justice during war (Orend 2000).

The second 'powerful' justification for being a killer has an ideological basis referring to Karabakh's century-long struggle with Azerbaijan. Gagik told us during our interview how he felt about facing the enemy: '... the enemy isn't a person and it's necessary to try not to pity the person, first of all he's an enemy, who suppressed our culture for centuries'.[38]

In many instances, this justification was stridently constructed in Karabakh society as events unfolded. In the beginning of this essay, we explained that extensive propaganda was conducted on both sides. Ideological propaganda, however, did not stop during the war: 'During war time, groups of 15–20 soldiers had to watch documentaries about the killings of Armenians by the Ottoman Turks. After watching these documentaries, we couldn't feel any pity for the enemy....'.[39]

Another justification for being a killer can be found in what could be called acts of vengeance for 'my father, my brother, my friend, and for the whole Armenian nation'. Although the Karabakh war was not a religious war, as justification religion or religious elements were sometimes pronounced: 'They turned Amaras [a holy church near the settlement of Machkalashen] into a sheep pen and kept sheep in it, can you imagine, in our church!'[40]

At the same time, there was an alternative discourse of fighting as an objective necessity. In such cases, young soldiers talked about their war participation from a

---

[37]Aram, 28 July 2009, Martuni.
[38]Gagik, 10 August 2009, Martuni.
[39]Gagik, 10 August 2009, Martuni.
[40]Gagik, 10 August 2009, Martuni.

distance, as if they were not really there, as if it was just a game in which they had to 'virtually' participate.

> Every time I took with me the gospel and put it inside my pocket of my coat and every time I prayed before the fighting started .... I vowed to hate Azerbaijanis for all this war ... I kind of think it's stupid to say and I shouldn't really say it but before fighting I swore to God that I'd fight to the last drop of hate! Simply, because this was like a game for me ... .[41]

The argument of having a fair fight not only helped to justify killings but also helped to find inner peace and establish an inner balance and harmony, as Aram (aged 17 in 1991) told us: 'I, for example, fought and killed, but during the whole war I didn't kill anyone who was defenceless, I never felt hatred and even today I don't feel hatred'.[42]

In this interview excerpt, Aram subconsciously refers to the de-personalisation of the enemy—the enemy has no name, but is everywhere. He demonstrates the ability to alienate oneself psychologically from the situation, and to protect one's emotions.

Before concluding, we want to remind the reader that despite dealing with the consequences of being a killer, these young men also had to deal with being the focus of enemy aggression and witnessing the deaths of their fathers, brothers, cousins, comrades or friends, as highlighted throughout this essay. In principle, the whole town of Martuni became one big target during air raids and shootings. In addition, many of these young men became targets for snipers. Aram (17 years in 1991), for example, told us how a two dollar coin saved him from being shot by a sniper. Thanks to the two dollar coin, the sniper's bullet only scratched his skin. Arsen (18 years in 1991) also told us that once a sniper fired several times at him at close range. However, it was obvious for Arsen that the sniper just wanted to play with him, not to shoot him otherwise he would have been killed with the sniper's first shot.

Despite being a target, these young men also witnessed the killings of their relatives or close friends. Manuk (aged 15 in 1991), for example, never told us himself that he saw the killing of his younger brother. Instead, his friend told us the story. Nonetheless, in view of Manuk's war experience it is noteworthy here that Manuk is one of the few young soldiers who dared to tell us his ambivalent feelings he had about the war:

> ... it was a strange day. We climbed up the mountain and suddenly saw ... many Azerbaijani soldiers. We only thought for one brief moment that they could be ours, Armenians. But Armenians usually patrol only in small groups. We took our positions and started to fire at them. Well, it was here when I felt pity ... I shot a couple of times and then stopped, I didn't want to shoot anymore ... I was terribly tired ... What a difficult day ... It's all nonsense, complete nonsense ... .[43]

[41]Hayk, aged 14 in 1991, 22 August 2009, Martuni.
[42]Aram, 28 July 2009, Martuni.
[43]Manuk, 17 July 2009, Martuni.

*Conclusion: researching youth in war and in post-war Karabakh*

Retrospectively, we find it valuable to think about the methodological and empirical contributions this investigation offers and possible future research directions. Throughout this essay we have demonstrated how the use of biographical interviews can facilitate an understanding of the changing and interrelated identities and actions of these young soldiers, explicitly because of their depth and detail. Every research participant we have interviewed for this research project had stories of violence, bereavement and loss to tell. They had fought in the war and had absorbed and responded to it in their own individual way. The identity transformations resulting from this war experience of these young soldiers are complex, contrasting structural and communal forces with the limited capacity to exercise agency in a war situation. It is beyond doubt that the Karabakh war had removed the possibility of choice for many of these young soldiers.

Even in the turmoil of war, these young men were not separated from the social relations and structure of their society. Research participants' experiences and conditions during wartime were strongly influenced by these factors. In this respect, the Karabakh experience of war can be usefully compared with the experience of war in Israel and Palestine, where violence and warfare not only resulted in suffering and alienation, but also in human and humane possibilities. This may indeed yield useful research in the future. On the whole, despite the lack of choice, these young soldiers have proved to be not merely young victims of war, but competent individuals capable of developing their own analysis of the situation and their own responses.

Unquestionably, wartime experience has a strong influence on post-war integration processes. In 'post-war' Karabakh society, old patriarchal gender norms have experienced a revival. In this context, it would be useful to investigate through the use of biographical interviews these young men's transitions from war to 'no war, no peace', in order to better understand post-war societal developments. In some ways, the revival of a patriarchal gender regime could be simply considered a strategy of resistance fostered by adults because they are directly connected to the memory of the war and the struggle for independence. In this case, it can take the place of a national idea, which has happened in other Eurasian regions fighting for independence (Sabirova 2008). However, if we consider Beck's (1992) *Risk Society*, then it could be merely a strategy these young men have used to cope with the many risks of post-war transformations by holding on to traditional gender roles. In any case, it is inevitable to explore everyday experiences of the 'post-war' generation of young men in Karabakh, especially as both states have not agreed on a peace settlement yet and fatalities continue to be part of everyday life despite the ceasefire.

*University of Winchester*
*Kuban Socio-Economic Institute*

*References*

Amone-P'Olak, K., Garnefski, N. & Kraaij, V. (2007) 'Adolescents Caught between Fires: Cognitive Emotion Regulation in Response to War Experiences in Northern Uganda', *Journal of Adolescence*, 30, 4, pp. 655–69.
Atkinson, R. (1998) *The Life Story Interview* (London, Sage).

Beck, U. (1992) *Risk Society: Towards a New Modernity* (London, Sage Publications).
Bloom, W. (1990) *Personal Identity, National Identity and International Relations* (Cambridge, Cambridge University Press).
Bonanno, G. L. (2004) 'Loss, Trauma, and Human Resilience: Have We Underestimated the Human Capacity to Thrive After Extremely Aversive Events?', *American Psychologist*, 59, 1, pp. 20–8.
Boyden, J. & de Berry, J. (2004) *Children and Youth on the Front Line* (New York & Oxford, Berghahn Books).
Brubaker, R. & Cooper, F. (2000) 'Beyond "Identity"', *Theory and Society*, 29, 1, pp. 1–47.
Bull, H. (1977) *The Anarchical Society: A Study of Order in World Politics* (London, Macmillan).
Butler, J. (1993) *Bodies that Matter: On the Discursive Limits of 'Sex'* (London, Routledge).
Butler, J. (1999) *Gender Trouble: Feminism and the Subversion of Identity* (London, Routledge).
Campbell, D. (1998) 'MetaBosnia: Narratives of Bosnian War', *Review of International Studies*, 24, 2, pp. 261–81.
Campbell, D. (2003) 'Cultural Governance and Pictorial Resistance: Reflections on the Imaging of War', *Review of International Studies*, 29.
Castells, M. (1997) *The Power of Identity*, Vol. II (Oxford, Blackwell Publishers).
Chorbaijian, L. (2001) *The Making of Nagorno-Karabagh: From Secession to Republic* (Basingstoke, Palgrave).
Chorbaijian, L., Donabedian, J. & Mutafian, C. (1994) *The Caucasian Knot, The History and Geo-Politics of Nagorno Karabagh* (London, Zed Books).
de Waal, T. (2003) *Black Garden: Armenia and Azerbaijan through Peace and War* (New York, New York University Press).
Denov, M. & Maclure, R. (2007) 'Turnings and Epiphanies: Militarization, Life Histories, and the Making and Unmaking of Two Child Soldiers in Sierra Leone', *Journal of Youth Studies*, 10, 2, May, pp. 243–61.
Enloe, C. (2000) *Maneuvers: The International Politics of Militarizing Women's Lives* (Berkeley, CA, University of California Press).
Evans-Pritchard, E. E. (1940) *The Nuer: A Description of the Modes of Livelihood and Political Institutions of a Nilotic People* (Oxford, Clarendon Press).
Feldman, A. (2002) 'X-Children and the Militarisation of Everyday Life: Comparative Comments on the Politics of Youth, Victimage and Violence in Transitional Societies', *International Journal of Social Welfare*, 11.
Goffman, E. (1959) *The Presentation of Self in Everyday Life* (Harmondsworth, Penguin Books).
Hall, S. (1996) 'Introduction: Who Needs Identity?', in Hall, S. & Du Gay, P. (eds) (1996) *Questions of Cultural Identity* (London, Sage Publications).
Hamilton, C. & Man, N. (1998) 'The Impact of Armed Conflict on Children in Kosovo', *Report of the Children and Armed Conflict Unit*, University of Essex, available at: www2.essex.ac.uk/papersandreports/kosreport.htm, accessed 17 March 2010.
Honwana, A. (2006) *Child Soldiers in Africa* (Philadelphia, PA, University of Pennsylvania Press).
Kaldor, M. (2001) *New & Old Wars: Organized Violence in a Global Era* (Stanford, Stanford University Press).
Kurkchiyan, M. (2005) 'The Karabagh Conflict: From Soviet Past to post-Soviet Uncertainty', in Kurkchiyan, M. & Herzig, E. (eds) (2005) *The Armenians: Past and Present in the Making of National Identity* (Abingdon & New York, RoutledgeCurzon).
Laitin, D. D. & Suny, R. G. (1999) 'Armenia and Azerbaijan: Thinking a Way Out of Karabakh', *Middle East Policy*, VII, October.
Malinowski, B. (1941) 'An Anthropological Analysis of War', *American Journal of Sociology*, 46, 4.
McBeth, S. (1993) 'Myths of Objectivity and the Collaborative Process in Life History Research', in Brettell, C. (ed.) (1993) *When They Read What We Write: The Politics of Ethnography* (London, Bergin and Garvey).
Neuman, I. B. (1992) 'Identity and Security', *Journal of Peace Research*, 29, 2.
Orend, B. (2000) *Michael Walzer on War and Justice* (Montreal, McGill-Queen's University Press).
Sabirova, G. (2008) 'Both War and Peace in the "Country of the Soul": The Young People of Abkhazia on War, Tradition and Independence', *Anthropology of East Europe Review*, 26, 1, pp. 51–68.
Shakhnazarian, N. (2008) 'Mal'chiki-mazhory karabakhskoi voiny: zhiznennye istorii voennoi "molodezhi"', *The Journal of Power Institutions in Post-Soviet Studies*, 8, available at: www.pipss.org/sommaire559.html, accessed on 12 February 2009.
Shahnazarian, N. (2010) 'National Ideologies, Survival Strategies and Gender Identity in the Political and Symbolic Contexts of Karabakh War', in Tsitsishvili, N. (ed.) (2010) *Cultural Archetypes and Political Change in the Caucasus* (Saarbrucken, Lambert Academic Publishing).

Somers, M. & Gibson, G. D. (1994) 'Reclaiming the Epistemological "Other": Narrative and the Social Constitution of Identity', in Calhoun, C. (ed.) (1994) *Social Theory and the Politics of Identity* (Oxford, Blackwell Publishers).

Suganami, H. (2002) 'Explaining War: Some Critical Observations', *International Relations*, 16, 3.

Suganami, H. (2008) 'Narrative Explanation and International Relations: Back to Basics', *Millennium: Journal of International Studies*, 37, 2.

Swaine, A. & Feeny, T. (2004) 'A Neglected Perspective: Adolescents Girls' Experiences of the Kosovo Conflict of 1999', in Boyden, J. & De Berry, J. (eds) (2004) *Children and Youth on the Front Line* (New York & Oxford, Berghahn Books).

Tajfel, H. (1982) 'Social Psychology of Intergroup Relations', *Annual Review of Psychology*, 33.

Tajfel, H. & Turner, J. C. (1986) 'The Social Identity Theory of Inter-Group Behavior', in Worchel, S. & Austin, L. W. (eds) (1986) *Psychology of Intergroup Relations* (Chicago, Nelson-Hall).

Verdery, K. (1993) 'Ethnic Relations, Economies of Shortage, and the Transition in Eastern Europe', in Hann, C. (ed.) (1993) *Socialism: Ideals, Ideologies, and Local Practice* (London, Routledge), pp. 172–86.

Waltz, K. (1959) *Man, the State and War: A Theoretical Analysis* (New York, Columbia University Press).

West, H. G. (2004) 'Girls with Guns: Narrating the Experience of War in FRELIMO's "Female Detachment"', in Boyden, J. & De Berry, J. (eds) (2004) *Children and Youth on the Front Line* (New York & Oxford, Berghahn Books).

Williams, M. C. & Neuman, I. B. (2000) 'From Alliance to Security Community: NATO, Russia, and the Power of Identity', *Millennium: Journal of International Studies*, 29, 2, pp. 357–87.

Wills, D. & Moore, C. (2008) 'Securitising the Caucasus: From Political Violence to Place Branding in Chechnya', *Place Branding and Public Diplomacy*, 4.

Ziemer, U. (2011) *Ethnic Belonging, Gender and Cultural Practices: Youth Identities in Contemporary Russia* (Stuttgart, Ibidem Verlag).

Ziemer, U. (2009) 'Narratives of Translocation, Dislocation and Location: Armenian Youth Cultural Identities in Southern Russia', *Europe-Asia Studies*, 61, 3, pp. 409–33.

# Co-optation or Empowerment? The Fate of Pro-Democracy NGOs after the Rose Revolution

BRIAN GRODSKY

*Abstract*

Western governments spend millions of dollars annually supporting the non-governmental sphere, and especially pro-democracy organisations, in non-democracies. The essay explores how inclusion of pro-democracy organisations into the state after democratic breakthrough can enhance or inhibit democratic consolidation, arguing inclusion can actually weaken the NGO community by creating rifts between one-time partners with suddenly disparate agendas. This argument is applied to the case of Georgia following the 2003 'Rose Revolution'. Evidence is based on elite interviews conducted in summer 2007.

IN NOVEMBER 2003, AFTER NEARLY 12 CONSECUTIVE years of rule, Eduard Shevardnadze was forced out of power in what is known as the 'Rose Revolution'. This peaceful uprising was the culmination of two apparently distinct processes: the gradual estrangement from Shevardnadze of political elites widely referred to as the 'young reformers' and the strengthening of pro-democracy non-governmental organisations (Devdariani 2004; Wertsch 2005). In the run-up to the 2003 parliamentary elections, Mikheil Saakashvili's New National Movement (*Ertiani Natsionaluri Modzraoba*), together with parties of other prominent oppositionists including Zurab Zhvania and Nino Burjanadze, were braced to perform strongly against the corruption-ridden incumbent. When the elections were deemed to have been rigged by local and international observers, oppositionists and NGOs mobilised thousands in protest. By 24 November, Shevardnadze publicly resigned and Georgia became what one scholar called 'one of the most important laboratories for democracy in the world' (Wertsch 2005, p. 519).

The United States may bear at least some responsibility for creating this laboratory. In the decade preceding the 2003 elections (1992–2002) the US budgeted $1.1 billion in assistance programmes to Georgia (Devdariani 2003, p. 8), and in 2002–2003 US assistance for democracy programmes was a combined $43.9 million (DOS 2004a; Devdariani 2003, p. 8). While generally a heavy aid recipient, Georgia is no outlier: the US and other Western countries annually spend millions of dollars on the development of the non-governmental sphere, seen as the 'building blocks of civil society', around the world (Wedel 1998, p. 85). This funding is frequently viewed as critical to the construction of a strong civil society that can challenge illiberal regimes and strengthen subsequent democratic ones (Herman 2006, p. 31).

But the very process of political change these organisations are supposed to engender may prove in the long term to be debilitating to those organisations that make it possible. This is particularly true, I argue, for pro-democracy groups which may, by nature, be the most politicised organisations, and thus most prone to enter the realm of electoral politics. What happens to these critical NGOs when their leaders abandon them to occupy newly freed space in the governing structures of the democratising state?

In this essay, I argue that relations between the non-governmental sphere and the government in the transition era are a function of institutionally determined objectives and inter-personal and professional relationships developed between members of the opposition to the previous regime. I focus my analysis on three distinctive types of pro-democracy organisations historically nurtured by the US: watchdogs (charged primarily with publicly pressing the government for political liberalisation and human rights), service providers (which focus more on technical assistance in the sphere of rule-of-law) and hybrids (including elements of both watchdogs and service providers). I find evidence that inclusion of various Georgian NGO members into the post-Shevardnadze state has at times weakened the country's NGO community by creating rifts between one-time partners who now find they have suddenly disparate agendas.

This essay is divided into three sections. In the first, I explore the phenomenon of civil society's politicisation and consider how politicised NGOs may be affected during the early phase of democratisation, especially how incorporation of NGO leaders into the new democratising state affects the relationship between the state and NGO actors. Next, I frame Georgian civil society in this broader theoretical framework, examining the rise of the political and civil opposition in Georgia from the 1990s to the Rose Revolution in 2003. Finally, I examine the case of Georgia after the 2003 Rose Revolution in an analysis based primarily on elite interviews conducted in summer 2007 with NGO activists and their one-time associates then in government. The results suggest that incorporation of NGO activists into the state can hurt the very NGOs one might expect to see most advantaged.

*Politics and civil society in non-democracies*

Civil society can be defined broadly as 'the realm of organised life that is open, voluntary, self-generating, at least partially self-supporting, autonomous from the state, and bound by a legal order or set of shared rules' (Diamond 1999, p. 221). According to this understanding, civil society actors are intermediaries between the private sphere and the state (Lewis 1992, p. 36; Diamond 1999, p. 221). By definition, civil society includes an array of distinct interests from the economic and cultural to the developmental and issue-oriented (including women, consumers and the disabled) (Diamond 1999, p. 222; Lewis 1992, p. 35). Through activities that can range from simply conveying information to mobilising the population and actually threatening political stability (for example through protests), civil society groups seek to 'change the terms of political discourse and so affect the content of public policy' (Dryzek 1996, p. 481; Berman 1997). Civil society, according to its proponents, is the vanguard and then guardian of democracy, ensuring the state remains accountable to the various concerns and demands of its citizens (Diamond 1992, p. 8).

Western policymakers have historically treated NGOs as fundamental elements of civil society (Wedel 1998, p. 85). In fact, civil society organisations range from these small professional groups to massive grassroots organisations (Schmitz 2001, p. 159; May 2005, p. 1; Diani 2006, p. 140; Friedman & Hochstetler 2002, p. 32). During the struggle for democracy, these various groups are united by the fact that they see themselves as 'trustee organisations' acting 'on behalf of largely silent constituencies' (Ottaway & Chung 1999, p. 107; Zakaria 1997). Fighting for democracy, organisational leaders claim to serve the greater population, and engage in mass mobilisation to realise their goals (Melucci, Keane & Mier 1989, pp. 78–9). These are 'principled' actors capable of shaping and mobilising opinion, and sometimes even strengthening new norms of legitimacy, at home and abroad (Sikkink 1993; Moravcsik 2000, p. 223).

While NGOs can serve several functions, from exerting important pressure on government and acting as a source of technical expertise and mobilising citizens, there is a vast literature that has raised questions concerning NGOs' representativeness and even internal democratic credentials (Carothers 2004, p. 100). Critics claim that NGOs are in fact elite-led organisations with little right to speak in the name of the public interest which is, as Carothers notes, 'a highly contested domain' (Carothers 2004, p. 101). Moreover, their dependence on foreign support often leaves them open to resource dependency and charges that their activities, designed to make them competitive on the foreign donor market, create a dysfunctional civil society sphere characterised by conflict rather than cooperation (Patterson 1998, p. 433; Henderson 2002, pp. 142–3; Kopecky & Mudde 2003, p. 5; Ikelegbe 2001, p. 11). Most importantly, their goals and output can make these organisations domestically isolated and irrelevant, depriving them *de facto* of the representativeness they claim lies at their core (Grodsky 2007; Mutua 2009, p. 29; Diamond 1999, p. 253).

Yet in many non-democracies, small NGOs have played a pivotal role in mobilising popular opposition to the incumbent regime—a testament to the fact that these organisations can reflect at least general elements of the popular will. In Central Europe, organisations such as the Czech Charter 77 (*Charta 77*), the Polish Workers' Defence Committee (*Komitet Obrony Robotników*), and the various Helsinki Committees throughout the Soviet Union played important roles in the opposition movements and popular anti-communist mobilisation (Havel 2005, p. 6; Bernhard 1993, pp. 313–15). Similarly, small non-governmental organisations were instrumental in organising or strengthening popular opposition in other illiberal countries such as the Philippines and Chile (Constantino-David 1998, p. 40; Puryear 1994, pp. 49–50). The most recent 'colour revolutions' highlight the role that NGOs continue to play in democratisation efforts around the globe. NGOs may be highly personalistic and internally divided, but they can play a lead role in social movements, which are themselves, as two leading social movement scholars have commented, 'highly precarious constructs' (Foweraker & Landman 1997, p. 39).[1]

---

[1] See also Schmitz (2001, p. 159); May (2005, p. 1); Diani (2006, p. 140); Friedman and Hochstetler (2002, p. 32).

According to many civil society proponents, NGOs serve simply as interest groups that, in the process of realising the interests of those political and economic constituents they claim to represent, demand better governance (Hearn & Robinson 2000, p. 244; Adamson 2002, p. 178). But better governance in non-democracies is usually synonymous with new forms of governance. This is particularly pertinent to pro-democracy organisations, which assign themselves the goal of improving the political system and are regarded as the 'vanguard of civil society' (Diamond 1999, p. 222) in many repressive states (Antoun 2000, p. 444). Ostensibly non-partisan, these organisations focus on activities such as promoting human rights and democratic norms, educating and mobilising the population and monitoring state-initiated mechanisms that are purported to enhance accountability (Diamond 1999, p. 222; Feldman 1997). Civil society groups and political opposition parties are formally separated by the fact that the former seek fundamental change rather than political power for themselves (Diamond 1999, p. 223; di Palma 1991, p. 68; Gershman 2004, p. 29), and may therefore be less susceptible to cooption by incumbent elites (Gilbreth & Otero 2001, p. 7).

In reality, though, the line between civil society actors and excluded political oppositionists in non-democracies is frequently very thin and porous (Fatton 1999, p. 214). Given their liberalising objectives, these organisations tend to be embedded in the political process, linked by mission or even personnel to opposition political parties (Waltz 1995, p. 155; An-Na'im 2001; Otero & O'Bryan 2002; Fatton 1999, p. 214; Bernhard 1993, p. 310; Kopecky & Mudde 2003, p. 5). At the most basic level, ostensibly neutral NGOs actively work to oppose (rather than support) a particular political group—usually the non-democratic incumbents (Bienen & Herbst 1996, p. 29; Ottaway 2001; Hachhethu 2007, p. 8; Mutua 2009, p. 21; Monga 1995, p. 367). Just as NGOs hope their political partners will facilitate their own role in future policy debates, opposition parties see a range of advantages in allying with NGOs, which can provide them with organisational support (Clarke 1998a, p. 43) and demand and monitor electoral processes (Ottaway 2001; Broers 2005; Devdariani 2004). Mass-based and elitist civil society organisations can also play key roles in popular mobilisation before and during elections (Duffy 1994, p. 100; Lanegran 1995, pp. 105–11; Fairbanks 2004; McFaul 2005; Carothers 2006; Herd 2005; King 2004). Their activities can be instrumental in creating an environment conducive to democratic breakthrough, but they also blur the civil society–political split so important to proponents of civil society.

If the goal of civil society were limited to ushering in democracy, this haziness would be inconsequential. But if the goal is to continue to safeguard the nascent democracy, effectively monitoring and checking political elites, then this phenomenon is far more important. Upon democratic breakthrough, opposition political elites naturally leave the former opposition movement for state positions. But other activists are also likely to move to the state sphere where they can pursue their activism in a more regular (and lucrative) fashion (Anderson & Dynes 1973). Having proven their skills through the struggle in such spheres as popular mobilisation, organisation and formulation of technical alternatives (Robertson 2004, p. 257), activists from civil society represent a trusted and available 'talent pool' (Gershman 2004, p. 31) for newly empowered political elites tasked with staffing and legitimising the new democratic state (Clarke

1998b, p. 188; Silliman & Noble 1998a, p. 288). Pro-democracy organisations are particularly hard hit by this phenomenon (Kopecky & Mudde 2003, p. 9). As one scholar pointed out in the case of post-1989 Eastern Europe: 'This migration left behind little or nothing in terms of oppositional public spheres. The gain was a liberal democratic state; the loss was a discursive democratic vitality' (Dryzek 1996, p. 485).

*Democracy now, what next?*

Transfers of NGO heads to political and state positions in new democracies carry risks, but also promise. In longer standing democracies, there is an acceptance that leaders from the non-governmental sector may seek inclusion into government temporarily as a means to better pursue their personal and organisational interests—and that they may exit the state when their positions no longer satisfy those goals (Downes 2000; Eaton 2003, p. 487). Similarly, movement of NGO actors into a newly democratising state (whether in parliament, government or administration) may provide new opportunities for social actors formerly excluded from influence to spread the ideas and policies espoused by their (former) organisations (Bell & Keenan 2004).

There is, thus, a bright side: if civil society strength is characterised by 'the ability of organisations within it to influence the exercise of power' (Bernhard 1993, p. 308) then the possibility of inclusion, particularly of organisations that have fought so long for the public welfare, may be positive. NGO leaders can be brought directly into a new government, even at the cabinet level, to elevate a country's international reputation (Eaton 2003, pp. 475, 488). Alternatively, NGOs with strong links to national parties may be strategically placed to 'establish networks of influence' that translate into desired political and economic reforms (Shin 2003, p. 702). Increased access, and perhaps similar ideological agendas, may enhance partnerships between state and NGO members (Bell & Keenan 2004; Hachhethu 2007, p. 8). The study of neo-corporatism, where select organisations directly influence government policies, highlights the potential advantages organisations receive from their new relationship (Schmitter 1974, p. 100; Lehmbruch 1979, p. 150; Wiarda 1997, p. 121).

Inclusion is not without its risks, though, the most evident of which is cooption. Cooption can be conscious or *de facto*, when new political elites bring NGO leaders into their government but give them little actual power (Dryzek 1996). Cooption can be prompted by, and include, a process of 'spoils politics', where outspoken NGO heads take top positions and a share of state resources in exchange for silence (Bartlett 2000, p. 446; Patterson 1998, p. 433). In other cases, NGO leaders remain, at least in principle, determined to make a difference, but are stymied by overruling political elites. Former NGO leaders acting as political elites may be allowed to participate in debate, but not influence outcomes. Concessions from the government might be limited to areas where the ruling regime has no particular conflict (Eaton 2003, p. 482), suggesting inclusion was not particularly important to this outcome.

Unfortunately, there has been very little analytical work on how immersion into the state of one-time civil society actors engaged in the democratic struggle affects relations between them and their former colleagues who remain in the non-governmental sphere. Given the intermingling of political and civil society during the opposition period, personal aspects of this relationship are core to this study. I argue that tensions between the non-governmental sphere and the government in the transition era result from a combination of institutionally-determined objectives and inter-personal and professional relationships developed between members of the opposition to the previous regime. Inclusion of NGO² members into the new political sphere may impede, rather than facilitate, relations between the NGO sphere and government as expectations of actors in the two categories clash. While certain NGOs may profit from their new connections to the state, organisations that continue to take the role of watchdog (at times critical of the government) may find their work more difficult with friends in power.

Every actor is subject to institutional constraints, the borders that define which objectives and actions are feasible and desirable. These are in large part defined by constituent demands. For NGO actors in much of the developing world, dependence on external donors sets these parameters; NGO leaders can be expected to pursue policies that will assure them future funding (Cooley & Ron 2002, p. 17; Henderson 2002; Sali-Teric 2001; Grugel 2000, p. 90; Hajjar 2001, pp. 31–4; Kopecky & Mudde 2003, p. 5). The transition from NGO to state involves a shift to a new constituency, and new political pressures. As one-time NGO leaders adapt to their new environment, they may feel certain actions or objectives they once espoused as activists are no longer feasible, or perhaps even desirable. Regardless of their ideals, their strategies, tactics and declarations will be altered as they sign onto the new regime that employs them. Outside observers may view these actors as co-opted, no longer true to what they long stood for.

Adaptation on the part of one-time NGO actors to new institutional constraints may set the grounds for conflict between civil society and the state, but this conflict is not inevitable. After all, it takes two sides to forge a relationship. Just as those abandoning non-governmental organisations acquire new goals and behaviours, those remaining or entering into the NGO sphere also face new choices (Bratton 1994, p. 64). Political changes may lead to new donor pressures or opportunities for state partnership that did not previously exist. Some pro-democracy organisations may maintain their watchdog functions, while others may concentrate more on provision of specialised services (for example training, advising, distribution of goods) to the new state. Activities and approaches to the new government, determined in large part by these new constraints, will play an important role in defining NGO–state relations.

Fundamental to this relationship is the personal dimension. Social activists, including actors in pro-democracy organisations, often have strong bonds that unite them (Jenkins 1983; McAdam & Paulsen 1993). Feelings of loyalty emerge from having spent years fighting for a common collective good (Chong 1991, p. 35; Polletta & Jasper 2001, pp. 289–90; Jenkins 1983, p. 530). The former illiberal regime's use of targeted repression may reinforce a sense of unity and 'intense subcultural solidarity' among these actors (Levite & Tarrow 1983, p. 298).² These strong ties create equally strong expectations on the part of both parties. NGO actors are likely to expect the new government to fulfil the idealistic programme on which they came to power. Government officials, by contrast, expect high levels of support from their former colleagues. These feelings should be particularly strong with respect to close friends or

²See also Tarrow (1994).

individuals who emerge from the same organisation. But conflicting institutional constraints on each party, described above, can render both sets of expectations unrealistic.

The result will be a break along lines defined by NGO function and personnel overlap. Relations should be best where NGOs focus on service provision, particularly (but not exclusively) when these organisations have members in the new government. Under these conditions, former colleagues find relations mutually advantageous; as in neo-corporatist relationships, state advantages (in the form of service contracts or endorsements) are given to trusted organisations that, in return, mute their own criticisms. In other words, organisations that adapt along with their now political leaders should be positioned to gain from the new conditions.

Relations should be considerably worse between the government and watchdog NGOs, those organisations that continue to monitor and speak out against the new government just as they did against the previous government. For those organisations without personal connections to the new regime, relations will be cold and the new government will probably continue to ignore or counter them in the same way the old one did (Bell & Keenan 2004, p. 348). By contrast, according to the argument here, relations between the state and critics will be worst when those critics are one-time partners from the opposition movement. It is here that the combination of institutionally defined objectives and personal expectations clash most dramatically, prompting disappointment and outrage between former colleagues and friends now in the state.

In summary, pro-democracy movements are composed of actors that frequently cross the line between civil and political society. The blurring of this line is a natural result of the inherently political objectives they demand, and occurs with respect to both mandate and personnel. When democratic breakthrough occurs, those on the strictly political side of the line move into the state, but they also bring with them former comrades from the civil society side, who may have needed skills or the prerequisite trust to help run the state. Non-governmental leaders who remain outside the state, as well as those who enter state positions, count on their previous colleagues for support. At the same time, both sets of actors face a new environment that can make or break relations. In cases where critical NGOs turn against their friends, the relations should be particularly negative.

*The case of Georgia*

In this section, I apply the above argument to the case of Georgia. I begin with a brief overview of Georgia's post-independence political development, and the evolution of Georgian civil society. Next, I explore the nature of state–civil society relations in Georgia following the 2003 events.

Eduard Shevardnadze rose to power by force, installed as chairman of the Georgian State Council and then head of state following a January 1992 coup against independent Georgia's first democratically elected president. Despite the violent nature of his rise to power, Shevardnadze was a welcome relief to those uncomfortable with the nationalist regime of President Zviad Gamsakhurdia, a former dissident who was labelled by opponents a 'fascist dictator' (Nodia 1995, p. 105) for his role in militarising the state against secessionist threats and cracking down on dissent (Areshidze 2007, p. 22). Shevardnadze, by contrast, was known as the last Soviet Foreign Minister who oversaw the peaceful demise of communism in the Eastern Bloc and helped usher in an unprecedented thaw in relations with the West (Cohen 2004, p. 80; Koslowski & Kratochwil 1994, p. 234; Kuran 1991, p. 34). For the first years of his rule, Shevardnadze further improved this image, bringing Georgia into major international organisations and promoting a Western-supported energy corridor through his territory (Devdariani 2003, p. 12; Cohen 2004, p. 84).

The international legitimacy Shevardnadze bestowed on his country was prized by constituents, who largely identified with Europe, but was largely dependent on Georgia's path of democratisation, which proceeded unevenly (Nodia 1995, p. 113; Broers 2005). For example, while Shevardnadze oversaw what were widely viewed as free and fair elections in 1992 and 1995, and allowed the opposition relative freedom, a strong presidential system and the personalistic nature of power marginalised political parties and ensured that authority remained centralised (Nodia 1995, p. 113; Broers 2005; Devdariani 2004). Similarly, though censorship in the media, which included a number of opposition outlets, was minimal, state-controlled media functioned essentially as a government mouthpiece (Nodia 1995, p. 113). Finally, Shevardnadze provided conditions that allowed Georgia in the mid-1990s to become known as an 'NGO heaven' in the region (Devdariani 2003, p. 13), but only so long as these civil society actors bolstered his democratic reputation in a non-threatening manner.

Western democracy promoters found Shevardnadze's Georgia a welcome home to the political and economic resources they poured into the civic associations they hoped would empower Georgia's citizenry. Civil society organisations initially emerged during the late 1980s when, as in other Soviet republics, they took up popular grievances unaddressed by the state (Broers 2005). At first these organisations focused on less overtly political issues, such as the environment and culture, but gradually they encompassed clearly political demands, including political liberalisation and autonomy. Although it had been weakened in the early 1990s by Gamsakhurdia's militarisation in the face of ethnic conflict in Abkhazia and South Ossetia, and then violence in the streets of Tbilisi, by the mid-1990s this nascent non-governmental sphere had revived under Shevardnadze. With it, Broers notes, 'a new elite of civic activists emerged, providing a new source of intellectual leadership' (Broers 2005, p. 338). As these activists strengthened their organisations, they became influential in shaping public opinion (Devdariani 2004, p. 97).

Shevardnadze's dedication to democratic reform and tolerance of civil society was tempered by political and economic challenges, including meagre economic growth and double-digit unemployment that steadily mounted throughout the 1990s (Cohen 2004). Civil war in Abkhazia and South Ossetia led to a decline in exports to Georgia's largest trading partner, Russia, as well as an influx of internally displaced citizens. The poor economic situation was also rooted in rampant corruption which emerged as a result of 'the progressive entrenchment of vested interests and the informalisation of Georgian politics' (Broers 2005, p. 334; Wheatley 2005, p. 109). Shevardnadze's failure to provide basic services and guarantee social welfare left him deeply unpopular and made democracy a threat (Baran 2002, p. 23; Broers 2005, p. 335). Charges of foul play in the 1999 parliamentary and 2000 presidential elections increased his unpopularity both at home and abroad, where the reputation he had spent years building was damaged (Cohen 2004, p. 84; Devdariani 2003, p. 14). By 2000, Shevardnadze's political position was attributed to electoral tricks and a weak and fragmented opposition (Baran 2002, p. 23; Broers 2005). His method of government, according to one scholar, 'was typical of a communist party boss... he believed that he was the source of power' (Wheatley 2005).

Nevertheless, thanks in part to Shevardnadze's earlier democratic reforms, political opposition was growing. A number of leaders dubbed the 'young reformers' (including Saakashvili and Zhvania) made their early political careers under Shevardnadze's personal tutelage in his Citizens' Union of Georgia (*Sakartvelos Mokalaketa Kavshiri*) (Cohen 2004, p. 82). As these individuals amassed political influence in parliament and the government throughout the 1990s, they worked closely with emerging civil society actors (Devdariani 2004, p. 97). By the end of 2001, the Citizens' Union was threatened by new, break-off opposition parties, including Saakashvili's National Movement (founded in November 2001) and Zhvania's United Democrats (*Gaertianebuli Demokratebi*, founded in June 2002). The new parties branded themselves the truly 'Western', pro-democracy choice.

These breakaway parties signalled the rise of a new period of politicisation in Georgian civil society. Ties between the 'young reformers' and non-governmental sphere became closer in the late 1990s as Shevardnadze more aggressively countered civil society. NGOs developed close relationships with the young reformers who served on parliamentary committees where NGOs proposed legislative changes (Wheatley 2005, p. 147). The government increasingly attacked the independent media and then sought to drown out the voice of independent NGOs by creating and backing pro-governmental organisations (Broers 2005, p. 339). Shevardnadze used state media to portray NGOs as grant-hungry individuals promoting foreign values and weakening the state, and sought legislation to clamp down on organisational activities (Broers 2005). Meanwhile, Shevardnadze's one-time protégés joined in NGO activities, for example leading street protests in defence of the independent television station Rustavi-2 between 30 October and 1 November 2001 (Devdariani 2004, p. 82). Many NGO leaders who were traditionally suspicious of personalistic political parties realised that political neutrality would mean a decline of democracy—and their own demise (Broers 2005, p. 340). In short, they, like many other pro-democracy activists around the world, allied themselves with the excluded (or, in this case, disadvantaged) opposition.

The relationship between Georgian civil society and political opposition was personal and ideological, but it was also influenced by structural factors. Western donors supported both, often simultaneously. In the run-up to the 2003 elections, for example, the United States spent an unprecedented amount on election transparency (Broers 2005, p. 341)—much of which consisted of training and funding both watchdog and service NGOs—which would, *de facto*, benefit the opposition. Western states also used diplomacy to bolster the opposition, such as the personal appeal by former US Secretary of State James Baker—a personal friend of Shevardnadze's—for free and fair elections (ICG 2003, p. 117; Areshidze 2007). Despite these efforts, there were numerous irregularities in the vote—from improper voter lists and contradictory electoral commission instructions to attacks on election monitors—that led to condemnation at home and abroad. Parallel vote tabulations and election monitoring conducted by local NGOs (including the local International Society for Fair Elections and Democracy (ISFED) and the Georgian Young Lawyers' Association (GYLA, *Sakartvelos Akhalgazrda Iuristta Asotsiatsia*)) were instrumental in proving deception. Two days after the elections, Zhvania announced the creation of a United Opposition Front (*Gaertianebuli Opozitsiuri Pronti*), which would include the National Movement, Burjanadze-Democrats (*Burdjanadze-Demokratebi*), and Unity (*Ertoba*), and Saakashvili threatened mass demonstrations if the electoral commission did not recognise opposition victory. In the end, it was these demonstrations, organised by opposition political elites and their non-governmental colleagues that became known as the Rose Revolution.

While there is no strong evidence that Western states actively planned the democratic revolutions that gripped Georgia (and then Ukraine and Kyrgyzstan), Western support at least played an important role in creating necessary pre-conditions for these events. External funding for key elements of civil society, such as independent media, vote monitoring groups and 'get out the vote' organisations, created a sphere of activity that would have faced significant challenges without external monetary and diplomatic support (McFaul 2005). Western-backed youth movements (supported in Tbilisi especially by George Soros's Open Society Georgia Foundation and the US-based National Democratic Institute) in each of these cases helped to broaden civic engagement (Carothers 2006; Herd 2005). Other pro-democracy and human rights NGOs used their ostensibly more objective stature to bolster opposition claims against incumbents and helped coordinate mobilisation efforts (Broers 2005; Devdariani 2004). As McFaul noted, 'foreign aid played no independent role in any of these breakthroughs (and rarely does), but contributed to the drama' (McFaul 2005, p. 16)

Following the 2003 events, Georgian civil society found itself facing a number of serious challenges. First, new political elites trying to fill the ranks of the administration, drew on the NGOs, in the words of one NGO member who became a political leader, as a 'hub for human resources' (Ugulava 2007).[3] This resulted in the closing of some smaller pro-democracy organisations, but many others—and all of the key organisations—were able to replace their outgoing leaders with members who had long been serving in more junior positions in the same organisation.[4]

Just as numerous organisations lost key personnel (Broers 2005, p. 345), Western donors began to redirect financing from the highly dependent NGO sector to the new, trusted government. For the fiscal year 2004, for example, US funding for democracy programmes had been reduced to $14.4 million, just over 60% of the 2002 level (DOS 2004b). In part, this resulted from the perception by US officials that Saakashvili and his associates were themselves among the top democracy promoters, leaving pro-democracy NGOs with no real role.[5] Financial limits led even more organisation

---

[3]G. Ugulava, Mayor of Tbilisi and former founder/director of non-governmental organisation ALPE, 21 July 2007, Tbilisi.

[4]Author's interviews with L. Tarkhnishvili, Head of Georgian Public TV, 24 July 2007, Tbilisi; N. Saakashvili, Executive Director of Horizonti, 16 July 2007, Tbilisi; M. Mullen, Former Georgia country director for National Democratic Institute, 26 June 2007, Telephone Interview; U. Nanuashvili, Executive director of the Human Rights Information and Documentation Center, 16 July 2007, Tbilisi.

[5]Anonymous interview with a United States Government Official, 5 January 2007, Washington, D.C.

members to look for state (and sometimes non-state) employment, and led to a decrease in the size of organisations (GYLA, for instance, cut 10% of its 120 personnel in the months after the democratic transition had begun).[6] As a result of personnel transfer, resource constraints and an apparently transformed political environment, Georgia's pro-democracy civil society organisations were forced to reassess their positions.

NGOs were not the only ones adjusting to the new environment. Georgia's new political elites and many ex-NGO leaders who moved to positions within the state similarly struggled to fit their pre-democracy idealism—which still dominated the NGOs they left behind—with the serious tasks dictated by their new institutional positions. Facing a legacy of corruption, serous internal and external security threats, and a society demanding swift economic improvements, the former pro-democracy leaders now working within the state adopted policies they might once have condemned. 'When you come to the government and when you have to do real work instead of theories, you see how hard [it is]', explained one high-ranking government official who emerged from the NGO sector.[7] 'I prefer, personally, to avoid huge political risks rather than have a theoretically-balanced constitution'. The head of Georgia's Supreme Court, another ex-NGO leader, similarly conceded that democratic lapses in the short-term were designed to bring about a stronger democracy in the long-term, commenting that, 'In this period there will be rights violations. We're not surprised'.[8]

Pro-democracy NGOs expecting the political environment to be far more liberal under Saakashvili were thus quickly disappointed. Within months of taking power, Saakashvili strengthened his own presidential hand at the same time that many NGO actors remained hesitant to criticise their former colleagues (Broers 2005, p. 345). Over time, the scenario became increasingly difficult for pro-democracy actors who, some loudly and some quietly, questioned the country's direction. Saakashvili's apparent departure from the democratic path—epitomised by the state of emergency in the autumn of 2007, but preceded (and followed) for years by questions concerning executive power, judicial independence, media freedom and the treatment of political opposition—has been reflected in international NGO reports. Since 2007, and after a very minor post-2003 improvement, Freedom House scores for political and civil rights in Georgia have fallen back to those witnessed during the 'partly free' Shevardnadze period. How, then, did leaders of pro-democracy organisations address this tendency and, more generally, manage relations with their former partners now in power?

*With us or against us?*

In this section, I examine more closely the evolving relationship between Georgia's post-2003 pro-democracy NGOs and their one-time leaders in government. In summer

---

[6]A. Dolidze, Former Chair of the Georgian Young Lawyers' Association (2005–2006), 10 July 2007, Telephone Interview.
[7]Anonymous interview with a Government of Georgia Official, Tbilisi.
[8]K. Kublashvili, Chairman of the Supreme Court of Georgia, 23 July 2007, Tbilisi.

2007, I conducted approximately 40 interviews with primarily two types of actors: political elites who came to power from the NGO sphere and leaders of active non-governmental human rights or pro-democracy organisations whose memberships had in part moved to the new government. My interviewees were initially chosen through consultations with several foreign and local actors who were involved in Georgia during and preceding the Rose Revolution. I was interested in speaking to representatives of all major human rights and pro-democracy organisations that were active preceding the 2003 events, as well as high-level political leaders who subsequently moved to state positions. I built on my initial list of interviewees using the 'snowball method', asking interviewees what other organisations might be of interest to this study. All of the organisation leaders with whom I spoke were heads of national (rather than regional) organisations, based in Tbilisi.

Interviews, conducted in Russian and English, were semi-structured, based on a broad list of questions. These included topics such as motivations for leaving or remaining in the non-governmental sphere and perceptions about the evolving relationship between the government and various non-governmental organisations. Most of my questions were open-ended and my goal was to gauge personal perceptions or private views. While I did not have previous contacts with these people, I found most to be very open—not surprising, given the public level of contention between the groups.

The organisations included in this study, almost all of which were founded before 2003 by local Georgians wary of the Shevardnadze regime, can be broken down into three basic types: 'service providers', 'watchdogs' and 'hybrids'. While any rigid typology is in some ways artificial, given the argument posed here it is useful to categorise these organisations in a way that more broadly interprets their mission. I do this through a combination of two methods: by examining their declared mission (in the organisation's literature); and through perceptions of mission (gleaned from interviews with organisation leaders). Service providers include those organisations that primarily focus on training, educational programmes, technical assistance and similar activities. I include here Liberty Institute (*Tavisuplebis Instituti*, which before 2003 was a central watchdog organisation), ALPE,[9] the Civil Society Institute (*Samokalako Sazogadoebis Instituti*), and the United Nations Association of Georgia (*Sakartvelos Gaeros Asotsiatsia*). By contrast, I include under watchdog organisations those primarily oriented towards monitoring and actively contesting state structures. These include the Human Rights Information and Documentation Center (*Adamianis Uplebata Tsentri*), Article 42 (*Konstitutsiis 42-e Mukhli*), the Egalitarian Institute (*Egalitaruli Instituti*), and Former Political Prisoners for Human Rights (*Kopili Politpatimrebi Adamianis Uplebebistvis*).[10] Finally, organisations that split their time, performing both functions are labelled 'hybrids'. They include the Georgian Young Lawyers' Association; Transparency International; and the International Society for

[9]'About Alpe', ALPE Foundation, available at: http://www.alpe.ge/alpe/about_alpe/, accessed 5 March 2012; UNA, 'About United Nations Association of Georgia, United Nations Association of Georgia', available at: http://www.una.org.ge/unag.html, accessed 6 January 2008.

[10]Human Rights Information and Documentation Center (HRIDC), 'Mission', available at: http://www.hridc.org/eng/mission.php, accessed 6 January 2008.

Fair Elections and Democracy.[11] Each of these organisations was primarily financed by Western donors prior to 2003 and almost all continue to depend on Western support today.

In addition to NGO leaders, I conducted interviews with former NGO actors (especially from the above-mentioned organisations) who have occupied high-level positions in the post-2003 state. These include senior-level representatives of the Office of the Prosecutor; the Constitutional Court; the Supreme Court; Tbilisi Mayor's Office; Georgian Prison Administration; Internal Affairs Ministry; parliamentary Human Rights Committee; Board of Public Television; and the Ombudsman's Office. I also spoke with various members of parliamentary opposition parties who were before November 2003 leaders of non-governmental organisations.

The purpose of these interviews was to establish how members of the two categories of elites saw their relationships with former colleagues now on the other side of the government–NGO divide. In fact, the categories established here are in some ways artificial since borders are frequently crossed—precisely the *raison d'etre* of this study. Political context, which now separates these two groups into NGO and state, until 2003 bound them together as the leaders of Georgia's opposition movement. Throughout the 1990s these NGOs grew into well paid, professional organisations which provided technical assistance to young reformers (especially in the form of draft legislation) (Devdariani 2004, p. 97). Private connections quickly grew between young reformers and NGO actors. While I do not have precise demographic data concerning my respondents, they are overwhelmingly young (25–40 years old), well-educated and exposed to the West through travel or formal training—characteristics that helped initially connect the young reformers and NGO activists in the 1990s. The commentaries of these individuals concern people who are not seen as 'others', but former colleagues and often close friends who now stand on opposing sides of the fence.

There were early indications that the relationship between Georgia's one-time NGO heads in government and those remaining outside the state would not be easy. Organisations devoted to the study of civil society have recognised that many NGOs functioning in Georgia soon began to feel that the new government, with so many former NGO leaders now at the helm, was dismissive of their voices. 'There is a general message that the government does not need NGOs anymore', commented the leader of one such organisation.[12] As one scholar noted early after the political turnover, NGOs also faced peer pressure not to criticise their former colleagues, and access to governmental leaders was reserved first for those civil society groups that had helped empower the new leadership and subsequently supported it (Broers 2005, p. 345).

In fact, the primary division appears to be between those NGOs who maintain a predominantly watchdog function and those that are focused more on providing services to the government. As predicted above, I find the worst relations between the

---

[11] Other organisations whose members were interviewed include *Horizonti* and the International Center for Civic Culture (organisations dedicated to the development of civil society); the Caucasus Institute for Peace, Democracy and Development (an independent think tank); representatives from the independent TV station Rustavi II; and representatives from various international organisations previously involved in opposition support (Open Society Georgia Foundation, Eurasia Foundation, National Democratic Institute).

[12] N. Saakashvili, Executive Director of *Horizonti*, 16 July 2007, Tbilisi.

government and watchdog NGOs. But while those watchdog organisations with few or no close personal connections to state actors face ostracism, those with close connections are subject to more open state attacks. By contrast, service NGOs, particularly with a high membership contribution to the state, have the most positive relationship with the Georgian government today. In this section I briefly overview local perceptions of the NGO–government relations, with respect to watchdog, service and hybrid organisations.

## *Watchdogs*

Those exclusively watchdog organizations that largely opposed or stayed out of the Rose Revolution and did not subsequently see their leaders go to government are by and large ignored or quietly condemned by the government. Whether or not these organisations actively opposed the Rose Revolution (as did the Former Political Prisoners for Human Rights) or not, members have alleged government harassment in the post-2003 period.[13] For those who fight the government in the courtroom (for example, representing victims of abuses who challenge the state in court) rather than in the media, the situation is neither dire nor constructive: 'We didn't have bad relations before, we don't have bad relations now', commented the leader of organisation 'Article 42', an organisation that provides human rights monitoring and legal council for rights victims. 'We always kept our distance, then and now'.[14]

These organisations all share the perception that the human rights situation in Georgia has deteriorated since 2003. They especially voice wariness about the lack of judicial independence, pressures on the media, and impunity for law enforcement officials. They allege that the new government has quickly consolidated power and used its anti-corruption campaign as a way to silence potential opposition. One NGO leader explained: 'We believe they are violating rights more now, because they are doing it in a more skilled way. The same torture done earlier was very open; now the methods of torture have changed—this is not necessarily physical torture, it can be psychological'.[15] By frequently showing on public television news footage of live, large-scale arrests of the allegedly corrupt, the government is intent, critics say, on keeping opponents sidelined.[16]

Since few or none of these organisations' members have moved to government, they lack personal relations that might create a particular reaction. In fact, according to one leader, their criticisms tend to be met by silence.[17] Government leaders are usually

---

[13]Author's interviews with U. Nanuashvili, Executive director of the Human Rights Information and Documentation Center, 16 July 2007, Tbilisi; N. Kakabadze, Head of Former Political Prisoners for Human Rights, 16 July 2007, Tbilisi; and G. Nikoleishvili, Deputy head of Former Political Prisoners for Human Rights, 16 July 2007, Tbilisi.

[14]M. Chokheli, Executive Director of the organisation 'Article 42 of the Constitution', 18 July 2007, Tbilisi.

[15]M. Chokheli, Executive Director of the organisation 'Article 42 of the Constitution', 18 July 2007, Tbilisi.

[16]A. Dolidze, Former Chair of the Georgian Young Lawyers' Association (2005–2006), 10 July 2007, Telephone Interview.

[17]M. Chokheli, Executive Director of the organisation 'Article 42 of the Constitution', 18 July 2007, Tbilisi

not eager to partner with them on projects, leaving them isolated. As one outspoken human rights NGO leader commented, 'Cooperation now between NGOs and government is illusory'.[18] The leader added that a lack of government attention to domestic criticism leads him to pursue international networks that might put pressure on the government for change: 'The Georgian government understands only two words, "international NGOs"'.[19]

For their part, state leaders accuse watchdog (as well as hybrid) NGOs of incessant criticism and a refusal to give credit where credit is due, perhaps a legacy of the anti-regime role NGOs adopted during the Shevardnadze era.[20] 'When the situation changed they didn't change. They didn't want to see the changes and the challenges', commented one senior level official.[21] When asked whether in 2002 Shevardnadze might have similarly described their own (NGO) criticisms as overly critical and unfair, one leader responded: 'The wording might be the same, I agree. But the real steps, the changes in the law, are obvious'.[22] If NGOs want to be useful, they must adapt their activities to the new realities, Tbilisi's mayor continued. 'They should fill the gap between government and society, what government can't deliver can be delegated [to] this civil sector'.[23]

*Service providers*

Just as watchdogs are ostracised, it is similarly predictable that government officials have been far friendlier to organisations that are less vocal in their opposition and more supportive of particular government programmes. Some of these organisations, such as the United Nations Association and Civil Society Institute, have historically focused on service provision. Perhaps more surprising, others have shifted from watchdog activities to service provision as the result of perceived demand after 2003. By steering clear of dissent and focusing instead on providing goods and services, these organisations—which were sometimes extraordinarily outspoken prior to 2003—have been able to use connections to thrive in Georgia's new political climate. Liberty Institute, which played a critical role in facilitating the Rose Revolution and whose members and associates took a number of senior positions afterwards, has followed such a strategy.

The combination of Liberty's close relations with government and its pro-government activities has led many to refer to it as a Government-Organised NGO (GONGO). But to Liberty's co-founder and leader, Levan Ramishvili the organisation

---

[18] U. Nanuashvili, Executive director of the Human Rights Information and Documentation Center, 16 July 2007, Tbilisi

[19] U. Nanuashvili, Executive director of the Human Rights Information and Documentation Center, 16 July 2007, Tbilisi

[20] Author's interviews with G. Ugulava, Mayor of Tbilisi and former founder/director of non-governmental organisation ALPE, 21 July 2007, Tbilisi and K. Kublashvili, Chairman of the Supreme Court of Georgia, 23 July 2007, Tbilisi.

[21] Anonymous interview with a Senior Government of Georgia Official, Tbilisi.

[22] G. Ugulava, Mayor of Tbilisi and former founder/director of non-governmental organisation ALPE, 21 July 2007, Tbilisi.

[23] G. Ugulava, Mayor of Tbilisi and former founder/director of non-governmental organisation ALPE, 21 July 2007, Tbilisi.

has merely changed the nature of its activities in recognition of new political realities.[24] Liberty officials since 2003 have claimed their organisation is more akin to a think tank, with the important role of drafting legislation needed to quickly modernise the country. Close government connections have been instrumental in influencing the policy process, Liberty members claim. 'If you have some friends in parliament or some other government bodies, it's easier for you to communicate', commented one member.[25] Many of the legislative initiatives that Liberty began sending to parliament after 2003 were originally drafted when many current government officials were affiliated with them, while other initiatives have been drafted since. It is clear that incorporation of Liberty officials, together with the reduction of the organisation's watchdog functions, has given Liberty significant influence in post-Shevardnadze Georgia.

Critics of the current government, whether opposition parties or watchdog NGOs, frequently see Liberty and the ruling United National Movement as one entity, alleging that Ramishvili is 'the ideologist of today's leaders'.[26] This is in part a reflection of an overlap of membership; some of the most powerful post-2003 politicians, including highly influential legislators and Liberty co-founders Gigi Bokeria and Givi Targamadze, spent much of the decade preceding the Rose Revolution working at Liberty. Others, including President Saakashvili, closely cooperated with Liberty in their drive for power. But in part this is also a reflection of the radical change in Liberty's activities before and after the revolution. 'They don't yell against human rights violations', commented Georgia's ombudsman in 2007, himself a former Liberty member.[27] The fact that their activities are so heavily geared towards legislative preparation, and that this legislation frequently passes with little discussion through the parliament which is dominated by the National Movement, leaves Liberty open to charges of collusion. According to the head of parliament's human rights committee, a vocal opponent of Saakashvili's government, 'All of the legislation prepared in that Institute that then comes here is neither humanitarian nor liberal'.[28]

Liberty may be the best known of the service NGOs, but it is not the only one. Another interesting case is the ALPE Foundation, a service organisation supported in part by the EU, the Open Society Georgia Foundation and USAID (through the Eurasia Foundation). ALPE has traditionally engaged in a variety of projects, from education and promotion of tolerance of minorities to judicial reform. After the 2003 events, the head of ALPE moved into government, and then became mayor of Tbilisi. ALPE officials claim that close connections and a policy of not openly criticising the government have given the organisation an advantage: 'Basically they don't like to be criticised', said ALPE's director, Zurab Guntsadze. 'I don't make public statements

---

[24] L. Ramishvili, Head of Liberty Institute, 17 July 2007, Tbilisi.

[25] G. Meladze, Member of Liberty Institute and former member of *Kmara* (political youth organisation), 17 July 2007, Tbilisi

[26] G. Khaindrava, Former Minister for Conflict Resolution and current head of the Egalitarian Institute, 24 July 2007, Tbilisi

[27] S. Subari, Public Defender (Ombudsman) of Georgia, 18 July 2007, Tbilisi.

[28] E. Tevdoradze, Chair of the Human Rights and Civil Integration Committee, Parliament of the Republic of Georgia, 24 July, Tbilisi.

because I know if I do this it will be very difficult to do some other things that are much more important'.[29] But ALPE officials claim that, through quiet diplomacy, they have gained the trust of highly placed colleagues that makes them more influential. For example, referring to a case of property confiscation in Tbilisi, Guntsadze says he approached Mayor Ugulava and said: '"Look, this is ridiculous; look at this from your old eyes, not your new, mayor eyes"... He listened and he changed [his decision]'.[30] The combination of connections and motivations has empowered non-governmental service providers, these actors claim.

### *The hybrids*

Apart from the Liberty Institute, the NGO that contributed the most personnel to the post-2003 Georgian state was the Georgian Young Lawyers' Association (GYLA), which played a critical role in election monitoring and the subsequent anti-Shevardnadze mobilisation. The GYLA has historically been involved in both watchdog and service functions, providing training to government officials and proposing legislative initiatives. Since 2003, it has attempted to maintain both functions. The considerable difficulties it has faced in this endeavour highlight the tensions involved.

If inclusion is the key to influence, GYLA should have 'backdoor' access to the new government. Its members occupy or have occupied senior political positions, including ministers of Defence, Justice and the Environment, and have virtually controlled the judicial branch—serving as chair of the Supreme and Constitutional Courts and the top positions in the Prosecutor's Office. Yet, according to GYLA leaders and other watchdog organisations, independence of the judiciary is perhaps the biggest problem in Georgia. If Shevardnadze's judiciary was corrupt, they say, Saakashvili's is politically partial: 'The prosecutor's office is really strong and directly controls the judges', summarised GYLA's 2007 leader, who served for six months in the prosecutor's office after 2003. 'He is in the president's close circle'.[31]

While GYLA initially had better access to the new government, this honeymoon quickly ended with GYLA's opposition to the 2004 constitutional amendment increasing power of the executive.[32] Tensions gradually increased with each criticism GYLA made at state policy, reaching a crescendo with GYLA's opposition to the sacking of virtually the entire cadre of Supreme Court judges, ostensibly as part of an anti-corruption campaign. GYLA's objections that Supreme Court members were pressured to leave without due process and, moreover, without evidence of wrongdoing, resulted in a more formal criticism by (former) GYLA members in government. In January 2006, after GYLA had chosen to legally defend several of the judges, the Defence Minister, the Minister of Environment, the chairman of the

---

[29]Z. Guntsadze, Director of ALPE Foundation, 23 July 2007, Tbilisi.

[30]Z. Guntsadze, Director of ALPE Foundation, 23 July 2007, Tbilisi.

[31]G. .Chkheidze, Chairman of the Georgian Young Lawyers' Association (2007–2008), Tbilisi, 17 July 2007.

[32]Author's interviews with G. Chkheidze, Chairman of the Georgian Young Lawyers' Association (2007–2008), Tbilisi, 17 July 2007 and L. Chkhetia, Deputy Chair of the Georgian Young Lawyers' Association (2006–2007), Tbilisi, 17 July 2007.

Supreme Court and others attacked GYLA in the national media, accusing it of partisan politics.[33] Senior level state employees who once held leading roles in GYLA continue to believe the legal association crossed the line from NGO to political opposition.[34] 'You can't criticise like an opposition party', commented K. Kublashvili, head of the Supreme Court. 'It's an NGO and it shouldn't leave this sphere. If they want to, they should transform themselves into a political party, that's no problem'.[35]

GYLA leaders believe that their personal connections to people at the top, coupled with their watchdog role probably exacerbated conflict, rather than providing them with access and influence. According to GYLA's 2007 leader, former GYLA members personally felt under attack by GYLA criticisms and moved quickly away from their organisational relationship.[36] Recalling her defence of expunged Supreme Court justices, A. Dolidze, an outspoken earlier leader (2005–2006) of GYLA agreed: '[Supreme Court Chairman Kublashvili] expected more loyalty from GYLA's chair than I exhibited'.[37] As NGO actors have been incorporated into state structures they have changed their orientation and mission. Where they once supported and took part in criticism of the state, they now feel betrayed by similar shows of disapproval from their former colleagues. 'The personal relationship can influence a lot in Georgia, which is a small country', commented GYLA's deputy chair.[38] 'It was mostly bad for us to have some former members or former acting members of GYLA in this high office'.

Senior government officials confide that they feel betrayed by their former colleagues, whose support they counted on to strengthen the new leadership and to democratise institutions.[39] Some deflect criticism, arguing that NGO leaders are merely jealous of the power their former colleagues in government attained.[40] Government leaders frequently disparage their civil society partners: 'All the best people available came to government and came in power on various levels', commented the Tbilisi Mayor, a former NGO leader. 'What is left in the NGO society? Basically now they are no longer progressive. They became like the surrogates of opposition parties'.[41]

---

[33] A. Dolidze, Former Chair of the Georgian Young Lawyers' Association (2005–2006), 10 July 2007, Telephone Interview.

[34] Author's interviews with K. Kublashvili, Chairman of the Supreme Court of Georgia, 23 July 2007, Tbilisi; and with a Senior Government of Georgia Official, Tbilisi.

[35] K. Kublashvili, Chairman of the Supreme Court of Georgia, 23 July 2007, Tbilisi.

[36] G. Chkheidze, Chairman of the Georgian Young Lawyers' Association (2007–2008), Tbilisi, 17 July 2007.

[37] A. Dolidze, Former Chair of the Georgian Young Lawyers' Association (2005–2006), 10 July 2007, Telephone Interview.

[38] L. Chkhetia, Deputy Chair of the Georgian Young Lawyers' Association (2006–2007), Tbilisi, 17 July 2007.

[39] Anonymous interview with a Senior Government of Georgia Official, Tbilisi.

[40] G. Papuashvili, Chairman of the Constitutional Court and former Minister of Justice and Minister of Environment, Republic of Georgia, 25 July 2007, Tbilisi; and anonymous interviews with a Senior Government of Georgia Official, Tbilisi.

[41] G. Ugulava, Mayor of Tbilisi and former founder/director of non-governmental organisation ALPE, 21 July 2007, Tbilisi.

Transparency International, which like GYLA functions as both a watchdog and a service provider with respect to technical assistance in drafting legislation, provides an interesting contrast to GYLA experience. Unlike GYLA, none of Transparency's members moved to the government after 2003.[42] Similar to the watchdogs discussed above, once Transparency officials became openly critical of the government, they began to lose access. For example, according to Transparency's executive director in Georgia, Tamuna Karosanidze, it became difficult to have high-level meetings with government officials and Transparency was evicted from its permanent office in parliament—essential to providing legislative critiques in a country where bills are passed very quickly. The same government officials who so publicly attacked their former NGO colleagues took a very different position when they had no expectations of loyalty: 'They don't go radically against us, and they're not openly against us, they try to create technical problems', Karosanidze explained.[43] The leaders of Transparency complain that government officials attack them for 'talking just like the opposition', but add that the charges are levelled privately. 'They're saying it's a new time, a difficult time for Georgia', Karosanidze continued. 'Now it's not time to criticise. By criticising you're not really helping. You're playing the game of Russia or you're delaying the process of Georgia's NATO integration'.[44]

*Discussion*

Soon after the Rose Revolution, one political observer commented: 'The billion dollars in democracy and development aid that Georgia has received from the United States since 1991—by far Washington's largest *per capita* investment in any Soviet successor state—seem to have paid off' (King 2004). However, if civil society development, one component of this democracy aid, is designed to have long-term consequences, then this prognosis was premature. Around the world, pro-democracy organisations have been drawn into newly democratising states. The case of Georgia demonstrates that this can weaken rather than empower pro-democracy groups.

As discussed above, inclusion in government has a number of potential benefits for NGO actors that remain outside of government. According to the literature, one might hypothesise that state leaders who understand the valuable role civil society can play and, perhaps more importantly, who have personal connections to actors still in the NGO community, might produce bonds conducive to close cooperation. At first glance, incorporation of pro-democracy NGO members into a democratising government should bode well for democratic consolidation.

Yet the case of Georgia demonstrates the dangers inherent in the inclusion of NGOs into a new government. Former NGO actors whose allegiance is now with the state must deal with new constituencies and adopt new objectives. These institutionally defined priorities are likely to create tension in the relationship between new state leaders and their former organisations. As each category of actors operates with the expectation that its former partner will continue to support it, they are likely to clash.

---

[42]T. Karosanidze, Executive Director of Transparency International, 19 July 2007, Tbilisi.
[43]T. Karosanidze, Executive Director of Transparency International, 19 July 2007, Tbilisi.
[44]T. Karosanidze, Executive Director of Transparency International, 19 July 2007, Tbilisi.

In the case of Georgia, the greatest clash appears to have been between state leaders and their one-time NGOs. This follows from the theory of expectations elaborated above. While Georgia's political elites are not eager to cooperate with those who criticise, they appear to be most resentful towards those colleagues who were once the closest.

This does not, of course, mean that Georgia's new political elites are determined to avoid cooperation with the NGO sector. In fact, a government official claimed, 'when you work with NGOs you can achieve "more", and point to partnership successes that' have taken place in areas less prone to purported politicisation.[45] But, whether because they feel they know the NGOs better than the current NGO leaders or simply because they now feel in charge, Georgia's leaders have clearly expected partnerships to be on their own terms. As the case of the reborn Liberty Institute and other 'service organisations' discussed above suggests, such relationships can be mutually beneficial. But those organisations that go beyond political elites' expectations of them 'to do research and provide some expertise' are unlikely to find sympathy within government circles.[46] As one former NGO leader who now holds a high state position conceded, 'I don't think that there is any country in the world whose government would like NGOs to be stronger'.[47]

What have been the effects on Georgia's democratic consolidation? Georgia's political evolution provides at least some evidence that this incorporation has negatively affected the path of democratisation. Georgia's scores in the Freedom House 'Freedom in the World' survey only modestly improved in the first two years after the Rose Revolution, from 4/4 (political rights/civil liberties) during the final years of Shevardnadze's rule to 3/4 in 2005 and 3/3 in 2006. These changes were insufficient to move Georgia from a 'partly free' to 'free' country, according to the ranking criteria, and matched the assessment of other international NGOs and governmental organisations which remarked on the country's 'uneven human rights record' (HRW 2007) and warned that 'serious problems remained' (DOS 2007). Among these were allegations that the strengthened executive branch limited judicial independence, restricted freedom of expression and practically granted impunity to law enforcement officers (HRW 2007). Since that period, Freedom House scores for Georgia have fallen back to those witnessed during the Shevardnadze period, 4.0 in 2008, 2009 and 2010.[48]

But those who attack the government rarely claim it has been ineffective or simply a case of elite turnover. Instead, they argue that Georgia's new political elites have used strong-arm tactics in a genuine attempt to move Georgia from a failing state into a secure and democratic one.[49] 'I don't think they've turned into dictators', said

---

[45]Anonymous interview with a Senior Government of Georgia Official, Tbilisi.

[46]T. Karosanidze, Executive Director of Transparency International, 19 July 2007, Tbilisi.

[47]I. Tsintsadze, Deputy Head of Department of Prisons, Republic of Georgia, and former head of Alternativa NGO, 25 July 2007, Tbilisi.

[48]Freedom House, '2012: Freedom in the World', available at: http://www.freedomhouse.org/report-types/freedom-world, accessed 5 March 2012.

[49]Author's interviews with T. Karosanidze, Executive Director of Transparency International, 19 July 2007, Tbilisi; and E. Tevdoradze, Chair of the Human Rights and Civil Integration Committee, Parliament of the Republic of Georgia, 24 July, Tbilisi.

one human rights leader, who added that while the country has made progress in some spheres human rights remain in danger. 'I think they feel that ideals are ideals and before we get to those ideals we have to go down this dirty road'.[50] 'They're making a lot of mistakes but, on the other hand, the direction is the right one', added the former Rustavi-2 owner, who assessed the chances of successful democratisation at '50–50'.[51]

It is impossible to attribute these negative phenomena to NGO-government relations alone, but it is at least significant that local NGOs that raise these issues are condemned privately or publicly and often depend on international organisations and state actors to speak for them. While some of the findings in this study are not surprising, and most would expect the government's relationship with watchdogs to be significantly worse than that with service providers (Gyimah-Boadi 1994, p. 132), the personal factor analysed here adds a new dimension to this puzzle. Those hybrids engaged in watchdog functions that had close colleagues in the state apparatus were more often the targets of government-based vitriol than were similar critics without personal connections. In a world where civil and political society are so often intertwined during the struggle for democracy, this phenomenon is neither unique nor good for democracy. If former colleagues are prone to attack rather than to respond to the comments of non-state monitors, the path to democratic consolidation may be particularly challenging.

Establishing a link between incorporation and failed democratic consolidation is further complicated by the fact that on top of the overwhelming tensions that have characterised government–NGO relations in Georgia, Georgian NGOs have also suffered from a general crisis caused by shifts of external funding away from civil society and towards the new government (Bell & Keenan 2004, p. 356; Bienen & Herbst 1996, p. 29). The dislocation this has involved is also not atypical for transition states, where resource dependency is often the rule rather than the exception, and foreign donors, viewing pro-democracy NGOs as redundant, redirect aid to democratic forces in power (Bell & Keenan 2004, p. 356; Bienen & Herbst 1996, p. 29; Carothers & Barndt 1999–2000; Sali-Teric 2001). To some extent, it may represent a difference in how donors and recipients understand the notion of an NGO and democratisation at large (Grugel 2000, p. 90; Schaffer 1998).

But the phenomenon in Georgia suggests that the West, and the United States in particular, was too optimistic at the dawn of the Rose Revolution. The US government's transfer of resources away from the organisations that helped bring democratic breakthrough may have served to further encourage the new government that, indeed, the role of a critical civil society had ended. As one former NGO leader and member of the parliamentary opposition commented in 2007, 'This is how it was up until 2000. They felt that Shevardnadze was a democrat, a pro-Western politician'. The difference is in the years since Georgia's Rose Revolution of 2003, few outside observers believe the country has moved closer to democratic consolidation. Instead,

---

[50]T. Karosanidze, Executive Director of Transparency International, 19 July 2007, Tbilisi.

[51]E. Kitsmarishvili, Former head of Rustavi 2, 23 July 2007, Tbilisi.

critics inside and outside the country wonder how to get Georgia back on the track it appeared to be on in late 2003.

*University of Maryland, Baltimore County*

## References

Adamson, F. B. (2002) 'International Democracy Assistance in Uzbekistan and Kyrgyzstan: Building Civil Society from the Outside?', in Mendelson, S. & Glenn, J. (eds) (2002) *The Power and Limits of NGOs: A Critical Look at Building Democracy in Eastern Europe and Eurasia* (New York, Columbia University Press), pp. 177–206.
An-Na'im, A. A. (2001) ''Human Rights in the Arab World: A Regional Perspective', *Human Rights Quarterly*, 23, pp. 701–32.
Anderson, W. A. & Dynes, R. R. (1973) 'Organizational and Political Transformation of a Social Movement: A Study of the 30th of May Movement in Curacao', *Social Forces*, 51, 3, pp. 330–41.
Antoun, R. T. (2000) 'Civil Society, Tribal Processes, and Change in Jordan: An Anthropological View', *International Journal of Middle East Studies*, 32, 4, pp. 441–63.
Areshidze, I. (2007) *Democracy and Autocracy in Eurasia: Georgia in Transition* (East Lansing, Michigan State University Press).
Baran, Z. (2002) 'The Caucasus: Ten Years after Independence', *The Washington Quarterly*, 25, 1, pp. 221–34.
Bartlett, D. M. C. (2000) 'Civil Society and Democracy: A Zambian Case Study', *Journal of Southern African Studies*, 26, 3, pp. 429–46.
Bell, C. & Keenan, J. (2004) 'Human Rights Nongovernmental Organizations and the Problems of Transition', *Human Rights Quarterly*, 26, pp. 330–74.
Berman, S. (1997) 'Civil Society and the Collapse of the Weimar Republic', *World Politics*, 49, 3, pp. 401–29.
Bernhard, M. (1993) 'Civil Society and Democratic Transition in East Central Europe', *Political Science Quarterly*, 108, 2, pp. 307-26.
Bienen, H. & Herbst, J. (1996) 'The Relationship Between Political and Economic Reform in Africa', *Comparative Politics*, 29, 1, pp. 23-42.
Bratton, M. (1994) 'Civil Society and Political Transitions in Africa', in Harbeson, J.W., Rothchild, D.S. & Chazan, N. (eds) (1994), pp. 51-81.
Broers, L. (2005) 'After the "revolution": civil society and the challenges of consolidating democracy in Georgia', *Central Asian Survey*, 24, 3, pp. 333-50.
Carothers, T. (2004) 'Civil Society: Think Again', in Carothers, T. (ed.) (2004) *Critical Mission: Essays on Democracy Promotion* (Washington, DC, Carnegie Endowment for International Peace), pp. 99-106.
Carothers, T. (2006) 'The Backlash against Democracy Promotion: The Autocrats Push Back', *Foreign Affairs*, 85, 2.
Carothers, T. & Barndt, W. (1999–2000) 'Civil Society', *Foreign Policy*, 117, pp. 18–24, 26–9.
Chong, D. (1991) *Collective Action and the Civil Rights Movement* (Chicago, University of Chicago Press).
Clarke, G (1998a) 'Non-Governmental Organizations (NGOs) and Politics in the Developing World', *Political Studies*, 46, 1, pp. 36–52.
Clarke, G. (1998b) *The Politics of NGOs in South-East Asia: Participation and Protest in the Philippines* (New York, Routledge).
Cohen, A. (2004) 'Shevardnadze's Journey', *Policy Review*, 124, pp. 75–85.
Constantino-David, K. (1998) 'From the Present Looking Back: A History of Philippine NGOs', in Silliman, G. S. & Noble, L. G. (eds) (1998b), pp. 26–48.
Cooley, A. & Ron, J. (2002) 'The NGO Scramble', *International Security*, 27, 1, pp. 5–39.
Devdariani, J. (2003) 'The Impact of International Assistance', in *Building Democracy in Georgia: International Institute for Democracy and Electoral Assistance*, Discussion Paper No. 11, May (Stockholm, International Institute for Democracy and Electoral Assistance).
Devdariani, J. (2004) 'Georgia: Rise and Fall of the Façade Democracy', *Demokratizatsiya*, 12, 1, pp. 79–115.
di Palma, G. (1991) 'Legitimation from the Top to Civil Society: Politico-Cultural Change in Eastern Europe', *World Politics*, 44, 1, pp. 49–80.

Diamond, L. (1992) 'Introduction', in Diamond, L. (ed.) (1992) *The Democratic Revolution: Struggles for Freedom and Pluralism in the Developing World* (New York, Freedom House, 1992), pp. 1–27.

Diamond, L. J. (1999) *Developing Democracy: Toward Consolidation* (Baltimore, Johns Hopkins University Press).

Diani, M. (2006) 'The Concept of Social Movement', in Lipschutz R. D. (ed.) (2006) *Civil Societies and Social Movements: Domestic, Transnational, Global* (Burlington, Ashgate, 2006), pp. 129–53.

DOS (2004a) *Fact Sheet: U.S. Assistance to Georgia, Fiscal Year 2003* (Washington, DC, US Department of State, Bureau of International Information Programs).

DOS (2004b) *U.S. Assistance to Georgia—Fiscal Year 2004*, BoIIP (Washington, DC, US Department of State, Bureau of International Information Programs).

DOS (2007) *Country Reports on Human Rights Practices 2006* (Washington, DC, Bureau of Democracy, Human Rights, and Labor), available at http://www.state.gov/g/drl/rls/hrrpt/2006/78813.htm, accessed 28 August 2007.

Downes, D. (2000) 'The New Zealand Environmental Movement and the Politics of Inclusion', *Australian Journal of Political Science*, 35, 3, pp. 471–91.

Dryzek, J. S. (1996) 'Political Inclusion and the Dynamics of Democratization', *The American Political Science Review*, 90, 3, pp. 475–87.

Duffy, T. (1994) 'Toward a Culture of Human Rights in Cambodia', *Human Rights Quarterly*, 16, 1, pp. 82–104.

Eaton, K. (2003) 'Restoration or Transformation? "Trapos" versus NGOs in the Democratization of the Philipines', *The Journal of Asian Studies*, 62, 2, pp. 469–96.

Fairbanks, C. H. (2004) 'Georgia's Rose Revolution', *Journal of Democracy*, 15, 2, pp. 110–24.

Fatton, R. J. (1999) 'The Impairments of Democratization: Haiti in Comparative Perspective', *Comparative Politics*, 31, 2, pp. 209–29.

Feldman, S. (1997) 'The Role of NGOs: Charity and Empowerment: NGOs and Civil Society: (Un)stated Contradictions', *The Annals of The American Academy of Political and Social Science*, 554, 46.

Foweraker, J. & Landman, T. (1997) *Citizenship Rights and Social Movements: A Comparative and Statistical Analysis* (New York, Oxford University Press).

Friedman, E. J. & Hochstetler, K. (2002) 'Assessing the Third Transition in Latin American Democratization: Representational Regimes and Civil Society in Argentina and Brazil', *Comparative Politics*, 35, 1, pp. 21–42.

Gershman, C. (2004) 'Democracy Promotion: The Relationship of Political Parties and Civil Society', *Democratization*, 11, 3, pp. 27–35.

Gilbreth, C. & Otero, G. (2001) 'Democratization in Mexico: The Zapatista Uprising and Civil Society', *Latin American Perspectives*, 28, 4, pp. 7–29.

Grodsky, B. (2007) 'Looking for Solidarność in Central Asia: The Role of Human Rights Organizations in Political Change', *Slavic Review*, 66, 3.

Grugel, J. (2000) 'Romancing Civil Society: European NGOs in Latin America', *Journal of Interamerican Studies and World Affairs*, 42, 2, pp. 87–107.

Gyimah-Boadi, E. (1994) 'Associational Life, Civil Society, and Democratization in Ghana', in Harbeson, J. W., Rothchild, D. S. & Chazan, N. (eds) (1994), pp. 125–48.

Hachhethu, K. (2007) *Civil Society and Political Participation*, available at: http://www.democracy-asia.org/countryteam/krishna/Civil%20Society%20and%20Polotical%20Participation.pdf, accessed 8 June 2007, pp. 1–15.

Hajjar, L. (2001) 'Human Rigths in Israel/Palestine: The Histroy and Politics of a Movement', *Journal of Palestine Studies*, 30, 4, pp. 21–38.

Havel, V. (2005) 'The Emperor Has No Clothes', *Journal of Democracy*, 16, 4, pp. 5–8.

Harbeson, J. W., Rothchild, D. S. & Chazan, N. (eds) (1994) *Civil Society and the State* (Boulder, Lynne Rienner).

Hearn, J. & Robinson, M. (2000) 'Civil Society and Democracy Assistance in Africa', in Burnell, P. (ed.) (2000) *Democracy Assistance* (London, Frank Cass), pp. 241–62.

Henderson, S. L. (2002) 'Selling Civil Society: Western Aid and the Nongovernmental Sector in Russia', *Comparative Political Studies*, 35, 2, pp. 139–67.

Herd, G. (2005) 'Colorful Revolutions and the CIS', *Problems of Post-Communism*, 52, 2, pp. 3–18.

Herman, R. (2006) *Advocacy in the Europe and Eurasia Region: Progress, Promise and Peril* (Washington, DC, United States Agency for International Development).

HRW (2007) *World Report 2007: Georgia Country Summary*, available at: http://hrw.org/englishwr2k7/docs/2007/01/11/georgi14790.htm, accessed 28 August 2007.

ICG (2003) 'Georgia: What Now?', *International Crisis Group Europe Report*, 151, available at: http://www.crisisgroup.org/en/publication-type/media-releases/2003/europe/Georgia%20What%20Now.aspx, accessed 3 December 2003.

Ikelegbe, A. (2001) 'The Perverse Manifestation of Civil Society: Evidence from Nigeria', *The Journal of Modern African Studies*, 39, 1, pp. 1–24.
Jenkins, J. C. (1983) 'Resource Mobilization Theory and the Study of Social Movements', *Annual Review of Sociology*, 9, pp. 527–53.
King, C. (2004) 'A Rose Among Thorns: Georgia Makes Good', *Foreign Affairs*, 83, 2.
Kopecky, P. & Mudde, C. (2003) 'Rethinking Civil Society', *Democratization*, 10, 3, pp. 1–14.
Koslowski, R. & Kratochwil, F. V. (1994) 'Understanding Change in International Politics: The Soviet Empire's Demise and the International System', *International Organization*, 48, 2, pp. 215–47.
Kuran, T. (1991) 'Now Out of Never: The Element of Surprise in the East European Revolution of 1989', *World Politics*, 44, 1, pp. 7–48.
Lanegran, K. (1995) 'South Africa's Civic Association Movement: ANC's Ally or Society's "Watchdog"? Shifting Social Movement—Political Party Relations', *African Studies Review*, 38, 2, pp. 101–26.
Lehmbruch, G. (1979) 'Liberal Corporatism and Party Government', in Schmitter, P. C. & Lehmbruch, G. (eds) (1979) *Trends Toward Corporatist Intermediation* (Beverly Hills & London, Sage Publications), pp. 147–83.
Levite, A. & Tarrow, S. (1983) 'The Legitimation of Excluded Parties in Dominant Party Systems: A Comparison of Israel and Italy', *Comparative Politics*, 15, 3, pp. 295–327.
Lewis, P. M. (1992) 'Political transition and the dilemma of civil society in Africa', *Journal of International Affairs*, 46, 1, pp. 31–54.
May, R. A. (2005) 'Human Rights NGOs and the Role of Civil Society in Democratization', in May, R. A. & Milton, A. K. (eds) (2005) *(Un)civil Societies: Human Rights and Democratic Transitions in Eastern Europe and Latin America* (Lanham, Lexington Books, 2005), pp. 1–10.
McAdam, D. & Paulsen, R. (1993) 'Specifying the Relationship Between Social Ties and Activism', *The American Journal of Sociology*, 99, 3, pp. 640–67.
McFaul, M. (2005) 'Transitions from Postcommunism', *Journal of Democracy*, 16, 3, pp. 5–19.
Melucci, A., Keane, J. & Mier, P. (1989) *Nomads of the Present: Social Movements and Individual Needs in Contemporary Society* (Philadelphia, Temple University Press).
Monga, C. (1995) 'Civil Society and Democratisation in Francophone Africa', *The Journal of Modern African Studies*, 33, 3, pp. 359–79.
Moravcsik, A. (2000) 'The Origins of Human Rights Regimes: Democratic Delegation in Postwar Europe', *International Organization*, 54, 2, pp. 217–52.
Mutua, M. (2009) 'Human Rights NGOs in East Africa: Defining the Challenges', in Mutua, M. (ed.) (2009) *Human Rights NGOs in East Africa: Political and Normative Tensions* (Philadelphia, University of Pennsylvania Press), pp. 13–36.
Nodia, G. (1995) 'Georgia's Identity Crisis', *Journal of Democracy*, 6, 1, pp. 104–16.
Otero, G. & O'Bryan, J. (2002) 'Cuba in Transition? The Civil Sphere's Challenge to the Castro Regime', *Latin American Politics and Society*, 44, 4, pp. 29–57.
Ottaway, M. (2001) *Strengthening Civil Society in Other Countries: Policy Goal or Wishful Thinking?*, available at: http://www.carnegieendowment.org/2001/06/29/strengthening-civil-society-in-other-countries/cm3, accessed 7 March 2012.
Ottaway, M. & Chung, T. (1999) 'Toward a New Paradigm', *Journal of Democracy*, 10, 4, pp. 99–113.
Patterson, A. S. (1998) 'A Reappraisal of Democracy in Civil Society: Evidence from Rural Senegal', *The Journal of Modern African Studies*, 36, 3, pp. 423–41.
Polletta, F. & Jasper, J. M. (2001) 'Collective Identity and Social Movements', *Annual Review of Sociology*, 27, pp. 283–305.
Puryear, J. (1994) *Thinking Politics: Intellectuals and Democracy in Chile, 1973–1988* (Baltimore, Johns Hopkins University Press).
Robertson, G. B. (2004) 'Leading Labor: Unions, Politics, and Protest in New Democracies', *Comparative Politics*, 36, 3, pp. 253–72.
Sali-Teric, S. (2001) 'Civil Society', in Papic, Z. (ed.) (2001) *International Support Policies to SEE Countries—Lessons (Not) Learned in Bosnia-Herzegovina* (Sarajevo, Open Society Fund Bosnia & Herzegovina).
Schaffer, F. C. (1998) *Democracy in Translation: Understanding Politics in an Unfamiliar Culture* (Ithaca, Cornell University Press).
Schmitter, P. C. (1974) 'Still the Century of Corporatism?', *The Review of Politics*, 36, 1, pp. 85–131.
Schmitz, H. P. (2001) 'When Networks Blind: Human Rights and Politics in Kenya', in Callaghy, T. M., Kassimir, R. & Latham, R. (eds) (2001) *Intervention and Transnationalism in Africa: Global-Local Networks of Power* (New York, Cambridge University Press), pp. 149–72.
Shin, E. H. (2003) 'The Role of NGOs in Political Elections in South Korea: The Case of the Citizens' Alliance for the 2000 General Election', *Asian Survey*, 43, 4, pp. 697–715.

Sikkink, K. (1993) 'The Power of Principled Ideas: Human Rights Policies in the United States and Western Europe', in Goldstein, J. & Keohane, R. O. (eds) (1993) *Ideas and Foreign Policy : Beliefs, Institutions, and Political Change* (Ithaca, Cornell University Press), pp. 139–72.
Silliman, G. S. & Noble, L. G. (1998a) 'Citizen Movement and Philippine Democracy', in Silliman, G. S. & Noble, L. G. (eds) (1998b), pp. 280–310.
Silliman, G. S. & Noble, L. G. (eds) (1998b) *Organizing for Democracy: NGOs, Civil Society, and the Philippine State* (Honolulu, University of Hawai'i Press).
Tarrow, S. (1994) *Power in Movement: Social Movements, Collective Action and Politics* (New York, Cambridge University Press).
Waltz, S. (1995) *Human Rights and Reform: Changing the Face of North African Politics* (Berkeley, University of California Press).
Wedel, J. R. (1998) *Collision and collusion: the strange case of western aid to Eastern Europe, 1989–1998*, first edition (New York, St Martin's Press).
Wertsch, J. V. (2005) 'Georgia as a Laboratory for Democracy', *Demokratizatsiya*, 13, 4, pp. 519–35.
Wheatley, J. (2005) *Georgia from National Awakening to Rose Revolution: Delayed Transition in the Former Soviet Union* (Aldershot & Burlington, Ashgate).
Wiarda, H. J. (1997) *Corporatism and Comparative Politics: The Other Great 'ism'* (Armonk, M. E. Sharpe).
Zakaria, F (1997) 'The Rise of Illiberal Democracy', *Foreign Affairs*, 76, 6, pp. 17–31.

# A Broken Region: The Persistent Failure of Integration Projects in the South Caucasus

## THOMAS DE WAAL

### Abstract

This essay reviews failed historical attempts at regional integration in the South Caucasus since the early twentieth century, and in particular the failed Transcaucasian federations of 1918 and 1922–1936 and the breakdown of Soviet economic integration in the region. It argues that there is much that makes the South Caucasus a viable region in terms of geography, culture and economic potential, but political contradictions and persistent perceptions of insecurity make for a pattern of recurring fragmentation. Both Caucasians and outsiders have a role to play if voluntary integration is to work as a project in the future.

THE PLACE THAT USED TO BE THE TRANSCAUCASUS and which is now called the South Caucasus presents a paradox in that it can be plausibly described both as a region and as not a region. The debate over this definition is not merely a theoretical one and raises fundamental questions about how the problems of the South Caucasus should be addressed. Is regional integration an inherently flawed strategy, or has it merely been wrongly applied, or has it faced obstacles that were too great? In answering these questions, it is instructive to look at the attempts to achieve overarching regional integration that were attempted in the last century—the short-lived Transcaucasian Federation and the looser Soviet Transcaucasian Federative Republic of 1922–1936, as well the integrationist processes of the Soviet period as a whole—and understand why they failed. A broader look at the repeating historical patterns suggests that exclusive national projects tend to overwhelm regional ones and that recurring problems of insecurity undermine integration projects.

Despite its history of disorder and disintegration, there is a strong case to be made that the South Caucasus does constitute a region and outside policy makers should treat it as such—although without trying to impose overly rigid limits on how the concept

---

This essay is an elaboration of a paper given at the University of Birmingham conference on the Caucasus in July 2009 and then worked into a lecture delivered at the University of Ann Arbor, Michigan, in October 2009. I am grateful to both institutions.

should be applied. This is not a universally shared view. Some argue that the concept of a South Caucasus region is merely a post-colonial legacy, a construction that has outlived its historic usefulness. Some scholars prefer to locate Armenia, Azerbaijan and Georgia within a wider context, by putting an emphasis, for example, on a 'wider Black Sea region' (Cornell *et al.* 2006). Most policy makers in foreign ministries tend to see their relationship with the region as three bilateral official relationships with Baku, Tbilisi and Yerevan, paying little attention either to the three *de facto* breakaway states of Abkhazia, South Ossetia and Nagorno-Karabakh or to the South Caucasus regional dimension. Yet I want to make the argument that, although the boundaries of the South Caucasus are blurred and its identities are varied, it does make sense to talk about it as a region and to encourage efforts for consensual regional integration.

## *What binds the region together?*

Several elements make this a region. The first is geography. Its first two boundaries to the east and west, the Caspian and Black Seas are indisputable. The third, to the north, the Greater Caucasus mountain range, forms one of the strongest natural borders in the world, in Strabo's famous words, 'forming a rampart to the isthmus which separates one sea from another' (Strabo 1856, p. 226). The boundary is blurred only at three points, in Abkhazia, Dagestan and across the mountains of Georgia (on just three roads), with the result that the Abkhaz, Lezghins and Ossetians have a foot in both worlds of the North and South Caucasus. But the mountains make the distinction between the North and South Caucasus much sharper than that between, for example, European and Asian Russia. The barrier has given the two regions strongly diverging histories. The North Caucasus was subject to much more brutal and complete colonial subjugation by tsarist Russia than the south, in part due to the perception that the peoples of the North Caucasus were less 'civilised' and susceptible to imperial rule, but also, crucially, because of the resources the Russian empire could commit to each place. For centuries, the only good viable route to the southern Caucasus was along the shore of the Caspian Sea via the Dagestani city of Derbent—a road taken initially by Peter the Great and chosen subsequently by other invaders from the north, including the Bolsheviks in 1920. The route into Georgia through the Daryal Pass was much more difficult; even after the Russian takeover of Georgia in 1801 the imperial army still faced a hazardous journey on this route. In 1812, rebels led by Alexander, younger son of former Georgian King Erekle II, cut the road across the mountains and massacred an entire Russian garrison. The only road, the Georgian Military Highway, was poorly built, ran through thick forests and, at only 10 feet wide, was too narrow for artillery to negotiate. The 130-mile long highway, with bridges spanning the multiple gorges, was finally completed in 1817. In the North Caucasus, by contrast, the only physical obstacles to conquest were the thick beech forests and winding gorges of the highlands which eventually, tens of thousands of conscript troops would overcome. As a result, Russia was always constrained by the mountains in the military resources it could deploy in the south and tended to rely on consent and co-optation of elites to rule the region. The history of two small peoples with archaic customs living on either side of the mountains, the Balkars and the Svans makes for an instructive comparison. The North Caucasian Balkars were subjected to the full process of colonial subjugation and modernisation by Russians, which included, in the twentieth century, collectivisation, Nazi conquest, Soviet re-conquest and then mass deportation in 1944. The South Caucasian Svans were—and still are to a large extent—mostly left to their own devices and retain many of their pre-modern ways.

The fourth border of the South Caucasus, to the south and south-west, with Iran and Turkey, is the one chiefly defined by politics. The Iranian border, running mostly along the Araxes River, has been established since 1828, but it is basically a political line drawn on the map. The fact that Batumi is part of Georgia and Kars and Igdir are part of Turkey is a result of the shifting battle-lines of 1918–1921. And yet, I would argue, the experience of the Soviet Union, the Cold War and closed borders has given those boundaries a real historical solidity. Post-Soviet Azerbaijanis in their secularised way of life have more in common with post-Soviet Armenians than they do with either Turks or even Iranian Azerbaijanis. After the end of the Soviet Union, a major reason why Ajaria did not become a conflict flashpoint, as it had been in the 1915–1921 period, was that the Muslim Ajarians had grown apart from their ancestral patrons, the Turks, after the enforced separation of the years of the Cold War. The two had become part of different regions (de Waal 2010, pp. 145–47). This geography continues to shape the lives of residents of Armenia, Azerbaijan and Georgia. Eldar Ismailov and Vladimer Papava have made an interesting proposal to rename the geographical space of these countries 'The Central Caucasus', and redefine the 'South Caucasus' as parts of northern Iran and north-eastern Turkey. But connections across the borders of Iran and Turkey are currently too weak to make this more than a theoretical proposition (Ismailov & Papava 2006).

The second element that binds the South Caucasus together is a shared culture. The inhabitants of the South Caucasus share many customs and assumptions that a visiting anthropologist would quickly recognise. However much urban Europeanised intellectuals in Tbilisi and Yerevan prefer not to acknowledge it, the peoples of the region share an enormous amount in terms of social traditions, music, cooking, family behaviour and the way they celebrate great life rituals such as weddings and funerals. The Soviet era added a further layer of identity, giving Soviet Transcaucasians a *lingua franca* in Russian and a shared experience of being 'southerners' within the Soviet system. These affinities mean very little when political quarrels break out, but where different ethnic groups feel secure and on uncontested territory, as for example Armenians and Azerbaijanis do in Georgia, observers notice that they quickly find a rapport and *modus vivendi*.

There is also a persistent intellectual strain, which identifies shared Caucasian traditions formed by history and topography and celebrates the uniqueness of the region. The heyday of this common culture was probably the court of Irakli II in Tiflis in the eighteenth century, where the Armenian-born monk-turned-troubadour Sayat Nova composed songs in Armenian, Georgian and Persian and chiefly in the *lingua franca* of the day, Azerbaijani Turkish. In the twentieth century it was best exemplified in multi-ethnic Baku, but also survived in exile. It can be found in émigré publications, which were of course coloured by nostalgia, but also given a clarity of perspective by distance from local politics. In 1955, the Circassian scholar Aytek Namitok, in a programmatic essay entitled 'The Caucasus' wrote that:

> The Caucasus became a living museum of the ancient races, the repository of a deep and rich stratification of various cultures, protected by topography against all attacks from outside. This long past has left in the character of the peoples traces which may be found in the old traditional families: pride and the reflexes of honour and nobility. And as their ethnic conservatism is wedded among Caucasians to extreme individualism, they are naturally hostile to any system which reduces personality to one common level, and to any form of oppression as well. (Namitok 1955, p. 6)

Despite its romantic tint, Namitok's views point to a recurring dynamic of this region. A collection of small peoples are surrounded by larger neighbouring powers, Iran, Russia and Turkey. Although they seek protection from and alliance with these powers, they also resist assimilation and have more in common on a day-to-day level with local neighbours, even though they may be in a state of political conflict with them.

Finally, economics and trade cleave this region together. The geographic location of the South Caucasus between Russia and the Middle East and the Black and Caspian Seas has made it a natural east–west and north–south trade corridor. In medieval times it was a conduit for a northern branch of the old Silk Road, but this potential was only fully realised by nineteenth-century technology. Prior to that, there had been a strong east–west division into Ottoman and Persian spheres of influence. Modern-day Georgia was split, with Mingrelia, Guria and Imereti belonging more in the Ottoman world, and Kartli and Kakheti in the Persian world. The dividing line was the Surami Highlands east of Kutaisi. In 1890, Russian engineers made the biggest step towards reunifying the old Georgian lands since the days of Queen Tamar, when they blasted a railway tunnel through the Surami Highlands, linking the Black and Caspian Seas by train for the first time. In 1906 the world's first 'kerosene pipeline' from Baku to Batumi followed the same route. In Soviet times, this transport infrastructure was extended, linking Sukhumi, Yerevan and Nakhichevan and Ijevan, Kazakh and Tbilisi in interlocking railway networks. The potential is still there for these connections to be restored and for the South Caucasus to be the pathway between Russia and Iran and Turkey and the Caspian Sea.

## *Failed federations*

On the other hand, the South Caucasus has persistently failed to work as a region. Nothing serious was attempted until the turn of the twentieth century, and since then regional integration projects have failed. To talk of the Georgian kings David the Builder and Erekle II as integrationist is too anachronistic. The tsarist empire governed a collection of provinces named after their principal cities which slowly gained a loose regional identity within the imperial system, after a viceroyalty was established in Tiflis in 1844. At the end of the nineteenth century, with the technological advances of railways and communications, it became more feasible to look at the region as a distinct whole. The culmination of this was the only attempt to form a Trancaucasian state in the spring of 1918, which collapsed after just one month. However, the Transcaucasian Federation did not last long enough to bear serious scrutiny. It was an improvised strategy, devised in April 1918, when it was clear that Russia was too preoccupied with its own problems to care about the

Transcaucasus, and as an Ottoman invasion threatened the region. In November 1917, Georgian Menshevik leader Noe Zhordania still believed his country's best hopes lay through a more democratic Russia. He said, 'This union [with Russia in 1801] was not the result of some kind of personal caprice or a matter of simple chance. It was a historic inevitability. At that time, Georgia stood before a dilemma: the East or the West. And our ancestors decided to turn away from the East and turn to the West. But the road to the West lay through Russia, and consequently to go toward the West meant union with Russia' (Zhordania 1919, p. 52). Five months later, events made the Caucasian leaders change their mind. Russia was embroiled in a destructive civil war, leaving Turkey a free hand to pursue its ambitions in the Caucasus. Enver Pasha's Ottoman Third Army captured Erzerum, Ardahan and Batum in quick succession. On 22 April 1918, the leaders voted to form a Transcaucasian Federation, nominally so as to form a unified position in the face of the new Ottoman threat. Zhordania himself abstained on the vote. But, as Enver Pasha marched further, the Armenians were desperate to ward off an Ottoman takeover, while Azerbaijanis mostly welcomed the advance of their Turkic brethren. Zhordania secretly negotiated a new alliance with Germany and on 26 May 1918 declared Georgia independent and the federation bankrupt. 'At the present moment the Georgian people says it is ready to accept the dominion of anyone rather than fall under the dominion of Turkey', Zhordania declared (Zhordania 1919, p. 94). The Georgian move signed the death warrant of the federation, and left the other two Transcaucasian Republics no choice but to declare independence two days later. They did so on Georgian territory in a situation of extreme crisis. The Armenians had just managed to avoid complete destruction by the Ottoman Army by their actions at the Battle of Sardarapat. The Azerbaijani nationalists declared independence in the Hotel Orient in Tiflis and set up a provisional government in Ganja because the Bolsheviks were in control of Baku.

This was the context for the short-lived independence of Armenia, Azerbaijan and Georgia. In the autumn of 1919, the US general James Harbord was sent to the region by President Woodrow Wilson to study the feasibility of adopting independent Armenia under an American mandate. He painted a picture of the region at its most dysfunctional:

> The three Governments from an occidental standpoint are now thoroughly inefficient, without credit, and undoubtedly corrupt. Alone each faces inextricable financial difficulties. Religious differences, added to racial, threaten to embroil them unless brought under a common control. Two of them have no outlet to the Black Sea except through Georgia over the railroad. They have no present intermonetary, postal, or customs union, and, as stated, no definite agreement for common control and use of the railroad, and are in continual squabbles over boundaries. Azarbaijan has no educated class capable of well administering a government; Georgia is threatened by bolshevism; Armenia is in ruins, and partial starvation. (Harbord 1920, p. 14)

From integration it was a short step to disintegration—an interesting parallel to what happened to the region at the end of the Soviet period. General Harbord's conclusion in 1919 was dramatic, but utopian: 'All our investigation brings conviction that the people in each would welcome a mandatory [sic] by a trustworthy outside power' (Harbord 1920, p. 14).

In other words, if the small nations of the Transcaucasus could not sort out their problems, a bigger power should do it for them. As we know, the United States was too far away to take up this challenge and besides the situation on the ground was changing fast. In fact in 1919 only one power was willing and able to assume a mandate to govern the Transcaucasus as a single whole, but very much on its own terms, and that of course was Bolshevik Russia.

## The Soviet project

By the spring of 1921, the Bolsheviks had re-conquered the South Caucasus. They encountered strong resistance but also received support from workers and minorities, such as the Abkhaz, Ossetians and Karabakh Armenians. Integration was again the watchword. They used the breakdown and bloodshed of the preceding years as their chief rationale for their own attempt at top-down regional unification and, in their own brutal way, put an end to seven years of strife and disintegration. In April 1923, the chief Bolshevik in the Caucasus, Sergo Orjonikidze, made a spirited defence of the virtues of the Bolshevik-imposed integration in the form of the new Soviet Transcaucasian Federation.[1] Orjonikidze said the South Caucasus was a 'single economic organism' and that, 'Our enemies, the Mensheviks, Musavatists and Dashnaks understood this, they understood that the Transcaucasus is a single economic whole and when in power, they created not distinct republics but a Transcaucasian Republic'. However, he then went on to comment that the national leaders had failed to unite in 1918, with disastrous results:

> The formation of separate national republics led to a historically unprecedented worsening of national relations between the Transcaucasian peoples. Wars between the republics over frontiers—the war between Georgia and Armenia, the war between Azerbaijan and Armenia, wars inside the republics—the destruction and burning of South Ossetia by the Mensheviks, the war of the Mensheviks with the Ajarians, war with the Abkhaz, war with the Akhaltiskhe Muslims. The mutual slaughter, in the literal sense of this word, of Muslims and Armenians filled the atmosphere of the Transcaucasus with the poison of hatred. The republics shut themselves off from one another with a Chinese Wall of customs barriers.

> Soviet power intervened in this over-heated atmosphere of national hatred. The population sighed with relief. It sensed that an end had come to these horrors. At the height of massacres of Armenians by Muslims in the Shusha-Aghdam region in Azerbaijan, Soviet power was proclaimed and the Red Army instantly put a stop to the massacres by its intervention in Soviet Azerbaijan, was welcomed by the whole population as a saviour from bloody horrors, destruction and devastation. (Gornyi 1992, pp. 144–5)

Read straight off the page, without consideration of what was to follow, Orjonikidze's arguments read very well. Seen retrospectively from the 1980s however, the devising of the new ethno-territorial map of the Caucasus by Orjonokidze and his comrades was viewed as a cynical game of 'ethnic engineering' or 'divide-and-rule policies'. But historians and scholars, such as Arsène Saparov, Jeremy Smith, Valerii Tishkov and Anatolii Yamskov, have revealed more method and pragmatism in the

---

[1] *Pravda*, 12 April 1923.

decisions made by the Bolsheviks, seeing them as being also driven by concerns of conflict resolution and economic integration—what might be called a policy of 'combine-and-rule'. For example, analysing the creation of the South Ossetian Autonomous Region, Saparov wrote, 'Ossetian autonomy was a compromise solution the Bolsheviks adopted to solve the fierce civil war conflict. It was not a product of any deliberate policy to divide and rule' (Saparov 2010, p. 121). Yamskov has explained how one justification for putting the Armenian-populated highlands of Karabakh within Soviet Azerbaijan and making them into a new autonomous region of Nagorno-Karabakh was that it would allow shepherds to move their flocks from winter to summer pastures without crossing a republican border (Yamskov 1991, p. 20). Interpreting Bolshevik decisions in the North Caucasus in a similar light, Tishkov wrote, 'In reality, a prevailing motive behind this was to establish economically viable republics, with mountain and foothill resources and with natural communications and appropriate geographies—not to implement the "divide and rule" principle' (Tishkov 1997, p. 34).

Stalin and Orjonikidze also had plans for a single regional federation. In 1922 they founded a new Soviet Transcaucasian Federation, known chiefly by its Russian initials, the ZSFSR (*Zakavkazskaya Sovetskaya Federativnaya Sotsialisticheskaya Respublika*). This is not the place to revisit the 'Georgian affair' and the fierce arguments between the local Georgian Bolsheviks on the one hand and the Moscow Bolsheviks, led by two Georgians, Stalin and Orjonikidze, and supported by most Armenians and Azerbaijanis, on the other. Suffice it to say that the centralisers were not merely motivated, as is sometimes suggested, by a desire to impose direct and comprehensive rule from Moscow over the region—or rather this may have been their long-term aim, but they also had shorter-term objectives, the first of which was to stabilise the region by giving its restless minorities, such as the Abkhaz, Ajarians, Karabakh Armenians and Ossetians a stake in the new order. The bloodshed and chaos of the preceding years had been so intense that there were obvious attractions to erecting a single overarching Soviet structure to cover over all the old contradictions. The creation within that structure of four of the autonomous entities of the Soviet Transcaucasus: Ajaria, Abkhazia, Nagorno-Karabakh and South Ossetia, can be seen as an improvised solution to the conflicts that had been raging there over the previous four years.[2] A future scholar would be advised to study whether the Bolsheviks imposed a ready-made ethno-federal structure on the South Caucasus, or whether, in actual fact, they were compelled by force of circumstance in the fragile situation of 1921 to devise their complex ethno-federal system in order to manage the conflicts of the Caucasus; in other words, it would be worth investigating whether the Caucasus was the blueprint and the ethno-federal system the result rather than, as is frequently assumed, the other way round.

The ambitions of the Georgians were to be sacrificed to this goal of a larger federation. In the event, the ZSFSR project was approved but the Georgians succeeded in watering down its functions to essentially economic ones. In practice, the

---

[2]A fifth autonomous republic in Nakhichevan was evidently more a product of geography and Turkish interests, while the short-lived Red Kurdistan was abolished when the Stalinist regime began to persecute ethnic Kurds.

separate republics (initially, Abkhazia among them) kept most of their institutional powers. Lavrentii Beria, appointed head of the ZSFSR in 1931, was content to see it quietly dissolved in 1936 into the three Soviet republics of Armenia, Azerbaijan and Georgia. Beria stayed on as head of the Georgian Communist Party (*Sakartvelos Komunisturi Partia*) before he was moved to head the NKVD in Moscow in 1938 (Knight 1995; Rayfield 2004).

From that point on, the three South Caucasian republics maintained markedly independent traditions and grew further apart. Naturally, the Soviet Union made for integration on many levels, provided the *lingua franca* of Russian and many shared elements of a Soviet identity. But for Armenia, Azerbaijan and Georgia there was no longer a shared Transcaucasian structure, merely rule by Baku, Tbilisi, Yerevan and, of course, Moscow. As many scholars have noted, the Soviet Union preserved and sharpened ethnic and national differences. Despite their natural communications links, Trans-Caucasian trade was also surprisingly limited, due to the eccentricities of the USSR-wide command economy. After the death of Stalin, the leaders of the republics increasingly resembled feudal princes, who vied with one another for the patronage of Moscow and had little interest in regional cooperation. Each cultivated republican institutions, from party networks to academies of science, which then transmuted into the institutions of independent statehood in 1991. To cite but one case of intra-regional rivalry, Armenian and Azerbaijani Communist Party leaders, Karen Demirchian and Heydar Aliev, clashed in the 1970s and 1980s over what was supposed to be an intra-regional project, a highway from eastern Azerbaijan across Armenia into the Azerbaijani exclave of Nakhichevan. Demirchian succeeded in blocking what was supposed to be a project benefiting the Soviet Transcaucasus as a whole because he judged it deleterious to Armenian interests (de Waal 2003, pp. 135–36; Martin 2001; Suny 1993).

*Reasons for failure*

Why did integration in the South Caucasus fail? The contradictions of 1918 stand out clearly as you read the émigré journals of the 1920s and the 1930s and the essays of the leaders of the former independent republics. To study them is to read hand-wringing accounts of how the Caucasians forgot their common interests and allowed the Bolsheviks to take over. However the spin that different authors put on their defeat reveals how unbridgeable the divisions actually were: either the Caucasians were too close to the Bolsheviks or to Denikin, too close to the Turks or not firmly enough opposed to them. For example here is the Azerbaijani author Shefi Rustambeili writing in the Paris-based journal *Kavkaz* in 1935 and giving a very slanted version of how Azerbaijan fell to the Bolsheviks. He writes, 'By April 28 [1920], Azerbaijan, having endured a grave internal political crisis, drawn by the combined actions of the Armenian government and the command of the 11th Soviet army into battle with Armenian insurgents in Karabakh, with allied Georgia adopting a complete indifferent and passive position, was basically powerless to resist the armed forces of the attacking Red Army' (Rustambeili 1935, pp. 10–11). This is not a version of events that Karabakh Armenians, whose community in the town of Shusha had been ravaged by an Azerbaijani army in March 1920, would recognise.

The fundamental issue was—and remains—that the shorter-term political agendas of national groups out-trump broader economic interests. This can take extreme forms. On several occasions, Caucasian rebels have blocked the main economic arteries of the region—its railways—in the name of immediate political goals. In 1905 for example Georgian Marxist rebels blocked the tunnel through the Surami highlands with a captured engine and instantly cut the Transcaucasus in two. In 1990 Georgian nationalist leader Zviad Gamsakhurdia organised a blockade of Georgia's railway system, with disastrous economic repercussions, to try to force through the electoral law he wanted for the new Georgian Supreme Soviet. The Azerbaijani Popular Front (*Azerbaijan Khalq Jabhasi*) also severed rail links to Armenia and by doing so, helped cut off the Azerbaijani exclave of Nakhichevan from the rest of the republic.

These events illustrate a phenomenon widespread in many states in a state of breakdown but apparently especially marked in the Caucasus, that security is defined in extremely narrow terms—that of the survival of one's close national kin—and that all other notions of solidarity with others or broader ownership of an economy are secondary. This certainly is what seems to have happened with the quick—and from one perspective suicidal—collapse of the Transcaucasian Federation in 1918.

Geography is also kinder to some residents of the region than others. There is a kind of inbuilt asymmetry in the way, that the different countries in the region regard regional projects. Landlocked Armenia has a greater interest in them than does Georgia. Armenia needs a stable Georgia because in good times Georgia is Armenia's route to the west and the north, to Europe and Russia and in bad times, Armenia shares Georgia's problems and can do nothing about it. Russia's vengeful economic sanctions against Georgia in 2006 hit Armenia badly, while the continued closure of the railway through Abkhazia arguably damages Armenians even more than Georgians. During the 2008 conflict between Russia and Georgia, on 16 August 2008, the destruction of the Grakali railway bridge in central Georgia halted imports to Armenia for a week and cost the country an estimated half a billion dollars. The same geographical curse was almost fatal for Armenia during its worst ever crisis from 1915 to 1921. James Harbord, the US general identified many of the same problems:

> Georgia does not hesitate to embargo freight against Armenia, and from her position of vantage simply censors the railroad traffic to that unfortunate country. Azerbaijan controls the fuel supply and combines with Georgia against Armenia, which alone of the three has nothing by which to exert leverage. The railroad can neither be consolidated nor properly operated under native control. Roadbed and rolling stock are rapidly deteriorating. An example of the power of Georgia over Armenia is that the latter is not permitted to import either arms or ammunition, though under almost constant menace from its neighbours. (Harbord 1920, pp. 14-15)

In this unequal regional power geopolitics, Azerbaijan is in a stronger position than Armenia but it is weaker than Georgia. Separated from its closest ally Turkey and also from its own exclave of Nakhichevan by Armenia and Iran, Azerbaijan must rely on Georgia as its most stable route to Europe. But that cannot be taken for granted as was shown when its oil and gas pipelines through Georgia were shut down during the August 2008 war.

Finally, Georgia, the central country in the Caucasus, is the most blessed by geography and largely for that reason the one with the smallest vested interest in regional cooperation. Perhaps the problem is that it takes the benefits for granted and, as in May 1918, often has the freedom to avoid the risks. Sharing projects with Armenia and Azerbaijan means benefiting from Caspian Sea energy, having greater access to Iran and Turkey and lessening tensions with Georgia's Armenian and Azerbaijani minorities, but it also means taking on the burden of Armenia and Azerbaijan's problems—and by extension those of Turkey and Iran. At crucial moments, as we have seen, in May 1918 and in 1922 Georgian leaders decided that a regional federation was not in their interests and tried to withdraw from it.

The Georgian position may also explain the quiet death of the ZSFSR in 1936. As far as I am aware, there is no academic study of this process. Quite possibly, the dearth of the references to the ZSFSR in the scholarly literature reflects the fact that the new federation relatively quickly became a hollow and ineffective structure, with real power exercised by republican leaders in Baku, Tbilisi, Yerevan and of course Moscow. Certainly, as in 1918, without explicit Georgian support, any integrationist project was doomed to failure. The evidence suggests that Beria was more of a Georgian nationalist than Stalin. Beria's son, Sergo, a close if unreliable witness, writes, 'Of the Transcaucasian Bolsheviks only the Armenians had been favourable to this idea [of a federation]. They doubtless counted on reigning as masters over their new territory, by utilising the substantial minorities of their people living in Georgia and Azerbaijan. My father had been against the Federation from its creation and when he became its head he lost no time in causing it to disappear'. In Sergo Beria's words it is interesting to see anti-Armenian prejudice and zero-sum thinking transferred to the next generation (Beria 2001, p. 13; Rayfield 2004, pp. 333–44).

Georgian political thought also has its own strong particularist tradition which urges the country down its own separate path. It was most strongly expressed in the introverted tradition of Georgian nationalism embodied by Zviad Gamsakhurdia, who saw Georgia as a unique Caucasian civilisation that was set apart from the rest of the world. In a less malign way it has found expression in the views of Mikheil Saakashvili, who, after some brief flirtation with Europe during his first years in office, identified the United States as his main ally and model. More recently he has talked about turning Georgia into 'Switzerland with elements of Singapore'. What the two have in common is the idea that Georgia is not to be bound by its geographical location but can pursue its own individual political destiny with only passing reference to its neighbours.

Foreign officials have frequently expressed their frustrations at what they see as the suicidal tendencies of Caucasian politicians in times of crisis. Amidst the turbulence of the first republics, at the 1919 Paris peace conference, British Foreign Office official Robert Vansittart was vexed by the failure of the Caucasian politicians to unite: 'In the circles of the Supreme Council many are of the opinion that the Transcaucasian Republics have no future at all, as they are unable to achieve any sort of solidarity, and are exhausting themselves in conflicts with each other ... Is it not clear to you that the despatch of arms and munitions for you has been delayed precisely because of your divergences, because of the fear that these arms would be used in your conflicts with each other?' (Lang 1962, p. 221).

Yet Vansittart was being a little disingenuous. A servant of the British Empire, he knew only too well that there was an external dimension to the problems of the Caucasus. Its conflicts would have been much more liable to resolution but for the fact that Caucasian nations played the role of proxies in Great Power politics. This could be called the problem of 'asymmetrical security': small nations are unable to defend themselves against a determined invader with vastly greater manpower and that in turn means that they ally themselves with a rival Great Power to survive. That is how small communities such as Karabakh Armenians or Ossetians have got sucked into the major international rivalries of the day. To get involved means fighting a war, but to do nothing is to risk being destroyed.

There are some tragic illustrations of this unhealthy dynamic in Caucasian history. The Georgians learned this lesson in 1795 when their capital Tiflis was completely destroyed by a Persian army and they entered into union with tsarist Russia. Faced by the 50,000 men of Enver Pasha's Ottoman Third Army in 1918, the 70,000 men of the Bolshevik 11th Army in 1920—or indeed the Russian Army of 2008—you need a powerful defender and that will not be a neighbour, but a Great Power of equal ferocity. That could be the Russia of Catherine the Great, it could be NATO, but it will not be someone local. This is the dynamic by which the combination of local quarrels and Great Power politics pulls the Caucasus apart.

*Towards voluntary integration*

Given the frequent failures to unite and the darker pages of the Soviet era, it is tempting to say that regional integration in the South Caucasus is a utopian project best left alone. Soviet top-down integration imposed from outside eventually contained within itself the seeds of disintegration. Yet the experience of the past 20 years supports the argument that independence without inter-dependence is not a good option either. In 1991, for understandable reasons, Georgia, Armenia and Azerbaijan set out on different and distinct paths but it is now painfully clear that in doing so they created further problems. Despite all the terrible parts of its legacy, the Soviet Union bequeathed the South Caucasus an integrated transport and communications network and an educated elite speaking Russian as a *lingua franca*. By jettisoning this, the new leaders of Armenia, Azerbaijan and Georgia weakened their own statehood. In 2010, two decades after the end of the Soviet Union, Armenia and Georgia were still extremely poor countries, with Gross Domestic Product purchasing power parity (GDP PPP) *per capita* of only around $5,000, a pitifully long way behind Russia and Turkey, let alone the Baltic states. Azerbaijan's relatively better score of around $10,000 *per capita* reflects an influx of oil and gas revenues that have not benefited much of the population. In all three cases, the conflict and disorder of 1988–1994 still leaves a heavy legacy. With hindsight, it should be obvious that three small countries, with many overlapping interests, located in a small region surrounded by three larger neighbours, will gain a great deal if they can work on mutually beneficial regional projects.

Bleak though the picture is, in the early twenty-first century it is still much more favourable than it was a century ago. The 'Great Powers' are still inclined to clash in Georgia (although not so much in Armenia and Azerbaijan) but the age of mass invasion is over. Tragic though the August 2008 war and Russia's military intervention into Georgia were, the five-day conflict was, relatively speaking, a light skirmish compared to the kind of bloodshed the region saw in the years 1915–1921. South Ossetia itself suffered even more greatly in the war with the Mensheviks in 1920. The conflict also focused minds on what is and is not possible in the South Caucasus. Regional cooperation between Georgia and its neighbours has improved. Huge obstacles to successful integration remain, however the first of which is the unresolved Armenian–Azerbaijani conflict over Nagorno-Karabakh. All regional projects are carried out in the shadow of this dormant volcano and in the knowledge that if it were to re-erupt, it would devastate the whole region.

It is logical to see the European Union, the exemplar of 'soft power', as providing the impetus for successful integration that the other more old-fashioned 'Great Powers' with an interest in the South Caucasus cannot provide. Yet the EU continues to be a hesitant partner for the region. Consider the European Union's Transport Corridor Europe–Caucasus–Asia (TRASECA) project, launched in 1993 for the eight countries of Central Asia and the South Caucasus and which has spent less than €200 million since then—far less than BP, Gazprom or USAID has spent in the region, to name three other foreign actors. Certainly, the EU in and of itself represents a successful model of shared sovereignty and economic integration, but it is unrealistic to expect that it can extend that as far east as the South Caucasus. Even before the latest economic crisis to hit the European project, it was showing signs of 'enlargement fatigue'. Those countries with clear membership ambitions and an obvious European destiny, in the first instance Croatia and perhaps Serbia, may still manage to join the EU. The prospects for three countries bordering Russia and Iran, beset by poverty, conflict and corruption, are much bleaker and there is a fundamental question mark over whether the three actually aspire to be full parts of Europe. Even Georgia, which is the most self-consciously 'European' of the three has a distinctly ambiguous relationship with the EU economic model, as a powerful libertarian economic group still holds significant influence (de Waal 2011; European Stability Initiative, ESI 2010). Projects such as the Eastern Partnership program, promising better trade opportunities and visa facilitation with the EU, can have beneficial results for the region. But they are also premised on working with a region that is actively interested in adopting a European-style economic and political model. The semi-authoritarian leaders of the South Caucasus are at best ambiguous about this. This provides a sad contrast with the way that the Turkey of the *Adalet ve Kalkınma Partisi* (AKP, Justice and Development Party) has made reforms that have moved it towards Europe, even though its membership perspective is at best dim.

The most successful European project in the South Caucasus comes not from the EU but from the Council of Europe (CoE) in which all three countries are members, having joined almost simultaneously in 1999 and 2000. It is successful mostly because it is modest and nudges the three countries to behave better. It has set up the European Court of Human Rights as the final recourse for all citizens of these countries. Yet it is not a powerful instrument: Georgia has still not fulfilled its obligations on the return of Meskhetian Turks and Armenia and Azerbaijan have both held very flawed elections in defiance of the CoE. This suggests that Caucasian leaders are more comfortable with organisations that can provide expertise but do not require them to delegate power.

On the ground, ordinary people are even further away from this kind of European aspiration. The experience of the last 20 years shows that local people in the South Caucasus are interested in economic collaboration, but in a very idiosyncratic way, that would be anathema to the EU. Two wholesale markets on the borders of Georgia exposed reserves of popular grassroots diplomacy and mutual confidence that most Western non-governmental organisations could only dream of. The Ergneti market on the border of South Ossetia and Gori region brought together Georgians and Ossetians in daily trade until it was closed down by the Saakashvili government in 2004. It was so large that traders travelled from one end to another by motorcycle. The Sadakhlo market on the Georgia side of the Armenian–Georgian border saw thousands of Armenians and Azerbaijanis do thriving business in many products. Both of these markets showed that, in the right environment, ordinary people were ready to forget about political conflict and do business together. Unfortunately, as neither market was properly regulated or taxed, they were identified as criminal zones that were to be closed down for the sake of propping up state budgets. Government economics trumped cross-conflict confidence building. The underlying message here is that there are untapped resources of entrepreneurial cross-border energy in the South Caucasus. If they are interested in promoting prosperity, the task of domestic governments should be to channel this energy into more and more legitimate trade, rather than merely suppressing it.

*Conclusion*

For many reasons, the South Caucasus would benefit greatly from closer regional integration. If it were to function as a single organism, especially in economic terms, it would recover invaluable missed potential as a single market, communications hub and international crossroads. Closer integration would help overcome the region's chronic poverty and isolation and soothe majority–minority disputes.

Reaching that position is much harder, however. While pragmatic and cultural interests may cleave ordinary South Caucasian people together, shorter-term politics and security concerns—or, to put it in more everyday language, fear—generally drive them apart. The history of the South Caucasus can be seen as a battle between centripetal integrationist processes and centrifugal tendencies in which the latter are more powerful. Since the break-up of the Soviet Union, the most recent phase of fragmentation has been aided both by traditional Great Power rivalries, real and perceived, between Russia, the United States, Europe, Turkey and Iran, and by the persistence in a new post-Soviet guise of political and economic monopolies, backed up by powerful nationalist narratives which entrench difference.

This essay makes the case that efforts at Caucasian integration do, however, rest on underlying geographical, cultural and economic realities. Currently, persistent attempts at cooperation, as witnessed in the two markets of Ergneti and Sadakhlo cited above, continue in the private sphere, even as central governments spin hostile narratives against one another.

In the past, efforts at integration in the South Caucasus have either been driven from above or by contingencies of the day. They failed because they could not withstand a change in geopolitical fortunes. The late tsarist period began to see slow economic integration, with the building of railways and pipelines connecting the Black and Caspian Seas, but this was swept aside by an upsurge in revolutionary and nationalist politics. The independent Transcaucasian state of 1918 did not survive long enough for even its citizens to notice its existence and quickly fell victim to intra-Caucasian rivalries and contradictory attitudes to the Ottoman military advance.

The most successful example of Caucasian integration, that of the Soviet period, was more an instance of integration with Russia, accompanied by exclusion from the region's two other neighbours, Iran and Turkey—than cross-Caucasian partnership. The Bolsheviks had an economic vision for the region and did a great deal to tie it together; for all the brutality of their methods, accusations of them implementing a 'divide-and-rule' policy are not well founded. But the Bolshevik–Soviet system, against its own declared goals, preserved national difference. An irremediably authoritarian system, the Soviet Union failed to foster horizontal connection and civic identities strong enough to over-ride ethnic distinctions when turbulence again broke out in the 1980s.

However, just because integration has persistently failed in the South Caucasus, that in itself is not an argument that it cannot work again in the future, if it is embarked on in a different way that is more inclusive and attractive to ordinary people.

Although trade may be the future it is probably not the best place to start. Recent academic literature on regional integration suggests that it is unrealistic to expect that business and economics will drive reconciliation and union. In his extensive study of successful instances of conflict resolution Charles Kupchan writes that only one of the 20 case-studies he cites was driven by economic incentives. He writes of the 'causal *in*significance' of economic integration as a factor in peace processes, arguing however that, 'Economic integration does advance stable peace during later phases, when societal linkages serve to consolidate reconciliation and promote cooperation and trust' (Kupchan 2010, pp. 399–400, emphasis in original). In his analyses of the unions of Switzerland and the United Arab Emirates, two cases where economic motives might have been expected to play a leading role, Kupchan argues that other factors—strategic restraint, compatible social orders, cultural commonality—were more important in earlier stages of conflict resolution, with economics and trade playing a greater role later (Kupchan 2010, pp. 286–339).

In the case of the South Caucasus, this analysis confirms the impression that political difference continues to outweigh rational economic interest. That in turn leads to the (perhaps fairly self-evident) conclusion that Caucasian regional security needs to be addressed in the first instance before regional integration can be countenanced. So long as Armenia and Azerbaijan on the one hand and Georgia and the regions of Abkhazia and South Ossetia (supported by Russia) on the other live in a state of profound mutual insecurity, little can be done to advance a common regional interest. The region's persistent and chronic security problems pose a challenge to outside powers, who also stand to benefit from a South Caucasus that is integrated, stable and open for international business. To promote that goal, the bigger foreign powers are well advised to declare a truce in their geopolitical clashes (both perceived and real) in the region and promote the concept of a South Caucasus which, precisely because it is in no one's sphere of influence, is set free to rediscover its own internal unity and lost connections.

*Carnegie Endownent for International Peace*

## References

Beria, S. (2001) *My Father: Inside Stalin's Kremlin* (London, Duckworth).
Cornell, S., Jonsson, S., Nilsson, N. & Häggström, P. (2006) *The Wider Black Sea Region: An Emerging Hub in European Security*, Silk Road Paper (Washington, DC & Upssala, Central Asia-Caucasus Institute & Silk Road Studies).
de Waal, T. (2011) *Georgia's Choices: Charting a Future in Uncertain Times* (Washington, DC, Carnegie Endowment).
de Waal, T. (2010) *The Caucasus: An Introduction* (Oxford, Oxford University Press).
de Waal, T. (2003) *Black Garden: Armenia and Azerbaijan Through Peace and War* (New York, New York University Press).
European Stability Initiative (2010) *Reinventing Georgia: The Story of a Libertarian Revolution*, available at: http://www.esiweb.org/index.php?lang=en&id=322&debate_ID=3, accessed 29 August 2011.
Gornyi, V. (ed) (1992) *Natsional'nyi vopros na perekrestke mnenii* (Moscow, Nauka).
Harbord, J. (1920) *Conditions in the Near East: The American Military Mission to Armenia* (Washington, DC, Government Printing House).
Ismailov, E. & Papava, V. (2006) *The Central Caucasus: Essays on Geopolitical Economy* (Stockholm, CA&CC Press).
Knight, A. (1995) *Beria: Stalin's First Lieutenant* (Princeton, Princeton University Press).
Kupchan, C. (2010) *How Enemies Become Friends: The Sources of Stable Peace* (Princeton, Princeton University Press).
Lang, D. (1962) *A Modern History of Soviet Georgia* (New York, Grove Press).
Martin, T. (2001) *The Affirmative Action Empire* (Ithaca, Cornell University Press).
Namitok, A.M. (1955) 'The Caucasus', *Caucasian Review*, 1, pp. 5–11.
Rayfield, D. (2004) *Stalin and his Hangmen* (New York, Random House).
Rustambeili, Sh. (1935) 'Iz Pechal'nogo Proshlogo', *Kavkaz*, 7–8/19–20, July–August.
Saparov, A. (2010) 'From Conflict to Autonomy: The Making of the South Ossetian Autonomous Region 1918–1922', *Europe-Asia Studies*, 62, 1.
Strabo (1856) *The Geography of Strabo* Vol II [Translated by H. C. Hamilton and W. Falconer] (London, Henry G. Bohn), Book XI, Chapter 2, p. 226.
Suny, R. (1993) *The Revenge of the Past: Nationalism, Revolution and the Collapse of the Soviet Union* (Stanford, Stanford University Press).
Tishkov, V. (1997) *Ethnicity, Nationalism and Conflict in and after the Soviet Union: The Mind Aflame* (Oslo, Geneva & London, PRIO, UNRISD & Sage).
Yamskov, A. (1991) 'Ethnic Conflict in the Transcaucasus: The case of Nagorno-Karabakh', *Theory and Society*, 20, 5.
Zhordaniya, N. (1919) *Za dva goda: Doklady i rechi* (Tiflis).

# Re-thinking Citizenship in the South Caucasus

## LALE YALÇIN-HECKMANN

*Abstract*

This essay presents research results from a Max Planck Research Group project in which six researchers examined the three components of Marshall's concept of citizenship in Georgia, Armenia, Azerbaijan and Turkey. The essay compares these components with other approaches to citizenship, arguing that processes such as migration, the stricter enforcement of borders and the introduction of new global players and markets to the region allow citizenship concepts to be played against one another.

WHY RE-THINK CITIZENSHIP IN THE SOUTH CAUCASUS when the urgent and relevant issues seem to be ethno-nationalism and ethnic conflicts? What can one learn from looking at citizen–state relations in this region that goes beyond what one knows from histories of colonial regimes, contested territorial units and the multiplicity of ethnic, religious, linguistic and local identities? The region is, after all, 'known' for ethnic complexity, for conflicts which are mostly seen as being rooted in ancient animosities (Minogue & Williams 1992; Saroyan 1996; Swietochowski 1993). Furthermore, ethno-nationalism is often presented as playing a crucial role in the process of state building in the post-Soviet period (Suny 1993; Cornell 2001; Hille 2010). With such questions in mind, and in contrast to the conventional approaches to understanding the state and society in the region, this essay argues for focusing on the meanings and workings of citizenship, for examining citizenship beyond ethno-national principles and for studying it from below, that is, from the perspective of citizens themselves, through their lives and their interactions with one other and with the state. The arguments developed here challenge the predominance of the frameworks of conflictology and

Various versions of this essay were presented at conferences in Birmingham, Philadelphia and Berlin. I would like to thank the participants of all these meetings, as well as the anonymous reviewers of this essay, for their useful comments. The shortcomings remain, as usual, mine alone. The research results presented here reflect the work of the research group Caucasian Boundaries and Citizenship from Below at the Max Planck Institute for Social Anthropology in Halle/Saale, Germany. The researchers Milena Baghdasaryan, Florian Mühlfried, Teona Mataradze, H. Neşe Özgen and the author worked together between 2006 and 2009 and were later joined by Nino Aivazishvili. I would like to thank them all for allowing me to refer to their partly unpublished but forthcoming work, and the Max Planck Institute for generously supporting the research.

regional security and advocate an alternative approach to the study of citizenship in the three South Caucasian states by looking at how state–citizen relations are conceptualised and perceived, and how they are embedded in the everyday lives of ordinary people.

The ground for exploring state–citizen relations in everyday life has been well established in the anthropology of the state (Sharma & Gupta 2006; Das & Poole 2004) and the anthropology of politics (Vincent 2002), even if citizenship issues have been for the most part implicit in these studies. We believe the anthropology of the state and the anthropology of politics provide useful points of entry to understanding the changes and continuities of state–citizen relations in the South Caucasus, especially because there have been such major changes in the ways the state has been present or absent in people's lives since the fall of the Soviet Union.

Studying citizenship in the South Caucasus is somewhat of a novelty also from the perspective of citizenship studies in general. Citizenship is typically the subject of theoretical work about Western democracies, where the experience of extensive and long-term labour immigration and the influx of refugees of various kinds have been interpreted as a challenge to the notions of identity and belonging, nation-statehood and sovereignty (Taylor 1994; Soysal 1997; Kymlicka 2003). In most contemporary scholarly work, citizenship is associated with social movements and claiming rights.[1] Here we present a range of research results on citizenship in which there is no obvious and observable social movement for citizenship rights (cf. Sharma 2008); moreover, the predominantly rural and small-town setting that we have chosen to analyse in the South Caucasus has thus far not been examined with regard to citizenship regimes and politics. Hence in this aspect as well, we claim to break new ground for broadening citizenship studies thematically, contextually and, we hope, theoretically.

The analysis of citizenship is imperative primarily because of the emergence of new national and political systems of order, hence new citizenship and border regimes, as well as new patterns of mobility and migration in the South Caucasus following the breakup of the Soviet Union. Not only were ethno-national groups affected by these new regimes in the post-Soviet and post-Cold War era, but the lives of many individuals and groups who cannot necessarily be defined according to some ethno-national principle alone were also disrupted, such as petty traders and participants in informal economies active in their own countries or as migrants. Moreover, the analysis of social inequality and poverty, which are exacerbated in post-war and post-socialist settings (Pine & Bridger 1998; Dudwick *et al.* 2003; Babajanian 2008), also demands a different framework for understanding state–citizen relations. We need to look particularly at how citizens cope with these new inequalities, which can cause problems even for citizens who culturally, ethnically and in terms of nationality belong to the present independent states of the region and may even belong to the ethnic majority.

Citizenship has been a much discussed concept in the social sciences in general. One of the classics in this field is T. H. Marshall's (1950) account of how citizenship developed

---

[1] See for instance the works on citizenship and urban movements (Holston 1999), civil society organisations (Hann & Dunn 1996), transnational processes of European extension (Ruegg 2006) and globalisation (Ong 1999).

out of a popular demand for civil, political and social rights in Western Europe. In this work, Marshall discussed three components of citizenship: the civil component was related to the achievement of individual freedoms and referred to such elements as freedom of speech, the right to own property and the right to justice. The political component entailed the rights necessary to participate in the exercise of political power, in particular the rights to free elections and a secret ballot (Marshall 1998). Marshall's final and most famous component of social citizenship has the following—and for many of us anthropologists, frustratingly evasive—definition: 'the whole range from the right to a modicum of economic welfare and security to the right to share to the full in the social heritage and to live the life of a civilized being according to the standards prevailing in the society' (Marshall 1998, p. 69).[2] These components were developed in a certain historical context, and they have been much criticised since then (Turner 2001; Bulmer & Rees 1996; Joppke 2007). Bryan Turner, for instance, argues that Marshall's paradigm offers a historically specific and evolutionary explanation for the emergence of these components; the evolution of the three components corresponds to the institutional development and differentiation in Western democracies in the form of 'the courts of justice, parliament and councils of local government, and the educational system and the social services' (Turner 2001, p. 190). Turner maintains that Marshall's evolutionist approach cannot provide 'an effective analysis of the causal mechanisms that produced an expansion of citizenship' (Turner 2001, p. 190),[3] in part because it treats citizenship as a uniform concept. Although Marshall's model cannot explain post-Marshallian historical developments and struggles which produced and still produce active citizens,[4] his initial model of citizenship with these components has become a global paradigm, the traces of which can be found in many states around the world. Even if we agree with the critique that Marshall's paradigm fails to take into consideration the regional, cultural, racial and ethnic divisions that societies might have, which admittedly do not fit neatly into Marshall's hypothetical model of heterogeneity based on social class (Turner 2001, p. 190), we still have many reasons to believe that issues of social class, of social inequality, of losers and winners and of new regimes of inclusion and exclusion need to be reconsidered, especially in the region of the South Caucasus. This is the main reason for reassessing the relevance of Marshall's categories in our research. Other researchers studying post-socialist forms of citizenship in the former Soviet Union discuss state–citizen relations in the Soviet and socialist model, as

---

[2]Marshall does somewhat specify and elaborate the idea of the 'civilized life' when he focuses on the development of social welfare in the twentieth century and the state-guaranteed minimum: '[T]here is a general enrichment of the concrete substance of civilised life, a general reduction of risk and insecurity, an equalization between the more and the less fortunate at all levels' (Marshall 1998, p. 108). He remains critical, however, concerning the debate about what the 'guaranteed minimum' should be, and asks 'whether ... there are natural limits to the contemporary drive towards greater social and economic equality' (Marshall 1998, p. 108).

[3]Turner points to the differences between the American and British debates concerning the growth of social rights and notes that different cultural issues were involved, as well as 'unintended consequences of modern warfare', i.e. that war, in addition to strengthening market forces, stimulated a national self-critique that led to calls for social change and equality, especially in Britain (Turner 2001, p. 191).

[4]Especially, as Turner (2001, p. 190) indicates, those instances in which transnational processes demand that citizens interact not only with their own states in a passive way, but take action beyond the states in which they happen to be living.

well as in the current era under the influence of global forces, from the perspective of Marshall's concept of social citizenship (Rasell 2010; Thelen *et al.* 2011). As I shall illustrate in this essay, the emerging practices of citizenship in the South Caucasus are deeply embedded in these new states' struggles for independence and autonomy, which have produced military conflicts, wars, ethnic cleansing, waves of refugees and internally displaced persons; but they are also deeply and simultaneously embedded in the social and economic inequalities of the transition period. We argue that these processes and their entanglement with one another can be best analysed through Marshall's citizenship model. We differentiate between the three components and explore the contextual and strategic highlighting of one component over the other by various social actors. We challenge Turner's proposition (2001) that social citizenship has been eroded,[5] and suggest instead that social citizenship is one of the principle means through which citizens encounter the state, actively practice their citizenship rights, and claim entitlements for having been worker-citizens of the former Soviet state. Recognising the rootedness of 'statehood' and notions of the procuring state in both the historical and current periods in the region, we work with Marshall's traditional components, expanding them when necessary to enter into a dialogue with more recent concepts of citizenship, such as cultural and transnational citizenship, and processes of inclusion and exclusion. Finally, we explore how the ordinary residents of the newly independent states of the South Caucasus define, signify and practice citizenship.

## *The research and findings*

What kinds of issues, therefore, have we examined? In which areas of social, political and economic life have we explored local people's notions of and interactions with the state, citizenship and citizenship rights? The Caucasus Research Group in Halle took up the following issues, all of which were significant and observable themes in the research localities: first, forced migrants (refugees and internally displaced persons) and their citizenship practices in relation to legislation and different levels of the state, and *vis-à-vis* international organisations; second, the memories and practices of the former Soviet state, as well as more *longue durée* cultural and historical notions of citizenship and their effect on contemporary notions and practices of citizenship; third, the effect of labour migration on the locality and population that the migrants leave behind, and how this migration impacts and interacts with citizenship regimes; fourth, the effects of new borders, new border regimes and new border economies on notions and practices of citizenship; and fifth, the interaction between the different components of citizenship (i.e. social, political, civil and cultural), especially under

---

[5]In an inaugural lecture at the University of Cambridge in 2000 (subsequently published in the *British Journal of Sociology*—see Turner 2001), Bryan Turner argues that the Marshallian paradigm of social citizenship has been eroded 'because the social and economic conditions that supported postwar British welfare consensus have been transformed by economic and technological change' (2001, p. 189). Turner argues that economic and technological changes have deeply affected the social identity of citizens, whom in the past could be classified as 'worker-citizens, warrior-citizens and parent-citizens' (Turner 2001, p. 189). These identities are no longer the basis for claiming rights from the state because technological and economic changes have also changed the character of rights, such that it is now more appropriate to talk of environmental, aboriginal and cultural citizenship principles.

the present conditions of changing social support policies and market-economic processes.

The projects were located in Georgia (two researchers), Armenia (one researcher), Turkey (one researcher) and Azerbaijan (two researchers). The principal findings are summarised below.

*Integration of refugees in Armenia*

One of the main issues shaping citizenship regimes in the region emerges from the histories and processes of war and ethnic cleansing, which turned thousands of people into refugees and internally displaced persons. Milena Baghdasaryan's research on Armenian refugees from Azerbaijan shows that after forced migration from Azerbaijan during the Karabakh conflict (1988–1994), many refugees settled in Armenia, but their political and economic situation is still far from well-integrated into Armenian society. Baghdasaryan has been working with a particularly disadvantaged group of refugees, those who have been for the most part living in refugee 'spaces' since the time of their arrival in Armenia (i.e. in dormitories and buildings given to or taken over by refugees at the time of their arrival, or in small housing units built with the help of such international refugee organisations as the United Nations High Commissioner for Refugees (UNHCR)). Many of these refugees suffer from acute financial problems and have difficulties integrating into the labour market and gaining access to proper housing. Baghdasaryan examines the reasons for these disadvantaged life trajectories and seeks to explain her informants' relative success or lack thereof in coping with being a refugee and living in a transition economy. More specifically, she looks at the patterns of political and legal integration of different groups of these refugees, for example, those who have become naturalised citizens and those who have chosen to forego naturalisation in order to maintain their refugee status.

Baghdasaryan's findings highlight the process of 'becoming local' despite still being refugees after nearly two decades. This anomaly and incongruence in categories, governmental technologies and social practices is represented in how people define their various attachments to the former state of which they were subjects (i.e. the Soviet Union and the Azerbaijan Soviet Socialist Republic); how they selectively remember and reconstruct the state and their own citizenship practices; and how laws and legislation, political ideologies and housing policies interact with the present-day concepts and practices of being 'national citizens' while at the same time being 'excluded from political citizenship' because of their refugee status.

Not all of the Armenian refugees from Azerbaijan stayed in Armenia; many chose to migrate further, primarily to Russia. Access to family networks, cultural capital, jobs and property in Armenia seems to be a primary factor in determining whether this double migration will occur or not. Considering the significance of out-migration from Armenia in general, Baghdasaryan cautiously concludes that choosing formal citizenship is a different matter from engaging in expressions of cultural citizenship and national belonging. While the refugee Armenians she has been working with believe on the whole that Armenia as a country and as a state is the ultimate homeland for all Armenians, especially after having been expelled from another location that they considered their homeland, many nevertheless out-migrated to Russia, especially during the 1990s, and chose to become citizens of the Russian Federation. Baghdasaryan's material, therefore, suggests that even at times of heightened nationalist feelings and discourses (Dudwick 1994; Platz 2000) and post-war traumas of displacement and loss, political citizenship, which determines legal belonging to a particular state, can be detached from feelings of national belonging if the conditions for social citizenship are such that a different country appears to be a better alternative than the national homeland.

*Restricted mobility in the Georgian highlands*

New border regimes and differentiated memories of belonging and transborder movement have been central to Florian Mühlfried's study. He explores the meaning of citizenship for the Tushetians, a transhumant ethnic group traditionally settled in the Georgian highlands bordering Chechnya and Dagestan, and asks 'how memories of the programmatically anti-bourgeois Soviet state shape or ... compete with present-day notions and practices of citizenship' (Mühlfried 2010, p. 94). In order to go beyond the standard notions of citizenship expressed in political, historical and social terms, Mühlfried used pile-sorting and ranking methods and applied a cognitive analysis to interpret these data in an explorative way. One of his findings, for example, is that 'women tend to sympathize with the "caring state", while men feel somewhat more attracted to centralized political authority' (Mühlfried 2010, p. 104–5). Mühlfried's most significant finding, however, pertains to his insight that 'belonging' and 'entitlement' are two crucial and contrasting concepts of citizenship among the Tushetians. The notion of entitlement is, as in other projects of the research group, strongly historically embedded in the Soviet notion of the strong, supportive and patronising state. Mühlfried uses additional quantitative data to discuss the distinction made by respondents between the current nation-state and citizenship within it:

> Whereas the first is almost universally appreciated and preferred to the Soviet Union, present-day citizenship is generally dismissed as being inferior to Soviet citizenship. A crucial criterion for this differentiation is freedom, which is conceptualised in two ways: on the one hand, freedom refers to the nation and denotes its independence and statehood. On the other hand, freedom translates as mobility, which is considered to be limited by the boundaries of the contemporary nation-state (Mühlfried 2010, p. 94).

Mobility is crucial to the transhumance of Tushetians and to the different symbolic, historical and social meanings Tushetians attach to lowlands and highlands. With this mobile lifestyle and settlement pattern, Tushetians see the state as enabling or restricting their freedom and evaluate the citizenship regimes accordingly. The Tushetians have had a relatively high degree of autonomy in organising their daily local administrative issues and cultivated a special and historical self-understanding as 'the guards of the border' under the socialist regime. They were able to draw extra benefits from this status, such as a degree of control over border trade and the freedom to pasture their herds on either side of the border, as well as the authority to conduct local-level 'diplomatic' relations and resolve conflicts with similar border-zone administrative bodies in Dagestan. With the change of the border regimes, Tushetians lost this limited yet locally significant flexibility in managing their own political and economic interests across the border. Now their 'freedom' of movement is managed by the closer political centre, Tbilisi, rather than by the more distant former power centre in Moscow, leading to a differentiated understanding of citizenships that either close borders and prevent mobility or open up borders and allow freedom of movement across them (Mühlfried 2011; Yalçın-Heckmann 2007).

### *The challenge of out-migration to citizenship in Georgia*

Out-migration is a dominant theme and issue throughout the South Caucasus. How those who remain behind cope with the positive and negative effects of the absence of family members and how the migration process interacts with the citizenship practices of the remaining family members are topics that have been taken up by Teona Mataradze. She explores citizenship practices in a rural settlement with a high incidence of out-migration in western Georgia. This particular region was highly dependent on state-subsidised coal operations and tea plantations. Both industries were in decline in the late socialist period and were dissolved, privatised or downsized in the post-socialist period. Apart from those working in agriculture and the few remaining state and health resort jobs, the inhabitants are oriented towards out-migration.[6] Even if through remittances migrants manage to support their families left behind and perform the role of the state (in terms of social provisioning), financial support and the prestige gained through it nevertheless do not completely compensate for the symbolic loss felt by families that are left without the male head of the household or the wife and mother (Shakhnazarian 2005).

Apart from supporting the family and covering basic costs, remittances are used to invest in the education of the family's children. Mataradze found that most of those who manage to go on to higher education come from families with migrant parents. Remittances are not used to change the overall economic structure of the village; they are enough to sustain families in the rural locality, but when they become more substantial, the investment is in education and/or flats in the urban centres, not in job-creating sectors. Hence, while the state has been withdrawing from its commitment to guarantee equal access to higher education, thereby restricting the social citizenship of members of non-migrating households, at the same time it could be said that the state profits from remittances because the social citizenship deficiencies are alleviated through the remittances of migrants.

Mataradze was able to observe the insecurity of migrants' lives as well. She witnessed several cases of deportation of labour migrants back to Georgia during the diplomatic crisis between Russia and Georgia in 2007. Her discussions with the deported and their families illustrate how vulnerable labour migrants with Georgian citizenship are in Russia, and how the passport and visa regimes limit their possibilities and force them to be creative in subverting bureaucratic and diplomatic regulations. Nevertheless, all of these efforts and strategies are carried

---

[6]A total of 17% of the surveyed households had at least one migrant abroad, and 10% of the households had a migrant within Georgia, mostly in the capital city, Tbilisi.

out on an individual basis, and Georgian citizenship is not necessarily activated in people's search for citizenship rights, legal protection or in an effective remediation of the unjust economic situation. Hence migrants' experiences do not necessarily act as a corrective to the deficiencies of political and legal aspects of Georgian citizenship.

While the rural Georgians Mataradze has been working with have a strong inclination to out-migrate and cope with the economic difficulties of the transition to a market economy by becoming 'absent citizens', for those remaining behind social support expected from the state continues to be central to their practice of social citizenship. When a programme for poverty reduction was being implemented during her stay in her field site, Mataradze (2011) observed how the state-determined criteria for identifying 'the poor'—i.e. those eligible for various kinds of financial and social assistance—were challenged by local people's notions of poverty, social equality and deservingness. At the local level, many people feel entitled to state assistance not because they are poor, but because they have worked for the state. Here we see how Turner's (2001) idea of claiming social citizenship on the basis of being worker-citizens (in this case, having been state-worker citizens) is still valid here. David Kideckel (2009, p. 119) also focuses on the process of claiming citizenship rights and observes that in some post-socialist societies such as Romania, rights are claimed on the basis of grievances: 'Citizens see themselves as supplicants to and claimant groups are often pitted against each other. The demands grievants present are less rights people are likely to achieve than claims they will probably be denied. Similarly, grievance-based citizens are organizationally alienated and shy from participation in local groups, though they often address their concerns to international organizations'. Kideckel finds the roots of this grievance-based citizenship in the historical command–obey type of Romanian statehood, which he argues has been further strengthened through socialism: 'The net effect of these [rights-claiming] actions produced an angry citizenry, alienated from the state, atomized, and protective of individual interests' (Kideckel 2009, p. 119). Even if Mataradze's rural Georgians can be characterised as having had a similar command–obey and alienated kind of relationship with the state and powerful authorities representing the state, they nevertheless seem less atomised in this rural community. This may be because they are more concerned with comparing their own fate with that of others in their immediate social surroundings and define social justice and equality through comparison with their neighbours. In this way, they maintain their notion of community by emphasising shared notions of equality and justice. Social citizenship for them is something rooted in the locality and community, not to be dictated from above by using some international scientific criteria and techniques for judging the 'poor'.[7] They consider themselves to be not the 'in need' poor but the 'deserving' poor, having earned support through former work for the state. Mataradze's material therefore suggests a fine nuance to Kideckel's 'grievance-based citizenship', since the grievance is not only or primarily due to some historical-cultural mind-set, but rather is based on challenging the

---

[7]See also Mataradze (2011).

present by claiming one's history of work and entitlements and acknowledging the social justice of the past.

### *Transcending nationalism in the Turkish–Georgian–Armenian border region*

With the end of the Soviet Union, the South Caucasian region border regimes have developed in contradictory ways. On the one hand, the Iron Curtain between Turkey and the former Soviet Union has fallen, and the Turkish–Georgian border and border region have been fundamentally transformed (Hann & Bellér-Hann 1998; Pelkmans 2006). On the other hand, further to the south, the Turkish–Armenian border is still officially closed due to the post-Karabakh war diplomacy, whereby Turkey supports Azerbaijan's claims for the return of occupied territories. Such changes in border regimes and their consequences are tackled by Neşe Özgen, who has been looking at changes in property and citizenship regimes in the border region where Georgia, Turkey and Armenia meet. This is a complex area in terms of depopulation and re-population, and ownership, use, claiming and expropriating of land, processes which have been going on for at least two centuries. The border was tightly guarded and closed during the Soviet period, and after the dissolution of the Soviet Union, the area came under the influence of new relationships and new patterns of movement of goods and people.

Özgen argues that on the Turkish side of the Iron Curtain, the local border communities had built up an image of themselves as 'protecting democracy and the West' from the Soviet Bloc. This image can no longer be maintained, and the residents have to justify their cultural belonging in a different way, beyond the simple formula of being 'patriotic border keepers'. Özgen found that such rewriting and renegotiating of belonging and discourses of being 'good citizens' also involve reclaiming and rewriting the history of land and power in the region. The new Baku–Tbilisi–Ceyhan oil pipeline going through the region opens new possibilities of evaluating land and claiming it as property by invoking citizenship entitlements. Özgen, using historical narratives, draws attention to how families of renown and power were able to use their citizenship as a privilege. They were able to bargain with the state during the Iron Curtain years, but now their power needs to be re-established through the strategic use of legislation and governmental technologies, especially for enforcing land registries. Land and land rights had been relatively unimportant until recently, and the poor soil and severe climate had led to out-migration, leaving migrants' remittances and state employees' salaries in the border towns of Kars and Ağrı as the primary sources of income. With the fall of the Iron Curtain and the construction of the pipeline, new strategies and discourses for accessing wealth have come to the fore, no longer based simply on national citizenship but on principles of global governmentality, rights and entitlements. The citizens on the Turkish side of the border have not been subjected to any formal change of citizenship regime; however, changes in border regimes coupled with the region's stronger integration into global economies have nevertheless upset existing political orders, where nationalist rhetoric is no longer the dominant or sufficient discourse for claiming citizenship rights. Nationalist claims to land and territory continue to occupy political imaginations, particularly of those with right-wing tendencies; nevertheless, international human rights and neoliberal good governance discourses have started offering alternative discursive spaces for claiming legitimate citizenship rights.[8]

*Caught between cultural and political citizenship in the Azerbaijan–Georgia borderlands*

Borders are contested, and not only along the former border between the non-socialist and socialist regimes of Turkey and the former Soviet Union. The presence of borders in people's everyday lives and their contestation in determining citizenship and belonging is a central theme in Nino Aivazishvili's research. Her preliminary findings illustrate what living on the border in a South Caucasus post-socialist country might mean nowadays: her research site lies in north-western Azerbaijan, on the border with Georgia. Although the village is only 15 km from the actual border and there is a road that crosses the border, it is not in fact possible to cross the border there as it is not an official border post. Local people remember that the border was barely noticeable during the Soviet period; they used the bridge and a simple river boat to travel back and forth between Georgia and Azerbaijan. Georgians came to the Azerbaijani border villages to sell maize and wheat, and to buy walnuts; from the Azerbaijani side, the ethnic Ingiloy, with whom Aivazishvili works, would go to the Georgian side for jobs on *kolkhozy* (collective farms) or construction projects because the pay there was better. This flexibility of the border regime does not exist anymore; the Ingiloy feel on the one hand encapsulated within Azerbaijan (similar to the way the Tushetians studied by Mühlfried feel enclosed within Georgia), as they have less freedom to travel to Georgia and have to acquire new passports for longer trips (Yalçın-Heckmann & Aivazishvili 2011). On the other hand, there are some efforts to maintain ethnic identity and language (Ingiloy speak a dialect of Georgian) by using the official Azerbaijani discourse of a multi-cultural Azerbaijani state (Orudzhev 2003). Ingiloy ethnic leaders play a delicate game of stressing their loyalty towards the Azerbaijani state (by, for instance, attending public ceremonies to commemorate former President Heydar Aliyev, similar to the ceremonies held in all other parts of Azerbaijan), but at the same time seeking special ethnic and cultural rights as minority citizens. They also justify maintaining religious contacts with the Georgian Church by stressing their mediatory role and 'bridge function' between the states of Georgia and Azerbaijan. Overall, compared to Soviet times, the cultural component of their citizenship seems to have become more of a liability for them, as they are perhaps more often reminded of the 'religious divide' between the Georgian-speaking Muslim and Christian

---

[8] The contested public space of claiming land, territory and history in this border region was very present in the Turkish media in September 2010. On 19 September, a religious ceremony, led by the Armenian Church in Turkey, was held in the ancient restored Armenian Church on the island of Ahtamar in the province of Van (see www.radikal.com.tr, 19 September 2010, accessed 19 September 2010). This was seen in general as a step towards reconciliation with Turkey's Armenian history. In response, the Turkish right-wing Nationalist Movement Party (*Milliyetçi Hareket Partisi*) declared a week after this much-publicised ceremony that it intended to commemorate the arrival of Seljuk Turks and their conquest of Anatolia by holding Muslim prayer ceremonies on Friday 1 October in the ruins of the ancient Ani Armenian monastery complex in the border province of Kars (see: www.radikal.com.tr, 28 September 2010, accessed 28 September 2010). Land continues to be territory, hence historically contextualised and contested (see also Yalçın-Heckmann *et al.* 2003).

populations in this region. Their cultural distinctiveness is articulated in secretive everyday strategies by ordinary Ingiloy, who talk about 'our language' and 'our people' (in Georgian *chveneburebi*) as being distinct from both the ethnic Azerbaijanis and the Christian Georgians across the border. One can conclude that the new citizenship regime encloses the Ingiloy even more than before and forces them to reckon with the political implications of their daily activities, of spoken languages and public or private rituals, hence raising the significance of the 'cultural' for them above 'political'.

### *The trials and tribulations of petty traders in an Azerbaijani border town*

While in the past the Ingiloy travelled to and from Soviet Georgia to take advantage of labour markets and better prices for consumer goods, today internationally produced goods are available in most of the big cities of the region. Ironically, however, people seem to have been economically more mobile during the socialist period than in the present-day free-market economy era. As my own research in a small town in western Azerbaijan shows, goods and traders are not moving in accordance with the market economic logic of reducing costs and optimising benefits. I have been studying transactions and the economic behaviour of traders and small businessmen in local markets in different districts of western Azerbaijan. Traders from the small town of Ağstafa, for instance, even though they live on the Georgian border only 50 km from Tbilisi, the capital of Georgia, are compelled to travel to the wholesale market in Baku, some 450 km away, to buy goods and bring them back to the border town to sell in the local market. This is, obviously, following not the logic of economics, but the logic of new citizenship regimes coupled with the flow of international products to the region; in other words, new passports, travel documents (Pelkmans forthcoming) and neoliberal production and consumption networks determine livelihood strategies.[9] Tbilisi is close but inaccessible for petty traders; it is the centre where many Western consumer goods arrive, but it is commonly believed that the trade in these goods is controlled by monopolistic trader clans and networks. Because of this, small traders cannot simply go and buy goods in Tbilisi; rather they must go to the wholesale market in Baku.[10]

---

[9] For a similar discussion of difficulties in border crossing for social and economic reasons between two other post-Soviet states, see Reeves (2007). Reeves (2009) further explores post-socialist border regimes and discusses the impact on states of representational politics for managing border regimes in Central Asia, particularly between Tajikistan and Kyrgyzstan, where the states' territoriality, ethnicity and sovereignty are constructed and implemented differently at different scales of the polity and society.

[10] See the report by Radio Free Europe's broadcasting station in Azerbaijani, 'Ucuz pazarlıq üçün Gürcüstana', *Azadlıq Radiosu*, 20 May 2010, available at: www.azadliq.org/content/article/2048090.html, accessed 20 May 2010). The reporter observes that Azerbaijani citizens from Ağstafa go to the bazaar in Tbilisi in order to buy cheaper products, but when they want to bring them across the border the Azerbaijani customs officers do not allow the goods in. The reporter notes that this does not necessarily follow any Azerbaijani customs laws, but rather is a practice aimed at protecting internal trade monopolies. Similar arbitrary practices seem to rule in the southern Azerbaijani—Iranian border town of Astara as well (see 'Verilişlr, "Kişmiş, hurma monopoliyası"', *Azadlıq Radiosu*, 5 September 2011, available at: http://www.azadliq.org/content/article/24317946.html, accessed 5 September 2011).

The economic activities of petty traders and small businessmen and women in this part of the country create the link to economic citizenship, a central theme of my ongoing research. Anthony Woodiwiss, in his overview of how economic rights, which have been 'basic and central to the development of citizenship' (2008, p. 53), are threatened through globalisation, focuses on labour rights in post-national and post-colonial countries to illustrate how economic citizenship varies greatly. My take on economic citizenship starts from the other end of the argument: what happens to people's economic citizenship when they do not have any secure employment at all and are not covered by legally guaranteed and bargained for labour contracts, as is the case in many transition countries and neoliberal economies of the margins?[11] As many of the former employees of the socialist system in Azerbaijan are now 'self-employed' in petty trade or in small businesses, one needs to explore how this new economy and trade 'cascade' not only into the realm of mutuality, as Stephen Gudeman argues,[12] but also into the practices of economic citizenship. Where and how do men and women in this economy, and practicing these economic activities, define the space of the state and engage with it as citizens? How do they compare their economic citizenship to that of the Soviet period?

Similar to Mataradze's rural Georgians, Azerbaijani petty traders and small businesspeople remember the Soviet state as protecting them and providing work, even if they also remember that work was not only offered but also assigned, and hence compulsory. Many of the traders of the contemporary era engage in their trading activities out of necessity—they do not have secure government employment and are not able to manage financially otherwise. But beyond this point, the degree to which they are able to exercise freely their economic right to open up a business and have a realistic prospect of developing their economic activities depends on their connections and political networks as much as it depends on having the necessary capital, skills and knowledge to run a business. This is where I argue that the trader-citizen perceives the state, personified as 'those in power' (in Azerbaijani, *hakimiyyettekiler*), as controlling scales of trade and access to certain goods and markets.[13] Trader-citizens learn about their own as well as others' economic 'rights' within this framework, and can either choose not to challenge the monopolies and expand their businesses by seeking protection from power holders at the top, or opt for out-migration and become 'absent citizens'.

*Conclusion*

We conclude that our findings and ongoing work contribute to the overall theory and debates on citizenship in the following ways: many recent works, including some from anthropologists on citizenship issues, have asserted the erosion of social citizenship (Turner 2001; Isin & Turner 2008a). Others argue that new varieties of citizenship,

[11] See Ong (1999); Kideckel (2009).

[12] Here I am using Stephen Gudeman's concept of trade cascading into the 'realm of mutuality' (of social relations, which he also calls 'the base'), which 'embodies values, such as equity, equality, age, gender, position and merit' (Gudeman 2008, p. 14), and to which I add kinship solidarity and familism.

[13] This is what Mitchell (1991) has called the 'state-effect'. As a petty trader in the bazaar in Ağstafa commented in our conversation, 'Azerbaijan is probably the only state in the world with a monopoly over trade in bananas!' (author's field notes).

such as transnational, post-national, denationalised, multicultural, flexible and biological citizenship, have become more relevant than the traditional model of nation-state citizenship. These developments are attributed to global processes of migration, multicultural movements, global human rights discourses and neoliberal economic and political processes. Yet other authors, such as Christian Joppke (2007) and Ayşe Çağlar (2004), suggest that the self-value of citizenship in Western societies is diminishing, and that it would be more appropriate to talk about 'citizenship light'. We believe that our findings counter these arguments to a considerable degree; citizenship as a general category of formal belonging, with its political and economic implications, plays a crucial role in people's lives in the South Caucasus. More important is the differentiation between different components of citizenship in the classic Marshallian terms: social citizenship is taken seriously in terms of entitlements from a withdrawing state. Historical concepts of citizenship are strongest when this social aspect of citizenship is evoked, less so when the civil aspect of citizenship is at stake. Even ethnic belonging can be seen as succumbing to social citizenship when the actors prefer to out-migrate and consent to insecure or non-existent political citizenship as a trade-off for some degree of economic security in better-off countries. Freedom of movement has become a criterion for differentiating and judging between the national state and the social state, and between political citizenship and social citizenship.

Hence, we argue that different aspects of citizenship can be differentiated from one another and selectively activated; which aspect of citizenship takes precedence in a given situation depends on historical experiences and contemporary economic and political issues. It is therefore crucial that the traditional understanding of citizenship as outlined by Marshall not simply be dismissed as irrelevant in modern global times; rather, it needs to be empirically studied, re-evaluated and re-thought, drawing as much as possible from the insights of the anthropology of the state. After all, what we do as anthropologists is examine not only changing notions and practices of citizenship from below, but also evolving notions and practices of the state, and the ever-changing relationship between the state and its citizens.

*University of Pardubice*

*References*

Babajanian, B. (2008) 'Social Welfare in Post-Soviet Armenia: From Socialist to Liberal and Informal?', *Post-Soviet Affairs*, 24, 4, pp. 383–404.

Bulmer, M. & Rees, A. M. (eds) (1996) *Citizenship Today: The Contemporary Relevance of T.H. Marshall* (London, University College London Press).

Çağlar, A. (2004) '"Citizenship Light": Transnational Ties, Multiple Rules of Membership, and the "Pink Card"', in Friedman, J. & Randeria, S. (eds) (2004) *Worlds on the Move: Globalization, Migration, and Cultural Security* (London, Tauris).

Cornell, S. E. (2001) *Small Nations and Great Powers: A Study of Ethnopolitical Conflict in the Caucasus* (Richmond, Curzon).

Das, V. & Poole, D. (2004) 'State and Its Margins: Comparative Ethnographies', in Das, V. & Poole, D. (eds) (2004) *Anthropology in the Margins of the State* (Oxford, James Currey).

Dudwick, N. (1994) *Memory, Identity and Politics in Armenia*, Unpublished PhD Dissertation (Ann Arbor, University of Michigan).

Dudwick, N., Gomart, E., Marc, A. & Kuehnast, K. (eds) (2003) *When Things Fall Apart: Qualitative Studies of Poverty in the Former Soviet Union* (Washington, DC, The World Bank).
Gudeman, S. (2008) *Economy's Tension: The Dialectics of Community and Market* (New York & Oxford, Berghahn).
Hann, C. & Dunn, E. (eds) (1996) *Civil Society: Challenging Western Models* (London, Routledge).
Hann, C. & Bellér-Hann, I. (1998) 'Markets, Morality and Modernity in North-East Turkey', in Wilson, T. M. & Donnan, H. (eds) (1998) *Border Identities: Nation and State at International Frontiers* (Cambridge, Cambridge University Press).
Holston, J. (ed.) (1999) *Cities and Citizenship* (Durham, NC, Duke University Press).
Hille, C. (2010) *State Building and Conflict Resolution in the Caucasus* (Leiden & Boston, Brill: Eurasian Studies Library).
Isin, E. F. & Turner, B. S. (2008a) 'Citizenship Studies: An introduction', in Isin, E. F. & Turner, B.S. (eds) (2008b).
Isin, E. F. & Turner, B. S. (eds) (2008b) *Handbook of Citizenship Studies* (Los Angeles & London, Sage Books).
Joppke, C. (2007) 'Transformation of Citizenship: Status, Rights, Identity', *Citizenship Studies*, 11, 1.
Kideckel, D. (2009) 'Citizenship Discourse, Globalization, and Protest: A Postsocialist–Postcolonial Comparison', *Anthropology of East Europe Review*, 27, 2.
Kymlicka, W. (2003) *Multicultural Citizenship: A Liberal Theory of Minority Rights* (Oxford, Clarendon Press).
Marshall, T. H. (1950) *Citizenship and Social Class and Other Essays* (Cambridge, University of Cambridge Press).
Marshall, T. H. (1964) *Class, Citizenship and Social Development* (London, Heinemann).
Marshall, T. H. (1998) 'Citizenship and Social Class', in Shafir, G. (ed.) (1998) *The Citizenship Debates: A Reader* (Minneapolis & London, University of Minnesota Press).
Mataradze, T. (2011) 'Is the State Social or the Computer Inhuman? Claims for State Support and Citizenship in Post-socialist Georgia', *Citizenship Studies*, 15, 3–4, June.
Minogue, K. & Williams, B. (1992) 'Ethnic Conflict in the Soviet Union: The Revenge of Particularism', in Motyl, A.J. (ed.) (1992) *Thinking Theoretically about Soviet Nationalities: History and Comparison in the Study of the USSR* (New York, Columbia University Press).
Mitchell, T. (1991) 'The Limits of the State: Beyond Statist Approaches and their Critiques', *The American Political Science Review*, 85, 1, March.
Mühlfried, F. (2010) *Being a State and States of Being*, Unpublished Habilitation thesis (Halle-Wittenberg, Martin-Luther University).
Mühlfried, F. (2011) 'Citizenship Gone Wrong', *Citizenship Studies*, 15, 3–4, June.
Ong, A. (1999) *Flexible Citizenship: The Cultural Logics of Transnationality* (Durham, NC, Duke University Press).
Orudzhev, G. (2003) 'Azerbaijan's National Minorities Today', *Central Asia and the Caucasus*, 4, 22.
Pelkmans, M. (2006) *Defending the Border: Identity, Religion, and Modernity in the Republic of Georgia* (Ithaca, Cornell University Press).
Pelkmans, M. (forthcoming) 'Powerful Documents: Passports, Passages, and Dilemmas of Identification on the Georgian-Turkish Border', in Bacas, J. L. & Kavanagh, W. (eds) (forthcoming) *Asymmetry and Proximity in Border Encounters* (Oxford, Berghahn).
Pine, F. & Bridger, S. (eds) (1998) *Surviving Postsocialism: Local Strategies and Regional Responses in Postsocialist Europe and the Former Soviet Union* (New York, Routledge).
Platz, S. (2000) 'The Shape of National Time: Daily Life, History, and Identity During Armenia's Transition to Independence, 1991–1994', in Berdahl, D., Bunzl, M. & Lampland, M. (eds) (2000) *Altering States: Ethnographies of transition in Eastern Europe and the Former Soviet Union* (Ann Arbor, University of Michigan Press).
Rasell, M. (2010) *Social Citizenship, Disability and Welfare Provision in Contemporary Russia: Views from Below*, Unpublished PhD Dissertation (University of Birmingham, UK).
Reeves, M. (2007) 'Travels in the Margins of the State: Everyday Geography in the Farghana Valley Borderlands', in Sahadeo, J. & Zanca, R. (eds) (2007) *Everyday Life in Central Asia: Past and Present* (Bloomington, Indiana University Press).
Reeves, M. (2009) 'Materialising State Space: "Creeping Migration" and Territorial Integrity in Southern Kyrgyzstan', *Europe-Asia Studies*, 61, 7, September.
Ruegg, F. (ed.) (2006) *Interculturalism and Discrimination in Rumania: Policies, Practices, Identities and Representations* (Berlin & Münster, LIT Verlag).

Saroyan, M. (1996) 'Beyond the Nation-State: Culture and Ethnic Politics in Soviet Transcaucasia', in Suny, R. G. (ed.) (1996) *Transcaucasia, Nationalism and Social Change: Essays in the History of Armenia, Azerbaijan and Georgia* (Ann Arbor, University of Michigan Press).

Shakhnazarian, N. (2005) 'The Virtual Widows of Migrant Husbands in War-torn Mountainous Karabagh', in Haukanes, H. & Pine, F. (eds) (2005) *Generations, Kinship and Care: Gendered Provisions of Social Security in Central Eastern Europe* (Bergen, University of Bergen, Center for Women's and Gender Research).

Sharma, A. (2008) *Logics of Empowerment: Development, Gender, and Governance in Neoliberal India* (Minneapolis & London, University of Minneapolis Press).

Sharma, A. & Gupta, A. (eds) (2006) *The Anthropology of the State: A Reader* (Malden, MA & Oxford, Blackwell).

Soysal, Y. (1997) *Limits of Citizenship: Migrants and Postnational Membership in Europe* (Chicago, University of Chicago Press).

Suny, R. G. (1993) *The Revenge of the Past: Nationalism, Revolution and the Collapse of the Soviet Union* (Stanford, Stanford University Press).

Swietochowski, T. (1993) 'Russia's Transcaucasian Policies and Azerbaijan: Ethnic Conflict and Regional Unity', in Buttino, M. (ed.) (1993) *In a Collapsing Empire: Underdevelopment, Ethnic Conflicts and Nationalisms in the Soviet Union* (Milan, Fondazione Giangiacomo Feltrinelli).

Taylor, C. (ed.) (1994) *Multiculturalism: Examining the Politics of Recognition* (Princeton, Princeton University Press).

Thelen, T., Dorondel, S., Szöke, A. & Vetters, L. (2011) '"The Sleep has been Rubbed from their Eyes": Social Citizenship and the Reproduction of Local Hierarchies in Rural Hungary and Romania', *Citizenship Studies*, 15, 3–4, June.

Turner, B. S. (2001) 'The Erosion of Citizenship', *British Journal of Sociology*, 52, 2, June.

Vincent, J. (ed.) (2002) *The Anthropology of Politics: A Reader in Ethnography, Theory, and Critique* (Malden, MA, Blackwell).

Woodiwiss, A. (2008) 'Economic Citizenship: Variations and the Threat of Globalization', in Isin, E.F. & Turner, B.S. (eds) (2008b).

Yalçın-Heckmann, L. (2007) 'Openings and Closures: Citizenship Regimes, Markets and Borders in the Caucasus', in Grant, B. & Yalçın-Heckmann, L. (eds) (2007) *Caucasus Paradigms: Anthropologies, Histories, and the Making of a World Area* (Münster & Berlin, LIT Verlag).

Yalçın-Heckmann, L., Behrends, A. & Leutloff-Grandits, C. (2003) *Property Regimes in the Context of War and Displacement: Chad, Croatia and Azerbaijan in Comparison*, Working Paper 62 (Halle, Max Planck Institute for Social Anthropology).

Yalçın-Heckmann, L. & Aivazishvili, N. (2011) 'Scales of Trade, Informal Economy and Citizenship at Georgian-Azerbaijani Borderlands', in Bruns, B. & Miggelbrink, J. (eds) (2011) *Subverting Borders: Doing Research on Smuggling and Small-scale Trade* (Wiesbaden, VS Verlag für Sozialwissenschaften).

# Re-making a Frontier Community or Defending Ethnic Boundaries? The Caucasus in Cossack Identity

## ANTON POPOV

*Abstract*

The essay focuses on the notion of the Caucasus as a reference point in the construction of Cossack identity in southern Russia. Since the late Soviet period, the Cossack revivalist/nativist movement has emerged in the territories which constituted the frontier zones of Tsarist Russia. Arguably, the historical Cossack hosts were established as a kind of frontier community which played an important role in the expansion of the Russian Empire. This essay examines how post-Soviet Cossacks reinterpret the meanings of the Caucasus as a spatial and cultural realm where, or in relation to which, they produce their identity as a distinct ethnic and cultural community.

SINCE THE LATE SOVIET PERIOD, THE COSSACK REVIVALIST MOVEMENT has emerged in the territories which constituted the frontier zones of Tsarist Russia. As a phenomenon in the political and cultural life of the post-Soviet period, Cossacks reappeared here in 1989 as an ethno-nationalist movement which traced its origin to the historical Cossack hosts. Some observers, such as Markedonov (2003, 2004a, p. 527) and Derluguian and Cipko (1997) have suggested defining the 'renaissance' Cossacks with the term 'neo-Cossacks' in order to emphasise the contemporary sources of political ideology and the particularities of the Cossack identity being founded in post-Soviet Russia. The neo-Cossack revival can be conceptualised as a 'nativist' movement since the claim of a particular status as a 'native people' (*korennoi narod*) in the 'historical' territories of Cossack hosts (so called *kazachii prisud*) has constituted its ideological core (Markedonov 2004b, p. 538). At the same time, there is no agreement among neo-Cossacks about an ethnic nomenclature term which would unambiguously define their ethnic status in relation to Russians or Ukrainians. However, the description of Cossacks as a 'subethnos' of Russians seems to have become the most acceptable for both the Russian state and the neo-Cossack mainstream (Derluguian & Cipko 1997, p. 1490). The particularity of the Cossacks is emphasised through their frontier past, or origin, as a community. The notion of 'native territory' here is particularly important, since in accordance with the Cossack ideology they have ancestral rights to these lands which were brought to Russia at the cost of Cossacks' blood. The south Russian steppes north of the Black Sea and the hills of the North Caucasus are claimed by neo-Cossacks as their historical homeland and native territory.

This essay focuses on the notion of the Caucasus as a reference point in the construction of Cossack identity in southern Russia. It examines how post-Soviet Cossacks reinterpret the meanings of the Caucasus as a spatial and cultural realm where, or in relation to which, they produce their identity as a distinct ethnic and cultural community. This approach follows scholars, such as Stuart Hall (1996) who argue that dialogical relationship with the 'other' constitutes the core of the identification process. By looking at the meaning of the Caucasus in the Cossack revivalism, this essay seeks to problematise the vision of historic and contemporary Cossackdom as a 'frontier' and 'ethnic' one—the two notions central to the ideology and imagination of many neo-Cossacks in southern Russia. The essay aims to demonstrate how the construction of neo-Cossack identity as ethnically defined, and with inherently frontier characteristics, is experienced by young people who participate in the Cossack revival.

The essay draws upon ethnographic research which was conducted among young Cossacks (members of officially registered and informal Cossack clubs) in Krasnodar *Krai* and Rostov *Oblast'* of the Russian Federation between spring and autumn 2007.[1] The majority of my informants were young people (15–30 years old), although the research involved a few people of the older generation. In order to protect informants' identity, their names and/or nicknames, by which they prefer to be called, as well as titles of official and informal clubs have been changed. The network of informants consists of members of at least four officially registered Cossack clubs (*kureni* or *khutorskie obshchestva*) which are part of the Kuban Cossack Host (*Kubanskoe kazach'e voisko*, KKV), which since 1998, has become the only state-recognised (*reestrovoe*) Cossack organisation in the region (Popov & Kuznetsov 2008, p. 240). A young officer at one of these clubs, who I will call the '*Kuren*", acted as a gatekeeper and my point of access to the network of informants, and through contact with them, I was also introduced to a number of young history re-enactment enthusiasts. In addition to the fieldwork diary which included participant observation notes, 26 interviews were recorded with 23 informants.[2] The main settings of fieldwork were Krasnodar, a capital city of the region, and Sochi, a city on the region's Black Sea coast. Other locations of the ethnography included the towns of Azov (Rostov *Oblast'*) and Taman (Krasnodar *Krai*). The analysis of the Cossack nativist ideology is based on books and newspaper articles published by neo-Cossacks as well as online

---

[1]The 'Cossack case study' was conducted as part of a three-year EU FP6 project 'Societies and Lifestyles: Towards Enhancing Social Harmonization through Knowledge of Sub-cultural Communities' (Contruct No: STREP-CT-CIT5-029013). This large international collaborative project was coordinated by Vitautas Magnus University, Lithuania.

[2]In September 2007, I was joined in the field by Hilary Pilkington (University of Warwick). Several audio interviews were recorded by both researchers jointly or separately. The fieldnotes and interview transcripts were word processed and coded for analysis using the Nvivo 7 software.

resources, the most significant of which have been two so-called 'ethnic Cossack' websites—*Vol'naya stanitsa* and *Kazarla*.[3]

## Ethnicisation of Cossack identity

In his historiographical study, Sergei Markedonov (2004b, p. 529) defines the issue of the Cossackdom's origin as 'the core question of Cossack studies'. Markedonov outlines 'migration' and 'autochthonous' approaches to this problem, which provide radically opposite positions on the issue at hand and could be traced from the historiography of imperial Russia. Briefly, according to the so-called 'migration theory', the Cossack communities are closely tied to mainland Russia from which their ancestors had migrated as run-away serfs and military men (*sluzhilye lyudi*) since the end of the fifteenth century. On the contrary, the proponents of 'autochthonous conception' insist that Cossacks emerged from the ancestral ethnic groups indigenous to the south Russian steppes and the North Caucasus which had a complex ethnic origin, including Iranian, Turkic, Caucasian and, crucially, Slavic elements. The Cossacks, thus, are represented as a Turko-Slavic amalgamation native to the steppes. These two approaches to Cossackdom's origin have been extended to two competing, if not conflicting, political ideologies in the representation of Cossack identities. The 'migration theory' is closely associated with the vision of Cossacks as an undivided part of the Russian people which has been expressed by the (Russian) state-centred party (*derzhavniki*), whereas an 'autochthonous' origin of the Cossacks has entailed claims for the recognition of the Cossackdom as a separate ethnic entity by parties which sometimes define themselves as Cossack-nationalist or *Kazakiitsy*.

Holquist (2009) traces these two visions of the Cossackdom (both as political ideologies and semi-official public discourses) back to the turbulent time of the Civil War when the first attempts at building Cossack nations were undertaken by the 'autonomists' on the territories of the Cossack Hosts supporting the Whites (importantly, sometimes together with the *gortsy* (highlanders) of the North Caucasus). Arguably, the ethnicisation of the Cossack identity was well on its way during the imperial period, due to the Cossack's particular military status and privileged landowner rights that created clear cultural and economic boundaries in relation to the majority of the Russian peasant population. After the Whites' defeat, the émigré Cossacks developed the idea of the independent federative state of *Kazakia* (hence, the term for the Cossack nationalists) which would be created on the territories of the so-called European Cossack hosts, including the steppes of the North Caucasus. The ideas of the *Kazakiitsy* had been epitomised by the publication in the USA of three volumes of *The Cossack Encyclopaedia* (*Kazachii slovar'-spravochnik*) edited by Gubarev and Skrylov (1992).

Ironically, the ethnic vision of Cossackdom, albeit with a significantly different understanding of the nature and origin of Cossack ethnicity, was promoted in the interwar period by the Soviet state also (Holquist 2009, p. 2). The Bolshevik policy towards the Cossacks during the 1920s and 1930s was driven by the suspicion towards

---

[3]'Vol'naia stanitsa', available at: http://fstanitsa.ru/, accessed 12 September 2011; 'Kazarla: etnicheskoe kazach'e ob''edinenie', available at: http://www.kazarla.ru/, accessed 12 September 2010.

them as counter-revolutionary elements who had actively fought against the Soviet rule during the Civil War. Cossack communities experienced a disproportional amount of violence and repression directed against *kulaks* (rich peasants) during the collectivisation of 1928–1934. This period of deportation and starvation of entire Cossack villages was followed by an unexpected political and cultural campaign for the 'Soviet Cossackdom' (*za sovetskoe kazachestvo*) which began in 1935. However, due to Bolshevik suspicions and, unlike other (properly) recognised ethnic groups, the Soviet Cossacks were never granted territorialised national autonomy in the course of the *korenizatsiya*, although such desires were expressed by some of them (Skorik 2008, pp. 206–7). Thus, lacking institutionalised forms of cultural particularism, the Cossack population were driven even closer to the Russian majority of the region.

After the Soviet victory in the Great Patriotic War, Cossackdom seemed to become a part of history, which had been publicly represented through ethnographic and folkloristic performances of Cossack choirs and dancing ensembles (Olson 2004, p. 162). Significantly, the memories of the Cossack past (and mostly its tragic periods) had been transmitted through intimate family histories, firmly occupying a rather private domain in the cultural, if not ethnic, identities of Cossack descendants in the region (Toje 2006, p. 1072). Thus, Brian Boeck suggests that contemporary Cossack nationalism and identity are 'influenced by the fact that modernisation and Soviet rule coincided, transforming traditional Cossack [identity] into largely an ethnic identity' (1998, p. 652).

### Frontier communities and ethnic boundaries

The attempts to approach the past of the Cossack communities within the paradigm of frontier studies seem to be justifiable (Markedonov 2004b, p. 566; Boeck 2001; Sen' 2006). However, the extent to which the same conceptual framework can be applied to the neo-Cossack movement constitutes one of the questions for this essay.

Geographers distinguish between 'boundary' as a line and 'frontier' as a zone (Prescott 1978, p. 31). Historians conceptualised frontiers of the past as areas of contact and hybridisation where political boundaries do not correspond with cultural diversity but rather form zones of overlapping political, cultural and economic boundaries (Parker 2002; van Dommelen 1997). White calls these zones the 'middle ground' where different peoples meet and engage in practices through which their differences are adjusted. New shared meanings and practices are emerging, often through the production of, and responses to, misunderstandings of the values and practices of the other (1991, p. x). Therefore, Kopytoff (1987) seems to be right in pointing out that the frontier is characterised by the conditions in which reproduction of previous 'traditions' become impossible or undesirable and as a result frontiers act as 'incubators' for the creation and development of new communities. This corresponds with White's (1991, p. xiv) principle of avoiding the use of the term 'traditional' in description of cultural systems emerging on frontiers. He also argues against ethnohistorical techniques of 'upstreaming' when ethnologies of contemporary groups are used to interpret frontier communities of the past. Thus, cultural fluidity, ethnic heterogeneity and relative mobility across substantial territory are among the features of groups that have been emerging and existing in frontier zones (Parker 2002, p. 374).

This argument might be extended to question whether the concept of ethnicity can indeed be used to adequately describe such frontier communities as historical Cossackdom. Within a social constructivist approach to ethnicity, cultural identities as an important aspect of ethnic identification are seen as a 'never finished process' of social construction (Hall 2000, p. 2). Therefore, ethnic identities are not based on stable and fixed cultural traits shared by all members of the ethnic group and/or nation, but are defined by articulating the differences between these groups and other groups. Thus, Barth (1996) writes about 'ethnic boundaries' as a result of interaction between different groups, during which ethnic differences are constructed and maintained. However, as has been stated earlier, the frontier situation is characterised by fluidity of all sort of boundaries, which results in hybrid cultural forms that sometimes make it difficult to talk meaningfully about group identity in relation to groupings larger than a 'village' (White 1991, p. 16).

In her critical reassessment of a racialised notion of ethnicity, Gould argues that this concept is closely linked to the development of nation states as a product of Western modernity which had been imported to other parts of the world (including the Caucasus) with the process of modernisation in the twentieth century (Gould 2007, p. 162). Therefore, it is not accidental that a new level of ethnicisation of Cossackdom in the North Caucasus and southern Russia coincided with the collapse of the imperial system. Indeed, the analysis of neo-Cossack nativism has to be situated within the context of the Soviet legacies of ethno-federalism and nation building in the Caucasus which effectively was part of the broader Soviet project of modernisation (Slezkine 1996, p. 214–25). Thus, the *korenizatsiya* produced territorially bounded ethnic entities in the region. This does not mean that such ethnic groups had not existed before the Soviet period, but rather that power was articulated differently in the past (Gould 2007, p. 161). In the Soviet Union, ethnicity (or *natsional'nost'*) became perceived in a rather primordialist way as determined by fixed cultural traits, language, religion and attachment to territory. Underpinning this understanding of ethnicity as a form of cultural identity is the principle of common origin and/or common experiences of all members of the group (Grossberg 1996; Staring *et al.* 1997, p. 11). Such a vision of ethnic groupings was elaborated within the 'theory of ethnos' (Bromlei 1973, 1981) which dominated the Soviet ethnology from the early 1980s and still remains influential in post-Soviet nationality policy (Tishkov 1997).

## *The Caucasus and (neo-)Cossacks*

Although Soviet historiography and ethnology (*etnografiya*) tended to see Cossacks as a subethnic group (subethnos),[4] it never questioned the 'migrant origin' of the Cossacks as a part of the Russian ethnos. However, this mainstream narrative was challenged by historian and ethnologist, Lev Gumilev, who, in the 1960s to 1980s, developed a highly controversial socio-biological, and fundamentally primordialist, theory of ethnogenesis of peoples living on the vast territory of Eurasia within the borders of Russia. According to this theory, Cossacks of the South Russian steppes are direct descendants of the

---

[4]This is how it was used as an example by Bromlei (1981, p. 48), a founder of the Soviet 'theory of ethnos'.

ancient Khazars who reigned over the territory between the Caucasus Mountains in the south and the Don and Volga rivers in the north (Gumilev 2009). This theory represents the Cossack history in the region as the continuous presence of the group indigenous to the North Caucasus and the northern coast of the Black Sea.

Although Gumilev's theory is, in general, criticised and dismissed by the majority of scholars working in the mainstream social sciences and humanities, it has gained great popularity among radical Russian nationalists (Shnirel'man 2010). The Cossack nativists also argue in favour of their 'Khazarian origin' because it, on the one hand, explains their ethnicity as different from Russians. On the other hand, it roots Cossacks in the Caucasus and provides them with a basis to claim their rights to exist as a separate ethnic entity in a region which is characterised by growing ethno-nationalism (Nikitin 2007, p. 162).

It seems that the KKV leadership is in favour of such ethnicist interpretations of Cossack identity. Vladimir Gromov, the former *ataman* of the Kuban Cossack Host (from 1992 to 2008), states that Cossacks are part of the 'North Caucasian civilisation' and share their 'traditions, culture [and] way of life' with *gortsy* ('mountain peoples') whose national autonomies are neighbouring Krasnodar *Krai* (Gromov 2002a, p. 3, 2002b, p. 8). The close association of neo-Cossacks with other North Caucasian ethnic groups is manifested in their celebrations of the anniversaries of the Russian parliament's adoption of a Bill on Rehabilitation of Oppressed Peoples and Cossacks in 1992. Neo-Cossacks see this bill as the Russian state's acknowledgement of Cossacks as a distinct ethnic group which shares its tragic history of Soviet persecutions with other 'punished peoples' in the North Caucasus (the Kalmyks, Chechens, Ingush, Karachai and Balkars). In April 2007, the fifteenth anniversary of the Bill coincided with the 'repatriation' to the Kuban from the USA of Kuban Cossacks' regalia which were taken to the West by emigrating White Cossacks in 1920. This was celebrated with a great parade gathering more than seven thousand uniformed Cossacks who marched through the central streets and squares of Krasnodar.

Although my informants do not question the ethnicist ideology of the KKV leadership, they worried about the potential negative consequences of such unscrupulous uses of history, ethnic terminology and, significantly, the association with the Caucasus as a region. Daniil, who is a member of the official (registered) organisation within the KKV and a ceremonial guard in Cossack uniform on the payroll of the *Krai* administration, makes a comparison to Cossack ethnicity claims in the early 1990s with 'ethnic conflicts' in the neighbouring Caucasian regions. In a way his comments confirm, albeit unexpectedly, that the Caucasus is a firm reference point for the Cossack revival in the region:

> At the beginning of the Cossack revival, some were shouting that they are Cossacks that Cossacks are a people, they went so far to suggest even a secession of the Kuban. So they shouted let's separate from Russia. This is what my father told me. God prohibits this. At that time there were Chechnya, Abkhazia, all these hot spots. It could be such a [bloody] war in the Kuban, oh, my God ... .[5]

---

[5]Daniil, born 1984, 24 April 2007, Krasnodar.

At the same time, on several occasions, young Cossacks articulated their differences with the Russian majority by positioning themselves in relation to the Caucasus and the 'Caucasians'. Thus, Viktor (born in 1977 in Sochi), a young officer at the Sochi Cossack organisation, generalised the Kuban Cossacks' attitudes towards Russian media reports that Cossacks were lining up to volunteer to join Russian troops during the Russo-Georgian 'August War' in 2008, in the following words: 'If Russia wants to fight, it's her business but not again at the cost of Cossack blood. We are, anyway, too close to there'.[6] However, Viktor emphasised that he knew only one Cossack from his organisation who was proactively searching for an opportunity to go to South Ossetia to fight, although he acknowledged that the majority were very pro-Ossetian and did not question the official anti-Georgian propaganda.

It is, perhaps, symptomatic for the Russian discursive construction of the region that my informants talk about the Caucasus in terms of conflict and violence (see more about this further in the essay). However, at least some of these narratives emphasise the specific Cossack position 'in-between' in relation to Russia and the Caucasus and 'Caucasians'. This was especially vividly articulated by Ingvar, a re-enactment enthusiast and member of a registered Cossack organisation:

> Once we happened to be in an epicentre of a conflict in [the middle of] the Krasnaia Street [the boulevard in Krasnodar city centre]. We were returning after one of our [re-enactment] theatrical performances ... with different weapon and so on ... we suddenly found ourselves in between two fighting parties—the skinheads and some Adygs, or, I do not remember who were they. And we were thinking for some time who [we would join] in the fight. Well, to our best, we waited and waited, and [at the end] we walked away from the temptation.[7]

In the ethnicist or nativist vision of modern Cossackdom in the North Caucasus and southern Russia, the Caucasus, as a geographically, historically and culturally defined region, seems to play a dual and contradictory role. This duality is characterised by historic claims to the region which were produced both in reference to, and in denial of, rival claims by the (ethnic) 'other'. Such conditions are best defined by the phrase 'ourselves and others' which Mackridge and Yannakakis (1997, p. 11) use in relation to the complex cultural situation which has emerged from the nationalist struggle over frontier zones in the Balkans.

Among my informants, there were quite a few who studied history at the regional universities. Many were reading popular-science versions of different historical and ethnological theories. Gumilev's volumes often occupied a prominent place on their bookshelves.[8] Many were also familiar with the émigré literature, which became available in the late Soviet Union and the Russian Federation as reprints or more

---

[6]Telephone conversation with the author, 14 November 2008.
[7]Ingvar, born 1987, 9 April 2007, Krasnodar.
[8]'Kazach'ya set', Lev Nikolaevich Gumilev o kazakakh, not dated, available at: http://cossackweb.narod.ru/kazaki/r_gmlkz00.htm, accessed 19 June 2010.

recently in electronic format.⁹ My research findings also suggest that this imagined online Cossack frontier community was enacted offline by some of my informants, who used such electronic resources to feed their ethnic and historical imagination.

*Historical re-enactment of the Cossack frontier on the Black Sea coast*

Despite White's (1991) warning, in their reinterpretation of the past, the Cossack nativists implement 'ethnic upstreaming' and search for their 'ancestors' among groups that historically lived in the Steppe zone northwards of the Black Sea. However, the history is not only revisited by the Cossack revivalist, it is also re-enacted by some of them.

Following my network of informants, I was introduced to young people in Sochi and Krasnodar who were interested in the re-enactment of military history. At the time of my fieldwork, they grouped around a club of historical re-enactment, called '*Bunchuk*' hereafter, led by its founder nicknamed 'Sarmat' (born 1980). Sarmat considers himself a hereditary Cossack (*potomstvennyi kazak*) and represents his organisation as an 'informal Cossack youth organisation'. In fact, there are very few Cossack descendants in his organisation. The majority of its members are mere enthusiasts of medieval Russian and Steppe military-history reconstruction.

Moreover, the '*Bunchuk*' reconstructs not only military history, but the Cossack ethnogenesis as well. As the following extract from an interview with 'Comandor', one of the activists of '*Bunchuk*' in Sochi, suggests, the emplacement of these history re-enactment activities in the region plays a critical role in the reconstruction of the Cossack identity as both a frontier and an ethnic community:

> *Polovtsy*—many trace Cossacks from them, meaning that ... they were blonde, an absolutely Slavic type. Well, see, these *Polovtsy* were one of the Golden Horde's provinces (*ulus*) as the Moscow principality was as well; the Russian Tmutarakan' principality—[where modern] Taman is situated—later became a province of the Golden Horde. Well, so, on the one hand, the Rus' was the pagan Horde, but on the other hand [it was] the Muscovites (*moskali*) ... . [In this way] we reconstruct this southern frontier.¹⁰

Sarmat and Comandor are both critical towards official (registered) Kuban Cossackdom, despising its leadership for their lack of commitment to the ethnic revival of the Cossacks as a people, reducing it to army-like activities such as uniformed marching. However, by representing the '*Bunchuk*' as a Cossack organisation, re-enactment enthusiasts continue to collaborate with the structures of the official KKV, receiving logistical support for the club's activities in exchange for performing historical fencing as a form of 'ancient Cossack martial arts' at public events organised by the KKV (participation in one such event was mentioned by Ingvar in the interview extract cited earlier).

---

⁹The digitalised version of the Gubarev and Skrylov's volumes (1966–1970) can be found as *Kazachii slovar'-spravochnik*, available at: http://www.cossackdom.com/enciclopedic/encyclopedic.htm, accessed 15 June 2010. It also became a foundation for so-called *Donskoi kazachii slovar'*, available at: http://silverhorseshoe.narod.ru/voc/voc.htm, accessed 15 June 2010, hosted on one of the Neo-Cossack websites. See also, Cossack National Alliance, 'Karta Kazakii', 1962, available at: http://old.fstanitsa.ru/3/114_1.shtml, accessed 19 June 2010.

¹⁰Comandor, born 1984, 1 April 2007, Sochi.

One of the fruits of such collaboration between the Cossackdom and historical reconstruction movement in Krasnodar *Krai* became the historical re-enactment festival 'The Black Sea Frontier' (*Chernomorskoe porubezh'ie*) which took place in May 2007. The emphasis in this festival was placed on the historical presence of the Slavs (Kiev Rus') in the Tmutarakan' principality that between the eleventh and thirteenth centuries was located on the Taman peninsula and the north-eastern cost of the Azov Sea. The Cossack nativists see the population of Tmutarakan' as being among their ancestors. At the same time, in the media coverage of the event, as well as in its title, the entire region was represented as a frontier zone of the medieval Russian principalities. The festival activities, for example, due to infrastructural and convenience reasons took place not on the Taman peninsula, but in the Gelendzhik district which is situated more than 100 km south along the coastal line.

'The Black Sea frontier' festival and other history re-enactment events, including the 215th anniversary of the Cossack landing from Bessarabia on the Taman peninsula celebrated by the KKV in September 2007 and sponsored by the Krasnodar *Krai* administration, can be understood as a process of cultural appropriation of the north-western Caucasus by Cossacks, or even more broadly, by the Russian majority of the region's population. In the course of such appropriation of the historical, cultural and ethnic heritage of the region, the Cossack, and indeed Russian, colonisation of the region in the eighteenth and nineteenth centuries is reimagined as a 'return' to the territory where Cossacks, Slavs or Russians are historically rooted.

## *Appropriation of the Caucasus*

The North Caucasus, of course, was appropriated by Russians in the course of the Caucasian War (1816–1864) and as a result of the several Russian–Ottoman treaties of the eighteenth and nineteenth centuries. The Cossacks acted both as a military force and as agrarian colonists who were settled in the areas conquered by the Russian Empire which were often depopulated after displacement of its Muslim population (various Turkic peoples and Circassians) (Babich *et al.* 2007, pp. 74–8). However, in the neo-Cossack discourses of Cossack autochthonous status in the region, their colonising past (which implies a migrant origin) is downplayed, while the presence of Cossack communities in the pre-colonial period (such as *Grebenskii* Cossacks in the Terek area) is emphasised.[11] The KKV leadership even went so far as to claim that the Cossacks were also victims of the Tsarist colonial policy in the Caucasus because they were forced to fight against 'other North-Caucasian peoples' and endured significant losses in the course of the Caucasian War (Gromov 2002a, p. 3).

One of the most frequently cited arguments for Cossack rootedness in the Caucasus which I heard from my informants is the 'Caucasian traditions' of the Cossacks which made them different from other East Slavs and non-Cossack Russians in particular. These traditions are understood as a core aspect of ethnic identification which in accordance with the 'theory of ethnos' is inseparable from other characteristics of the

---

[11]See, for example, Kazarla, 'Grebenskie kazaki. Kazachii slovar'-spravochnik, A. I. Skrylov, G. V. Gubarev', not dated, available at: http://www.kazarla.ru/index.php/historyview/864, accessed 20 June 2010.

ethnic group, such as the historical territory of living (Bromlei 1973). Thus, Daniil explains this connection between Cossacks and the Caucasus by means of traditions in an almost socio-Darwinist fashion, positioning Cossacks as survivors of the harsh frontier conditions of the region:

> If a particular tradition came from a particular territory, [this was because] it helped a people (*narod*) [who lived there] to survive on this territory. Therefore, since Cossacks had come to the Kuban they undoubtedly used traditions which existed among Circassians, Adygs, I don't know who else, other ethnic groups (*etnosy*) that used to live here, Greeks ... .[12]

Interestingly, in an article published in the Cossack ethnic journal *Kazarla*, the Caucasus and Cossacks are linked via the particular tradition of winemaking. In the article, Cossack winemaking is represented as traces of ancient tradition indigenous to the Caucasus, as well as peoples who lived there (for example, the Scythians, Khazars and South Slavs) whom Cossack nativists count among their ancestors (Kovalev 2009, p. 15).

Perhaps partly due to the Soviet institutionalised tradition of Cossack singing and dancing (Olson 2004), music is seen by my informants as the most obvious way of manifesting and transmitting traditions. Thus, during the Azov historical re-enactment festival organised by Cossack and re-enactment organisations in August 2007,[13] the Cossack version of the *lezginka* (a fast Caucasian dance) was performed on several occasions during the socialising at the camp-site by Sarmat and some other festival participants who explicitly identify themselves as 'hereditary Cossacks' (mostly from Krasnodar *Krai* and Rostov *Oblast'*).[14] Among the '*Bunchuk*' members, there were also popular couplets which they sang as the old Cossack song '*Shamil*", imitating the rhythmic structure and style of North-Caucasian singing with a typical refrain '*oisya-ta-oisya*'. However, these couplets had facetious content, sometimes with sexist and xenophobic connotations directed against the Caucasians, as in the following example:

| | |
|---|---|
| *My slavyanskaya druzhina* | We are Slavic guards, |
| *My bolshaya seks-mashina* | We are a big sex-machine, |
| *Otymeem vsekh podryad* | Will fuck everybody up, |
| *V zhopu vstavim kolovrat.* | Will stick a sun wheel in [your] ass.[15] |
| *Oisya-ta-oisya* | *Oisya-ta-oisya,* |
| *Ty menya ne boisya.* | Don't you be afraid of me. |
| *Otymeem vsekh podryad* | We will fuck everybody up, |
| *Ty ne bespokoisya* | Be sure [about this]. |

---

[12]Daniil, born 1984, 24 April 2007, Krasnodar.

[13]The Azov festival is dedicated to the Don Cossacks' defence of the fortress of Azov against the Ottoman Turks in 1637–1641, the so-called '*Azovsoe osadnoe sidenie*'. These festivals have been run by one of the Don Cossack military-history re-enactment clubs in the contemporary town of Azov in the Rostov *Oblast'* since 2005. The members of the '*Bunchuk*' are among the most active participants of these festivals.

[14]The popularity among Terek and Kuban Cossacks of *gorskii* dances such as the above mentioned *lezginka* before the revolution is well documented (see, for example, Eleseev 2001).

[15]The *kolovrat* or sun wheel is a Slavic pagan symbol dedicated to *svarog*, the sun god. Some of my informants interpreted the *kolovrat* as a 'symbol of fire, strength and power' (Comandor, born 1984, 1 April 2007, Sochi). A few of the '*Buchuk*' members, including Sarmat himself, belong to a neo-pagan sect of *Rodnovery*. For more details on this, see Pilkington and Popov (2009).

In a way the hyper-sexual, or even in a way homosexual, connotations of such couplets in combination with the quasi-Caucasian refrain can be interpreted as a Russian xenophobic parody of the stereotypical Caucasian man. The authentic '*Shamil*" song also had lyrics which ridiculed 'Chechens', or mountain counterpart of the Cossacks, in general, imitating their accent and borrowing some terms from their languages. These couplets, 'Caucasian' in their form but with anti-Caucasian content, might be considered as a continuation of the Cossacks' complex relationships of 'othering' (Hall 1996) with their mountain neighbours. Although sang in jest, such couplets convey the meaning of Cossack, Slavic or Russian dominance.

In relation to this, it is interesting that Georgii, an active member of the '*Bunchuk*' who also acted as a history instructor at the '*Kuren*", in his interview while talking about the hypothetical possibility of marrying a 'Caucasian' woman explained his liking of Caucasian (Georgian and Circassian) music as a cultural tradition to which Cossacks are exposed:

> Well, Adygean girls ... By the way I, in general, like Caucasian music. All in all, we live side by side, we have no other option but to know it. We should not go away from it. Let's put it like this, bit by bit we have to learn the culture of other people. We have no choice but have to know the culture of the people we live next to. This is how God made it, we live side by side therefore we have to know their mentality, what is acceptable and what is not in their [culture]. That's it.[16]

It seems that in the nativist discourses, the Caucasus is appropriated by the Cossacks through appropriation of the Caucasian 'traditions'. The Cossack Caucasian-ness is materialised and, therefore, looks especially convincing in such material artefacts as *cherkeska* (Circassian coat) and *kinzhal* (Caucasian dagger) which they share with North-Caucasian *gortsy* (highlanders) (Leutskii & Babenko 2008, pp. 5–7). This Cossack attire has become a most visible symbol of the Cossack revival in the region which is manifested through uniformed performances. Ironically, this aspiration for authenticity has provoked the most hostile reaction from the majority of the population in the region (including those who consider themselves to be Cossack descendents). An offensive expression '*ryazhennye kazaki*' (masquerading Cossacks) which implies a fake, non-authentic behaviour is often used towards 'traditionally dressed Cossacks' in the region.

However, Stepanych (born 1956), a middle-aged *ataman* (head) of a small Cossack organisation and 'spiritual leader' of many of my younger informants, recently published a book about the Cossack traditional culture in which, as he told me, he proves that *cherkeska* has a pure Cossack origin and has nothing to do with Circassians. Thus, it seems that the next step in the Cossack-nativists' appropriation of the Caucasus might be the deprivation of Caucasians of 'their traditions', as they had been deprived of a significant part of their territory some 150 years ago, in the same way as other Caucasians, labelled as 'migrants', are rejected as culturally alien to, and historically uprooted from, the territories Cossacks claim for themselves.

---

[16]Georgii, born 1982, 23 August 2007, Krasnodar.

## Rejection of the 'Caucasians'

The Cossack revival movement is often criticised for its xenophobia and extreme nationalism. The members of the neo-Cossack organisation in Krasnodar *Krai* are notorious for violence against ethnic minorities and migrants from Central Asia and Transcaucasia, which led to a series of pogroms of Armenian and Turkish population of the region in the 1990s (Osipov & Cherepova 1996, pp. 81–3). Responding to this accusation of violation of human rights and discrimination against minorities, the Cossacks often blame Russian central authorities for ignoring the problems of so-called 'ethnic migration' (Gromov 2002b). The central authorities are accused of betraying Slavs' interests in the region for the sake of Western values which are uncritically accepted by authorities as norms of 'civilised society'. It is interesting that in the following extract, Stepanych explains this opposition through the spatial metaphor of a walled town and the uncivilised or savage places and people outside it, drawing the picture of the imagined frontier that, in his opinion, is similar to the one which existed on the borders of the Roman Empire. His emphasis on a 'town' being alien to the Kuban suggests the indigenous origin of Cossacks:

> Thus the civilised ones tell us, 'You are not civilised'. But what is a civilisation, in general? 'Civil' has a Roman origin, it means 'someone who lives inside a town's walls', thus, the one who is outside the wall he is a savage, a pagan (*paganets*). Yes, we are pagan, yes, we are not good, and we do not conform to the town's rules. But we didn't ask to build towns. You are the ones who came to us, so you either follow our lifestyle or ... we don't keep anyone here [against their will] (laughter).[17]

Interestingly, this opposition of Cossacks as an autochthonous population to 'civilised newcomers' could be extended to include the 'Caucasian migrants' and Armenians, in particular, as elements which are culturally alien to Cossacks. Later, in this interview, Stepanych explained that Cossacks managed to keep peace in the region in the pre-revolutionary period because they acted as a buffer between Russians and North Caucasian *gortsy* (highlanders) with whom they shared many traditions, including dress code and warrior ethos. In his opinion, due to suppression by the authorities of the 'true revival' of the Cossackdom in the region, the Russians suffer in the North Caucasian autonomous republics and even in the 'Russian provinces', such as Krasnodar *Krai*, where the 'Caucasian migrants' have started dictating their rules to the Russian majority.

Through the discursive appropriation of the Caucasus, Cossacks are constructed as a group which has the rights of 'hosts' (meaning local and 'native' population) as opposed to non-native 'guests' that are migrants who interestingly are defined ethnically as 'Caucasians' (*kavkaztsy*). Expressing his rather xenophobic attitudes towards Caucasian migrants in Sochi, Comandor refers to the historical right of Cossacks to take the place of natives in the area after capturing the place from Adygs in the course of the Caucasian War:

---

[17]Stepanych, born 1956, 12 September 2007, Krasnodar.

> When I hear an argument between an Armenian and Georgian about who owns the city of Sochi. [I am saying] guys, you are not from here, you used to live over there, so if you want to argue for some rights, go to Armenia, to Georgia, argue over there. Yes, I can understand if Adygs, Ubyhs, who are remaining here, start claiming their rights. Yes, they indeed used to live here. But those guys are not from here .... [18]

Importantly, Comandor himself moved to Sochi from his native Kabardino-Balkaria two years before the interview took place. Nevertheless, he does not consider himself to be a migrant but names the Armenians, who have constituted a significant proportion of the Sochi district population since the late nineteenth century, as 'newcomers'. Comandor was also reproducing an anti-migrant discourse promoted by Krasnodar regional authorities (Popov & Kuznetsov 2008; Osipov & Cherepova 1996). In the Russian Federation, in general, the quasi-ethnic concepts of 'Caucasians' or 'those of Caucasian nationality' (*litsa kavkazskoi national'nosti*) are used extensively by the state agencies (such as the police and the Federal Migration Service) as well as by 'ordinary' citizens, creating the image of migrants from this region as both corrupt and culturally alien to the ethnically Russian (or 'Slavic') population.

Paradoxically, although Caucasians are rejected as non-native to the Kuban, the native status of the Cossacks in the region and their cultural distinction is expressed through comparison with Caucasian neighbours. An interview with a young member of the '*Kuren*'', Vania is indicative in this respect. In order to make sense of the Cossacks as a people, he compares their 'traditions' with Adygean:

> For example, if in Russia, the Victory Day is a common celebration, yeah, we celebrate the 215th anniversary of [the Cossack] landing in Taman—this was the most recent celebration. But it is celebrated only by the Cossacks because it is a purely Cossack celebration. The other people have their own rites, their own celebration on particular days. In Adygea, I don't remember when they have this celebration, in my opinion sometime in January, they celebrate a sacrifice with their entire *aul* (village). ... All the same, everyone has their own lifestyle. Of course we try to defend the majority in our territory—the Cossacks, because the Kuban is a Cossack region, Cossacks always lived and ruled here.[19]

The image of 'ethnic frontier' emerges from such a comparison; Vanya's narrative also implies a conflict and need to defend Cossacks (the Russian majority) from their Caucasian neighbours. The choice of the word 'defence' might be understood quite literally in this context. The interview with Vania took place a few days after he came from Taman where he participated with other '*Kuren*'' members in the celebration of the anniversary mentioned in the extract above. At the festival venue, the Krasnodar Cossack delegation was camping in a military style on the big field where the horse-riding performance, one of the central events of the festival, was held. The night before the performance the Cossacks were woken up by full military alarm because one of the patrols guarding the camp stopped a car with a woman looking for 'Asker' (a Muslim name common in the North Caucasus) who had something to do with horses. The

---

[18] Comandor, born 1984, 1 April 2007, Sochi.
[19] Vania, born 1985, 12 September 2007, Krasnodar.

rumours spread that some 'Chechens' were going to raid the camp and steal horses that were kept nearby in the makeshift stables. The patrols of young Cossacks in full army gear with deactivated Kalashnikovs were reinforced. It turned out that the 'Asker' was one of the Adygean circus riders invited by the festival organisers due to a lack of skilful horsemen among the KKV members to perform at the main event. Ironically, Adygeans were performing dressed in the 'traditional' Kuban Cossack uniform, confirming critics' scepticism about neo-Cossacks' claims of authenticity.

The conditions in which contemporary Cossackdom has been revived are perceived by the neo-Cossacks and Russian nationalists as a form of a frontier between the so-called Slavic population of the 'Russian regions' in southern Russia and representatives of 'titular' and other non-Russian ethnic groups of the autonomous and independent republics on both sides of the Caucasus. Therefore, the Cossack revivalism has to be linked also with the growth of Russian nationalism after the collapse of the Soviet Union. At the same time, the nationalist ideas might be appealing to some people due to the nationalists' instrumental use of culturally and historically conditioned stereotypes of Russia's ethnic minorities and/or entire regions, such as the Caucasus.

Thus, since the imperial period conflict and violence as the context for Russo-Caucasian relations has been romanticised in Russian popular culture. Grant argues, for the Russian audience, the Caucasus has become 'an everyday idiom' for a zone of violence where Russians are 'ever the noble victim' (2005, p. 47). More recently, following the Chechen war and other so-called 'ethnic conflicts', the peoples of the Caucasus are often portrayed in the Russian media as, by nature, violent (Grant 2005, p. 39).

Despite the claim of a shared cultural heritage with the Caucasians, the Cossack identity is constructed as ethnically exclusive and hostile towards the 'other Caucasus'. In the final section of this essay, I will examine how the notion of a frontier origin of the Cossackdom and its shared history and even ancestry with other Caucasians is experienced and contested in the individual biographies of young Cossacks.

### *Imagined and untold frontier genealogies*

Today the mixed ethnic origin of the old (pre-revolutionary) Cossack families has become almost common knowledge among the members of the Neo-Cossack organisations. In his rather confusing and contradictory account of Cossack history, the *ataman* of the Great Brotherhood of Cossack Hosts, Valerii Nikitin draws the following picture of the frontier conditions of the North Caucasus where Cossacks 'were formed as a specific ethnos' (2007, p. 163):

> Due to the resettlement of Armenians in the North Caucasus, their communities were formed in different regions and in a number of places Armenians lived in mixed communities with other peoples. Since there were many Cossack settlements in this area, Armenians, Georgians, Ossetians, Chechens had settled in the Cossack villages ... and gradually mixed with the native Cossack population. The most interesting fact is that newcomers imperceptibly became included in Cossackdom. The integrated groups of 'highlander Cossacks' (*gorskie kazaki*) started emerging among the Don, Kuban and Terek Cossackdom .... (Nikitin 2007, p. 169)

Indeed, many Cossack descendants, including some of my informants (such as Daniil, born 1984; Georgii, born 1982, and Viktor, born 1977), would state that they of course have mixed ethnic background because their Cossack ancestors used to marry captured Turkish, Tatar and Circassian women. This perception of Cossacks as a frontier group characterised as 'mixed race' is firmly established in the public imagination in a way that sometimes leads to undermining of the nativists' cause in constructing Cossackdom as an ethnic entity. Thus, Yura, a member of the Sochi Cossack organisation, in his answer to my question whether Cossacks are a people or estate, rejected the idea of Cossacks' ethnic distinction, pointing out their heterogeneous background:

[Being] a Cossack, as I understood, is simply a spiritual state (*sostoyanie dushi*). ... In general, it is not like saying look, if you have fair hair (*rusyi*) and an aquiline nose then you are not a Cossack, but if you have black curly hair, are two metres tall and wave a sword above your head then you are a Cossack. Look, Jews and Armenians were accepted in Cossackdom. There was an entire Armenian unit in the [Kuban] Host, wasn't there?[20]

For some of my informants, the ethnically mixed genealogies of the historical Cossack families justify the enrolment of people who do not have Cossack ancestry in the neo-Cossack organisations. However, priority is given to Russians, or 'Slavs', as Dima, a junior officer in the Krasnodar '*Kuren*' organisation, explains:

In general, they try, we try [to enlist people] of Slavic origin, or at least by [their] confessional characteristics. Well, fine, he is an Ossetian, but they [the Ossetians] are Christians, anyway. There are Abkhazian Christians; there is an Abkhaz Department [of the KKV] where there are a lot of Abkhazians; there are such people .... [21]

However, when Caucasians, or people of mixed Russian–Caucasian origin participate in the Cossack movement, they try to downplay their non-Russian genealogy. Dima's father, for example is an Ossetian, and although Dima was brought up by his Russian (Kuban Cossack) mother, he is proud of his Caucasian heritage. Perhaps this explains his interest in ethnic diversity among historical Cossack hosts and his exceptionally broad knowledge of the cultures and ethnicities present in the Caucasus. However, Dima is not open about his Ossetian extraction and I doubt that many members of his organisation are aware of his 'mixed origin'. Even I learned about his Ossetian father only several months after our first meeting, despite the fact that Dima was my key informant in Krasnodar.

Perhaps, Ingvar's story is especially indicative of the attitudes towards Caucasian ancestry among neo-Cossacks. Ingvar is a member of both the '*Bunchuk*' and a registered Cossack organisation in Krasnodar. He starts his story with his interest in the Cossackdom and participation in the revival movement with his Cossack father stressing, partly in jest, the importance of the 'genes':

---

[20]Yura, born 1979, 13 September 2007, Sochi.
[21]Dima, born 1982, 21 March 2007, Krasnodar.

Four years ago I started actively participating [in the Cossackdom] when I enlisted in the '*Bunchuk*'. Well, I became fascinated with the idea. I don't know, somehow I knew that my father originates from Cossacks, but it was just something I knew that I was not interested in before ... . But you could not argue with your genes and in a very short time I became 'ours' (*svoim*) in this environment. I am not distinct from others whether it is in respect of my folklore knowledge or speaking *balachka*.[22] Thankfully, in my [grandmother's] farmstead *balachka* was spoken, although the farmstead is considered to be ... , but I was told fairytales in *balachka*. There were no problems with the language, although I cannot say that I speak [*balachka*] very well.[23]

Ingvar's narrative is also important because of what was not told or remained silent in it. Although, Ingvar structures his 'Cossack biography' around his father's Cossack origin, he has never seen his father, who left his mother before he was born. Ingvar's mother is an Armenian local to Krasnodar *Krai* and he was brought up spending a lot of time with his maternal grandparents in their village—the grandmother's farmstead mentioned in the interview—which is a compact settlement of Hamshen Armenians, 30 km from Krasnodar. Ingvar has an Armenian surname, but he prefers to be called by the Russian name which sounds close enough to his given Armenian name. He is known to the majority of his friends and acquaintances in the Cossack movement and the military history reconstruction circle by his history re-enactment nickname. Ingvar is an enthusiast of the 'traditional Cossack martial arts' and an active member of the Krasnodar Ukrainian Society which he attends to learn the Ukrainian language, perhaps in order to improve his command of *balachka*. The majority of Ingvar's acquaintances are aware of his Caucasian origin (they are sometime unsure whether he is Armenian or Georgian though) and consider him an exceptional case of a 'Caucasian' turned into Cossack.

Dima's and Ingvar's stories are a good example that despite the discursive production of the Cossack collective genealogy as an imagined ethnic community attached by cultural and ancestral roots to the Caucasus, the real stories of cultural interaction between different ethnic groups in the region, which include mixed marriages and split families remain untold, downplayed and silenced. The real life histories of the 'Caucasian frontier' were and still are more complex and multi-vocal than those which are told by nativists to represent a neo-Cossack ethnic identity.

## *Conclusion*

In this essay, I discuss the place and role of the Caucasus as a geographically and culturally defined region in the construction of neo-Cossack identity. My aim has been to problematise the construction of the neo-Cossack identity as both ethno-national and possessing inherently frontier characteristics. This has been achieved, at the conceptual level, through the discussion of problems with the application of ethnicity as an

---

[22]*Balachka* is a commonly used word for the local Ukrainian dialect which some Kuban Cossack nativists consider to be a distinct Cossack language.

[23]Ingvar, born 1987, interview with the author, 9 April 2007, Krasnodar. I quote this interview with all its inconsistency and abrupt stops of phrases because it demonstrates how uneasy and inconsistently the Cossack identity is constructed and represented in the narrative which leaves part of the story untold.

analytical concept to frontier situations which are characterised by overlapping political, cultural and economic boundaries, as well as relatively high spatial mobility that results in hybrid and unstable cultural forms which are difficult to describe in ethnically defined categories. On the other hand, the outline of the history of Cossack nativism demonstrates that the historical, geographical and cultural specificity of the Caucasus as a region created conditions for the prevalence of ethnic (and nationalistic) discourses in reimagining the Cossackdom as a socio-political phenomenon. Significantly, these factors include such diverse processes as Cossack struggles against (and eventual defeat from) the Bolsheviks in the Civil War; the early Soviet policy of *korenisatiya* in the region; post-Soviet regionalism; the growth of ethno-nationalism in the north Caucasian autonomies and the emergence of Russian nationalism after the collapse of the USSR. All of these make the Cossack identity in the region, what Boeck (2004) calls 'functional ethnicity', which is employed by people in order to understand their experiences (including traumatic family histories) within a shifting social environment. In these conditions, the Cossacks nativists use the Caucasus as an identifier which marks their border position in relation to the Russian state, Russians and the non-Russian peoples of the region. Here, the meaning of the Cossackdom as an 'indigenous group' to the Caucasus has strong ethnic connotations since in Russian public discourses the region is associated with different manifestations of ethnic particularism, for example, ethno-nationalism, ethnic conflicts and Caucasian separatism.

At the empirical level, the essay examines how the meanings of the Caucasus are reinterpreted, internalised and converted in actions by young members of the Cossack movement in the course of their imaginative work for making sense of contemporary Cossackdom. The ethnographic findings demonstrate how the Caucasus is apprehended by the neo-Cossacks discursively through ethnic upstreaming and looking for 'traditions' which would root them in the region. These are the techniques that White (1991) criticises as counter-productive for the interpretation of frontier communities of the past. They, however, become essential for demarcating ethnic boundaries against which neo-Cossacks define themselves. As a frontier community, historical Cossackdom was seen as a defender of imperial boundaries, with neo-Cossacks claiming the same role for themselves in the North Caucasus; but now the boundaries are drawn along ethnic lines and it is the 'Caucasians' (migrants) against whom the Cossacks defend their 'native' territory. Paradoxically, in their rejection of the Caucasians, the Cossacks try to claim part of the Caucasus for the ethnic Russians, or Slavs. Thus, despite neo-Cossacks' ethicist claims, which are partly directed against the Russian majority, those observers who see the Cossack revival in southern Russia and the North Caucasus as a 'particularist form of Russian nationalism' are correct (Derluguian & Cipko 1997, p. 1498).

*The University of Warwick*

*References*

Babich, I., Bobrovnikov, V., Kazhurov, V. & Solov'eva, L. (2007) 'Kavkazskie gortsy i kazaki na granitsakh imperii', in Bobrovnikov, V. & Babich, I. (eds) (2007) *Severnyi Kavkaz v sostave Rossiiskoi imperii* (Moscow, Novoe literaturnoe obozrenie), pp. 59–86.

Barth, F. (1996) 'Ethnic Groups and Boundaries', in Hutchinson, J. & Smith, A. D. (eds) (1996) *Ethnicity* (Oxford, Oxford University Press), pp. 75–82.
Boeck, B. (2004) 'From the Verge of Extinction to Ethnic Distinction: Cossack Identity and Ethnicity in the Kuban' Region, 1991–2002', *Ab Imperio*, 2, pp. 617–45.
Boeck, B. (2001) 'Frontir ili pogranich'e? Rol' zybkikh granits v istorii donskogo kazachestva', in Manuilov, A. (ed.) (2001) *Sotsial'naya organizatsiya i obychnoe pravo: materialy nauchnoi konferentsii (Krasnodar, 24-26 avgusta 2000 g.)* (Krasnodar, RITs 'Vol'nye masters'), pp. 147–61.
Boeck, B. (1998) 'The Kuban' Cossack Revival (1989–1993): The Beginnings of a Cossack National Movement in the North Caucasus Region', *Nationalities Papers*, 26, 4, pp. 633–57.
Bromlei, Y. (1973) *Etnos i etnografiia* (Moscow, Nauka).
Bromlei, Y. (1981) *Sovremennye problemy etnografii* (Moscow, Nauka).
Derluguian, G.M. & Cipko, S. (1997) 'The Politics of Identity in a Russian Borderland Province: The Kuban Neo-Cossack Movement, 1989–1996', *Europe-Asia Studies*, 49, 8, pp. 1485–500.
Eleseev, F. I. (2001) *Kazaki na Kavkazskom fronte, 1914–1917* (Moscow, Voenizdat), available at: http://grwar.ru/library/Eliseeff-Kazaki/index.html, accessed 13 October 2011.
Eley, G. & Suny, R. (eds) (1996) *Becoming National. A Reader* (Oxford, Oxford University Press).
Gould, R. (2007) 'Language Dreamers: Race and the Politics of Etymology in the Caucasus', in Grant, B. & Yalçın-Heckmann, L. (eds) (2007) *Caucasus Paradigms: Anthropologies, Histories and the Making of a World Area* (Berlin, Lit Verlag), pp. 143–66.
Grant, B. (2005) 'The Good Russian Prisoner: Naturalizing Violence in the Caucasus Mountains', *Cultural Anthropology*, 20, 1, pp. 39–67.
Gromov, V. (2002a) 'Ne budet spokoistvya v dome kazaka, esli dom gortsa razrushen ...', *Kubanskie novosti*, 13 March.
Gromov, V. (2002b) 'Kuban' ne mozhet vmestit' vsekh zhelayushchikh', *Kuban' segodnya*, 15 March.
Grossberg, L. (1996) 'Identity and Cultural Studies—Is that all There is?', in Hall, S. & du Gay, P. (eds) (1996) *Questions of Cultural Identity* (London, Sage Publications), pp. 87–107.
Gubarev, G. V. & Skrylov, A. I. (eds) (1992) *Kazachii slovar'-spravochnik. T. 1-3* (Moscow, TO 'Sozidanie').
Gumilev, L. N. (2009) *Otkrytie Khazarii* (Moscow, Airis-Press).
Holquist, P. (2009) 'From Estate to Ethnos: The Changing Nature of Cossack Identity in the Twentieth Century', unpublished paper presented at the conference *National Identity in Eurasia*, Oxford, 23–24 March, Oxford, Oxford University.
Hall, S. (2000) 'Introduction: Who needs "Identity"?', in Hall, S. & du Gay, P. (eds) (2000) *Questions of Cultural Identity* (London, Sage Publications), pp. 1–17.
Hall, S. (1996) 'Ethnicity: Identity and Difference', in Eley, G. & Suny, R. (eds) (1996), pp. 339–49.
Kopytoff, I. (1987) *The African Frontier: The Reproduction of Traditional African Societies* (Bloomington, IN, Indiana University Press).
Kovalev, D. (2009) 'Chapurka svezhego chikhirya', *Kazarla: etnicheskii kazachii zhurnal*, 1.
Leutskii, V. P. & Babenko, A. A. (2008) *Traditsionnyi muzhskoi kostyum kubanskikh kazakov* (Krasnodar, Tsentral'noe raionnoe kazach'e obshchestvo Ekaterinodarskogo otdela Kubanskogo kazach'ego voiska).
Mackridge, P. & Yannakakis, E. (1997) 'Introduction', in Mackridge, P. & Yannakakis, E. (eds) (1997) *Ourselves and Others: The Development of a Greek Macedonian Cultural Identity Since 1912* (Oxford, Berg), pp. 1–22.
Markedonov, S. (2004a) 'Kazachestvo: edinstvo ili mnogoobrazie?', *Ab Imperio*, 2, pp. 521–8.
Markedonov, S. (2004b) 'Osnovnoi vopros kazakovedeniya: rossiiskaya istoriografiya v poiskakh "drevnego" kazachestva', *Ab Imperio*, 2, pp. 529–66.
Markedonov, S. (2003) 'New Cossacks in the South of Russia: Ideology, Values, and Policies', *Central Asia and Caucasus*, 29, 5, pp. 161–74.
Nikitin, V. (2007) *Kazachestvo: natsiya ili soslovie?* (Moscow, 'Yauza', 'Eksmo').
Olson, L. J. (2004) *Performing Russia: Folk Revival and Russian Identity* (London, Routledge Curzon).
Osipov, A. & Cherepova, O. (1996) *Narushenie prav vynuzhdennyh migrantov i etnicheskaya diskriminatsiya v Krasnodarskom krae (polozhenie meskhetinskikh turok)* (Moscow, Pravozashchitnyi tsentr "Memorial").
Parker, B. J. (2002) 'At the Edge of Empire: Conceptualizing Assyria's Anatolian Frontier ca. 700 BC', *Journal of Anthropological Archaeology*, 21, 3, pp. 371–95.
Pilkington, H. & Popov, A. (2009) 'Understanding Neo-paganism in Russia: Religion? Ideology? Philosophy? Fantasy?', in Williams, C., Ramanauskaite, E., McKay, G., Goddard, M. & Foxlee, N. (eds) (2009) *Subcultures and New Religious Movements in Russia and East-Central Europe* (New York, Peter Lang), pp. 253–304.

Popov, A. & Kuznetsov, I. (2008) 'Ethnic Discrimination and the Discourse of "Indigenization": The Regional Regime, "Indigenous Majority" and Ethnic Minorities in Krasnodar Krai in Russia', *Nationalities Papers*, 36, 2, May, pp. 223–52.

Prescott, J. R. V. (1978) *Boundaries and Frontiers* (Totowa, NJ, Rowman and Littlefield).

Sen', D. V. (2006) 'Kazachestvo Dona i Severo-Zapadnogo Kavkaza v kontse 17 v.—18 v.: praktiki vzaimootnoshenii frontirnykh soobshchestv s musul'manskimi gosudarstvami Prichernomor'ya (v kontekste zadach i perspektiv izucheniya mezhdunarodnykh otnoshenii v regione)', in *Istoricheskoe znachenie Kubani: stanovlenie i tendentsii razvitiya (konets 18—nachalo 20 v.): Materialy nauchnoi konferentsii* (Krasnodar, Diapazon-V), pp. 81–8, available at: http://www.cossackdom.com/articles/s/sen_kazdon.htm, accessed 15 June 2010.

Shnirel'man, V. A. (2010) 'Evraziitsy i evrei', *Forum noveishei vostochnoevropeiskoi istorii i kul'tury*, 1, pp. 46–78.

Skorik, A. P. (2008) *Mnogolikost' kazachestva Yuga Rossii v 1930-e gody: ocherki istorii* (Rostov-on-Don, Izdatel'stvo SKNTs VSh YuFU).

Slezkine, Y. (1996) 'The USSR as a Communal Apartment, or How a Socialist State Promoted Ethnic Particularism', in Eley, G. & Suny, R. (eds) (1996), pp. 202–38.

Staring, R., Kalb, D., Van der Land, M. & Tak, H. (1997) 'Localizing cultural identity', *Focaal*, 30–31, pp. 7–21.

Tishkov, V. A. (1997) *Ethnicity, Nationalism and Conflict in and after the Soviet Union: The Mind Aflame* (London, Sage Publications).

Toje, H. (2006) 'Cossack Identity in the New Russia: Kuban Cossack Revival and Local Politics', *Europe-Asia Studies*, 58, 7, pp. 1057–77.

van Dommelen, P. (1997) 'Colonial Constructs: Colonialism and Archaeology in the Mediterranean', *World Archaeology*, 28, 3, pp. 305–23.

White, R. (1991) *The Middle Ground: Indians, Empires, and Republics in the Great Lakes Region, 1650–1815* (Cambridge, Cambridge University Press).

# Post-Soviet Ethnic Relations in Stavropol'skii *Krai*, Russia: 'A Melting Pot or Boiling Shaft'?

## ANDREW FOXALL

### Abstract

According to the Russian NGO SOVA Center, 20 people were killed and at least 148 were injured in racist and neo-Nazi attacks in 2011 in Russia. Although a decline on 2007 (when 89 people were killed and at least 618 injured), the figure remains worryingly high. These people, as well as many others who are not included in these statistics, are victims of Russia's violent geographies of ethnic relations. Through research conducted over the course of two years in 2008 and 2009, supplemented by an analysis of research conduced by NGOs and independent researchers, I document post-Soviet ethnic relations in Stavropol'skii *Krai*.

THE BOMB ATTACK IN MAY 2010 OUTSIDE THE House of Culture and Sport in Stavropol', Stavropol'skii *Krai* was a reminder that ethno-nationalist tensions and violence are an everyday reality for people in that territory. In expressing his views on the attack, Vladimir Nesterov, head of the neo-nationalist 'Union of Slavic Communities of Stavropol'" (*Soyuz Slavyanskikh Obschestvennikh Organizatsii Stavropol'ya*), suggested that public expressions of ethnic Caucasian identity were 'unacceptable' to the *krai*'s majority ethnic Russian population (Kommersant 2010). The 2011 US Annual Report on Human Rights, published in early 2012, declared that while the number of racially motivated crimes in Russia had declined since 2010, ethnic discrimination and violence was still a matter of concern and skinhead violence (primarily against individuals from the North Caucasus) was a serious problem (US Department of State 2012). Indeed, despite having their basic human rights guaranteed under Article 19 of The Russian Constitution, discrimination of ethnic minorities is widespread, with Amnesty International (2006) reporting that Russian authorities have created a state of 'impunity' against ethnic discrimination and violence. Scholarly research supports this conclusion,

Research for this essay was supported by a CEELBAS Doctoral Studentship from the ESRC that the author held at the University of Oxford between 2007 and 2010. The author would like to thank Judith Pallot, the Guest Editors and two anonymous reviewers for their supportive comments and suggestions on earlier drafts, as well as numerous contacts, friends and research participants in Russia without whom this research would not have been possible.

showing that the authorities actively discriminate against minorities (Swerdlow 2006; Popov & Kuznetsov 2008). Anyone with a relative or friend who has been the victim of ethnic discrimination or violence is a victim of Russia's continuing failure to deal with these problems. Nor should the 1.4 million people employed in the Ministry of Internal Affairs' (*Ministerstvo vnutrennikh del*, MVD) *militsiya* (and other security services) be forgotten.[1] They are also participants in Russia's violent geographies of ethnic relations (Pain 2007, pp. 900–1). Amnesty International (2004) reported that Russian authorities target visible minorities for racial profiling, resulting in unnecessary registration and passport checks, searches, and arbitrary arrest and detention. It is indicative that the Federal Migration Service (*Federal'naya migratsionnaya sluzhba*) remains part of the MVD, which is *a priori* engaged in tackling crime. 'Such an institutional structure', Chebankova (2007, pp. 450) notes, 'creates an atmosphere in which most ethnic minorities are immediately classed as those who fall under the jurisdiction of the law enforcement agencies'. As a result, ethnic minorities in Russia, particularly those from the North Caucasus, are subjected to a double marginality. 'People of Caucasian nationality' (*litsa kavkazskoi natsional'nosti*) face widespread intolerance by ethnic Russians (and Slavs, more broadly) and institutionalised discrimination from the Russian state through its security services. In October 2002, Lyudmilla Alekseyeva, Chair of the Moscow Helsinki Group, identified anti-Caucasian feelings (so-called *Kavkazofobiya* or Caucasus-phobia) as 'definitely the most serious problem that Russia is faced with today. It is very widespread among the population in general, at all levels' (Russell 2005, p. 112).

In the North Caucasus, post-Soviet ethnic relations must be understood in the context of political change, economic liberalisation, military conflict and demographic processes (Zayonchkovskaya 2000). Traditionally considered a multi-ethnic region, in the post-Soviet years Stavropol'skii *Krai* has become a primary destination for migrants from the North Caucasus republics because of its attractive opportunities for employment (O'Loughlin *et al.* 2007a). Rapid population growth and high levels of out-migration in North Caucasus republics (well-established processes) contrast with the natural population decrease of ethnic Russians and the high natural increase of ethnic Caucasians in Stavropol'skii *Krai*. As a result, while ethnic Russians remain the majority population in Stavropol'skii *Krai* in many ways they consider themselves as an embattled minority group (Belozerov 2005). This is clearly evident in the growing territorial and ethnic differentiation of the *krai*'s population.[2] Research on ethnicity in the North Caucasus has shown that ethnicity became increasingly politicised during the 1990s (Cornell 2001; Lapidus 2002) and that a complex ethnic geography increases the risk of ethnic conflict (Zürcher 2007, pp. 4–5). These issues are captured in the question '*Stavropol'e: plavil'nii kotel ili oboronitel'nii val?*' ('Stavropol': a melting pot or boiling shaft?') (Markedonov 2007). Through a series of initiatives, authorities in

---

[1]See http://inmoscowsshadows.wordpress.com/2010/01/01/the-latest-russian-police-reform-the-kremlin-is-likely-to-be-the-only-beneficiary, accessed 19 July 2012.
[2]In the 1990s, this process of 'ethnic segregation' (Kolossov *et al.* 2001) led to calls for combining ethnic Russian dominated areas of Chechnya (Naurskii *Raion* and Shelkovskii *Raion*) and Dagestan (Kislyarskii *Raion* and Tarumovskii *Raion*) with Stavropol'skii *Krai* (Matveeva 1999, p. 42).

Stavropol'skii *Krai* have developed an interest in the role played by geography in ethnic relations. Most notably, in 2008 the *Etnicheskii Atlas Stavropol'skogo kraya* (Ethnic Atlas of Stavropol'skii *Krai*) was published jointly by academics at Stavropol' State University and the 'Committee of Stavropol'skii *Krai* for National and Cossack affairs' (*Komitet Stavropol'skogo krai no delam natsional'nostei i kazachestva*) in Stavropol' (Belozerov *et al.* 2008).[3] Reviewing the Atlas, Vasilii Shnukov, former chairman of the 'Committee of Stavropol'skii *Krai* for National and Cossack affairs',[4] argued that the work would allow authorities to 'solve questions of interethnic attitudes' as 'experience shows that the transformation of [ethnic] Russians into the minority populations in multi-ethnic regions increases the probability of different sorts of conflicts, including interethnic, occurring' (Shnukov 2009). A similar conclusion was drawn by Bassin (2009, p. 131) who, writing about the appearance of *ethnopolitika* (ethno-politics) in post-Soviet Russia, highlighted the need for detailed and comprehensive studies of the 'volatile ethno-demographic situation' in many parts of Russia which 'provides abundant opportunities for future [ethnic] conflict'.

This essay explores post-Soviet ethnic relations in Stavropol'skii *Krai*. The territory provides a remarkable site for the study of ethnic relations, as it occupies a key place in contemporary Russian politics—it is the only territory within the North Caucasus Federal District (created in January 2010) with an ethnic Russian majority population— and holds a symbolic place in the history of Russian control over the North Caucasus.[5] Research on ethnicity in the North Caucasus has emphasised connections with religion (Yemelianova 2003; Gammer 2008) and noted how ethnicity became 'politicised' in post-Soviet transition (Lapidus 2002). Elsewhere, Cornell and Starr (2006, p. 25) group ethnic nationalism with radical Islam, the influence of kinship-based networks, the slow pace of democratisation and the prominence of organised crime as the foremost challenges to peace in the Caucasus. Writing on security, Cornell (2001, p. 3) notes that, 'inter-ethnic relations in the Caucasus pose actual and potential threats to the security of Eurasia, and by extension the international community in general'. Yet, as Tishkov (2004, p. 9) has observed, the utility of such grand geopolitical theorising is questionable as in North Caucasus 'big theories fall short'. To mark this essay out from existing literature, I draw on a growing literature within political geography (and critical approaches within the social sciences more broadly) concerned with 'everyday life' (see, for example, Megoran 2006; Pain & Smith 2008; Ramadan 2009) and focus on the 'everyday' scale of ethnic relations, something that is often ignored and left unexplored in much existing literature. In doing so, this essay connects with wider work on the spatiality of instability within the North Caucasus beyond Chechnya. As Vendina *et al.* (2007, p. 178) note in their study on Chechnya, 'most attention [on the North Caucasus] has been focused on the military campaigns and the impacts of rampant violence, but very little attention has been paid to the non-military dimensions of these devastating wars, both within Chechnya and beyond'. Alluding to the wider dimensions of the wars, Tishkov (2004, p. xviii) has noted how the Second Chechen War 'destroys human lives and health far beyond the battlefield', but he does not go on to explore this beyond a

---

[3]See also, Foxall (forthcoming).
[4]See http://www.stavkomnat.ru/, accessed 19 July 2012.
[5]See, for example, Kolossov *et al.* (2001); O'Loughlin *et al.* (2007a).

limited analysis of the impact of the War on family life (2004, pp. 151–63). Similarly, Cornell (2001, p. 1) has written that the 'humanitarian burden' of the two Chechen Wars 'has been borne by the people of the region more than by the international community', but he is not forthcoming with how such a 'burden' was embodied or played out in individuals' everyday lives. This essay begins to refocus attention on the spatiality of geopolitical instability beyond Chechnya in the North Caucasus through exploring the impact of instability on ethnic relations in Stavropol'skii *Krai*. In doing so, this essay explores (rather than assumes) the importance of ethnicity in everyday life and can contribute to a better understanding of the ethnic situation in Stavropol'skii *Krai* and Russia as a whole.

The remainder of this essay is structured as follows. In the next section, I explain the methodological issues associated with conducting research on ethnic relations in Russia. I then briefly examine the geographer's traditional explanatory variables—the time and space of ethnic groups in Stavropol'skii *Krai*. In the following section—Post-Soviet ethnic relations in Russia—I draw on the work of NGOs and independent researchers to analyse the current situation of ethnic relations in Russia and Stavropol'skii *Krai* in particular. Next, I make use of my own research in Stavropol'skii *Krai* to explore how ethnic Russian and non-ethnic Russian citizens experience and negotiate ethnic relations in their everyday life, focusing on the ways through which citizens experience ethnic discrimination. Finally, I offer some concluding remarks on the prospects for improving ethnic relations in Russia.

*Methodological issues*

It is necessary to use an eclectic range of sources when conducting research on ethnic relations in Russia as authorities traditionally do not welcome the interest of outsiders on the issue. Although reports from the Moscow-based EAWARN ('The Network of Ethnological Monitoring and Early Warning for the Prevention of Conflicts') suggest that ethnic relations have turned increasingly violent since the early 1990s, exact figures for instances of ethnic conflict—as well as for discrimination against ethnic minorities—are hard to obtain due to chronic under-reporting (Kozhevnikova 2009). Authorities, for example, frequently charge perpetrators with the less serious offence of 'hooliganism' (Amnesty International 2006, p. 20). Therefore, I have had to follow the time-honoured method of research into 'closed' aspects of Russian society by piecing together data from a variety of sources (Pallot 2007). As Pallot notes, the accuracy of research in this context 'is inevitably open to question' as it relies upon research by NGOs and independent researchers (2007, p. 572). I have been able to supplement these sources with my own research, conducted over the course of two years between 2008 and 2009 as part of an ESRC-sponsored CEELBAS Doctoral Studentship, in Stavropol'skii *Krai*. My research involved semi-structured interviews with 50 people and five focus-group interviews. Since the objective of my research was to develop an idea of the state of ethnic relations in Stavropol'skii *Krai*, I interviewed 20 individuals who could provide informed answers and who could direct me to other people who could answer specific questions, including academics, politicians, policy makers, political commentators and other opinion formers. These interviews had a dual purpose in that the interviewee was both informed and offered an informed opinion. This allowed me to excavate the opinion formers' range of opinions and to see to what extent their, on the whole, measured views were internalised by the population through 30 interviews which I conducted in Stavropol' with a variety of people, including students, workers, the retired and unemployed. A secondary aim of these interviews was to gauge the everyday opinions of citizens in Stavropol' about ethnic relations. The results of this research are the subject of other publications (Foxall 2010, 2011), but some information is relevant to the present discussion.

The two principal sources of data are EAWARN and the SOVA Center ('The SOVA Center for Information and Analysis'). Created in 1993 by Valerii Tishkov, EAWARN is a joint project of the Institute of Ethnology and Anthropology, Russian Academy of Sciences (RAS) and the Conflict Management Group based in Boston, Massachusetts. The goal of EAWARN is to undertake ethno-political monitoring within the post-Soviet states, particularly regions within Russia with multi-ethnic populations and complex ethno-political situations, for the purpose of conflict prevention and conflict management. Since 1994, EAWARN has published a bi-monthly bulletin (*Byulleten'*) and special reports available to an international academic audience and political institutions, national and regional power structures in Russia, NGOs, experts, policy makers and practitioners. The information produced by EAWARN is stored in the computerised 'Data-Bank on Ethnicity and Conflict' at the Institute of Ethnology and Anthropology, RAS. For my study, I was given full access to this Russian-language data-bank. This amounted to nearly 200 pages of reports on the ethno-political situation in Stavropol'skii *Krai*. These data are not available via the EAWARN website.[6] SOVA, meanwhile, is a human rights NGO and think-tank, based in Moscow. Formed in 2002 by members of the Moscow Helsinki Group and the Russian research centre 'Panorama', SOVA conducts sociological research on the development of nationalism and racism in contemporary Russia. SOVA produces regular reports and recommendations regarding ethnic conflict, hate crimes, racist violence and other manifestations of nationalism that are widely used and cited by OSCE, Amnesty International, Pulitzer Centre on Crisis Reporting, and other human rights and political organisations.[7]

*Demography and geography in Stavropol'skii* Krai

According to the 2010 All-Russian Census, Stavropol'skii *Krai* has a population of 2,786,281 people. While 80.9% are ethnic Russian, 5.9% of its residents are Armenians, 1.8% are Dargins, 1.2% are Greeks, 1.1% are Roma, 1.1% are Ukrainian and 0.8% are Nogai, along with a scattering of smaller groups. In their study of the ethnic geography of Stavropol'skii *Krai*, O'Loughlin *et al.* (2007a) identify the most salient characteristics of ethnic geography in the *krai* as the low net in-migration of ethnic Russians (and Slavs more broadly); high in-migration of Armenians; renewed out-migration of Chechens after nearly a decade (1996–2004) of in-migration; and large-scale net in-migration of Avars and Dargins (from Dagestan). Owing to these

---

[6]http://www.eawarn.ru, accessed 19 July 2012.
[7]http://sova-center.ru, accessed 19 July 2012.

(and other) processes, they argue that a trend of 'de-Russification', reflecting the in-migration of ethnic Caucasians and out-migration of ethnic Russians (combined with a low rate of natural increase), is manifest in a noticeable reduction in the ethnic Russian share of the *krai* population; 80.9% in 2010 compared with 84% in 1989 and 91.3% in 1959. While such figures, however, do not give a sense of the very real spatial segregation of ethnic groups in Stavropol'skii *Krai* (see Belozerov 2005), it is clear that there is increasing internal ethnic differentiation within Stavropol'skii *Krai*, which is seen as politically sensitive for the Kremlin and Russian society as the retreat of ethnic Russians from the *krai* has long been equated with losing control over the North Caucasus (Dzutsev 2009). Between 1989 and 2010, the ethnic Russian population in the North Caucasus republics fell by around 466,500 people as Russians have fled conflict and what they perceive to be increasingly hostile policies (Tsvetkov 2006). This is part of a more long-term 'de-Russification' of the North Caucasus republics: in 1959 ethnic Russians accounted for 38.8% of the population in the seven republics of the North Caucasus and by the time of the 2010 census this figure had dropped to 9.3%. In absolute terms, the number of Russians living in the North Caucasus republics dropped by 1,086,600 people in this period (1959–2010). At the same time, the non-ethnic Russian population of the republics has dramatically increased: from around 3,929,000 in 1989 to 6,189,800 in 2010. It is owing to such contemporary demographic processes that Markedonov (2009) argues 'Stavropol' has become a frontier, a unique border line dividing "the Russian world" and "the Caucasus world"'.

*Post-Soviet ethnic relations in Russia with particular reference to Stavropol'skii* Krai

There was a considerable level of resistance to all forms of ethnic conflict and violence in the early 1990s (as well as ethnic discrimination) as the officially enforced 'Soviet' identity (which proclaimed the equality of all ethnic groups in the Soviet Union) was still strong (Gudkov 2006). However, ethnic relations became increasingly violent throughout the mid-1990s in Russia as ethno-nationalism grew to 'astonishing levels' (Harding 2009). The rise in ethno-nationalism can be seen as a reaction to the collapse of the Soviet Union and the chaos of financial (and societal) reforms, and went hand-in-hand with a growth of support in Russia for 'conservative' political parties—the KPRF (Communist Party of the Russian Federation, *Kommunisticheskaya Partiya Rossiiskoi Federatsii*) and the LDPR (Liberal Democratic Party of Russia, *Liberal'no Demokraticheskaya Partiya Rossii*) (Clem & Craumer 2004). At the same time, Russian neo-nationalist organisations, for example, the 'Movement against Illegal Immigration' (*Dvizhenie Protiv Nelegal'noi Immigratsii*) and 'Russian National Unity' (*Russkoe natsional'noe edinstvonatsiona'lnoe edinstvo*), began to appear in the so-called 'red belt' of territories stretching along the southern border of Russia, particularly Stavropol'skii *Krai*, where they received official support from the authorities,[8] seeing

---

[8]There is reason to believe that Dmitri Kuzmin (Major of Stavropol' *gorod* in 2007) sympathised with ultra-nationalists. During an investigation into allegations of official misconduct, he was found to have kept Nazi paraphernalia in his office. See von Twickel (2009).

themselves as 'defenders' of Russia from immigrants.[9] In the 1990s,'Russian National Unity' (now disbanded) found official support from the Stavropol'skii *Krai* authorities; members of the group 'patrolled' public parks and city streets, gradually becoming an arm of the regional government. However, in 1998 Yuri Luzhkov, Mayor of Moscow, forbade a planned Russian National Unity gathering as part of a larger federal campaign. The influence of the group began to wane after that, and two years later it split into a number of smaller factions, some of which are still active today in Stavropol'skii *Krai*. The most notable of these groups is the 'Union of Slavic Communities of Stavropol'. The rebirth of the Cossack movement—like ethnic, cultural and religious groups in general—during *perestroika* also explains the rise in ethno-national tensions, as descendants of the Kuban Cossacks in Krasnodar *krai* and the Terek Cossacks in Stavropol'skii *Krai* reformed into Cossack hosts (*voisko*) (Boeck 1998; O'Rouke 2007). Cossacks, who operate as a vigilante force not answerable to any government authority although they are closely associated with some officials, were given government authority in the mid-1990s to conduct joint patrols with police units. In 2001, Vasily Bondarev (occupying positions as both Ataman of the Terek Cossacks and Secretary of the Stavropol'skii *Krai* Security Council) explained that Cossacks had established 33 self-defence detachments and dozens of volunteer patrols and security firms, bringing together some 8,000 Cossacks, in Stavropol'skii *Krai*. Bondarev also claimed that Terek Cossacks had formed patrols in the *raiony* bordering on Chechnya and Dagestan, for which they received an annual R18 million allocation from the *krai* budget (Mukhin 2001). In the name of law enforcement, Cossacks and other authorities frequently commit ethnic violence. Indeed, while skinheads are the perpetrators of ethno-national attacks in most Russian regions, in the North Caucasus such violence is primarily associated with Cossacks.[10] Table 1 shows statistics of Racist and Neo-Nazi Attacks between 2004 and 2011 in Russia. Nationally, Moscow and Moscow *Oblast'* and St Petersburg and Leningrad *Oblast'*, as the two largest cities and their environs, had the highest recorded number of attacks (1558 and 484 respectively), but with concentrations in other large regions, including Stavropol'skii *Krai* (64). Coverage of ethnic violence is incomplete, and data frequently do not include the North Caucasus republics.

One feature of ethnic relations in Russia is that, until recently, they had been increasingly violent. Although 2008 saw the first decrease in the number of recorded victims of racist and neo-Nazi attacks since 2004, the number of attacks in 2008 (615

---

[9]In 1991, there were only a handful of these groups operating in Russia, but in 2004 their number stood at more than 33,000. On 11 March 2001, the 'National Anti-Terrorist Committee' (*Natsional'ni Antiterroristicheskie Komitet*, NAK) released a report that cited data from the MVD (a member of the NAK) suggesting that right-wing extremist movements had 200,000 members. These are official figures, but experts agree that the number of Russians in ultra-radical nationalist organisations is greater. See Jamestown Foundation (2009).

[10]These groups are not necessarily mutually exclusive though; in 2005, SOVA reported that Cossacks had begun to coordinate with skinheads, seeing each other as 'comrades-in-arms' (Kozhevnikova 2005).

## TABLE 1
### Statistics of Racist and Neo-Nazi Attacks between 2004 and 2011, by City

| | 2004 | | 2005 | | | 2006 | | | 2007 | | | 2008 | | | 2009 | | | 2010 | | | 2011 | | | Total. 2004-9 |
|---|---|---|---|---|---|---|---|---|---|---|---|---|---|---|---|---|---|---|---|---|---|---|---|---|
| | Killed | Beaten, wounded | Total victims | Killed | Beaten, wounded | Total victims | Killed | Beaten, wounded | Total victims | Killed | Beaten, wounded | Total victims | Killed | Beaten, wounded | Total victims | Killed | Beaten, wounded | Total victims | Killed | Beaten, wounded | Total victims | Killed | Beaten, wounded | Total victims | |
| Total in Russia | 50 | 218 | 268 | 49 | 419 | 468 | 66 | 522 | 588 | 89 | 618 | 707 | 116 | 499 | 615 | 93 | 440 | 533 | 42 | 401 | 443 | 20 | 148 | 168 | 3800 |
| **Top ten regions by total number of attacks** | | | | | | | | | | | | | | | | | | | | | | | | | |
| Moskva *Oblast'* | 18 | 62 | 80 | 16 | 179 | 195 | 40 | 228 | 268 | 57 | 224 | 281 | 64 | 223 | 287 | 41 | 153 | 194 | 20 | 177 | 197 | 11 | 45 | 56 | 1558 |
| Leningrad *Oblast'* | 9 | 32 | 41 | 4 | 45 | 49 | 4 | 56 | 62 | 11 | 118 | 129 | 15 | 40 | 55 | 19 | 46 | 65 | 2 | 50 | 52 | 3 | 28 | 31 | 484 |
| Nizhny Novgorod | 1 | 5 | 6 | 4 | 12 | 16 | 0 | 36 | 36 | 1 | 44 | 45 | 4 | 21 | 25 | 6 | 31 | 37 | 5 | 21 | 26 | 0 | 2 | 2 | 193 |
| Sverdlovsk *Oblast'* | 1 | 7 | 8 | 6 | 6 | 12 | 0 | 6 | 6 | 3 | 17 | 20 | 1 | 16 | 20 | 1 | 20 | 21 | 0 | 5 | 5 | 2 | 1 | 2 | 93 |
| Voronezh | 1 | 2 | 3 | 1 | 21 | 22 | 1 | 6 | 7 | 0 | 17 | 17 | 2 | 23 | 25 | 0 | 5 | 5 | 3 | 3 | 5 | 1 | 4 | 4 | 86 |
| Irkutsk *Oblast'* | 3 | 0 | 3 | 2 | 5 | 7 | 0 | 8 | 8 | 1 | 53 | 54 | 0 | 1 | 1 | 2 | 4 | 6 | 0 | 4 | 5 | 0 | 4 | 4 | 84 |
| Primorye | 5 | 9 | 14 | 1 | 3 | 3 | 2 | 18 | 20 | 1 | 3 | 4 | 3 | 6 | 9 | 2 | 13 | 15 | 1 | 2 | 3 | 0 | 0 | 0 | 70 |
| Krasnodar | 2 | 32 | 34 | 0 | 3 | 3 | 0 | 7 | 7 | 0 | 11 | 11 | 1 | 6 | 7 | 0 | 7 | 7 | 0 | 3 | 3 | 0 | 2 | 2 | 69 |
| Novosibirsk | 2 | 12 | 14 | 1 | 9 | 10 | 0 | 9 | 9 | 1 | 5 | 6 | 3 | 2 | 3 | 1 | 11 | 12 | 1 | 2 | 2 | 0 | 1 | 1 | 64 |
| Stavropol' | 0 | 0 | 0 | 0 | 21 | 21 | 0 | 1 | 1 | 1 | 8 | 9 | 3 | 10 | 13 | 2 | 11 | 13 | 1 | 5 | 6 | 1 | 0 | 1 | 64 |
| **Bottom ten regions by total number of attacks** | | | | | | | | | | | | | | | | | | | | | | | | | |
| Buryat | 0 | 0 | 0 | 0 | 0 | 0 | 0 | 0 | 0 | 1 | 1 | 2 | 0 | 0 | 0 | 1 | 1 | 2 | 0 | 0 | 0 | 0 | 2 | 2 | 6 |
| Smolensk | 0 | 0 | 0 | 0 | 2 | 2 | 0 | 0 | 0 | 0 | 0 | 0 | 0 | 0 | 0 | 0 | 2 | 2 | 0 | 2 | 2 | 0 | 0 | 0 | 6 |
| Astrakhan | 0 | 0 | 0 | 0 | 2 | 2 | 0 | 0 | 0 | 0 | 0 | 0 | 0 | 0 | 0 | 0 | 2 | 2 | 0 | 0 | 0 | 1 | 2 | 3 | 5 |
| Orenburg | 0 | 0 | 0 | 0 | 0 | 0 | 1 | 1 | 2 | 1 | 1 | 2 | 0 | 0 | 0 | 1 | 0 | 1 | 0 | 0 | 0 | 0 | 0 | 0 | 5 |
| Petropavlovsk-Kamchatskiy | 0 | 0 | 0 | 0 | 0 | 0 | 0 | 0 | 0 | 1 | 0 | 1 | 0 | 0 | 0 | 0 | 0 | 0 | 0 | 3 | 3 | 0 | 1 | 1 | 5 |
| Chita | 0 | 0 | 0 | 0 | 0 | 0 | 1 | 0 | 1 | 0 | 3 | 3 | 0 | 0 | 0 | 0 | 0 | 0 | 0 | 0 | 0 | 0 | 0 | 0 | 4 |
| Sacha (Yakutia) | 0 | 0 | 0 | 0 | 0 | 0 | 0 | 0 | 0 | 0 | 2 | 2 | 0 | 0 | 0 | 0 | 0 | 0 | 0 | 2 | 2 | 0 | 0 | 0 | 4 |
| Evreiskaya avtonomnaya *Oblast'* | 0 | 0 | 0 | 3 | 0 | 3 | 0 | 0 | 0 | 0 | 0 | 0 | 0 | 0 | 0 | 0 | 0 | 0 | 0 | 0 | 0 | 0 | 0 | 0 | 3 |
| Yuzhno-Sakhalinsk | 1 | 0 | 1 | 0 | 0 | 0 | 0 | 0 | 0 | 0 | 0 | 0 | 0 | 0 | 0 | 0 | 0 | 0 | 0 | 0 | 0 | 0 | 0 | 0 | 1 |
| Pskov | 0 | 1 | 1 | 0 | 1 | 1 | 1 | 0 | 0 | 0 | 0 | 0 | 0 | 0 | 0 | 0 | 0 | 0 | 0 | 0 | 0 | 0 | 0 | 0 | 1 |

*Source*: SOVA Center website: http://www.sova-center.ru/en/xenophobia/reports-analyses/2012/04/d24088, accessed 24 July 2012.

victims) was more than double that in 2004 (268 victims) (see Table 1).[11] In 2011, the figure stood at 168 victims. Ethnic violence is found in virtually all regions and each Russian city has its own particular distribution of violent attacks. Instances of racist and neo-Nazi attacks are more common in Russia's violent 'heartland'—Moscow and Moscow *Oblast'*, St Petersburg and Leningrad *Oblast'*, Nizhnii Novgorod *Oblast'*, Sverdlovsk *Oblast'*—than in regions along Russia's southern border.[12] Nevertheless, of the 3,800 racist and neo-Nazi attacks in Russia between 2004 and 2011, 2,321 (or 61%) occurred in these four regions. Ethnic violence tends to be concentrated in areas with high levels of immigration, and where the impacts of changing demography are felt most acutely. Whilst this means that ethnic violence is most common in cities or other urban settlements, it also occurs in rural peripheries.

In an attempt to explore the geographic distribution of violent attacks, Table 2 shows the ethnicity of the victims of racist and neo-Nazi attacks. Unfortunately, data that are available do not reflect 'actual' identity of victims, but rather the identity given to them by the attackers. In other words, if a Slavic person were mistaken for a Caucasian, he or she would be registered as a 'person from the Caucasus'. According to these data, the number of attacks rose steadily from 269 in 2004 to 716 in 2007, before falling to 168 in 2011. However, as the table makes clear, some groups of people suffer disproportionately from Russia's violent geographies of ethnic relations; for example, the number of attacks against people from the Caucasus increased from 53 (of 268) in 2004 to 103 (of 561) in 2008, before falling to 20 (of 168) in 2011, following the pattern for racist and neo-Nazi attacks as a whole. Overall, 561 out of 3,800, (15%) racist and neo-Nazi attacks between 2004 and 2011 were committed against people from the Caucasus. Table 2 shows how this compares with other victims of the same violence.

At the same time, statistics for the number of convictions for violent crimes with a recognised hate motive roughly map onto the pattern of racist and neo-Nazi attacks in the same 2004–2011 period (see Table 3). Thus, while Moscow and Moscow *Oblast'* and St Petersburg and Leningrad *Oblast'* are the locations of the majority of attacks, there were a number in Stavropol'skii *Krai*. Indeed, in 2007, there was the same number of attacks in Stavropol'skii *Krai* as in St Petersburg and Leningrad *Oblast'*. This is due to the six weeks of intermittent ethnic rioting in May and June 2007, when two ethnic Russian students and one ethnic Chechen student were killed (Foxall 2010).[13]

### *'Everyday' ethnic relations and discrimination in Stavropol'skii* Krai

In Russia, racist and neo-Nazi attacks and violent hate crimes are not the only manifestations of ethno-nationalism. Rather, ethnic discrimination is important to

---

[11]I use the term 'neo-Nazi' here only because it is the term used by Russian authorities to identify the groups in question. In reality, as Laquer (1996, pp. 178–96) notes, National Socialism defined Slavs as racially inferior *Untermenschen* and thus this ideology appeals to few people in Russia. Instead, Russian neo-Nazi groups are characterised by: racism; anti-Semitism; Islamophobia; and extreme xenophobia towards people from Asia and the Caucasus. See Laquer (1996).

[12]In 2004, there were approximately 6,000 young neo-Nazis in Moscow, over 3,000 in St Petersburg and well over 2,500 skinheads in Nizhni Novgorod. See Tarasov (2004).

[13]For an overview of the state of interethnic relations in Stavropol'skii *Krai* in 2007, see Astvatsaturova (2007).

## TABLE 2
### Statistics of Racist and Neo-Nazi Attacks in 2004–2011, by Categorisation of Victims

| Year | | Dark-Skinned | Central Asian | Caucasian | Middle Eastern or North African | Other Asian | 'non-Slav' appearance | Members of youth subcultures, anti-fascists and leftist youth | Other, or not known | Total |
|---|---|---|---|---|---|---|---|---|---|---|
| 2004 | Killed | 1 | 10 | 15 | 4 | 8 | 2 | 0 | 10 | 50 |
|  | Beaten or wounded | 33 | 23 | 38 | 12 | 30 | 22 | 4 | 57 | 219 |
| 2005 | Killed | 3 | 18 | 12 | 1 | 3 | 3 | 3 | 5 | 49 |
|  | Beaten or wounded | 38 | 35 | 52 | 22 | 72 | 72 | 121 | 21 | 419 |
| 2006 | Killed | 2 | 17 | 15 | 0 | 4 | 4 | 3 | 21 | 66 |
|  | Beaten or wounded | 32 | 60 | 72 | 11 | 52 | 69 | 119 | 107 | 522 |
| 2007 | Killed | 0 | 35 | 27 | 2 | 2 | 20 | 5 | 2 | 93 |
|  | Beaten or wounded | 38 | 82 | 64 | 21 | 45 | 90 | 195 | 88 | 623 |
| 2008 | Killed | 2 | 63 | 27 | 2 | 1 | 11 | 4 | 6 | 116 |
|  | Beaten or wounded | 23 | 123 | 76 | 13 | 41 | 56 | 87 | 80 | 499 |
| 2009 | Killed | 2 | 40 | 17 | 0 | 14 | 9 | 5 | 6 | 93 |
|  | Beaten or wounded | 59 | 89 | 76 | 2 | 36 | 62 | 77 | 39 | 440 |
| 2010 | Killed | 1 | 18 | 5 | 0 | 3 | 7 | 3 | 5 | 42 |
|  | Beaten or wounded | 26 | 80 | 45 | 1 | 18 | 99 | 64 | 68 | 401 |
| 2011 | Killed | 1 | 10 | 6 | 0 | 0 | 1 | 0 | 2 | 20 |
|  | Beaten or wounded | 18 | 25 | 14 | 0 | 8 | 21 | 26 | 36 | 148 |
| Total |  | 279 | 728 | 561 | 91 | 337 | 548 | 716 | 553 | 3800 |

*Source*: SOVA Center website: http://www.sova-center.ru/en/xenophobia/reports-analyses/2012/04/d24088/, accessed 24 July 2012. Note: This table does not include victims of attacks in the ethnic republics of the North Caucasus. Nor does the table include attacks committed on homeless people with an ideological motivation.

TABLE 3
STATISTICS OF CONVICTIONS FOR VIOLENT CRIMES WITH A RECOGNISED HATE MOTIVE IN 2004–2011

| Year | | Moscow | St Petersburg | Stavropol' | Total in Russia |
|---|---|---|---|---|---|
| | | \multicolumn{3}{c}{City} | |
| 2004 | Number of convictions | 4 | 2 | 0 | 9 |
| | Number of offenders convicted | 11 | 10 | 0 | 26 |
| | Including suspended sentences of release from punishment | Unknown | 4 | 0 | 5 |
| 2005 | Number of convictions | 2 | 2 | 0 | 17 |
| | Number of offenders convicted | 4 | 10 | 0 | 56 |
| | Including suspended sentences of release from punishment | 0 | 4 | 0 | 5 |
| 2006 | Number of convictions | 5 | 3 | 0 | 33 |
| | Number of offenders convicted | 11 | 10 | 0 | 109 |
| | Including suspended sentences of release from punishment | 1 | 4 | 0 | 24 |
| 2007 | Number of convictions | 4 | 2 | 2 | 23 |
| | Number of offenders convicted | 11 | 11 | 2 | 65 |
| | Including suspended sentences of release from punishment | 0 | 3 | 0 | 18 |
| 2008 | Number of convictions | 7 | 4 | 1 | 35 |
| | Number of offenders convicted | 40 | 9 | 2 | 118 |
| | Including suspended sentences of release from punishment | 4 | 2 | 1 | 31 |
| 2009 | Number of convictions | 11 | 2 | 1 | 52 |
| | Number of offenders convicted | 41 | 3 | 2 | 132 |
| | Including suspended sentences of release from punishment | 7 | 0 | 0 | 35 |
| 2010 | Number of convictions | 10 | 6 | 4 | 91 |
| | Number of offenders convicted | 36 | 32 | 30 | 320 |
| | Including suspended sentences of release from punishment | 3 | 18 | 6 | 120 |
| 2011 | Number of convictions | 8 | 3 | 0 | 58 |
| | Number of offenders convicted | 30 | 39 | 0 | 199 |
| | Including suspended sentences of release from punishment | 4 | 16 | 0 | 74 |

*Source*: SOVA Center website, available at: http://www.sova-center.ru/en/xenophobia/reports-analyses/2012/04/d24088, accessed 24 July 2012.

consider. For victims, the violent geographies of ethnic relations are exacerbated by ethnic discrimination. Although discrimination affects access to employment, services, transport and many other aspects in life, one of the ways that it is manifest most clearly is in access to housing. According to research carried out by the Centre for Ethnopolitical Studies in Moscow in 2002, of 400 newspaper articles advertising private housing for rent surveyed in Stavropol'skii *Krai*, 140 announcements (or 35% of all announcements) stated they were only available to '[ethnic] Russians' (Table 4). Approximately the same share of announcements in other media (for example, street advertisements or other notices) also stated that the accommodation was only available to ethnic Russians. Analysis of the advertisements show that expressions containing the phrases 'for Russian family' (*dlya Russkie sem'e*) or 'Russian' (*Russkie*) were the most common way in which this discrimination was made apparent, while

TABLE 4
PRIVATE ADVERTISEMENTS BY LANDLORDS WITH THE INDICATION OF THE NATIONALITY OF
A TENANT, 2002 AND 2003

|  | December 2002 | | | October–December 2003 | | |
| --- | --- | --- | --- | --- | --- | --- |
|  | | 'For [ethnic] Russians' | | | 'For [ethnic] Russians' | |
|  | All announcements | Number | % | All announcements | Number | % |
| Private advertisements in newspapers | 400 | 140 | 35 | 355 | 47 | 13.2 |
| Private advertisements in other media | 100 | 33 | 33 | 208 | 60 | 28.8 |
| All | 500 | 173 | 34.6 | 563 | 107 | 19 |

*Source:* http://www.indem.ru/Ceprs/Minorities/mainStDER.htm, accessed 24 July 2012.

phrases such as 'for Slavs' (*dlya Slavyanam*), 'Slavic family' (*Slavyanskie sem'e*) or 'for a respectable Russian family' (*dlya prilichnoi Russkoi sem'e*) appeared less often. There are also more explicit demands, for example, 'only Russian' (*tol'ko Russkie*) and 'only to Slavs' (*tol'ko Slavyanam*). There was no mention of any ethnic groups in the advertisements, except for ethnic Russians and Slavs.

The fact that landlords prefer to rent apartments to Slavs is well understood by potential renters, who emphasise their ethnicity when looking for an apartment. Here, phrases like 'for Russian family' (*dlya Russkie sem'e*), 'Russian men' (*Russkie muzhchin*') or 'Russian women' (*Russkie zhenshchini*) are more common. Similarly, in all advertisements, Russian is the only ethnicity mentioned. Of the 500 advertisements placed in newspapers by potential tenants in December 2002, 135 (or 27%) stated that they were only 'For [ethnic] Russians' (*dlya Russkikh*). At the same time, of the 100 advertisements placed in other media 28 also stated they were meant for ethnic Russian landlords. Table 5 shows these data for both December 2002 and December 2003. These figured can be supplemented by interview data from Stavropol'.

The interviews that I conducted in Stavropol'skii *Krai* confirm these prior reports of ethnic discrimination in the sphere of accommodation. For most, ethnic discrimination first occurs after the process of migration has been completed and accommodation is required. I was told by many ethnic Caucasian interviewees that they had been forced to move frequently by landlords unwilling to rent to them for extended periods or to register them as resident in the dwelling; most explained that having one of the North Caucasus republics listed as their area of origin in their internal passport meant that they had been refused accommodation. It emerged from a small number of interviews, however, that the longer ethnic Caucasians had lived in Stavropol'skii *Krai* the less difficultly they had in finding housing. At the same time, the interviews also revealed other types of discrimination. I was frequently told how in the agricultural sphere ethnic minorities are given the best land by authorities and ethnic Russians are given the worst land often without water supply (Pallot & Nefedova 2007). Other interviewees told me how they had been treated differently to ethnic Russians when applying to receive or renew documents and how they frequently face other difficulties on account of their ethnicity. For example, I was told by several interviewees how the

TABLE 5
PRIVATE ADVERTISEMENTS BY POTENTIAL TENANTS WITH THE INDICATION OF THE NATIONALITY OF A LANDLORD, 2002 AND 2003

|  | December 2002 | | | October–December 2003 | | |
| --- | --- | --- | --- | --- | --- | --- |
|  |  | 'For [ethnic] Russians' | |  | 'For [ethnic] Russians' | |
|  | All announcements | Number | % | All announcements | Number | % |
| Private advertisements in newspapers | 500 | 135 | 27 | 1030 | 207 | 20.1 |
| Private advertisements in other media | 100 | 28 | 28 | 51 | 13 | 25.5 |
| All | 600 | 163 | 27.2 | 1,081 | 220 | 20.4 |

*Source*: http://www.indem.ru/Ceprs/Minorities/mainStDER.htm, accessed 24 July 2012.

police frequently check the passports of ethnic Caucasian men, who are forced to pay bribes since they often do not have valid documents. This limits their ability to move freely in their area of residence and around the country. Other restrictions on movement, for example, checkpoints and roadblocks, are a regular occurrence in Stavropol'skii *Krai* and the North Caucasus more broadly. Yet, while these restrictions apply to all citizens, particular people are disproportionately affected owing to their vehicle registration plates. One interviewee told me how:

> My car is registered in Kabardino-Balkaria . If your vehicle has number plates from one of the [North Caucasus] republics, they [Russian police officers] always stop you . What are the checkpoints for? Any terrorist can get around them, so they are useless as security barriers...[14]

These (and other) forms of discrimination are a particularly harsh introduction to Russia's violent geographies of ethnic relations for many migrants in Stavropol'skii *Krai*. For many, this discrimination compounds the hardship of forced migration associated with fleeing the Chechen Wars and other geopolitical instability in the North Caucasus republics. Whilst not all migration is forced, even those migrants who migrate for economic reasons are open to forms of discrimination.

Nevertheless, the distribution of racist and neo-Nazi attacks and the ethnicity of the victims of these attacks are only one element of the problematic violent geographies of ethnic relations in Russia. In what follows, I draw on semi-structured interviews conducted in Stavropol' *gorod* (city), Stavropol'skii *Krai*, to highlight how ethnic Russian and non-ethnic Russian citizens understand and negotiate ethnicity in their everyday lives. Figure 1 shows Stavropol'skii *Krai* in its geographical context. As I explained earlier, in the 1990s Stavropol'skii *Krai* was the primary destination for Caucasian migrants fleeing geopolitical instabilities in Chechnya and other republics in the North Caucasus (O'Loughlin *et al*. 2007b). The legacy of this migration is that, according to the 2010 census, there are more Chechens in Stavropol'skii *Krai* than in any federal subject except Chechnya itself, Ingushetia, Dagestan and Moscow city.

[14]Ethnic Azeri, 25, female shop worker, 27 July 2009, Stavropol'.

FIGURE 1. STAVROPOL'SKII *KRAI* IN ITS GEOGRAPHICAL CONTEXT.

The impacts of migration in the 1990s on Stavropol'skii *Krai* were geographically uneven, with *raiony* in the south (Kurskii, Stepnovskii and Andropovskii *raiony*) and west (Kochubeevskii, Trunovskii and Grachevskii *raiony*) receiving the most significant migration flows from Chechnya. In 2007, in the two *raiony*, Neftemkumskii *Raion* and Kurskii *Raion*, of Stavropol'skii *Krai* that border Chechnya and Dagestan, non-ethnic Russians comprised 62.4% and 48.5% of the population respectively (Belozerov *et al.* 2008, pp. 175, 180). In conditions of economic crisis and hardship, ethnic conflicts (although not always violent) have occurred around more banal and 'everyday' issues such as land ownership, land distribution, migration policy and access to education.

## 'Everyday' ethnic relations in Stavropol'skii Krai

The narratives of citizens in Stavropol'skii *Krai* of their experiences of ethnic relations show how attempts by the post-Soviet state to promote interethnic harmony and a Russian civic identity run up against the practical difficulties associated with war and peace, demographic and migration processes, economic stagnation and crisis in the North Caucasus. In this sense, my interviews can be read for what they convey about how citizens experience Russia's violent geographies of ethnic relations in everyday life.

The interviewee quoted below is a middle-aged Chechen male. It is included here to give meaning and perspective to how wider geopolitical events in the North Caucasus have affected ethnic relations in Stavropol'skii *Krai*; the interviewee describes the Second Chechen War (1999–2001) as the 'turning point' in ethnic relations in the *krai*.

> I have lived in Stavropol' for 15 years since 1994. From 1994 to 1999 it was ok. Before the Second Chechen War ... if you worked hard and stayed within the law then everything was ok. But now, it is different. Now people are aggressive towards me and my people ... some people fear being seen by the *militsiya*. The moment a police officer sees me, he becomes aggressive.[15]

It is obvious that the fear that the Chechen male spoke about, while occasionally misplaced, is most often well founded. For such fear to operate, individuals do not have to have experienced violence themselves. In the most extreme example of this, Akhmedova and Speckhard (2006) found that suicide terrorists in Chechnya were motivated not only by their own experiences of violence, but also by a wish to avenge the deaths (and experiences) of relatives and friends. In Stavropol'skii *Krai*, the experiences of friends, relatives and acquaintances are bound up in narratives surrounding 'fear' of ethnic violence. Within Russia, ethnic-motivated violence is a crime punishable by prison. However, perceptions or fear of ethnic-motivated violence have no place in law. As the extract above shows, the people who are victims to the latter are, in a sense, quasi-victims; located at the interface between the direct power over the body exercised by physical (or verbal) violence and the more diffuse power of fear of violence and conflict.

At the same time as ethnic Caucasian discrimination, ethnic Russians (and other nationalities) also feel discriminated by the process of migration, particularly the movement of ethnic Russians from the southern *raiony* of Stavropol'skii *Krai*. The two interviewees below reflect on these issues in the context of a large-scale riot between ethnic Dargins and ethnic Nogais in Stepnovksii *Raion* on 21 June 2009.

> In the south the ethnic Caucasians are the majority populations in certain towns and *raiony*. Although they lived there during Soviet times, the [levels of] migration increased in the 1990s. Ethnic Russians have left these places because they do not like to be dominated by people from the republics. If you were ethnic Russian, then would you want to live there? No.[16]

> If the current migration processes continue on their own without governmental policies and without restriction and control, without any calculation as to the social impacts that it will have, then of course it will lead to conflict. And nowadays you can see what this has led to in Stepnovsky *Raion*, between Nogais and one of the nationalities from Dagestan. Nogais understand themselves as the local people and they understand Stepnovsky *Raion* as their territory ... And people from Dagestan are migrating there because of poor economic and social conditions there [Dagestan], for example a lack of free land and work ... There are over 40 national groups in Dagestan, but once they leave [Dagestan] they act as one. They settle in the same area, give each other jobs, and colonise. The same process is happening in almost every *raion* in eastern Stavropol'skii *Krai*.[17]

Like all migration processes, the local population in Stavropol' have their own perspective on forms of discrimination. As the narratives above indicate, ethnic Russians problematise the migration experience. For many of the local ethnic Russian

---

[15]Ethnic Chechen, 45, unemployed male, 10 July 2009, Stavropol'.
[16]Ethnic Russian, 51, business man, July 2009, Stavropol'.
[17]Ethnic Ossetian, 68, business man, 17 July 2009, Stavropol'.

population, the issue is not ethnic Caucasians who have migrated to Stavropol'skii *Krai per se*, but rather the time they have stayed in the *krai* and the extent to which they have integrated into the local population.

> Fifteen years ago, Chechens and other North Caucasian peoples came here to flee the [First Chechen] War for what should have been just a couple of months or years. From the beginning, they have taken advantage of the hospitals, schools, and other services. Because they have stayed here for too long, they have not properly integrated and have not accepted our [ethnic] Russian way of life ...[18]

> There are German and Greek people who live here [in Stavropol'skii *Krai*], Polish too. And they are civilised compared to the Caucasians. I have friends from these ethnic groups, they don't have any problems with us [ethnic Russians] and we don't have any problems with them ... People are fleeing. In Neftemkumskii, Kurskoi, Budyennovsk there are just a few, a handful, of ethnic Russians left. The border with the North Caucasus is moving. At the moment, the border is in Stavropol'skii *Krai*. But it will go to Rostov and Krasnodar. Two years ago, [former] governor [Aleksandr] Chernogorov [of Stavropol'skii *Krai*] said that the unity of the Caucasus republics is such a problem that it needs to be discussed in Moscow ... And when Chernogorov built the highway from Budyennovsk it was symbolic of a new road or channel to unite the Caspian and Black Sea ... But this road makes it easier for the Caucasians to move to Stavropol'skii *Krai*. If there are more Caucasians and fewer [ethnic] Russians then we will be discriminated against even more [than now]. And there will be more violence.[19]

In their study of the localised geographies of violence in the North Caucasus between 1999 and 2007, O'Loughlin and Wittmer (2010, p. 186) note how the Caucasian Federal Highway (M-29), the main highway of the region which links Makhachkala (Dagestan) to Grozny (Chechnya), Nazran (Ingushetia), Nal'chik (Kabardino-Balkaria), Mineral'nye Vody (Stavropol'skii *Krai*) and Rostov-on-Don (Rostov *Oblast'*), is marked 'by the clusters of violence at its major towns and cities' along its route. This gives substance to the claim made by the interviewee above that the new highway would bring 'more violence' to Stavropol'skii *Krai*, albeit in a way other than which the interviewee intended.

Like most Russian regions, the issue of the declining ethnic Russian population in Stavropol'skii *Krai* is particularly sensitive. As has been noted elsewhere, the meaning of the border between Stavropol'skii *Krai* and the North Caucasian republics is in flux, and in daily life its significance is increasingly important (Riklin 2005; Markedonov 2007, 2009). This makes many ethnic Russians in Stavropol'skii *Krai* uncomfortable as they fear inclusion of the territory into the affairs of the North Caucasus 'proper' (i.e., the republics): what Malashenko (2009) has called Russia's 'internal abroad'. In the excerpt above, the interviewee explained how the building of a highway in southern Stavropol'skii *Krai* will facilitate the migration of ethnic Caucasians to Stavropol'skii *Krai* in the future. In the first excerpt below, the interviewee complains about the current ethnic composition of the *krai*. The interviewee describes how people from the Caucasus, despite being a minority population, make up the majority of people in

---

[18]Ethnic Russian, 38, unemployed male, 23 July 2009, Stavropol'.
[19]Ethnic Russian, 27 male shop worker, 24 July 2009, Stavropol'.

hospitals in Stavropol', meaning that Russians do not have equal access to emergency services and are thus discriminated against. In the second excerpt below, the interviewee complains about unequal access to education, highlighting the role of corruption. As these (and other) excerpts suggest, concerns surrounding the provision of services (and who benefits from those services) are widespread.

> The population of Stavropol'skii *Krai* is over 80% ethnic Russian, but people from the Caucasus live here and work here too, and they have businesses here ... And also hospitals. Over half of the people in hospitals are from the republics. But they are only 20% of the population. Why aren't [ethnic] Russians or Slavs in these hospitals?[20]

> They [ethnic migrants] come from the [North Caucasus] republics to here [Stavropol'skii *Krai*] because it is cheaper for them to enter into our universities. But for us [Cossacks], it is impossible to enter into the universities. For example, a girl came from a Cossack school with a gold-diploma and tried to enter university. They told her that she wouldn't enter university unless she gave them money. They had a quota for individuals from the Caucasus which they had to fill. How could she have this amount of money? Why do the authorities privilege the Caucasians? Why are we discriminated against?[21]

A number of interviewees complained about a quota system in education, yet while this system (as well as for other services) existed during the Soviet period (Zaslavsky 1994), as far as I am aware no such system exists at the time of writing. Nevertheless, for these interviewees acceptance of the conditions of the 'system' in return for attending university underlies the discrimination, and unequal nature of ethnic groups, in Stavropol'skii *Krai*. Other interviewees accepted that the declining ethnic Russian population combined with the increasing ethnic Caucasian population in Stavropol'skii *Krai* meant that there would be a change in those ethnic groups using certain services and needing particular provisions; for example, the low birth rate of ethnic Russians compared to the high birth rate of ethnic Caucasians means that ethnic Caucasians are more likely to use nursery schools and kindergartens. Nevertheless, most ethnic Russians with whom I spoke argued that they had developed a 'defensive consciousness' in light of the large-scale immigration of ethnic Caucasians. One interviewee said:

> A defensive consciousness has developed amongst [ethnic] Russians ... For those people in Russia who are patriots and those people who have nowhere to go, then when the war with the Caucasians begins they will come here to help defend Russia ... They will defend their families and Russia. Right to the end. Until death. It will come to this, unfortunately ... People have guns not because they desire one, but because they need one. The *militsiya* is useless ... But it will be so huge that you cannot imagine the scale of violence and death ... Here there will be so much blood, because it is the Caucasus ... If something happens here between ethnic groups, then nobody can say where the violence will stop and who it will involve ... .[22]

---

[20]Ethnic Russian, 51, business man, 10 July 2009, Stavropol'.
[21]Ethnic Russian (Cossack), 71, retired male, 20 October 2008, Stavropol'.
[22]Ethnic Russian, 68, male shop owner, 3 August 2009, Stavropol'.

Judging from other interviews, corruption—a problem throughout post-Soviet Russia—is particularly problematic in the North Caucasus, jeopardising national security and undermining state and social institutions. Former President Medvedev has alluded to this on several occasions, most notably in his Federal Address of November 2009, and more recently in addressing human rights activists at a meeting of the Council for Civil Society in May 2010.[23]

> I think that, of course, the situation [in Russia] would be different without the national republics ... [In Stavropol'skii *Krai*] We are saying that we want factories and an economy, a programme for our children, a project of houses, but nobody hears us. Instead the money is going over there to the territories of the republics. And they get money under the table and steal things. And this money from Russia just disappears. Nobody [in Russia] asks where this money is spent.[24]

As these extracts show, ethnic discrimination and corruption go hand-in-hand in Stavropol'skii *Krai*, permeating most aspects of life; from pro-natal incentives for individuals from the ethnic republics to ethnic 'quotas' in education institutions. Compounding this, as I suggested above, ethnic groups are subject to different crime and punishment. One person with whom I spoke told me that Russian authorities often charge assailants of violent conflict from the Caucasus with 'lesser' charges, such as hooliganism, compared to ethnic Russians, in an effort to downplay the significance of ethnic conflict, perhaps in the face of pressures emanating from Moscow:

> ethnic conflicts appear [in Stavropol'skii *Krai*] everyday. We have a statistic according to which it is likely or not whether you go to prison. If Russians are fighting against non-Russians, then Russians are sentenced according to the law on 'ethnic' violence. And if the non-Russians are sentenced they are charged only with bad behaviour. Another example [is] the Chechen War. Russian officers are put in to prison as killers. And all the people who fought against us in the name of 'anti-Russian' forces, they now have streets named after them and all sorts of awards. It was the genocide of the Russian population in Chechnya. Russian officers were forced to go there, and nowadays they give them long sentences in prison. And that's why people are angry. I am saying this because the behaviour of governmental [*vlast'*] structures forces us to fight against each other. In other words, if we are all citizens of the Russian Federation regardless of what nationality we have, if there is a law, defined by an administrative decree or by the constitution, then everybody is supposed to follow this law. But nowadays we have the situation that the law is there for some people, and other people are given privileges. We can see it, we are not stupid.[25]

In their research on the geography of crime and punishment in post-Soviet Russia, Moran *et al.* (2011) note that the North Caucasus region has both the highest number of penal institutions in Russia (61) and the highest number of people detained (74,000

---

[23] For an overview of human rights in Stavropol', see Selyukov (2008).
[24] Ethnic Russian, 42, male politician, 13 July 2009, Stavropol'.
[25] Ethnic Russian, 34, male academic, 24 October 2008, Stavropol'.

inmates). However, these data are not disaggregated by ethnicity and it is difficult, in the context of Russian authorities' close and secretive treatment of its penal institutions, to make any concrete assessment of whether, as the interviewee suggested, ethnic Caucasians and ethnic Russians are charged with different 'crimes' after committing similar offences.

*Concluding remarks*

The current state of ethnic relations has repercussions for the whole of Russian society. Understanding this, regional authorities throughout Russia attempt to manage ethnic relations in various spheres of life. Building on the work of Brubaker (1996), Popov and Kuznetsov (2008, p. 227) argue that this is achieved through the 'securitization of interethnic relations', whereby 'relations between the state and minorities are seen not as an object of democratic politics but as a sphere of state security' (Wæver 1995). This works to consolidate the power of the state, leading to the violation of civil and minority rights and curtailing society's control over the power of the state (Osipov 2002, p. 62; see also, Avksentiev et al. 2002). In part because of this, the prospects for improvements in ethnic relations in Russia are not, in the short term, encouraging.

Because so many people are affected (directly or otherwise) by ethnic relations, it might be reasonable to think that the Russian population will constitute a force for change and oppose ethnic discrimination and violence. Research that has been done on ethnic relations in Russia suggests otherwise. Alexander Verkhovskii, of the SOVA Centre, has noted that 'Xenophobic prejudice is widespread in Russia ... More than 50% [of Russians] support the idea that ethnic Russians should have privileges over other ethnic groups ... More than 50% believe that ethnic minorities should be limited or even expelled from their region' (Harding 2009; Gudkov 2008). Popov and Kuznetsov, who researched ethnic discrimination in Krasnodar *krai*, concluded that, 'the Soviet principle of the institutionalisation of ethnicity continues to dominate unchallenged post-Soviet public consciousness and political practices, thus creating the conditions for ethnic discrimination, racism and xenophobia' (2008, p. 245). Shlapentokh reaches a similar conclusion, suggesting that ethnic conflict 'indicates that the deep-seated ills of Russian society [which] could have powerful implications for the country's future' (2010, p. 199). All of this points to an inability by ethnic Russians to accommodate non-Slavic peoples in a way that is essential if the country is to develop.

*Queen's University Belfast*

*References*

Akhmedova, K. & Speckhard, A. (2006) 'A Multi-casual Analysis of the Genesis of Suicide Terrorism: The Chechen Case', in Victoroff, J. I. (ed.) (2006) *Tangled Roots: Social and Psychological Factors in the Genesis of Terrorism* (Amsterdam, IOS Press), pp. 324–55.
Amnesty International (2004) 'Russian Federation: Out of Control: Anti-Chechen Sentiment in Moscow Post-Metro Blast', 18 February, available at: http://www.amnesty.org/en/library/asset/EUR46/007/2004/en/6f3db1c2-fabd-11dd-b6c4-73b1aa157d32/eur460072004en.pdf, accessed 24 July 2012.

Amnesty International (2006) 'Russian Federation: Violent Racism Out of Control', 3 May, available at: http://www.amnesty.org/en/library/info/EUR46/022/2006, accessed 24 July 2012.
Amnesty International (2008) 'Amnesty International Report 2008: The Russian Federation', available at: http://www.amnesty.org/en/region/russia/report-2008, accessed 24 July 2012.
Astvatsaturova, M. (2007) 'Stavropol'skii *Krai*: Mezhetnicheskie otosheniya v etnopoliticheskom landshafte', *Kazanskii Federalist*, 3–4, available at: http://www.kazanfed.ru/publications/kazanfederalist/n23-24/10/, accessed 24 July 2012.
Avksentiev, V. A., Babkin, I. O., Medvedev, N. P., Khop, A. Yu. & Shnukov, V. V. (2002) *Stavropol'e: Etnokonfliktologicheskii portret* (Stavropol', Stavropol' State University Press).
Bassin, M. (2009) 'The Emergence of Ethno-Geopolitics in Post-Soviet Russia', *Eurasian Geography and Economics*, 50, 2, pp. 131–49.
Belozerov, V. S. (2005) *Etnicheskaya karta Serverogo Kavkaza* (Moscow, OGI).
Belozerov, V.S., Panin, A.N. & Chikhichin, V.V. (2008) *Etnicheskii Atlas Stavropol'skogo kraya [Ethnic Atlas of Stavropol' krai]* (Stavropol', Stavropol' State University Press).
Boeck, B. J. (1998) 'The Kuban' Cossack Revival (1989–1993): The Beginnings of a Cossack National Movement in the North Caucasus Region', *Nationalities Papers*, 26, 4, pp. 633–57.
Brubaker, R. (1996) *Nationalism Reframed: Nationhood and the National Question in the New Europe* (Cambridge, Cambridge University Press).
Chebankova, E. (2007) 'Implications of Putin's Regional and Demographic Policies on the Evolution of Inter-ethnic Relations in Russia', *Perspectives on European Politics and Society*, 8, 4, pp. 439–59.
Clem, R. S. & Craumer, P. R. (2004) 'Redrawing the Political Map of Russia: The Duma Elections of December 2003', *Eurasian Geography and Economics*, 45, 4, pp. 241–61.
Cornell, S. (2001) *Small Nations and Great Powers. A Study of Ethnopolitical Conflict in the Caucasus* (Richmond, Curzon Press).
Cornell, S. E. & Starr, F. S. (2006) *The Caucasus: A Challenge for Europe*, Central Asia-Caucasus Institute & Silk Road Studies Program, A Joint Transatlantic Research and Policy Center of Johns Hopkins University and Uppsala University, available at: http://www.silkroadstudies.org/new/docs/Silkroadpapers/0606Caucasus.pdf, accessed 24 July 2012.
Dzutsev, V. (2009) 'North Caucasus' Ethnic Russian Population Shrinks as Indigenous Populations Grow', *Eurasian Daily Monitor*, 6, 120, available at: http://www.jamestown.org/single/?no_cache=1&tx_ttnews%5Btt_news%5D=35730, accessed 24 July 2012.
EAWARN (2005) 'Ideologiya mezhnatsional'nikh otnoshenii na regional'nom urovne: Printsipi, napravleniya, tekhniki i tekhnologi', *Byulleten' seti etnologicheskogo monitoring i rannego preduprezhdeniya konfliktov*, 61.
Foxall, A. (2010) 'Discourses of Demonisation: Chechens, Russians, and the Stavropol' Riots of 2007', *Geopolitics*, 15, 4, pp. 684–704.
Foxall, A. (2011) 'Developments in Inter-Ethnic Relations in Stavropol'skii *Krai*', *Russian Analytical Digest: Russian Nationalism, Xenophobia, Immigration and Ethnic Conflict*, 93, 10 March, pp. 12–4.
Foxall, A. (forthcoming) 'Mapping Ethnic Relations: Cartography and Conflict Management in the North Caucasus, Russia', in Mahapatra, D. A. (ed.) (Forthcoming) *Conflict and Peace in Eurasia* (Basingstoke, Routledge), pp. 54–72.
Gammer, M. (ed.) (2008) *Ethno-Nationalism, Islam and the State in the Caucasus: Post-Soviet Disorder* (London & New York, Routledge).
Gudkov, L. (2006) 'Xenophobia: Past and Present', *Russia in Global Affairs*, 7 February, available at: httpr://eng.globalaffairs.ru/numbers/14/998.html, accessed 24 July 2012.
Gudkov, L. (2008) 'Photofit of the Average Russian Citizen: Xenophobia', *Novaya Gazeta*, 3 September, available at: http://en.novayagazeta.ru/data/2008/63/06.html, accessed 24 July 2012.
Harding, L. (2009) 'Putin's Worst Nightmare', *The Guardian*, 8 February, available at: http://www.guardian.co.uk/world/2009/feb/08/russia-race, accessed 23 July 2012.
Human Rights Watch (2004) '"Glad to be Deceived": The International Community and Chechnya', January, available at: http://www.hrw.org/wr2k4/7.htm, accessed 23 July 2012.
Jamestown Foundation (2009) 'Russian Neo-Nazi Movement Facing State Crackdown', *Eurasian Daily Monitor*, 6, 96, 19 May, available at: http://www.jamestown.org/single/?no_cache=1&tx_ttnews[tt_news]=35011, accessed 24 July 2012.
Kolossov, V. A., Galkina, T. A. & Krindatch, A. D. (2001) 'Territorial'naya identichnost' i mezhetnicheskie otnosheniya (Na primere vostochnykh raionov Stavropol'skogo kraya)', *Polis (Political Studies)*, 11, 2, pp. 61–78.
Kommersant (2010) 'Bomba ostalas' nezamechennoi' [The bomb went unnoticed], May 28, available at: http://www.kommersant.ru/doc/1376316, accessed 21 August 2012.

Kozhevnikova, G. (2005) 'SOVA Center: Radical Nationalism and Efforts to Oppose it in Russia in 2005', 25 February, available at: http://www.sova-center.ru/en/xenophobia/reports-analyses/2006/02/d7366/, accessed 19 July 2012.
Kozhevnikova, G. (2009) 'Radical Nationalism in Russia, and Efforts to Counteract It in 2008', *SOVA Center for Information and Analysis*, available at: http://xeno.sova-center.ru/6BA2468/6BB4208/CCD6D21, accessed 24 July 2012.
Lapidus, G. W. (2002) 'Accommodating Ethnic Differences in Post-Soviet Eurasia', in Beissinger, M. & Young, C. (eds) (2002) *Beyond State Crisis? Post-Colonial Africa and Post-Soviet Eurasia in Comparative Perspective* (Washington, DC, Woodrow Wilson Center and Johns Hopkins University Press), pp. 323–58.
Laquer, W. (1996) *Fascism: Past, Present and Future* (New York, Oxford University Press).
Malashenko, A. (2009) 'U nikh tut portreti Putina, Medvedeva, no oni za shariyat', *Slon*, 3 December, available at: http://www.slon.ru/articles/203931/, accessed 23 July 2012.
Markedonov, S. (2007) 'Stavropol'e: Plavil'nii kotel ili oboronitel'nii val?', *Politkom.ru*, 16 March, available at: http://www.politcom.ru/4293.html, accessed 24 July 2012.
Markedonov, S. (2009) 'Na Stike Mirov Stavropol'skii *Krai*: Fornost russkikh ili zone integratsii?', *Chastnii Korrespondent*, 25 June, available at: www.chaskor.ru/p.php?id=7827, accessed 23 July 2012.
Megoran, N. (2006) 'For ethnography in political geography: Experiencing and re-imagining Ferghana Valley boundary closures', *Political Geography* 25, 6, pp. 622–640.
Moran, D., Pallot, J. & Piacentini, L. (2011) 'The Geography of Crime and Punishment in the Russian Federation', *Eurasian Geography and Economics*, 52, 1, pp. 79–104.
Mukhin, V. (2001) 'Cossacks Return to Roots in Caucasus', *The Russia Journal*, 29 June, available at: http://www.russiajournal.com/node/5020, accessed 24 July 2012.
O'Loughlin, J., Panin, A. & Wittmer, F. (2007a) 'Population Change and Migration in Stavropol' Kray: The Effects of Regional Conflicts and Economic Restructuring', *Eurasian Geography and Economics*, 48, 1, pp. 249–67.
O'Loughlin, J., Kolossov, V. & Radvanyi, J. (2007b) 'The Caucasus in a Time of Conflict, Demographic Transition, and Economic Change', *Eurasian Geography and Economics*, 48, 2, pp. 135–56.
O'Loughlin, J. & Witmer, F. (2010) 'The Localized Geographies of Violence in the North Caucasus of Russia, 1999–2007', *Annals of the Association of American Geographers*, 101, 1, pp. 178–201.
O'Rouke, S. (2007) *The Cossacks* (Manchester, Manchester University Press).
Osipov, A. (2002) 'Konstruirovanie Etnicheskogo Konflikta i Rasistskii Diskurs', in Voronkov, V., Karpenko, O. & Osipov, A. (eds) (2002) *Rasizm v Yazyke Sotsial'nykh Nauk* (St Petersburg, Aletei).
Pain, E. A. (2007) 'Xenophobia and Ethnopolitical Extremism in Post-Soviet Russia: Dynamics and Growth Factors', *Nationalities Papers*, 35, 5, pp. 895–911.
Pain, R. & Smith, S.J. (eds.) (2008) *Fear: Critical Geopolitics and Everyday Life* (Aldershot, Ashgate).
Pallot, J. (2007) ''Gde muzh, tam zhena'' (Where the Husband Is, So Is the Wife): Space and Gender in Post-Soviet Patterns of Penality', *Environment and Planning A*, 39, 3, pp. 570–89.
Pallot, J. & Nefedova, T. G. (2007) *Russia's Unknown Agriculture: Household Production in Post-Soviet Rural Russia* (Oxford, Oxford University Press).
Popov, A. & Kuznetsov, I. (2008) 'Ethnic Discrimination and the Discourse of "Indigenization": The Regional Regime, "Indigenous Majority" and Ethnic Minorities in Krasnodar Krai in Russia', *Nationalities Papers*, 36, 2, pp. 223–52.
Ramadan, A. (2009) 'A Refugee Landscape: Writing Palestinian nationalisms in Lebanon', *ACME*, 8, 1, 69–99.
Riklin, A. (2005) 'Mi ego meryaem', *Ezhednevnii Zhurnal*, 7 July, available at http://www.ej.ru/?a=note&id=1394, accessed 24 July 2012.
Russell, J. (2007) *Chechnya—Russia's 'War on Terror'* (London, Routledge).
Sapozhnikova, G. (2008) 'Migrantka iz Kirgizii: "Russkie takie dobrie. Pochemu oni nas ubivayut?"', *Komsomol'skaya Pravda*, 28 April, available at: http://www.kp.ru/daily/24088.5/320353/, accessed 24 July 2012.
Selyukov, A. I. (2008) *Zaschita prav i svobod cheloveka na Stavropol'e (Istoriya. Teoriya. Praktika)* (Stavropol', Unknown Publisher).
Shlapentokh, D. (2007) 'The Ethnic Riots in Stavropol'', *Prague Watchdog: Reporting on conflict in the North Caucasus*, 26 June, available at: http://www.watchdog.cz/?show=000000-000004-000002-000032&lang=1, accessed 21 July 2012.
Shlapentokh, D. (2010) '"Kondopoga"—Ethnic/Social Tension in Putin's Russia', *European Review*, 18, 2, pp. 177–206.

Shnukov, V. (2009) 'Etnicheskii atlas Stavropol'skogo kraya podgotovlen so trudnikami SGU', *Stavropol'skaya Pravda*, 24 October, available at: http://www.stapravda.ru/20081024/Etnicheskij_atlas_Stavropolskogo_kraya_podgotovlen_sotrudnikami_33756.html, accessed 24 July 2012.

Swerdlow, S. (2006) 'Understanding Post-Soviet Ethnic Discrimination and the Effective Use of U.S. Refugee Resettlement: The Case of the Meskhetian Turks of Krasnodar Krai', *California Law Review*, 94, 6, pp. 1827–78.

Tarasov, A. (2004) *Nazi-skiny v sovremennoi Rossii*, Analytical Report by Moscow Bureau for Human Rights (Moscow, Moscow Bureau for Human Rights).

Tishkov, V. (2004) *Chechnya: Life in a War-Torn Society* (Berkeley, University of California Press).

Tsvetkov, O. (2006) 'Ethnic Russians Flee the North Caucasus', *Russian Analytical Digest*, 7, pp. 9–13.

US Department of State (2012) 'Country Reports on Human Rights Practices for 2011: Russia', available at: http://www.state.gov/j/drl/rls/hrrpt/humanrightsreport/index.htm?dlid=186397, accessed 19 July 2012.

von Twickel, N. (2009) 'Stavropol's Ex-Mayor Detained in Austria', *The Moscow Times*, January 30, p. 2.

Vendina, O. I., Belozerov, V.S & Gustafson, A. (2007) 'The Wars in Chechnya and Their Effects on Neighboring Regions', *Eurasian Geography and Economics*, 48, 2, pp. 178–201.

Wæver, O. (1995) 'Securitization and Desecuritization', in Lipschutz, R. (ed.) (1995) *On Security* (New York, Columbia University Press), pp. 46–86.

Yemelianova, G. (2005) 'Kinship, Ethnicity and Religion in post-Communist Societies', *Ethnicities*, 5, 1, pp. 51–82.

Zayonchkovskaya, Z. A. (2000) *Migratsii: Naselenie Rossii 1999* (Moscow, Knizhnyi dom Universitet), pp. 119–56.

Zürcher, C. (2007) *The Post-Soviet Wars: Rebellion, Ethnic Conflict, and Nationhood in the Caucasus* (New York, New York University Press).

# Suicide Bombing: Chechnya, the North Caucasus and Martyrdom

## CERWYN MOORE

### Abstract

This essay analyses Chechen-related suicide attacks, locating them within the historical and political context of the anti-Russian insurgency in the North Caucasus and the different factions of the anti-Russian armed resistance movement in the period between the first and second Russo-Chechen wars. The core of the essay is an analysis of the different character of two waves of suicide operations, (2000–2002) and (2002–2004). The first wave was linked to nominally Islamist groups, whereas the second set of attacks were linked to Operation Boomerang devised by Shamil Basaev. Finally, the essay considers other attacks that do not fit into either of these two waves of terrorism.

IN THE YEARS SINCE THE SECOND RUSSO-CHECHEN WAR, violence across the North Caucasus has persisted. While major combat operations stopped some years ago, the ongoing regional conflict continues to cause concern for the Russian authorities and the Russian-backed Chechen administration based in Grozny. Aspects of the current struggles hark back to an earlier period of instability, which is the subject of this essay. This essay offers a reading of Chechen-related suicide attacks between June 2000 and August 2004, locating them within the historical and political context of the anti-Russian insurgency in the North Caucasus.[1] While these attacks occurred during the wake of the second Russo-Chechen war (1999–2004), in order to understand them, it is necessary to look at the earlier inter-war period (1996–1999)

---

I would like to thank the British Academy who funded fieldwork in Russia and the Caucasus in 2004, as part of an ongoing project analysing the insurgency in the North Caucasus. Versions of the essay were presented at, amongst other places, BISA in December 2004, as part of an ESRC workshop in January 2005, and finally at BASEES in 2009, in a panel session chaired by Galina Yemelianova. I would like to thank the panel organisers and audiences at these and other sessions, the reviewers, Beverley Brown, Matthew Frear, NK, KA, JK and VK for their comments and support, and finally Madina, Zarina and Volodya for their help in the field.

[1] I use the terms 'suicide attacks', 'suicide operations' and 'suicide missions' interchangeably, following Gambetta (2005) and Moghadam (2008). In addition, the phrase 'Chechen-related' is used to illustrate that some of the attacks between 2000 and 2004 were not conducted by Chechens.

and the different factions of the armed resistance movement that existed, emerged, grouped and regrouped. It is also necessary to situate the role played by the Special Purpose Islamic Regiment (*Islamskij Polk Osobogo Naznačenija/al-Jihad-Fisi-Sabililah*, SPIR) and Islamic Battalions (*Islamskij Batal'on*), and thereafter, the development of a system of military *jama'ats* which operated across the North Caucasus.[2] Many aspects of the second Russo-Chechen War also need to be revisited and analysed.

There has been some insightful ethnographic and sociological analysis of the local social dynamics and historical backdrop that shaped the two Russo-Chechen conflicts of the 1990s (Gammer 2006; Tishkov 2004; Dunlop 1998; Souleimanov 2007), and also some interesting political and military analysis (German 2003; Kramer 2005; Blandy 2004; Williams 2003). Other interventions, largely stemming from anthropology, have offered some insight into local cultural dynamics in the North Caucasus, and religious radicalism in the former Soviet Union more generally (Yemelianova 2002, 2010; Bobrovnikov 2004; Naumkin 2005). However, little has been done to explore, analyse and understand the groups that employed terrorism during and after the second conflict or the rationales behind their use of violence.[3] In addition, with some key exceptions that I build on here, much of the scholarly work analysing terrorism linked to Chechnya and the North Caucasus[4] suffers from methodological flaws, either in its attempts at quantitative analysis or in approaching the area solely through the disciplinary lens of Russian studies (this literature and its problems are discussed in more detail in the next section).

In contrast, exploring the context of the armed resistance movement sheds light on the use of suicide attacks, not only by tracing the complex networks between groups and individuals but also by indicating the strategic capability and capacity of different groups within the insurgency as they relate to shifting aims. Hence, the significance of the argument here that suicide operations should be grouped into two main clusters or 'waves' (2000–2002 and 2002–2004)—with a significant increase in the use of this tactic in the second wave. It should be noted that the phenomena of mass hostage-taking with suicidal intent, notably the Moscow Theatre/Dubrovka House/Nord Ost siege (October 2002, hereafter referred to as Nord Ost) and the Beslan School Siege (September 2004), have been analysed in detail elsewhere (Dunlop 2006; Dolnik 2007).

I begin by offering an introductory account of suicide attacks and the way that Chechen-related 'martyrdom operations' have been analysed, before further specifying the approach taken here. Then, I turn to examine the inter-war years, looking at how the Chechen separatist movement fragmented, followed by the formation of the different factions of the anti-Russian armed resistance movement. Here, I draw attention to four

---

[2]*Jama'at* is an Arabic term, which literally means group or community. It has taken on a particular meaning in a military context, being used to refer to various clandestine anti-Russian groups (i.e. Ingush *jama'at*; *Jama'at Shariat* in Dagestan).

[3]I recognise the problems associated with labelling different actors as separatists, insurgents or terrorists. These terms are used descriptively throughout, and no value should be attached to their usage herein.

[4]I use the terms 'Chechnya' and the 'North Caucasus' throughout the essay. The first war focused on Chechnya alone, while the second conflict always had a regional character, effectively beginning in Dagestan in the summer of 1999.

factions—militant groups, namely the titular Islamist paramilitary groups known as the Islamic Battalions and SPIR; an indigenous pan-Caucasian faction of Islamists, including Zelimkhan Yandarbiyev, and their paramilitary allies; a group of foreign volunteers inspired by classical accounts of *jihad*; and a moderate (separatist) faction in the Chechen-led anti-Russian movement. Although there were overlaps between these four groups, each had shifting capabilities and differing goals which were, in part, shaped by federal policies in the North Caucasus. The next part of the essay explores the adoption of terrorist tactics with the onset of the second Russo-Chechen conflict in 1999 through to the end of major Russian combat operations in 2002. This section discusses the first wave of suicide attacks (June 2000–2002) organised by groups, for the most part, from the town of Urus-Martan. The essay then moves on to consider the second wave of suicide attacks, situating them within the terrorism campaign, called Operation Boomerang, directed by Shamil Basaev, which drew on support from the multi-ethnic military *jama'at*s that operated outside of the administrative borders of Chechnya (principally the Stavropol', Shelkovskii and Ingush groups). Finally, the essay explores two residual attacks, shaped by personal revenge, that do not fit into either of the two identified waves of attacks, before offering concluding remarks.

## *Analysing suicide attacks*

Suicide attacks—in which the death of the perpetrator is a key component of the success of the mission—have received considerable attention in a range of disciplines, particularly since 9/11.[5] Many features of suicide operations have been analysed, and their occurrence in various geographical regions surveyed, but the case of Chechnya has been touched upon only in passing in these scholarly works (Gambetta 2005; Richardson 2006; Pedazhur 2006). Work that focuses on the motives for suicide operations also offer only fleeting references to the Chechen case, although the analysis herein would support some arguments in the more insightful work on this issue (Moghadam 2008; Hafez 2007). At the same time, there has also been some more popular and very influential literature that seeks to identify general trends in suicide attacks through statistical analysis; here too, operations by groups in the North Caucasus have received only cursory attention (Pape 2005). Pape's work in particular has received a number of critical responses that highlight wider debates about the applicability of quantitative analysis to different case studies (Moghadam 2006; Cook 2007). While a chapter in a recent co-authored monograph (Pape & Feldman 2010) offers a more sustained reading of the Chechen case, the methodological problems remain unresolved, including the over-reliance on some superficial secondary literature and the omission of key works on suicide attacks and terrorism linked to the North Caucasus. Although widely read, Pape's work draws on incomplete data sets and fails to address campaigns of terrorism, including failed attacks, leading to a limited appreciation of groups, networks and individuals that have used radical tactics. In turn, Pape's account of incidents related to Chechnya tends to divorce attacks from the context in which they occurred.

[5]See Cronin (2003) for a useful review of the literature.

It could be argued that such problems are endemic not only with popular studies but quantitative approaches to terrorism more generally. The heavy dependence on secondary literature is particularly unfortunate, given that the available secondary literature on Chechnya and North Caucasus is frequently unreliable, especially in conflating different groups, aims and motives. The overzealous use of a statistical approach also limits any appreciation of the intricate group relations which impacted on the use of radical tactics. Much of the secondary literature also reads Chechnya through the lens of Russian studies which clouds analysis.[6] This is compounded further by the limited use of statements by Chechen fighters themselves. The outcome is inevitably a misreading of the insurgency and the use of radical tactics by particular groups. All in all, both academic and popular work on suicide attacks remains incomplete, while studies of terrorism specifically linked to the North Caucasus often fail to understand or accurately contextualise the case of Chechnya.[7]

Instead, the analysis here seeks to add to the currently limited stock of knowledge on suicide attacks. This includes John Reuter's (2004) report on Chechen suicide operations. However, the report was drafted prior to the end of the second wave of suicide attacks, offering only partial insight into the context needed to address different types and waves of attacks. Others, such as Nabi Abdullaev (2007) also provide insight into the phenomena of Chechen-related suicide operations, examining the motives associated with particular attacks. Both works acknowledge the indigenous roots of suicide attacks linked to Chechnya and recognise the internal radicalisation in the armed resistance movement. The process of radicalisation manifested itself in the use of Islamist religious rhetoric by some groups, including, for instance, labelling suicide bombers as 'martyrs' (*shahid*), thereby invoking honorific Arabic terminology to describe attackers who died fighting for the defence of their homeland.[8] Similarly, other area specialists (Souleimanov & Ditrych 2008; Matveeva 2004; Markedonov 2010), detailed ethnographic work (Sokirianskaia 2008; Yarlykapov 2007; Yemelianova 2010) and informed work on political Islam (Wilhelmsen 2005; Yemelianova 2002) offer much needed insight into the motivations of groups involved in the second conflict. Earlier work by the present author which touches on suicide operations (Moore & Tumelty 2008, 2009) also seeks to avoid aforementioned methodological problems and will be built on in this essay.

---

[6]For example, Arab volunteers are often mistakenly viewed as *al-Qaeda* operatives, while factions or groups in the insurgency are frequently lumped together as 'Wahhabi', which the federal authorities use as a derogatory catch-all label to refer to anti-Russian units. The term is also often used to refer to Islamists which are not Sufi. Of course, Wahhabism does have a specific meaning outside of its usage by federal groups in Russia.

[7]It is beyond the scope of this essay to engage with or present the range of debates either about suicide attacks in general, or even themes such as female suicide operations, Islamism and the spread of martyrdom attacks in Chechnya, although these themes are touched on.

[8]The Arabic word *shahid* (noun *shahed*) is often transliterated from Russian as *shaheed*. A *shahid* is both a martyr and witness. Although not part of Chechen culture, terminology of this kind was increasingly used by some groups so as to give particular attacks a meaning within an anti-Russian and Islamist narrative. I expand on arguments about the role of Salafism, constituent parts of the foreign fighter movement, and *jihad* in Chechnya, in a research paper entitled 'Beyond Jihad in Chechnya: Foreign Fighters and the insurgency in the North Caucasus' (Moore 2012).

The argument advanced here—that Chechen-related suicide attacks should be seen as constituting two distinct waves—is built on a careful and evidenced depiction of the different factions of the armed resistance movement. The initial turn to radical tactics in the first wave of suicide attacks, and the increase and strategic usage of such tactics as a development from the first to the second wave of suicide attacks is strongly contextualised in a shifting historical setting and supported by qualitative material, employing statements by key members of armed resistance movement to substantiate claims.

A strategic reading of terrorism considers its utility as a 'military strategy employed by actors who believe, rightly or wrongly, that through such means they can advance their goals' (Neumann & Smith 2008, p. 6). To this end, a strategic reading of terrorism considers the use of 'military means to fulfil the ends of policy' (Neumann & Smith 2008, p. 6). Groups involved 'seek to achieve their political aims through terrorist violence' while 'legitimacy and relative military weakness are important variables in strategic terrorism' (Neumann & Smith 2008, p. 11). In a sense then, strategic initiatives such as Operation Boomerang, which included the use of suicide attacks, served long-term objectives as part of an attempt to establish a wider regional insurgency, whereas the cluster of attacks beginning in 2000 were small-scale actions which served a larger purpose of resistance to federal operations in Chechnya. Accordingly, the aim is to develop a specific argument that there have been two waves of attacks which are different in character. It situates the first wave (2000–2002), while culminating with Nord Ost, as local initiatives organised by groups, namely the Islamic Battalions and the SPIR, based in Urus-Martan. This wave of attacks, which occurred in Chechnya, was designed to support the war effort by these groups. The attacks focused on military and paramilitary targets and involved predominantly male attackers, some of whom were converted to Islam.

The second wave of suicide attacks (late 2002–2004) had a strategic character. A number of attacks were part of Operation Boomerang, a campaign of terrorism in part orchestrated by Shamil Basaev. This wave of attacks included the more explicit use of female bombers, targeting facilities inside and outside of Chechnya, while many of the 'martyrs' themselves came from the highland villages in Chechnya and the Nogay community. Unlike the first wave of attacks, the groups largely responsible for suicide attacks, which increased between December 2002 and 2004, were often linked to the *Riyad-us-Saliheyn*, a 'martyr battalion' led by Shamil Basaev.[9] The groups involved were often multi-ethnic, while the attacks occurred not only inside Chechnya, but in the wider North Caucasus region and even further afield in Moscow. The targets were military and political, while the methods used included truck-bomb attacks and individual assassination attempts. The attacks reflected the changing character of the insurgency, which increasingly developed a regional form, reacting to the situation in

---

[9]The *Riyad-us-Saliheyn* was an informal network of supporters from across the North Caucasus, led by Shamil Basaev. The network was also frequently cited as the *Riyad-us-Saliheyn* Reconnaissance and Sabotage Martyr Brigade. The Arabic name is transliterated into English as the Gardens of the Righteous. Despite being formed around 2000, the *Riyad-us-Saliheyn* was barely heard of until Nord Ost in October 2002, and only became active later that year. It undertook operations on an *ad hoc* basis, drawing support from various *jama'at*s (Vedeno; Ingush; Stavropol'; Shelkovskii) across the region in the period from late 2002.

Chechnya which was shaped by a process of political normalisation. In the final part of the essay, I consider other attacks that do not fit into either of these two waves of terrorism. With these points in mind, it is necessary to unpack the tensions, relationship and development of groups and networks in the interwar period, so as to identify how and why particular factions of the anti-Russian armed resistance movement adopted the use of suicide operations between 2000 and 2004.

*The rise and fall of the Chechen Republic of Ichkeria (ChRI)*

Following the Khasavyurt Peace Agreement, which ended the first Russo-Chechen war in 1996, elections were held in order to establish a political administration in the ChRI.[10] Aslan Maskhadov, who had been chief of staff in the Chechen armed forces, gained widespread support, winning through to become president in the first post-war elections of 27 January 1997. However, Chechen politics quickly became marked by infighting. Other defeated presidential election candidates—Zelimkhan Yandarbiyev and Movladi Udugov—began to move away from the largely nationalist and separatist agenda they had advocated in the early 1990s. Yandarbiyev, a poet and writer, had earlier served in Dudayev's administration, replacing him as interim president following Dudayev's assassination in April 1996. Yandarbiyev had used his position as interim president to introduce aspects of *Shari'ah* Law, granting a measure of power to Islam Khalimov, a religious advisor to Dudayev, and to Movladi Udugov, previously an information advisor to the late Chechen president.

In the period immediately after the elections, Maskhadov attempted to nullify the influence of his political rivals, who had adopted Islamist Salafi doctrine, by incorporating them into the newly formed administration.[11] Islam Khalimov became the head of the Ministry of the Interior, which he immediately renamed the Ministry of Shari'ah Security, while Khalimov's deputies, Abdul-Malik Mezhidov and Supyan Abdullayev, were linked to the *Shari'ah* Guard, a paramilitary group that served a symbolic role as part of the Maskhadov administration. Somewhat surprisingly, the (secular) president appointed Movladi Udugov, an Islamist, as foreign minister, while Zelimkhan Yandarbiyev became an ambassador-at-large for the ChRI.[12]

During the latter part of 1997, Maskhadov's former comrade-in-arms Shamil Basaev—another defeated presidential candidate—gradually became entwined with a

---

[10] With the dissolution of the Soviet Union in 1991, the Checheno–Ingushetia Autonomous Soviet Socialist Republic was split into the Ingushetian Federal Republic and the Chechen Federal Republic, i.e. part of the Russian Federation. In November of the same year, President Jokhar Dudayev announced the independence of the (renamed) ChRI, which was not recognised by the Russian federal government. With the end of the first Russo-Chechen war, the ChRI gained *de facto*, although still not formally recognised, independence, with Jokhar Dudayev as its first president.

[11] Salafiyya is a theological term that refers to a movement in which Muslims should strive to follow the pious fathers, or first three generations of Islam. The Salafi movement includes both militant groups, including some which are pan-Islamist and Umma-orientated, as well as peaceful branches of thought. Salafism—and more specifically the adoption and use of *jihad* by particular Islamist groups—is often shaped by local political dynamics, hence the need to provide a detailed reading of statements by key commanders and the context which shape the use of holy war.

[12] See the interview with Yandarbiyev for references to his adoption of radical Islam in *Vremya Novosti*, 27 December 2001.

pan-Islamist grouping made up of Arab *jihadi* volunteers led by Ibn Khattab and a small group of local Islamist volunteers that had formed in the course of the first war. Until 1995, the group was led by the elderly Jordanian–Chechen ideologue, Shaykh Ali Fathi al-Shishani, who had arrived in the North Caucasus in 1993. Shaykh Fathi had served in Afghanistan as an aid to the mujahedeen, working closely with the Afghan field commander Abu Sayyaf (Moore & Tumelty 2008). After arriving in Chechnya, Fathi established an Islamist group, known as *al-Jama'at al-Islmaiyya*, which incorporated the handful of Arab foreign fighters into its ranks upon their arrival in Dagestan in 1995. The Arab foreign fighters fought against the Russian forces in the first war and thereafter remained in the North Caucasus.[13] The Arab volunteers included not only fighters but financiers and ideologues, many of whom were from Saudi Arabia (Ibn Khattab; Hakim al-Medani; Yaqub al-Ghamidi; Abu Omar al-Sayf) and the broader diaspora community. They operated within a broad Salafi movement, establishing links to indigenous groups in the mountainous Chechen and Dagestani highlands. Although numbering little more than a few dozen, the Arab volunteers had fought in Afghanistan and Tajikistan as *mujahids*, where they had formed kinship bonds while also honing a classical reading 'holy war' derived from the pan-Islamist doctrine advanced by Abdullah Azzam (Moore 2012).

As Fathi's health worsened (he died in 1997), Khattab and his aides quickly took charge of the *jama'at*, using their military training and experience to launch a series of attacks in support of the broader Chechen war effort. The most notable of these operations, the ambush of a Russian armoured column at Yarysh Mardy, led to the death of dozens of Russian service personnel. These actions brought Khattab into the orbit of Basaev, who had established himself as a key field commander in the resistance. Basaev invited Khattab to stay in Vedeno as his guest, calling him 'brother'—a powerful symbolic gesture in Chechen customary tradition, which simultaneously granted him freedom of movement and protection (Moore & Tumelty 2008, p. 417). Basaev's patronage cemented an alliance with Khattab built on their respective military experiences, an alliance that gained momentum in the interbellum period.

The fluid political situation in the inter-war years was complicated further by the array of armed formations that had not demobilised at the end of the war. A number of field commanders, such as Salman Raduyev, retained influential private paramilitary forces. Younger fighters established their own small paramilitary groups, as the financial power of the Islamists was used to buy off local criminal groups. Arbi Barayev, with Zelimkhan Yandarbiyev acting as a benefactor, created the *al-Jihad-Fisi-Sabililah*, known as the SPIR, while the *Shari'ah* Guard, although disbanded by Maskhadov in 1998, retained influence as an informal militia supported by Zelimkhan Yandarbiyev. Other 'Islamic' or '*Shari'ah*' units were also established by the Akhmadov brothers and sub-commanders such as Magomed Tsagarayev, with one unit, called the Islamic Battalions, operating from Urus-Martan.

[13]The local Islamist irredentists (Udugov, Yandarbiyev and their paramilitary allies), as well as local and foreign fighters (Basaev and Khattab) operated within a pan-Islamist current, which itself, was enveloped in a larger Salafi *jihadi* movement. However, it is not feasible to identify how different elements of these groups formed alliances, partly because the actions of these groups changed over time, blurring the distinction between them. Importantly though, their actions were not shaped by the popular usage of Wahhabism.

The paramilitary groups linked to Yandarbiyev and Udugov, maverick field commanders like Raduyev, and the presence of Islamist factions associated with Basaev and Khattab undermined the nationalist/separatist movement that had served as a unifying force during the first Russo-Chechen war. Seeking to maintain a measure of control over the fluid political situation, Maskhadov formed a series of temporary alliances with different factions during the latter part of 1997. Maskhadov initially welcomed Islamist politicians into his government of national unity, but both Yandarbiyev and Udugov used ever more militant Islamist rhetoric. The Islamists subsequently organised alliances, with splinter groups and sections of government variously adopting mixed positions; in effect, the temporary alliances proved unsustainable. The year 1997 saw two government reshuffles but, by the middle of 1998, the political situation had further deteriorated, prompted by two crises.

The first crisis erupted in December 1997 when dozens of armed men led by Ibn Khattab slipped across the border into Dagestan, where they were joined by local volunteers, in a sortie directed against federal troops. In the early hours of the morning of 22 December, over 100 armed men led by Ibn Khattab attacked the garrisoned tank battalion of the 136th Mechanised Infantry Brigade, stationed in a suburb of the Dagestani town of Buinaksk. The raid left dozens of men injured. The attackers separated into small groups, retreating to the highland border region, pursued by Dagestani police and Russian army units. The federal authorities quickly accused supporters of the Dagestani Salafi community—namely the Karamakhi *jama'at*—of involvement in the raid (Matveeva 2004, p. 128). The sortie led to an escalation in tension between the local Dagestani Sufi authorities, and the conservative Salafi communities based in the highland villages (Murtazaliyev 1997, pp. 1–2). In the late December, Bagautdin Kebedov, one of the ideological leaders of the Dagestani Salafi communities, relocated to Chechnya. Tensions in Dagestan remained high, as federal officials, and the Sufi authorities sought to isolate the Salafi strongholds, leading dozens of families to relocate to Chechnya during the spring months of 1998. Around the same time, both Yandarbiyev and Udugov, still smarting from their defeat in the January 1997 presidential elections, were seeking to increase their influence through other political organisations. One of these, the Islamic Nation (*Islamskaya Natsiya*), led by Udugov, formed a bridge to the group led by Kebedov. In effect, the Islamist organisation led by Kebedov merged with the Islamic Nation (even though Udugov remained in the Maskhadov administration). Then, in April 1998, Udugov, Basaev and their supporters convened a Congress of Peoples of Dagestan and Ichkeria, the aim of which was the unification of the mountain peoples (Barakhova 1998, p. 3).

A second crisis erupted in July 1998 (Akhmadov 2010), this time in Chechnya, when the paramilitary groups led by Arbi Barayev and Abdul-Malik Mezhidov quarrelled with another militia group led by the Yamadayev brothers, leading to an armed confrontation in Gudermes. The fighting destroyed large parts of the groups loyal to Barayev and Mezhidov. Thereafter the group led by Barayev was integrated into the emerging Islamist political alliance opposed to Maskhadov. Significantly, neither Basaev nor the volunteer formations affiliated to Khattab had become involved in the skirmish at Gudermes, effectively cordoning off the Arab *mujahedeen* from direct involvement in political infighting. By the middle of 1998, a loose coalition including Yandarbiyev, Udugov and the younger generation of paramilitary volunteers associated with the Islamic Battalions and the SPIR consolidated their position in certain regions by embracing Salafi Islam—which was increasingly functioning as an ideological umbrella. It was only a few years earlier, during the first Russo-Chechen war, that the separatist movement had been supported by local Sufi religious leaders. Now many Sufi leaders, most notably the Chechen Mufti Akhmad Kadyrov, openly opposed the growing power of the Salafi Islamist factions, criticising Maskhadov's failure to curb their influence.[14]

By this time, Basaev's ties to Khattab had become closer, along with links to the local Lak, Lezgin and Avar communities in Dagestan, and the Nogay in the Stavropol' region in Russia. During the latter part of 1998, building on the April Congress, Basaev and his supporters established a pan-Caucasian movement designed to unite the peoples of Dagestan and Chechnya—a vision shaped by Basaev's experience in the Abkhaz Battalion in the early 1990s (Moore & Tumelty 2009). Acting independently of the Maskhadov administration, the movement brought together likeminded political, military and ideological groups, focusing on the unification of Islamic communities in Chechnya and Dagestan. With the mandate of the Congress in mind, Basaev and Khattab united to form a paramilitary group, the Islamic International Peacekeeping Brigade (*Islamskaja meždunarodnaja mirotvorčeskaja brigade*, IIPB), which operated outside the formal structure and geographical boundaries of the ChRI. The IIPB, numbering around 1,000 volunteers, was multi-ethnic, melding Khattab's *jama'at* with a host of Islamist volunteers from the region and from the transnational Salafi *jihadi* community. It maintained close ties to the towns of Serzhen-Yurt and Vedeno, where Khattab and Basaev were based. Meanwhile, the villages of Karamakhi, Kadar and Chabanmakhi in Dagestan had become centres of Salafi activity, hosting, amongst others, members of the local Avar and Lezgin sub-ethnic communities in the Karamakhi *jama'at* led by Jarulla Rajbaddinov. The young Chechen–Jordanian ideologue Abdurakhman al-Zarqi, a former aide to Shaykh Ali Fathi al-Shishani, and following Fathi's death in 1997, his ideological successor, had taken up residence in the mountain villages that bordered Chechnya, together with a number of his supporters.[15] Abdurakhman had relocated to Dagestan from Chechnya after the battle of Gudermes, further entrenching informal ties between groups in Vedeno and Dagestani groups in the Karamakhi *jama'at*. The agenda of Chechen and Dagestani unification was formalised politically in an announcement by Basaev on 9 February 1999. The announcement stemmed from a meeting attended by many factions, including those led by Raduyev, Yandarbiyev, and members of the Congress of Ichkeria and Dagestan (Udugov, Basaev, Khattab). The group came together for a *shura* or consultation, nominating Basaev as the military commander of the Congress and Islam Khalimov as the political secretary. The group sought to unify Salafi enclaves in Chechnya and Dagestan, advancing the need for *jihad* so as to curb perceived aggression by the federal authorities. Basaev's position as emir of the military council—the *Majlis al-Shura*—conferred upon him the authority to launch military operations.

---

[14]*Nezavisimaya Gazeta*, 11 August 1998.

[15]The use of the sobriquet 'al-Zarqi' points to the Abdurakhman's background as part of the Chechen Jordanian diaspora in Zarqa.

In the early August 1999, the vision of Chechen and Dagestani unification, and the creation of an autonomous Islamist State were given new momentum when the IIPB launched a large-scale military operation in Dagestan. The large-scale military incursion was, at least in part, a response to a request for aid made by Bagaudtin Kebedov, who had returned to Dagestan, thereby sparking further hostilities. Although the attack was routed, it led to calls by local groups for protective intervention by the Russian authorities—thus giving the Yelt'sin administration a rationale for preparing a military campaign to re-establish law and order in Chechnya. When a series of bomb blasts destroyed apartments and military barracks in Moscow, Dagestan and Volgodonsk, they were immediately attributed to Ibn Khattab by the Russian media. By 20 August, the Russian authorities were escalating their military build-up on Chechnya's borders, while Maskhadov called on the State Defence Committee to design a strategy to fend off the impending Russian assault.

Drawing together and elaborating the picture painted above: just prior to the outbreak of the second Russo-Chechen war, the nationalist/separatist movement had fractured in at least four ways. First, a group of Islamists began to coalesce around a radical Salafi agenda. This group, bolstered by the patronage of Zelimkhan Yandarbiyev and Movladi Udugov, grew in power and influence and challenged the authority of the Maskhadov administration throughout the latter part of the inter-war period. They advocated the adoption of *Shari'ah* Law, funded paramilitary groups and played a role forming coalitions that agitated against the secular Maskhadov administration. Second, the idea of a pan-Caucasian military movement, the IIPB, or at least a smaller-scale version that aimed to unite Chechen and Dagestani Islamists, also gained momentum in the interbellum. The military movement, supported by a small number of Dagestani ideologues including Bagaudtin Kebedov, had ties to foreign Islamists as well as the local Chechen Salafis, melding an anti-Russian agenda with a *jihadi* narrative. The close relationship between the two groupings was formalised in late 1998, following the creation of the military council or *Majlis al-Shura*. Third, and correspondingly, the Sufi character of the separatist movement in the first Russo-Chechen war was eclipsed in the interbellum. Most notably, a partial split occurred between the *Qadiriyya* and the *Naqshbandiyya* Sufi Brotherhoods—thereby significantly reducing Maskhadov's ability to shape coherent policies or maintain an effective ruling administration. Finally, a younger generation of agitators, primarily known as criminals, also became more influential in the inter-war years. The two most notable groups, associated with Arbi Barayev (the SPIR) and the Akhmadov brothers (the Islamic Battalions), operated from Urus-Martan. These groups maintained links with the indigenous Salafis and Basaev and Khattab's IIPB, although the Islamic Battalions and SPIR predominantly sought financial reward from criminal activities.

*The insurgency and the adoption of suicide operations: 2000–2004*

Russian troops reinvaded Chechnya in October 1999, sparking a second war. The threat of foreign invasion had forced the parallel organisations—the State Defence Committee linked to Maskhadov and the military council (*Majlis al-Shura*) linked to the Islamists—to work alongside each other organising the armed resistance. By January 2000, the Russian federal forces had surrounded Grozny. Some ChRI field commanders broke through the encirclement and retreated to the highlands. Even though Maskhadov had the support of loyal fighters and pockets of resistance throughout Chechnya, his ability to influence the military arm of the resistance waned as losses mounted. At the same time, the alliance of groups linked to the *Majlis al-Shura* had developed a remarkable capacity to control the information war, successfully propagating the image that the resistance had a rather limited, secular and Sufi, character.[16]

Federal operations set the stage for the adoption of radical tactics by elements of the armed resistance movement. On 12 June, Russian officials oversaw the inaugural ceremony, at an army base at Gudermes, of the pro-Kremlin leader, Akhmad Kadyrov, as head of an interim Chechen administration. While the appointment of Kadyrov paved the way for a federal policy of normalisation, it also marked the start of a determined campaign to eliminate the paramilitary organisations that had sprung up in the inter-war years. Two days after his inauguration, Kadyrov called on Chechen rebels to lay down their arms, stating that it was 'time to stop spilling blood for ideas [that are] alien to the Chechen people'.[17] While the explicit target was paramilitary groups, such as the Islamic Battalions and the SPIR, the implicit target was Salafi Islam. Kadyrov's statement thereby signalled a fundamental shift in the character of the conflict, as the former nationalist/separatist movement split further. Himself a Sufi religious leader, Kadyrov had staunchly opposed the increasing influence of Salafi Islam, disagreeing with the perceived policies of appeasement by the Maskhadov administration.[18] By the middle of June 2000, and in contrast to the first Russo-Chechen conflict, federal forces included a significant portion of pro-Kremlin Chechens from the Sufi *Qadiriyya tariqat*, setting the scene for a further wave of internecine violence.

Throughout May and June, forces loyal to Barayev's SPIR and the Islamic Battalions, led by the Akhmadov brothers, mounted a wave of attacks in Grozny. In the early June, federal forces surrounded Urus-Martan as part of a series of sweep operations. This was the moment when the SPIR employed its first suicide attack: 10 June 2000. The truck-bomb attack, which targeted a federal checkpoint, was undertaken by two people, one of whom was Barayev's (female) cousin Hawa. A *fatwa* was issued supporting the attack, as well as a video that celebrated the alleged Islamic character of the operation.[19] It was followed shortly afterwards by two car bomb attacks on 12 and 13 June. The first, directed against a temporary military *Blokpost* (checkpoint), was conducted by a member of Islamic Battalions.[20] A

---

[16]Maskhadov did have a network of supporters in foreign countries. Within the ChRI he had the support of a number of field commanders, including Akhmed Avtorkhanov and Vakha Arsanov, as well as the head of the Argun *jama'at*, Abdul Khalim Sadulayev. Beyond the borders, Maskhadov had support from official and unofficial ChRI representatives, such as Akhmed Zakayev, Umar Khambiyev, and informal support from others, including representatives in the diaspora.

[17]*Interfax*, 14 June 2000, the author retains a hard copy of this newswire report.

[18]For example, see the interview with Akhmad Kadyrov in *Al-Sharq al-Awsat*, 10 January 2000.

[19]The *fatwa* aimed to legitimise female martyrdom operations, linking the actions of Chechen rebels to the broader transnational Salafi movement. 'The Islamic Ruling of the Permissibility of Martyrdom Operations', available at: http://www.religioscope.com/pdf/martyrdom.pdf, accessed 15 June 2008.

[20]*ITAR-TASS*, 12 June 2000, the author retains a hard copy of this newswire report.

statement issued by Movladi Udugov, who had fled to Turkey, confirmed that the attack, in which four Russian soldiers died, had been undertaken by a Russian convert to Islam (Krasnov 2000). A day later, on 13 June, radical sources posted details of another 'act of self sacrifice' when a second suicide car bomber detonated explosives at a federal checkpoint near Grozny.[21] This attack was also conducted by a Russian convert to Islam.

In the early July, members of the Islamic Battalions and the SPIR launched five co-ordinated suicide attacks. The attackers drove five truck-bombs into federal installations in Gudermes, Urus-Martan and Argun. Barayev himself confirmed that the attack in Urus-Martan had been undertaken by a member of the SPIR, while Ramzan Akhmadov, the head of the Islamic Battalions, confirmed that his units had launched other attacks directed against federal groups loyal to the pro-Kremlin Kadyrov and the Russian administration.[22] The twin suicide truck-bomb attacks in Gudermes, the seat of power of the Kadyrov administration, targeted the barracks of *Ministerstvo Vnutrennykh Del* (MVD) units, and a military checkpoint, while the truck-bomb in Urus-Martan was also directed against interior ministry troops (Allenova *et al.* 2000). Although these three attacks caused few fatalities, the early morning truck-bomb attack directed against a hostel housing troops from the MVD, did kill dozens and wound scores of federal troops (Galkin 2000). Rebel news sources announced that the 'special operation' by 'martyrs' was an 'integral part of a large-scale plan' by the armed forces of the ChRI.[23] Statements by representatives of Maskhadov's State Defence Committee indicated that, on the contrary, they had neither planned nor sanctioned the attacks (Shihab 2000). Even though the tactical shift to use suicide attacks may have been influenced by foreign volunteers, the attacks in July were local all initiatives which were planned, initiated and undertaken by Chechen groups. By this time, Akhmad Kadyrov was openly targeting the Akhmadovs and the Tsagarayevs from Urus-Martan (Politkovskaya 2001, p. 200).

Although forced to operate more clandestinely, and greatly weakened by federal attacks, the SPIR and Islamic Battalions continued to mount military operations. In late December 2000, federal authorities in Grozny averted a suicide truck-bomb attack directed at a temporary police station. Again the attack was linked to the Islamic Battalions from Urus-Martan, and specifically Magomed Tsagarayev.[24] According to John Reuter, the driver of the Ural truck-bomb was a 16-year-old girl, Mareta Duduyeva, who 'had not lost any close relatives in the Chechen wars and had never been religiously devout' but who 'would nonetheless become the prototype for a prevalent Russian view on the origin of female suicide bombings' (2004, p. 7). Interestingly, as Reuter notes, stories in the Russian press surrounding Mareta Dudayeva focused on her kidnapping and manipulation.[25] The youth of the attacker,

---

[21]'Over 300 suicide fighters join special Chechen battalion', *Kavkaz Tsentr*, 13 June 2000.

[22]Nokhchi Information Centre, 3 July 2000. Although this pro-rebel news centre is now discontinued, the author is in possession of a transcript of this news report, translated from Russian.

[23]'Chechenskie Komandiry Slyshat Rezul'taty Napadenii na Rossiiskie Tseli', *Kavkaz Tsentr*, 4 July 2000.

[24]*Interfax*, 20 December 2000.

[25]See, for example, Yuzik (2003).

coupled with her alleged manipulation, served to draw attention to the brutality of the armed resistance movement, tarnishing it.

The suicide attacks in 2000 were initiated by the Islamic Battalions and SPIR, as federal pressure was directed against former strongholds, such as Urus-Martan. The attackers were drawn from the units loyal to Barayev and the Akhmadov brothers, as well as the sub-units linked to Magomed Tsagarayev, and endorsed by Udugov. In January 2001, Tsagarayev was killed in Grozny; a report of his death named him as 'the deputy amir [sic.] of the Urus-Martan military unit' led by Ramzan Akhmadov.[26] Around the same time, Ramzan Akhmadov himself was killed, while other members of the Islamic Battalions were detained or eliminated (Dyupin 2001). Six months later, in June, Arbi Barayev was killed. Thus, by the latter half of 2001, the groups and key facilitators who had organised the first wave of attacks had been killed or captured, undermining the SPIR and Islamic Battalions, and halting their capacity to launch suicide attacks.

The dwindling capacity of the Chechen groups precipitated a rapprochement between Basaev and Maskhadov. By mid-2002, Maskhadov's State Defence Committee had merged with the military council organised by Basaev and the radical wing of the resistance in 1998, forming the Supreme State Defence Committee of the *Majlis al-Shura*. Although Maskhadov remained the political leader of the resistance, he lacked an effective military support base, limiting his ability to co-ordinate large-scale attacks. The Salafi wing of the resistance, including Basaev, Khattab and the IIPB had also suffered severe setbacks throughout the first few years of the second war (Khattab was killed in March 2002). However, these groups retained the capacity to mount a guerrilla campaign in Chechnya, supported by the younger generation of fighters, willing to use radical tactics.

The culmination of this phase of attacks by the SPIR and Islamic Battalions was the mass hostage-taking event in October 2002, the Nord Ost siege (Shermatova & Tate 2003). Basaev and a group of loyalists planned the raid, while he appeared to have formally sanctioned the attack through his authority as Emir of the *Majlis al-Shura*, but his role seems to have been secondary to that of other key figures (Akhmadov 2010, p. 205). The attack on Nord Ost was, at least in part, also endorsed by Movladi Udugov and Zelimkhan Yandarbiyev. Although not a suicide attack, the use of Islamic dress by some of the hostage-takers points towards the influence of Middle Eastern Islamists and, on that basis, might be viewed as an attempt to secure further funds by factions of the resistance with ties to Middle East.[27] The *jihad*ist community in Saudi Arabia had long supported Khattab, viewing his actions as heroic, while other Middle Eastern Islamists sympathised with Chechen Islamists, such as Yandarbiyev. In a sense, the use of Islamist garb would appeal to potential benefactors from the Middle East. However, statements by the hostage-takers clearly indicated that the attack was designed to compel the Russian authorities to reconsider

---

[26]Nokhchi Information Centre, radio broadcast 5 January 2001. The author retains a transcript of the statement.

[27]Some female hostage-takers donned the *burqa*, dress usually worn in Islamic societies but which is not part of the traditional female dress in Chechnya, while banners in Arabic were displayed in the theatre.

their policy towards Chechnya. Shortly after, federal forces stormed the theatre and killed the hostage-takers, including their leader Mosvar Barayev (who had succeeded his uncle as head of the SPIR). Six days after the siege ended Shamil Basaev claimed responsibility for organising the 'Moscow operation by Mosvar Barayev's special unit'.[28] Maskhadov quickly relieved Basaev of his position as Emir of the military council, although he retained control over the *Riyad-us-Saliheyn* and effectively remained in control of a significant portion of the military wing of the movement.

To summarise: the initial wave of suicide attacks between 2000 and the autumn of 2002 were deployed by Barayev's SPIR and the Akhmadov brothers' Islamic Battalions in an attempt to counter the Russian federal attacks directed specifically against them. Despite being undertaken in the name of militant Islam, the attacks were localised initiatives organised by indigenous Chechen groups. Finally, while widely associated with female suicide bombers, both by the media and by their own early video legitimising female 'martyrdom', in fact the suicide operations were largely undertaken by men, as pressure and sweep operations were launched in Urus-Martan. The capacity of the SPIR and Islamic Battalions diminished after the death of key commanders, effectively ending the first wave of suicide attacks. Following Nord Ost, the remnants of these groups became integrated in Basaev's units.

### *The rise of the military* jama'ats

By the middle of 2002, the federal forces controlled most of Chechnya, initiating a campaign of normalisation designed to draw down the large-scale Russian military presence, with pro-Russian Chechen units undertaking military 'sweep' or 'cleansing' operations. These sweep operations were known as *zachistka*s, had been used in the first war, throughout 2000 and 2002, and thereafter on an *ad hoc* basis. Villages were surrounded and over the course of a number of days troops would systematically check houses for rebels, make arrests and detain suspected rebel sympathisers. This approach was conjoined with political change, whereby the interim pro-Kremlin administration would be replaced with a fully fledged Chechen government. Against this backdrop, the second wave of suicide attacks was predicated on very different terms, forms of organisation and ways of thinking. To understand this difference, it is necessary to explore the growth of the military *jama'at*s, going back to 1995.

The lack of cohesion in the Chechen armed resistance movement led to the use of informal regional networks, most notably the system of military *jama'at*s. *Jama'at*s vary in size and are variously comprised of local, tribal and clan communities, often affiliated to particular villages, playing political, social and economic roles in the wider mosaic of ethnic groups in the region. *Jama'at*s had been established in parts of the North Caucasus in earlier eras of Islamisation, particularly in parts of Dagestan. In military terms, *jama'at*s came to the fore at the end of the first Russo-Chechen war, when Ibn Khattab took over the leadership of Shaykh Fathi's group (*al-Jama'at al-Islamiyya*) in 1995. The Salafi military *jama'at*s grew exponentially from 1997, as regional volunteers participated in the training programmes organised in the camps

---

[28]'Chechen Warlord Basaev Takes Responsibility for Moscow Siege', *Kavkaz Tsentr*, 1 November 2002.

run by, amongst others, Ibn Khattab and his coterie of Arab foreign fighters (Moore & Tumelty 2008). By late 2002, the military *jama'at*s provided a vehicle through which Basaev could initiate a strategic campaign of terrorism, so as to respond to, and retaliate against, federal policies of normalisation in Chechnya.

Following the withdrawal of the ChRI government from Grozny in early 2000, a meeting of the State Defence Committee and the *Majlis al-Shura* led to the adoption of a strategy designed to expand the zone of conflict across the North Caucasus. Remnants of military units of the resistance—which included Ingush, Kabardin, Karachay, Avar, Nogay and Balkar volunteers—returned to their local communities and established small clandestine local networks outside of Chechnya that could be used to support a regional insurgency. At least some of the *jama'at*s sought to promote a conservative brand of Islam, which would indicate allegiance to the Salafi wing of the anti-Russian movement. The establishment of a network of *jama'at*s also served a strategic aim—broadening the zone of conflict beyond the confines of Chechnya, a move which Maskhadov endorsed (Fuller 2010).

Basaev's Avar interpreter, Raul Makasharipov, who had accompanied him on the 1999 incursion into Dagestan, established a group named *Dzhennet* (sometimes transliterated from Russian as *Jennet*; in Arabic, the word refers to paradise), which subsequently became the Dagestani *Jama'at Shari'at* (Moore 2010). Elsewhere, following the retreat from Grozny, the remnants of the Nogay Battalion, who had pledged allegiance to Basaev's cause in 1999, also returned to their villages. A number of these volunteers then established the Stavropol' and Shelkovskii *jama'at*s, made up of ex-members of the Nogay battalion. While most of the *jama'at*s were multi-ethnic, the Karachay and Nogay were almost exclusively mono-ethnic. Many volunteers remained loyal to Basaev and other field commanders in whose groups they had gained their combat experience.

Ingush volunteers had supported military operations in Grozny at the start of the second war, although a considerable number were killed and wounded defending the Chechen capital or in the subsequent withdrawal. Between 2000 and 2001, many Ingush volunteers were organised around small military *jama'at*s, which operated clandestinely, splitting into smaller sub-groups, and were largely geographically based (such as the Nazran *jama'at* and the Sleptov *jama'at*). Each sub-group established bases across the republic, aiding the broader war effort in the years after 2001. Acting as independent units, the *jama'at*s were difficult to identify, let alone counter, given the federal focus on Chechnya as the key site of the conflict. After 2001, although they retained a measure of independence, the Ingush groups became integrated into the broader system of military *jama'at*s, as the organisational structure of the Chechen-led resistance changed. The *jama'at* led by Ilyas Gorchkanov and Ali Taziev (known by the pseudonym Magas) was renamed, but in essence retained a core group of small clandestine units capable of supporting the broader Chechen-led war effort. Much like the groups in Dagestan, the Ingush *jama'at*s included volunteers from other ethnic and sub-ethnic groups, including Chechens, Balkars and a handful of Ossetians.

Another *jama'at*, named Yarmuk, was formed in Kabardino-Balkaria, by remnants of the IIPB. Established by Balkar and Kabardin volunteers, the group was led by Muslim Atayev, known as Amir Sayfullah, an ideologue who had trained in a camp run by Ruslan Gelayev. In 2002, the group helped Gelayev move from the Pankisi Gorge back into Ingushetia, and subsequently initiated a recruitment drive. Affiliates of the Yarmuk *jama'at* pledged allegiance to Shamil Basaev, providing support for operations they would later launch in 2005. Although their numbers remained small, the military *jama'at*s had many members with considerable combat experience; they could operate outside of the confines of Chechnya, giving them an important tactical capability. The military leadership headed by Basaev would draw heavily on the regional *jama'at* networks when Operation Boomerang was launched in late 2002.

### *The many faces of Operation Boomerang*

Following Nord Ost (October 2002), Basaev integrated some of the surviving members of 'Barayev gang'—Movsar's successor, Khamzat Tazabayev and some Akhmadov loyalists—into his military units, including the one that would be used to launch a wave of suicide attacks, the *Riyad-us-Saliheyn*. The shrinking capacity of the insurgency led its military leaders to consider radical tactics, harking back to Basaev's decision to launch a military *nabeg*[29] deep into Russian territory in June 1995 during the first Russo-Chechen war. In autumn 2002, the *Majlis al-Shura* incorporated a younger generation of fighters who had begun to take increasingly important roles in the hierarchy of the anti-Russian resistance (Sokirianskaia 2008, pp. 128–32). All the groups, including the *Riyad-us-Saliheyn*, drew upon the military *jama'at*s inside Chechnya and across the North Caucasus.

The first major act of terrorism after Nord Ost was a suicide attack attributable to the *Riyad-us-Saliheyn*. On 27 December 2002, two truck-bombs were driven into the main headquarters of the Chechen government in Grozny. The bombs completely destroyed the buildings, killing over 80 people and wounding hundreds of others. The attack was attributed to the radical wing of the resistance (Udugov 2003). A sharp upsurge in attacks followed in 2003. Basaev had spent almost two years garnering financial support for specific operations and designating targets. Following a meeting of the *Majlis al-Shura* in early 2003, Basaev—by then operating under the Arabic *nom de guerre* Amir Abdallah Shamil Abu Idris—announced Operation Boomerang. In the announcement, he stated that the policy of 'retaliation', using '*shaheeds*' (suicide bombers), had been initiated following the arrest or 'disappearance' of female relatives by Russian authorities (Basaev 2003a). It was federal operations that had led Basaev to 'launch Operation Boomerang in the homeland of those on behalf of [i.e. in the name of] the Russian people who are committing atrocities in the Chechen land' (Basaev 2003b). However, the familiar rhetoric of retaliation masked, at least in part, a new strategic aim: to escalate the campaign of terrorism to the wider North Caucasus region, and to target Moscow, as federal forces continued to mount operations in Chechnya and its environs.

---

[29] A *nabeg* is a lightening raid. It was traditionally used by different groups in the North Caucasus to capture cattle or hostages. The speed and style of these attacks generated fear and panic. Two independent raids, akin to militarised *nabegs*, were employed by Chechen groups in June 1995 and January 1996.

On 12 May 2003, another truck-bomb, driven by a male and female attacker, exploded at the entrance to a government security complex in Znamenskoye, in the northern part of Chechnya. The attack, claimed by Basaev as part of Operation Boomerang, partially destroyed the building, killed around 60 people and injured scores more, although it failed to kill Mairbek Khusiev, the regional head of the *Federalnaya Sluzhba Bezopasnosti* (FSB, Russian Federal Security Service) (Basaev 2003a). The attack on Znamenskoye also served a symbolic purpose, given its location in the northern plains of Chechnya, considered one of the safest places in the region and a seat of pro-Kremlin Chechen power. The two concerns—the strategy of taking the war to security organisations linked to the Russian and pro-Russian Chechen administration and the tactic of targeting of specific individuals—appear to have shaped the initial batch of attacks linked to Operation Boomerang from December 2002 through to late 2003.

*Adaptation and innovation*

It was not long before the federal authorities began to curtail the movement of Ural trucks and target the military *jama'at*s. Basaev shifted his tactics, turning to the use of individual or small groups of female attackers. Strategically, the move was designed to undermine the political process of normalisation in Chechnya, to foster a sense of insecurity in Russia and to give the militant underground much needed breathing space—particularly through further attempts at targeted assassination. A few days after the Znamenskoye truck-bomb attack, a lone female suicide attacker was arrested; according to reports, she had planned to blow herself up at the 9 May Victory Day parade in Grozny (Abdullaev 2003).

Then on 14 May, at a traditional religious festival at Islkhan-Yurt celebrating the Sufi Sheikh Kunta-Khadzhi Kishiev, an attempt was made to assassinate Akhmad Kadyrov.[30] The suicide attack, by two bombers killed 16 people and left approximately 150 injured, including some of Kadyrov's bodyguards. The innovative nature of the attack, in which the two women posed as journalists and carried explosives in their camera equipment, demonstrated the capacity of Basaev and his aides to learn, given that a similar method of attack had been used by *al-Qaeda*, killing Shah Masood in Afghanistan on 10 September 2001. For the radical groups associated with Basaev, the assassination of Akhmad Kadyrov would have been profoundly symbolic, given his presence at a Sufi festival organised by the pro-Kremlin United Russia (*Edinaya Rossiya*) party. Two and half months later, another failed suicide attack took place, this time directed against Kadyrov's son, Ramzan.[31] Russian authorities reported that the attack was conducted by a female attacker from a village in the Southern highlands of Chechnya (Barinov 2003). Even though the two attacks in May and the attack in July had not killed their intended targets, directing attacks at the assassination of influential members of the pro-Kremlin Chechen and Russian administration, who were in some way implicated in the suppression of, and 'cleansing' of the southern regions, became a distinctive feature of Operation Boomerang.

---

[30]'Female Bomber Kills 14', *Moscow Times*, 15 May 2003, p. 1.
[31]'Chechen Dies After Suicide Bombing', *The Moscow Times*, 29 July 2003, p. 3.

Between these three attempted assassinations, on 5 June there occurred the first attack in Mozdok, in the Federal Republic of North Ossetia-Alania, also undertaken by a female suicide attacker from a Chechen highland village. The attack was directed against a bus carrying federal air personnel to the Russian airbase in Mozdok and killed around 17 people (Bagrov 2003, p. 1). Much like earlier suicide attacks, the bombing invoked a sense of collective responsibility, given the role that Mozdok played in the federal air campaign. However, the potential for civilian casualties caused some debate within the insurgency. Against the dissenters, Zelimkhan Yandarbiyev argued that 'the Chechens or any other nation fighting for its liberation has a full and unconditional right to use any methods and means available' (Yandarbiyev 2003).

The key reason why the radical wing of the resistance deployed female bombers, and also why they used multi-ethnic groups from *jama'ats* outside of Chechnya, was to evade the punitive security measures adopted by the pro-Kremlin Chechen and Russian authorities, which tended to focus primarily on male members of the Chechen population. For example, the Mozdok attack was supported by an Ossetian, a man from Kabardino-Balkaria, an Ingush, while a Chechen, remaining in the background, had organised the bombing.[32] The timing of each attack was also planned strategically. A (failed) truck-bomb directed against a government compound in Grozny, which led to the death of two bombers, had been designed to challenge the political authority of pro-Russian Chechen authority, timed a day before a meeting of the temporary regional legislature.[33]

On 5 July 2003, the terror campaign escalated further when two female attackers were stopped by security guards as they attempted to enter a festival at the Tushino airfield, just outside Moscow. The first attacker failed to fully detonate her bomb, killing herself and a passer-by, while the second bomber killed around 15 people and injured approximately 30 bystanders. Up until then no further attacks had occurred in Moscow since Nord Ost; nor had civilians been the prime target of Chechen suicide bombers. Representatives of the *Riyad-us-Saliheyn*, including Basaev, did not claim responsibility in the immediate aftermath. This suggests that the attack may have been sanctioned by Basaev but organised independently by volunteers based in Ingushetia (Saradzhyan 2003, p. 3). Less than a week later, another attack in Moscow, again only circuitously linked to *Riyad-us-Saliheyn*, also failed. On this occasion, the female attacker left a bag filled with explosives in a cafe in Moscow. Confusion surrounds exactly what happened next. The bomb failed to detonate and the attacker was captured attempting to flee the scene. It is unclear if and how the attacks in Moscow in July—particularly the second attack—relate to Operation Boomerang or *Riyad-us-Saliheyn*, especially because of the targets—civilians—and the lack of any motive associated with the sites attacked. Operation Boomerang attacks were designed to 'speak' to punitive or political measures associated with the federal campaign in Chechnya or its environs. Nonetheless the Tushino airfield attack may have been designed to escalate the terror campaign. Tellingly, while Basaev did eventually claim some responsibility for the Tushino bombings, he did not acknowledge any

---

[32]'Four Go on Trial in Mozdok Suicide Blast', *The Moscow Times*, 10 August 2004, p. 3.

[33]*Interfax*, 20 June 2003, the author retains a transcript of this newswire report.

involvement in the second attack, indicating that he had neither commissioned nor sanctioned the operation. Thus, the decision to launch operations in Moscow in 2003 appears to have been made by affiliated groups, rather than being part of the orchestrated strategic campaign of terror related to Operation Boomerang.

Then, on 1 August, a truck-bomb was used to attack a military hospital, again in Mozdok, North Ossetia. Although directed against a soft target, a similar rationale was offered to justify the attack. The target was in North Ossetia, a republic viewed as a supporter of the federal campaign by the radical wing in the insurgency, while the hospital at the base housed injured military personnel who had participated in combat operations, particularly bombing raids, in Chechnya's mountainous regions (Sharia News Agency 2003a). According to reports, the attack was organised by volunteers from Chechnya, Ingushetia and Ossetia, having simply been commissioned by Basaev (Rechkalov 2004, p. 5).

Further attacks followed. In September 2003, two truck-bombs were used to attack the FSB compound in the Ingush capital, Nazran. The bomb attack, conducted by the members of the Nogay community, was a joint combat operation organised by the Stavropol' *jama'at* and *Riyad-us-Saliheyn* (Sharia News Agency 2003a). The attack failed, largely due to the security barriers in front of the building—although it did lead to the death of four bystanders and injured over a dozen others. The suicide operation again drew attention to the multi-ethnic nature of the military *jama'at*s with volunteers from Kabardino-Balkaria, Ingushetia and the Stavropol' region providing *ad hoc* support (Larintseva *et al*. 2003, pp. 20–2). Overall, a significant proportion of the attacks after December 2002 were undertaken by Nogay participants—supported by the Stavropol' and Shelkovskii *jama'at*s—and Chechens from highland towns, such as Vedeno and Shali.

The wave of attacks in 2003 concluded with a devastating bombing in December, well beyond the borders of Chechnya, and another failed attack in Moscow. What is known as the Yessentuki attack—which took place on 6 December 2003—appears to have been part of a cluster of operations designed to unnerve the Russian public in the build up to the Russian presidential elections. The attack targeted a morning commuter train *en route* from Kislovodsk to Mineralnye Vody. The blast occurred inside a train carriage just outside the resort town of Yessentuki, in Stavropol' province, Russia, near the north-west border of Chechnya. The blast killed around 40 people and injured nearly 200. According to Russian security officials, the suicide attacker was male, although three female accomplices were implicated.[34] The *modus operandi* of using grenades strapped to the bodies of a bomber was unsophisticated yet deadly. The location and timing of the operation, inside a crowded commuter train, compounded the death count.

However, the Yessentuki bombing is significant because it also served as an act of retaliation, following a June 2003 crackdown by the federal authorities on the Nogay Islamists from the Shelkovskii *Raion* of Chechnya and the Neftekumsky *Raion* of Stavropol' *Krai*. Thus, as well as serving a larger political purpose, the retaliatory

---

[34]"Chechen "Black Widows" Claim Responsibility for Yessentuki, Moscow Blasts', *Kavkaz Tsentr*, 23 December 2003, available at: http://kavkazcentrer.com/eg/content/2003/12/25/2196.shtml, accessed 25 July 2012.

attack also communicated a message of defiance to the federal forces in the North Caucasus. The attack highlighted the ineffective security measures of the Russian authorities, a symbolic point that added weight because it occurred just days before the Russian parliamentary elections. Following strategic logic, the December suicide attack highlighted the inability of the Russian state to protect its citizens, also creating fear and anxiety among the Russian population in the North Caucasus.

A week later, a further attack by a female suicide bomber occurred in Moscow. The bombs she was carrying exploded as she was passing the National Hotel, near to the Russian parliament building, the *Duma*. The attack killed five bystanders and wounded over a dozen others. Shortly after the Yessentuki and Moscow attacks, Basaev released a statement claiming responsibility on behalf of *Riyad-us-Saliheyn*, stating that the *Duma* had been the target of the Moscow attack, and that the Yessentuki attack had been launched by the Stavropol' *jama'at* (Basaev 2003c). Thus, the 2003 strategy consisted of attacks within the North Caucasus region alongside attacks in Moscow. For instance, following the March 2003 referendum which was used to establish a new constitution by the pro-Kremlin Chechen administration, attacks increased.

The wave of attacks in May, June, September and December 2003 also appears to have been reactions to the broader socio-political conditions in Chechnya proper, following as they did the March constitutional vote, which the local authorities had claimed would ensure the safety and security of the local population. Each attack demonstrated that punitive measures by the federal authorities could not halt—indeed would only provoke—the strategic escalation of Operation Boomerang. The July attacks in Moscow and the wave of attacks that followed the presidential elections in October 2003 were a little more difficult to place, but were in part tied into the State *Duma* elections in Russia, as well as the elections in Chechnya. At least in part, members of the *Riyad-us-Saliheyn* appear to have selected targets due to their political and economic importance, as part of the infrastructure of the Russian state. Targets were chosen and actions undertaken that expanded the conflict zone, as the foothold of the insurgents in Chechnya proper weakened, and as Chechen-on-Chechen violence spiralled. Selecting particular towns, and the context of the broader regional politics, helped to legitimise the attacks as part of Basaev's terror campaign. The two attacks in the North Ossetian town of Mozdok were sanctioned and funded by Basaev, partly because of the Russian military presence in the town, but also because of the long-standing role that Ossetia had played as 'Russia's fortpost [sic] in the North Caucasus'.[35]

### *The culmination of Operation Boomerang: terrorism in 2004*

Operation Boomerang concluded in 2004, a crucial year for understanding the changing dynamics in the insurgency. Prior to this, however, the Ingush *jama'at* was becoming increasingly active, broadening the conflict zone beyond the borders of Chechnya. Again, this manifested itself in targeted assassination attempts using

---

[35]Basaev made a series of pronouncement about Operation Boomerang in an interview for Channel Four news, on 3 February 2005. The text of the interview is available at: http://www.kavkazcenter.com/eng/content/2005/02/04/3500.shtml, accessed 9 July 2009.

suicide attackers. One such 'failed' attack on 6 April 2004 served to demonstrate the shift back to assassination. The former FSB general and then President of Ingushetia, Murat Zyazikov, survived an assassination attempt by a suicide car bomber. After the attack, Basaev stated that the terror 'is spreading into neighbouring regions, threatening the security of the country as a whole' (Sergievskii 2004). Not only did the assassination attempt lead, not long after, to an escalation of the violence in Ingushetia, it served to highlight the broadening zone of conflict, symbolically linking Zyazikov with repression in the North Caucasus, particularly given the close relationship he had with the Putin administration. The attack itself also occurred only days after Zelimkhan Yandarbiyev had been assassinated by Russian agents in a car bomb in Qatar, which Basaev used rhetorically to legitimise the assassination attempt on Zyazikov.

Then in May, at the Victory Day parade at the newly refurbished Dinamo Stadium in Grozny, a huge explosion killed Akhmad Kadyrov, Hussein Isaev, the Chairman of the State Council of the ChRI, and the Commander of the Unified Troops, General Valeri Baranov. Whether Kadyrov himself was the target of the attack is open to question, because he was not scheduled to attend the event. Nonetheless, the insurgents had severely weakened the federal hierarchy in Chechnya, having targeted an event that would necessarily be attended by high-ranking officials. Federal authorities quickly announced that they would run a new election campaign—at which point they were dealt another telling blow, a military *nabeg* was launched against the Ingush town of Nazran.

The audacious attack in late June—launched by over 150 fighters—not only targeted military barracks, FSB and Interior Ministry compounds but it also demonstrated the increasing importance of the Ingush *jama'at* and, more generally, the ability of the insurgents to launch large-scale attacks. The federal authorities embarked on numerous security sweeps in response to the *nabeg* and yet it was followed less than two months later by an upsurge in attacks in Chechnya, including the seizure of checkpoints by Chechen fighters in and around Grozny on 21 August.[36] Alongside, the upsurge in attacks directed against military targets, Basaev also continued to run a parallel terror campaign, including a series of attacks on Kadyrov's successor, Sergei Abramov. However, the culmination of this phase of attacks was yet to come, timed as it was to undermine the announcement of a new Chechen president, following the death of Akhmad Kadyrov, in late August 2004.

On 24 August, two internal flights heading for southern Russia left the newly refurbished and highly secure airport, Domodedovo, in Moscow. Two women had boarded the planes, having evaded stringent security measures; both were Chechen suicide bombers. The bombers—originally from highland towns—detonated their explosives, destroying the aircraft and killing 90 people; a statement released on the internet claimed responsibility on behalf of the Islambouli brigades. A week later on 31 August 2004, another female suicide attacker blew herself up, this time during rush hour at the Rizhskaya metro station in Moscow. The attack killed around a dozen

---

[36]Security sweeps following the Nazran raid did yield some results for the federal forces. Federal authorities killed Abu Queytyba, a logistical and financial expert, and an influential member of the Arab *mujahedeen*, who had helped organise the Nazran raid.

people and wounded nearly 70. Investigators quickly identified the bomber as a sister of the attacker who had blown up one of the two planes. A statement was again issued, claiming responsibility on behalf of the Islambouli brigades, although it quickly became apparent that the two attacks had been organised by the *Riyad-us-Saliheyn*.[37] It is thought that the claim was issued to garner financial support and link the attacks to the broader Salafi movement. In effect, therefore the three attacks served a tactical, symbolic and strategic purpose, demonstrating the inability of the Russian law enforcement agencies to provide security in the face of the escalation of the terror campaign using suicide attacks against soft targets.

These spectacular suicide attacks were followed by the Beslan school siege, which began on 1 September 2004. The attackers, numbering at least 32 people, surrounded the key entry points to the school and shepherded children and parents into the school gymnasium. The school had been chosen not only because of the role that North Ossetia was playing in the federal war effort, and its proximity to Chechnya and Ingushetia, but also because of the potential to incite further inter-ethnic clashes between the Ingush and Ossetians. The multi-ethnic group of attackers were well-prepared, although many appear not to have known that they would be attacking a school or holding children as hostages. The federal forces reacted slowly. The ensuing hostage-taking crisis was interrupted by the release of a set of demands—including, once again, the demand to halt the conflict in Chechnya. The situation worsened as the federal authorities rebuffed attempts at negotiation, and eventually culminated on 3 September in a drawn-out fire-fight that left hundreds dead and many more injured.

In February 2005, Basaev spoke about Operation Boomerang in an interview for Channel Four news. He acknowledged that it was because larger scale attacks had been hampered in 2003 that the Shura had accepted his proposals for using suicide attacks, which also enabled the longer term strategy of establishing a North Caucasus system of military *jama'at*s. He said, 'We have not stopped directing our operations against military and political targets on Russian territory. It's just that your knowledge and our capability to conduct military action are limited'.[38] After Beslan, Basaev had stated that 'we actively brought military operations to the territory of Russia in 2002 [referring to Nord Ost], at precisely the time when they began to conduct the Chechenisation of the conflict'.[39] While Chechenisation had clearly undermined the ability of the resistance to mount operations in Chechnya proper by late 2004, due to the capture and death of members of *Riyad-us-Saliheyn*, the

---

[37]The Islambouli Brigades are a small militant Islamist group which had launched a handful of attacks in Pakistan. Khalid Islambouli was a junior officer in the Egyptian army who planned and participated in the assassination the Egyptian president, Anwar Sadat, in 1981. Members of the Egyptian *al-Jihad* group responsible for the attack were quickly arrested. Khalid was sentenced to death by the Egyptian authorities in 1982, and thereafter became eulogised in radical Islamist circles as one of the first modern martyrs. The group had never launched attacks in Russia and no evidence was provided to support the statement claiming responsibility.

[38]3 February 2005. The text of the interview is available at: http://www.kavkazcenter.com/eng/content/2005/02/04/3500.shtml, accessed 9 July 2009.

[39]3 February 2005. The text of the interview is available at: http://www.kavkazcenter.com/eng/content/2005/02/04/3500.shtml, accessed 9 July 2009.

emergence of combat *jama'at* groups across the North Caucasus meant that the insurgency retained a military capacity and capability.[40]

### Retribution and revenge

At least two other attacks appear to have their roots in the second Russo-Chechen war: the attack by Elsa Gazueva in 2001 and the Moscow metro bombing in February 2004. The first attack was by Elza Gazueva, in which she detonated grenades in the presence of members of pro-Kremlin Chechen military commanders, having requested to see them. The attack took place on 29 November 2001. The explosion killed her and gravely wounded Gaidar Gadzhiev, chief of the military administration of Urus-Martan region. Gadzhiev—who had ordered the arrest of Gazueva's husband as part of a cleansing operation—later died as a result of his wounds.

The attack was followed by a series of arrests and attacks on the houses of family members and rebel sympathisers (Memorial 2001). No group claimed responsibility for the attack, indicating that it was an independent, indeed individual, act of retribution, a personal response to the brutality of the local pro-Kremlin Chechen authorities and the federal forces.[41] Importantly, however, Urus-Martan was a well-known centre of anti-Russian radicalism—as well as local support for key criminal groups, including the Akhmadov gang and associates of Magomed Tsagarayev. While evidence linking either Gazueva or her husband to these groups is circumstantial, a number of the families in Urus-Martan were certainly sympathetic to the Islamist groups from the town. Although the bombing was part of a cluster of suicide attacks between 2000 and 2002, the *modus operandi* and target indicate that it was more likely to be an individual reaction to the action of federal forces targeting the Tsagarayev family in and around Urus-Martan.

The second attack—the Moscow metro bombing in 2004—also has its roots in an earlier phase of operations by Russian forces. The attack took place at around 8.30 in the morning of 6 February 2004, in a crowded commuter metro carriage travelling between the Avtozavodskaya and Paveletskaya underground stations in central Moscow. Approximately 40 people were killed, with a further 145 injured in the blast. Information about the attack remains sketchy, although it does appear that the blast was linked to three attackers, one man and two women, who had boarded the train shortly before the explosion. The style of the attack appeared similar to the Yessentuki train bombing in December 2003.

Significantly, however, a statement released shortly after the attack by an unknown group named Gaston Murdash, led by Lom-Ali Chechensky—and perhaps the *modus operandi*—indicated another, more plausible, motive. The statement read, 'This was small, but good. Remember! This was revenge for the Aldy February 5–6 2000, and it

---

[40] For instance, Abu Bakr Bizambayev was killed while Rustam Ganiev was arrested. See the Ministry of Information (MOI) available at: http://eng.mvdrf.ru/news/337/?print, accessed 10 August 2010.

[41] The customary report on military operations published through the Kavkaz Tsentr mentioned the attack but Basaev, the *Riyad-us-Saliheyn* or any other group or individual did not claim responsibility. See 'Special Operations of the Chechen Mujahideen', *Kavkaz Tsentr*, 4 December 2001, available at: http://www.kavkazcenter.com/eng/content/2001/12/04/71.shtml, accessed 10 August 2010.

is only the beginning!'[42] At the time, the leadership of the separatist movement did not claim responsibility for the attack, which is telling, nor was the bombing accompanied by other attacks, which had become the key trademark of suicide attacks linked to *Riyad-us-Saliheyn*. Although not part of Operation Boomerang, nor sanctioned by Basaev, it does appear that the then leader of the Arab *mujahedeen*, Abu Walid, may have supported the attack. Nonetheless, the bombing appears to have been an act of personal retaliation—harking back to Chechen customary codes of revenge—for the savage Russian cleansing operation in Aldy in February 2000.[43]

As part of the first phase of the Russian advance in Chechnya, a number of villages and towns had been surrounded and subjected to *zachistk*i (cleansing operations) designed to flush out suspected rebels. Such tactics had been employed in the first war, although they became more widespread following a change in Russian strategy after the failures of the first conflict. Underpinned by a strategy of collective punishment, such attacks became commonplace as Russian troops advanced into Chechnya's highlands. *Zachistka*s became notorious because of the unrestrained brutality employed by the troops and *kontraktniki* (contract soldiers), which led to many civilian deaths. As a preventive measure, on 5 February 2000, Russian forces had launched a *zachistka* operation in the Chechen village of Novye Aldi. The operation lasted around two days, and led to the death of around 80 inhabitants, according to the human rights organisation, Memorial (2000).

## *Concluding remarks*

Since the end of the Cold War, numerous studies have predicted that the North Caucasus would be engulfed by conflict. However few, if any, have explained how and why particular campaigns of terrorism occurred. In contrast, this essay has argued that there have been two waves of attacks. The first, which started in June 2000, culminated with the Nord Ost siege in October 2002. At least in part, the suicide attacks resulted from federal pressured exerted on groups from Urus-Martan, notably the Islamic Battalions linked to the Akhmadov brothers, and the SPIR linked to Arbi Barayev. This wave of attacks, which largely occurred in Chechnya, was designed to support the war effort by these groups. The attacks focused on military and paramilitary targets and largely involved male attackers.

A second wave of suicide attacks which began in December 2002 and which culminated in the Beslan School Siege in September 2004 served a strategic purpose as part of a campaign of terrorism, known as Operation Boomerang, overseen by Shamil Basaev. Operation Boomerang drew on the then nascent system of military *jama'at*s, and the multi-ethnic organisational support networks outside of Chechnya, so as to expand the zone of conflict as a result of federal pressure exerted on both the moderate and radical wings of the resistance increased. More generally, the attacks were

---

[42]'Blast in Metro was revenge for Aldy?', 8 February 2004, available at: http://kavkaz.org.uk/eng/content/2004/03/01/2470_print.html, accessed 8 July 2009. See also, 'Unknown Rebel Group Claims Moscow Metro Blast', *Gazeta.ru*, available at: http://www.gazeta.ru/2004/03/02/oa_113618.shtml.

[43]The idea of 'blood revenge' being an essential component of the second conflict was raised more recently in the ethnographic work of Souleimanov and Ditrych (2008).

designed to retaliate and respond to the Chechenisation of the conflict. The second wave of attacks included the more explicit use of female bombers, targeting facilities inside and outside of Chechnya, while many of the 'martyrs' themselves came from the highland villages in Chechnya and the Nogay community. Unlike the first wave of attacks, the groups largely responsible for suicide attacks, which increased between December 2002 and 2004, were often linked to the *Riyad-us-Saliheyn*, a 'martyr battalion' led by Shamil Basaev. The attackers were often from Chechen highland towns or from the Nogay community. The groups involved were often multi-ethnic, while the attacks occurred inside Chechnya, in the North Caucasus and also further afield in Moscow. The targets were military and political, while the methods used included the use of truck-bombs and individual assassination attempts. Many of the attacks reflected the changing character of the insurgency, which increasingly developed a regional form. The *Riyad-us-Saliheyn* appears to have operated as a franchise organisation, with Basaev drawing on support from the Vedeno, Shelkovskii, Stavropol' and Ingush *jama'at*s. Although women were frequently used to overcome punitive security measures, a number of attacks were launched by men, while the targets and methods draw attention to the ways that the group innovated and adapted their usage of radical methods. At least some of the attacks in Operation Boomerang also appear to have been launched as independent initiatives, suggesting that they were simply funded by Basaev.

To conclude, the analysis in this essay serves to debunk many of the myths, often repeated in popular studies, associated with Chechen-related suicide attacks. The first batch of attacks were local initiatives directed and led by Chechen groups, using truck or car bombs, directed at military checkpoints, as opposed to heavily defended political targets. Although the July 2000 attacks were co-ordinated, again they used truck or car bombs, in support of operations launched by the SPIR and the Islamic Battalions led by Ramzan Akhmadov and Arbi Barayev, respectively. In contrast, the wave of attacks which followed used innovative methods and escalated throughout 2003 and 2004. The second wave of attacks started with truck-bombs used to attack a heavily defended political and military target in Chechnya. They were followed by a wave of individual attacks, often using female bombers in targeted assassination attempts, in Chechnya. Thereafter, a further batch of attacks using truck-bombs and individuals, directed at softer targets in North Ossetia, served a strategic aim designed to expand the zone of the conflict. At the same time, another batch of attacks occurred in Moscow. In Moscow, an attack was directed against the *Duma*, and it was followed by the attack on a train in Yessentuki, in the Stavrapol *Krai* region in 2003. Then in April 2004, an attempted assassination of the Ingush president, using a car bomb driven by a suicide bomber, occurred. The attack was followed in August by a series of even more sophisticated individual suicide operations in which bombers travelled to Moscow. On 24 August, two of the three female attackers breached the stringent security at Domodedovo airport, boarding planes to Southern Russia, before detonating their explosives, while a third bomber died a few days later in an improvised explosion at the Rizhskaya metro station. These three attackers could easily have been directed against other poorly defended targets. Instead, the attacks were part of a steady escalation and innovation in the use of radical tactics, directed by Shamil Basaev. Much like other acts of terrorism attributable to Basaev, many of the suicide operations were linked to a political strategy, responding to federal initiatives to normalise relations in Chechnya. Many of the attacks in Operation Boomerang demonstrated that Basaev retained a military capability, as well as a capacity to adapt and change methods of attack. Finally, this serves to underscore the point that the only other attack directed against the Moscow metro system, the February 2004 suicide operation, was both improvised and independent of Operation Boomerang.

*University of Birmingham*

## References

Abdullaev, N. (2003) 'Suicide Attacks Take Rebel Fight to a New Level', *Moscow Times*, 16 May.
Abdullaev, N. (2007) 'Unravelling Chechen "Black Widows"', *Homeland Defense Journal*, 5, 5, pp. 18–21.
Akaev, V. (2010) 'Islam and Politics in Chechniia and Ingushetiia', in Yemelianova, G. (ed.) (2010).
Akhmadov, I. (2010) *The Chechen Struggle: Independence Won and Lost* (New York, Palgrave Macmillan).
Allenova, O., Stulov, O. & Dyupin, S. (2000) 'Posle okonchaniya krovavykh boev pod Serzhen-Yurtom...' *Kommersant"*, 4 July.
Bagrov, Y. (2003) 'Female Suicide Bomber Blows Up Bus', *Moscow Times*, 6 June, p. 1.
Barakhova, A. (1998) 'Shamil Basayev ob'edinit Chechniyu I Daghestan', *Kommersant"*, 28 April, p. 3.
Barinov, V. (2003) 'Shekhidy Protaklivayut svoi Put' k Synu', *Gazeta*, 28 July.
Basaev, S. (2003a) 'Abdallah Shamil Announces Operation Boomerang', *Kavkaz Tsentr*, 24 May, available at: http://old.kavkazcenter.com/eng/content/2003/05/24/1349.shtml, accessed 8 November 2004.
Basaev, S. (2003b) 'Jihad is Only Starting to Flare Up in Ichkeria', *Kavkaz Tsentr*, 9 June, available at: http://old.kavkazcenter.com/eng/content/2003/06/09/1453.shtml, accessed 8 November 2004.
Basaev, S. (2003c) 'Chechen Independent Brigade Claims Responsibility for Bombings', *Kavkaz Tsentr*, 25 December, available at: http://old.kavkazcenter.com/eng/content/2003/12/25/2196.shtml, accessed 8 November 2004.
Basaev, S. (2005) 'Interview of Shamil Basaev to Channel Four News', Kavkaz Tsentr, 4th February, available at: http://www.kavkazcenter.com/eng/content/2005/02/04/3500.shtml, accessed 20 July 2011.
Blandy, C. (2004) *Chechnya: Centre of Unabated Instability and Conflict*, 20 May, available at: http://www.da.mod.uk/colleges/arag/document-listings/caucasus/, accessed 28 March 2010.
Bobrovnikov, V. (2004) 'Rural Muslims' Nationalism in the Post-Soviet Caucasus: The Case of Dagestan', in Gammer, M. (ed.) (2004).
Cook, D. (2007) 'A Critique of Robert Pape's 'Dying to Win', *The Journal of Strategic Studies*, 30, 2, pp. 243–54.
Cronin, A. (2003) 'Terrorists and Suicide Attacks', *U.S. Congressional Research Service Report for Congress*, 28 August, available at: http://www.fas.org/irp/crs/RL32058.pdf, accessed 10 February 2010.
Dolnik, A. (2007) *Negotiating the Impossible: The Beslan Hostage Crises* (London, Royal United Services Institute for Defence and Security Studies).
Dunlop, J. (1998) *Russia Confronts Chechnya: Roots of a Separatist Conflict* (Cambridge, Cambridge University Press).
Dunlop, J. (2006) *The 2002 Dubrovka and 2004 Beslan Hostage Crises: A Critique of Russian Counter-Terrorism* (Stuttgart, Ibidem-Verlang).
Dyupin, S. (2001) 'Obezglavlen Klan Golovorezov', *Kommersant"*, 12 March.
Fuller, L. (2010) 'Five Years after Maskhadov's Death, Situation in North Caucasus Remains Complex', *Radio Liberty*, 7 March, available at: http://www.rferl.org/content/Five_Years_After_Maskhadovs_Death_Situation_In_North_Caucasus_Remains_Complex/1976899.html, accessed 15 March 2010.
Gall, C. & De Waal, T. (1997) *Chechnya: A Small Victorious War* (London, Pan Books).
Galkin, G. (2000) 'Poka budut ubivat nashikh, ya ni rublya ne dam', *Kommersant"*, 4 July.
Gambetta, D. (ed.) (2005) *Making Sense of Suicide Missions* (Oxford, University of Oxford Press).
Gammer, M. (ed.) (2004) *The Caspian Region: Volume II* (London, Routledge).
Gammer, M. (2006) *The Lone Wolf and the Bear: Three Centuries of Chechen Defiance of Russian Rule* (London, Hurst & Co).

German, T. (2003) *Russia's Chechen War* (London, Routledge Curzon).
Hafez, M. (2007) *Manufacturing Human Bombs: The Making of Palestinian Suicide Bombers* (Washington, DC, United States Institute for Peace).
Kramer, M. (2005) 'Guerrilla Warfare, Counterinsurgency and Terrorism in the North Caucasus: The Military Dimension of the Russian-Chechen conflict', *Europe-Asia Studies*, 57, 2, pp. 209–90.
Krasnov, V. (2000) 'Chechen Rebels Launch Deadly Strikes Against Russians', *AFP*, 12 June.
Larintseva, A., Samedov, T. & Allenova, O. (2003) 'Kol'tso Kavkazskoi Natsional'nosti', *Kommersant Vlast'*, 38, pp. 20–2, available at: http://www.kommersant.ru/doc.aspx?DocsID=414826, accessed 24 July 2002.
Markedonov, S. (2010) *Radical Islam in the North Caucasus* (Washington, DC, CSIS).
Matveeva, A. (2004) 'Dagestahn: Inter-Ethnic Tensions and Cross Border Implications', in Gammer, M. (ed.) (2004).
Memorial (2000) 'Zachistka: Novii-Aldi, 5 Fevralya 2000 g.', *Doklad Provozashchitnogo Tsentr Memorial: Mezhdunarodnye Prestupleniya protiv Grazhdanskogo Naseleniya*, 2 (Moscow, Memorial).
Memorial (2001) 'Terror with Terror', 20 December, available at: http://www.memo.ru/eng/memhrc/texts/terror.shtml, accessed 7 June 2007.
Memorial (2002) 'Kontrterroristicheskaya Operatsii', *Doklad Provozashchitnogo Tsentr Memorial: Narushenie Prov Chelovek i Norm Gumanitarnogo Prav v Khode Vooruzhennero Konflikta v Chechne: Sentyabr' 1999 g.—Mai 2002 g. poselok Starye Atagi'*, 3 (Moscow, Memorial).
Moghadam, A. (2006) 'Suicide Terrorism, Occupation, and the Globalization of Martyrdom: A Critique of "Dying to Win"', *Studies in Conflict and Terrorism*, 29, 8, pp. 707–27.
Moghadam, A. (2008) 'Motives for Martyrdom: Al-Qaida, Salafi Jihad, and the Spread of Suicide Attacks', *International Security*, 33, 3, pp. 46–78.
Moore, C. (2010) 'The Roots and Transformation of the Dagestan Insurgency', 29 September, available at: http://www.jamestown.org/programs/edm/single/?tx_ttnews%5Btt_news%5D=36961&tx_ttnews%5BbackPid%5D=484&no_cache=1, accessed 20 April 2012.
Moore, C. (2012) 'Beyond Jihad in Chechnya: Foreign Fighters and the Insurgency in the North Caucasus', unpublished research paper.
Moore, C. & Tumelty, P. (2008) 'Foreign Fighters and the Case of Chechnya: A Critical Assessment', *Studies in Conflict and Terrorism*, 31, 5, pp. 412–33.
Moore, C. & Tumelty, P. (2009) 'Assessing Unholy Alliances in Chechnya: From Communism and Nationalism to Islamism and Salafism', *The Journal of Communist Studies and Transition Politics*, 25, 1, pp. 73–94.
Murtazaliyev, O. (1997) 'Security Assurances in Our Hands', *Dagestanskaya Pravda*, 249, pp. 1–2.
Naumkin, V. (2005) *Radical Islam in Central Asia: Between Pen and Rifle* (Oxford, Rowman & Littlefield).
Neumann, P. & Smith, M.L.R. (2008) *The Strategy of Terrorism: How it Works, and Why it Fails* (London, Routledge).
Pape, R. (2005) *'Dying to Win': The Strategic Logic of Suicide Terrorism* (New York, Random House).
Pape, R. & Feldman, J. (2010) *Cutting the Fuse: The Explosion of Global Suicide Terrorism and How to Stop it* (Chicago, University of Chicago Press).
Pedazhur, A. (ed.) (2006) *The Root Causes of Suicide Terrorism: The Globalization of Martyrdom* (Abingdon, Routledge).
Politkovskaya, A. (2001) *A Dirty War: A Russian Reporter in Chechnya* (London, Harvill Press).
Rechkalov, V. (2004) 'My Khotim Sovershit' Vzryvy v Gorode Mozdoke ...', *Izvestiya*, 12 August, p. 5, available at: http://www.izvestia.ru/incident/article265260/, accessed 20 April 2012.
Reuter, J. (2004) 'Chechnya's Suicide Bombers: Desperate, Devout, or Deceived?', *American Committee for Peace in Chechnya*, available at: http://www.jamestown.org/uploads/media/Chechen_Report_FULL.pdf, accessed 20 August 2010.
Richardson, L. (2006) *What Terrorists Want: Understanding the Enemy, Containing the Threat* (New York, Random House).
Saradzhyan, S. (2003) 'Suspected Organiser of July Attack Held', *Moscow Times*, 21 August, p. 3.
Sergievskii, S. (2004) 'Bomba dlya prezidenta', *Nezavisimaya Gazeta*, 7 April.
Sharia News Agency (2003a) 'We will be Forcing Russians to Peace ...', 8 September 2003, available at: http://old.kavkazcenter.com/eng/content/2003/09/08/1647.shtml, 8 November 2004.
Sharia News Agency (2003b) 'FSB HQ in Ingushetia was Exploded by Nogai Family', 23 September, available at: http://old.kavkazcenter.com/eng/content/2003/09/23/1691.shtml, accessed 8 November 2004.
Shermatova, S. & Tate, A. (2003) 'Eshyo Troe iz Baraevskikh', *Moskovskie Novosti*, 41, 21 October.

Shihab, S. (2000) 'Le représentant du président tchétchène, Ilias Akhmadov: On ne pas peut contrôler une vague de suicides', *Le Monde*, 5 July.
Sokirianskaia, E. (2008) 'Ideology and Conflict: Chechen Political Nationalism Prior to, and During, Ten Years of War', in Gammer, M (ed.) (2008) *Ethno-Nationalism, Islam and the State in the Caucasus: Post-Soviet Disorder* (London, Routledge), pp. 102–38.
Souleimanov, E. (2007) *An Endless War: The Russian-Chechen Conflict in Perspective* (Peter Lang, Frankfurt).
Souleimanov, E. & Ditrych, O. (2008) 'The Internationalisation of the Russian–Chechen Conflict: Myths and Reality', *Europe-Asia Studies*, 60, 7, pp. 1199–222.
Tishkov, V. (2004) *Chechnya: Life in a War-Torn Society* (London, University of California Press).
Udugov, M. (2003) 'Why Do Chechen Mujahideen Blow Themselves Up', *Kavkaz Tsentr*, 16 January, available at: http://www.kavkazcenter.com/eng/content/2003/01/16/800.shtml, accessed 6 January 2009.
Wilhelmsen, J. (2005) 'Between a Rock and a Hard Place: The Islamisation of the Chechen Separatist Movement', *Europe-Asia Studies*, 57, 1, pp. 35–59.
Williams, B. (2003) 'Jihad and Ethnicity in Post-Communist Eurasia: On the Trail of Transnational Islamic Holy Warriors in Kashmir, Afghanistan, Central Asia, Chechnya and Kosovo', *The Global Review of Ethnopolitics*, 2.
Yandarbiyev, Z. (2003) 'Chechen People have the Right to Their Defence', *Kavkaz Tsentr*, 17 June, available at: http://old.kavkazcenter.com/eng/content/2003/06/17/1431.shtml, accessed 8 November 2004.
Yarlykapov, A. (2007) 'Separatism and Islamic Extremism in the Ethnic Republics of the North Caucasus', *Russian Analytical Digest*, 22, pp. 6–11.
Yemelianova, G. (2002) *Russia and Islam: A Historical Survey* (London, Routledge).
Yemelianova, G. (ed.) (2010) *Radical Islam in the Former Soviet Union* (London, Routledge).
Yuzik, Y. (2003) 'Women Shahids of Nord Ost', *Komsomolskaya Pravda*, 22 October, available at: http://kp.ru/daily/23142/24174/, accessed 10 June 2011.

# List of Contributors

VICKEN CHETERIAN is the Director of CIMERA, a Geneva-based institution specialising in political governance (http://www.cimera.org). He holds a PhD from the Graduate Institute of International and Development Studies, Geneva. His research interests are contemporary political evolutions of post-Soviet space and the Arab world, including armed conflicts, environment and security, media and democratisation. His latest publications are *War and Peace in the Caucasus, Russia's Troubled Frontier* (Hurst & Columbia University Press, 2009) and the edited volume *From Perestroika to Rainbow Revolutions, Reform and Revolution after Socialism* (Hurst, forthcoming). *Address*: CIMERA, 1, Rue du Vuache, P.O. Box 1242, 1211 Geneva 1, Switzerland.

ANDREW FOXALL is Lecturer in Human Geography at Queen's University, Belfast. He holds a BSc (Hons) from the University of Plymouth, an MSc from the University of Birmingham and a DPhil from the University of Oxford. His research encompasses two main areas—geopolitics of ethnicity and nationalism, and the political geographies of energy and the environment—that are brought together through an empirical focus on post-Soviet Russia. *Address*: School of Geography, Archaeology and Palaeoecology, Queen's University Belfast, Elmwood Avenue, Belfast BT7 1NN, UK.

TRACEY GERMAN is a Senior Lecturer in the Defence Studies Department at the Joint Services Command and Staff College, King's College London. Her research interests include security in the Caucasus region, the impact of the Chechen conflict and energy security in the former Soviet states. Publications include *Regional Cooperation in the South Caucasus: Good Neighbours or Distant Relatives?* (Ashgate Publishing Ltd, 2012), *Russia's Chechen War* (Routledge, 2003) and the co-authored *Securing Europe: Western Interventions towards a New Security Community* (IB Tauris, 2009), as well as articles in journals such as *European Security, Small Wars and Insurgencies, Central Asian Survey, Vestnik analitiki* and *Politique étrangère*. *Address*: Defence Studies Department, King's College London at the Joint Services Command and Staff College, Faringdon Road, Shrivenham SN6 8TS, UK.

BRIAN GRODSKY is currently an Associate Professor of Comparative Politics at University of Maryland, Baltimore County, and a graduate of University of Michigan, Ann Arbor (PhD, August 2006). His research interests include human rights, transitional justice, democratisation, global civil society, social movements and US foreign policy. His two books include *The Costs of Justice* (University of Notre Dame Press, 2010) and *Social Movements and the New State: The Fate of Pro-Democracy Organizations When Democracy is Won* (Stanford University Press, 2012). His articles have appeared in journals including *European Journal of International Relations, Journal of Peace Research, Government and Opposition, Journal of Human Rights, Slavic Review, International Studies Review, Human Rights Review, World Affairs, Problems of Post-Communism, Central Asian Survey* and *Journal of Central Asian Studies*. *Address*: Department of Political Science, University of Maryland, Baltimore County 1000 Hilltop Circle, Baltimore, MD 21250, USA.

NINO KEMOKLIDZE is a PhD candidate at the Centre for Russian and East European Studies (CREES), University of Birmingham. In 2010–2011, she was a visiting researcher at the Department of Russian and Eurasian Studies, Norwegian Institute of Foreign Affairs (NUPI) in Oslo. Her dissertation topic concerns problems of nationalism and ethnic violence in Georgia. She has also published on the issues concerning self-determination and secession in Kosovo, Abkhazia and South Ossetia. She holds an MA degree in International Relations with Peace and Conflict Studies specialisation from the Australian National University and an MSc in Nationalism Studies from the University of Edinburgh. *Address*: Centre for Russian and East European Studies, School of Government and Society, Muirhead Tower, University of Birmingham, Edgbaston, Birmingham B15 2TT, UK.

CERWYN MOORE is a Senior Lecturer in International Relations at the University of Birmingham. He works on interpretive IR theory, critical approaches to security and conflict in the Caucasus and Central Asia. He has published widely on aspects of the conflicts in the North Caucasus, in journals such as *Studies in Conflict and Terrorism*, *International Affairs* and the *Journal of Communist Studies and Transition Politics*. His monograph, *Contemporary Violence: Post-modern War in Kosovo and Chechnya* (Manchester University Press), and co-edited (with Chris Farrands) collection, *International Relations Theory and Philosophy: Interpretive Dialogues* (Routledge), were both published in 2010. His work on IR theory has been published in leading journals including *Alternatives* and the *British Journal of Politics and International Relations*. *Address*: Department of Political Science and International Studies, School of Government and Society, Muirhead Tower, University of Birmingham, Edgbaston, Birmingham B15 2TT, UK.

ANTON POPOV received his PhD in Russian and East European Studies from the University of Birmingham. His research interests are in social anthropology (with a particular focus on post-socialist societies); memory studies; identity and transnationalism; and ethnicity and (non-Western forms of) civil society. He has conducted ethnographic research in Russia, Turkey, the United Kingdom and the South Caucasus. He has published a number of journal articles and chapters in edited volumes. *Address*: Department of Sociology, The University of Warwick, Coventry CV4 7AL, UK.

NONA SHAHNAZARIAN is a Lecturer in Social Anthropology at the Kuban Socio-Economic Institute, Krasnodar, Russia. She was an Associate Researcher at the Center for Caucasian and Pontic Studies from 1999 to 2010. Her main academic interests are ethnographic method, economic anthropology and gender studies. Her recent publications include the book *In the Tight Embrace of Tradition: Patriarchy and War* (KSEI/CISR 'Aleteia', 2011). *Address*: Kuban Socio-Economic Institute, Krasnodar, Russian Federation.

JEREMY SMITH is Professor of Russian History and Politics at the Karelian Institute, University of Eastern Finland. He has recently completed projects on the Khrushchev era and on Georgian nationalism and Soviet power in the 1950s. His research focuses on the non-Russian nationalities of the Soviet Union, with especial emphasis on the South Caucasus region, and he is also part of a team providing commentary and insight into contemporary relations between Europe and Central Asian countries in the 'EU-Central Asia Monitoring' project. His latest book, *Red Nations: the Nationalities Experience in and after the USSR* will be published by Cambridge University Press at the end of 2012. *Address*: Karelian Institute, University of Eastern Finland, Joensuu campus, P.O. Box 111, FI-80101 Joensuu, Finland.

THOMAS DE WAAL is Senior Associate in the Russia and Eurasia Program of the Carnegie Endowment for International Peace, Washington DC. He is a writer and analyst on the Caucasus, Russia and the Black Sea region. He is the author, most recently, of *The Caucasus: An Introduction* (Oxford University Press, 2010). In the 1990s, de Waal worked as a journalist in Moscow, specialising in Russian politics and events in Chechnya. He is the co-author with Carlotta Gall of *Chechnya, A Small Victorious War* (Picador, 1997) and sole author of *Black Garden: Armenia and Azerbaijan through Peace and War* (New York University Press, 2003). He has also worked for the BBC World Service and for the NGOs, the Institute for War and

Peace Reporting and Conciliation Resources. *Address*: Carnegie Endowment for International Peace, 1779 Massachusetts Avenue NW, Washington, DC 20036-2103, USA.

LALE YALCIN-HECKMANN studied sociology in Istanbul and anthropology at the London School of Economics. She worked at universities and research institutes in Germany and Turkey and currently is Docent at the University of Pardubice, Czech Republic. She is the author of *Tribe and Kinship among the Kurds* (Peter Lang, 1991), *The Return of Private Property: Rural Life after Agrarian Reforms in the Republic of Azerbaijan* (2010), is co-author of *Die Kurden: Geschichte, Politik, Kultur* (with Martin Strohmeier, C.H. Beck, 2000), co-editor of *Caucasus Paradigms: Anthropologies, Histories and the Making of a World Area* (with Bruce Grant, LIT Verlag, 2010), and numerous articles on Kurds, migration, Islam in Europe, and the anthropology of the Caucasus. *Address*: University of Pardubice, Studentska 95, 532 10 Pardubice 2, Czech Republic.

GALINA M. YEMELIANOVA is Senior Lecturer in Eurasian Studies at the Centre for Russian and East European Studies at the University of Birmingham. She heads the University of Birmingham Research Group on the Caucasus and Central Asia and teaches an MSc Pathway on the Caucasus and Central Asia. She has been researching history and contemporary politics in the Middle East and Muslim Eurasia for more than two decades. Her publications include *Yemen During the First Ottoman Rule (1538–1635)* (Nauka Press, 1988), *Russia and Islam: A Historical Survey* (Palgrave, 2002), *Islam in Post-Soviet Russia: Public and Private Faces* (co-editor and co-author, Routledge Curzon, 2003) and *Radical Islam in the former Soviet Union* (Routledge, 2010). *Address*: Centre for Russian and East European Studies, School of Government and Society, Muirhead Tower, University of Birmingham, Edgbaston, Birmingham B15 2TT, UK.

ULRIKE ZIEMER is a Lecturer in Sociology at the University of Winchester. Previously, she has worked as a Postdoctoral Research Fellow at the Centre for East European Language Based Area Studies (CEELBAS), School of Slavonic and East European Studies (SSEES), University College London. Her publications include the monograph *Ethnic Belonging, Gender and Cultural Practices: Youth Identities in Contemporary Russia* (ibidem Verlag, 2001). *Address*: University of Winchester, Sparkford Road, Winchester SO22 4NR, UK.

# Index

Note:
Page numbers in *italic* type represent tables

Abashidze, A. 27
Abdullaev, N. 173
Abdullayev, S. 175
Abdurrakhmanova, J. 16
Abkhazia 2, 6–11, 18–27, 40; armed forces 45; bases 40, 44–50; Battalion 178; border guards 47; and Georgia 22–4, 33; power struggle 24, 54; Russian military 31, 35; sovereignty recognition 33–4, 44, 48
Abramov, S. 190
Afghanistan 31, 64, 176, 186
Aivazishvili, N. 123
Ajaria 20, 104; Muslim 101
Akhaltisikhe Muslims 104
Akhmadov brothers 176, 179–83; death of Ramzan 182, *see also* Islamic Battalions
al-Qaeda 30, 186
Alekseyeva, L. 149
Aliev, H. 23, 26–8, 106
Aliev, I. 17, 28, 34
ALPE Foundation 85, 89–90
Amnesty International 149, 151, 152
Anderson, B. 8
Ankvab, A. 48
Arab volunteers 173, 184; Ingush 184, 187, 189; *jihadi* 176; *mujahedeen* 176–7
*Argumenty nedeli* (newspaper) 44–5
armed forces: Abkhazia 45
Armenia 2, 6–11, 16–21, 35, 51; and Azerbaijan 2, 6–7, 11, 16, 21–8, 35, 50–1, 110; Hamshen 144; refugees integration 118–19; sovereignty 22, 34; territorial demands 21, 34, *see also* Nagorno-Karabakh
Armenian refugee integration 118–19
arms race 28–32
Astemirov, A. 15–16
autochthonous conception 131; Cossack status 137
Azerbaijan 2, 6–7, 11, 21–2, 35, 50–1, 122; -Armenia conflict 2, 6–7, 9, 11, 16, 21–8, 35, 50–1, 110; base importance 30; -Georgia citizenship 123–4; military spending increase 31; Nagorno-Karabakh 2–7, 17–19, 23–5; nationalism 21, 36, 103; petty traders 124–5; Popular Front 23, 36; post-Soviet 101; recognition 34; resolution discussions 26

Bagapsh, S. 48
Baghdasaryan, M. 118–19
Baker, J. 82
Baku-Tbilisi-Ceyhan pipeline 7, 31, 122
*Banchuks* 136–9, 143–4
Baranov, V. 190
Barayev, A. 176–82; death 182; gang 185, *see also* SPIR
Barth, F. 133
Basaev, S. 27, 172–4, 178, 182–6, 189–94; *Riyad-us-Saliheyn* martyr battalion 174, 183–8, 191–4
Bassin, M. 150
Beck, U. 71
Beissinger, M. 18
Beria, L. 106
Beria, S. 108
blockades 25
Boden, D. 26
Boeck, B. 132, 145
Bokeria, G. 89
Bolshevik invasion 4
Bolsheviks 108, 112, 145; invasions 100–1, 106; policy towards Cossacks 131–2; Transcaucasian 108
Bondarev, V. 154
border guards 47, 119; Abkhazia 47
border nationalisms 122–4
borderlands 122–4; Azerbaijan-Georgia citizenship 123–4; and boundary definitions 132; bridge function 123; Georgia 122–4; guards 47, 119; petty traders 115, 124–5; regimes 117–18; Turkish-Georgian-Armenian nationalism 122–3
borders: integration projects 100–1
Bota, L. 26
boundaries: and communities 132–3

# INDEX

boundary definitions 132
British Petroleum (BP) 28, 110
Brubaker, R. 166; and Cooper, F. 59
Burjanadze, N. 74
Butler, J. 60

Carothers, T. 76
Carrière d'Encausse, H. 4
Catherine the Great 109
Caucasian Federal Highway 163
Caucasian War (1816–64) 137
Caucasus Research Group 11, 117
ceasefire agreements 23–5, 34; Karabakh 37; Medvedev-Sarkozy 49
Centre for East European Language Based Studies (CEELBAS) 148; Doctoral Studentship 151; network 10
Centre for Russian and East European Studies (CREES) 1
Chebankova, E. 149
Chechen Republic of Ichkeria (ChRI) 175–9, 184, 190
Chechensky, L-A. 192
Chechnya 5–6, 10, 16–17, 119, 142, 150–2, 160–1, 165; crisis eruptions 177–9; hostages and brutality 8; Ingush Autonomous Republic 19; military *jama'ats* 183–94; nationalism 27; rebels 9, 25–7, 31; Republic of Ichkeria (ChRI) 175–9, 184, 190; and Russia 2, 9, 12, 16, 22–7; Russian invasion 5, 37; Second War 150–1, 161–2; sovereignty 32; suicide operations 12, 162, 170–95; unification and Dagestan 178–9; union republic status 20; wars (1990s) 7, 18, 29, 170–95
Cheterian, V. 10, 15–39
Christianity 2
Cipko, S.: and Derluguian, G. 129
citizenship 114–28; absent 121, 125; Armenian refugee integration 118–19; border nationalisms 122–4; components 116; contrasting concepts 119; cultural and political 123–4; grievance-based 121; mobility restrictions in Georgia 119–20; out-migration challenges 120–6; and petty traders 115, 124–5; regimes 115–17; research and findings 117–18; South Caucasus 114–26
Civil Society Institute 85, 88
class 116
Clinton, President W. (Bill) 29
colour revolutions 76
combine-and-rule policy 105
commitment problem 9
Commonwealth of Independent States (CIS) 24, 35, 43
communities: and boundaries 132–3

Conflict Management Group 152
conflictology 11, 114–15
conflicts 2, 15–39, 104, 110; ancient hatreds 21; Azerbaijani-Armenian 2, 9, 16, 22–8, 110; ethnic theories 2, 8–9; ethno-religious 2; Georgia-Abkhaz 7–9; Georgia-South Ossetia 7–9; and histories 9; impacts on young soldiers 57–71; Ingush-Ossetian 2, 6; internationalisation 28–32; Kyrgyz-Uzbek 7; Nagorno-Karabakh 2–11, 16–27, 31, 36, 51–4, 110; origins 15–37; resolution attempts 23–8, 112; Russian-Georgian war 2; Russo-Chechen 2; and state-building 23–8; territorial 2; triangular 10, 17–23, *see also* ethnic conflicts
Congress of Peoples of Dagestan and Ichkeria 177
Cooper, F.: and Brubaker, R. 59
Cornell, S.: and Starr, F. 150–1
Correlates of War Project 7
corruption/fraud 35, 81–4, 87, 110, 165; judiciary 90; legacy 84
*Cossack Encyclopaedia, The* (Gubarev and Skrylov) 131
Cossack peoples 11–12, 129–47; *Banchuks* 136–9, 143–4; Bolsheviks policy towards 131–2; Caucasian rejection/separatism 140–2, 145; Caucasus appropriation 137–9; dress 139; ethnic boundaries 132–3; frontier communities 132–3; frontier genealogies 142–4; Great Brotherhood 142; historical re-enactments on Black Sea coast 136–7; identity 131–2; identity ethnicisation 131–2; *Kazakiitsy* ideas 131; KKV 134–7, 142; *korenizatsiya* 133; Krasnodar *Krai* 134, 137, 140; Kuban Host 130–1, 134–6, 154; *Kuren* 139–41; migrant origins 133; movement rebirth 154; nativism 133; neo- 129, 133–6; Sochi 135; Terek 154; traditions 136–9; White 131, 134; and xenophobia 138–40
Council of Europe (CoE) 110
crimes: violent 156, *158*
Croatia 110
Czech Charter 76

Dagestan 119, 161, 177, 184; attacks by Khattab 177–9; and Chechen unification 178–9; Salafi community 177
Dagomys Agreement (1992) 24
Dashnaks 104
David the Builder, King of Georgia 102
De Waal, T. 3, 11, 61, 99–113
Demirchian, K. 106
democracies 74–98; co-options 78; early phases 75; Georgia's path 80–95; and NGOs 74–95; non- 75–8; policies and civil

# INDEX

society 75–8; relationship forging 78–80; transition to state 78–80
Denisov, A. 48
Derluguian, G.: and Cipko, S. 129
discrimination 20; education quota system 164–5; and everyday relations 156–66; housing 158–61; movement restrictions 159–60; passport checks 159–60
displacement *see* refugees
divide-and-rule policies 104
Doijashvili, Z. 15
Dolidze, A. 91
Dudayev, D. 6; assassination 175
Duduyeva, M. 181
*Dzhennet* group 184

education quota system: discrimination 164–5
Egalitarian Institute 85
Elchibey, A. 23
elections 28, 48; free 116; Georgia 28, 82–3
elites, new 34–7
*émigrés* 4, 9; publications 101
enlargement fatigue 110
Erekle II, King of Georgia 100–2
ethnic boundaries: Cossack 132–3
ethnic conflict 8–9, 23, 142; and *ethnopolitika* 150; everyday relations and discrimination 156–66; and frontiers 141–4; hatred 15; landlords attitudes 158–61, *159–60*; likelihood factors identified 8–9; mobilisation justification 18–19; post-Soviet relations 153–6; racist and neo-Nazi attacks 154–7, *155–7*; and research 151–2; theories 9; violent crimes with hate motive *158*
ethnicity: functional 145
ethnos theory 133; boundaries and communities 132–3; and Cossack identity 131–2; frontier 141; and functional ethnicity 145
European Union (EU) 40, 46, 55, 89; Monitoring Mission 49; Transport Corridor Europe-Caucasus-Asia (TRASECA) 110
everyday relations: and discrimination 156–66
exports: gas/oil 29

Fathi al-Shishani, Shaykh Ali 176–8, 183
Fearon, J. 9
Federal Migration Service 141, 149
federations: failed 102–4
Forest Brothers 27
Former Political Prisoners for Human Rights 85
Foxall, A. 12, 148–69
fraud *see* corruption/fraud

Freedom House 84; Freedom in the World survey 93
frontier communities: Cossack 132–3
frontier genealogies: Cossack 142–4
frontiers: and ethnic conflict 141–4
funding: Georgia US 83, 92; NGOs 74–5, 83

Gabala radar station 42
Gadzhiev, G. 192
Galeyev, R. 185
Gammer, M. 27
Gamsakhurdia, Z. 15, 24, 33, 80, 81, 108
gas/oil fields 7, 36, 108; Caspian resources 28–9; and companies 35; deals 28–9; exports 29; kerosene 102; pipelines 28, 102, 107; revenues 29–31
Gaston Murdash group 192
Gazprom 110
Gazueva, E. 192
Gelayev, R. 28
genocide 62
Georgia 2, 6–7, 11, 24, 50; -Abkhazia conflict 7–9, 22–5, 33; aid 34; bloodshed and chaos 105; borderlands 122–4; Citizens' Union 82; Communist Party 106; democracy path 80–95; elections 28, 82–3; funding (US) 83, 92; for Georgians 15; highlands restricted mobility 119–20, 126; military spending increase 30–1; National Movement 20, 36, 74, 82, 89; NATO application 52–4; non-governmental organisations (NGOs) 80–95; out-migration 120–2, 125; and pro-democracy NGOs 80–95; recognition 34; Rose Revolution (2003) 11, 16, 24, 28–30, 74, 85, 94; Russian military bases 40–6; Russian war (Aug 2008) 2, 7, 11, 15–21, 27–8, 32–4, 107–10, 135; sanctions 107; -South Ossetia conflict 7–9, 23–4, 43–4; State Council 80; Supreme Court 84, 91; territorial integrity 33; Threat Assessment Document 53; Tiflis destruction 109; United Democrats 82; young reformers 74, 82
Georgian Young Lawyers Association (GYLA) 83–5, 90–2
German, T. 10, 40–56
Gibson, G.: and Somers, M. 60
Gorbachev, M. 61
Gorchkanov, I. 184
Gordian Knot 6
Gould, R. 133
Government-Organised Non-Governmental Organisations (GONGOs) 88
Grakali railway bridge 107
Grant, B. 142
Great Game centre 2–3
Great Power politics 109

# INDEX

Grodsky, B. 11, 74–98
Gromov, V. 134
Gubarev, G.: and Skrylov, A. 131
Gudeman, S. 125
Gumilev, L. 133–5
Gumri military base 25
Guntsadze, Z. 89–90
Gurr, E. 7

Hall, S. 59, 130, 133
Harbord, Gen J. 103, 107
hatred 15, 21, 156, *158*
Helsinki Committees 76; Moscow Group 149, 152
Holquist, P. 131
honour: and young soldiers 67–8
housing discrimination 158–61
Hovanissian, R. 4
human rights 165; European Court 110; US Annual Report 148; violations 87–9, 93–4
Human Rights Information and Documentation Centre 85

Ichkeria, Chechen Republic of (ChRI) 175–9, 184, 190
identity 115, 123; Cossack 11–12, 129–47
Ingiloy peoples 123–4
Ingush volunteers (*jama'at*) 184, 187, 189–90
Ingushetia 185; -Ossetia conflict 2, 6
Institute of Archaeology and Antiquity 1
Institute of Ethnology and Anthropology 152; Data-Bank 152
integration projects 99–113; Bolshevik invasion 4; borders 100–1; failed federations 102–4; failure reasons 106–11; most successful 112; region binding 100–2; Soviet 104–6; voluntary 109–11
International Olympics Committee (IOC) 52; and Sochi Winter (2014) 52
International Security Assistance Force (ISAF) 31
International Society for Fair Elections and Democracy (ISFED) 85–6
internationalisation: conflict 28–32
Irakli II 101
Iran 30, 35, 101–2, 108, 112
Iraq 30–1
Iron Curtain 122
Isaev, H. 190
Islam 2, 101; Akhaltiskhe 104; nationalist forces 17; radical 150; Salafi and IIPB 175–9, 182–4, 191; *Shari'ah* Law/Guard 175–6, 179; Sufi brotherhoods 179–80; Sunni Muslims 2; volunteers 3, 173, 184, *see also* Salafi
Islamic Battalions 172–4, 178–83, 193

Islamic International Peacekeeping Brigade 178
Islamic Nation 177
Islhan-Yurt festival 186
Ismailov, E.: and Papava, V. 101
Israel 71
*Izvestiya* (newspaper) 44

*jama'ats*: Chechnya military 183–94; and terrorism 183–94
*jihadi* volunteers 176
*jihadism* 2, 29, 176; ideologies 18, 27; *Salafi* 27, 32, 175; Saudi Arabia community 182
Joint Peacekeeping Forces (JPKF) 24–5
Judaism 2

Kadyrov, A. 31, 178–81; assassination 31, 186, 190
Kadyrov, R. 31, 186
Karabakh 9–21, 24, 34–7, 106, 118; Azerbaijani counter-attack (1993–4) 24–5; Baku-Moscow conflict 20; ceasefire agreement 37; Movement (Armenia) 36; post diplomacy 122; resolution attempts 28, *see also* Nagorno-Karabakh
Karasin, G. 49–50
Karosanidze, T. 92
*Kavkaz* (journal) 106
*Kazakiitsy* ideas 131
*Kazarla* (Cossack journal) 138
Kebedov, B. 177–9
Kemoklidze, N.: *et al* 1–14
kerosene 102
Key West summit (2001) 26–8
Khadzhimba, R. 47–8
Khalimov, I. 175, 178
Khasavyurt Peace Agreement (1996) 2, 16, 25–7, 175
Khattab (Saudi *mujahed*) 27, 176–9, 184; Dagestan attacks 177–9
Khusiev, M. 186
Kideckel, D. 121
Kishiev, Sheikh Kunta-Khadzhi 186
KKV 134–7, 142
Kocharian, R. 24–6
Kokoity, E. 47–8
Kokoshin, A. 43–4
*Komsomoloskya Pravda* 50
Kopytoff, I. 132
*korenizatsiya* 133
Kozyrev, A. 35
Krasnodar: *Krai* 134, 137, 140; Ukrainian Society 144
Kuban Cossack Host 130–1, 134–6, 154
Kublashvili, K. 91
Kupchan, C. 112
*Kuren* 139–41

# INDEX

Kuznetsov, I.: and Popov, A. 166
Kyrgyz-Uzbek conflict 7

labour migration 117, 120
Laitin, D.: and Suny, R. 8
land rights 122
landlords attitudes: and ethnic conflict 158–61, *159–60*
Lavrov, S. 52
legitimacy 81
Liberty Institute 85, 88–9, 93
Luzhkov, Y. 154

McFaul, M. 83
Mackridge, P.: and Yannakakis, E. 135
*Majlis-al-Shura* 180; Supreme State Defence Committee 182–4
Makasharipov, R. 184
Malashenko, A. 163
Malinowski, B. 57
Markedonov, S. 129–31, 153
Marshall, T.H. 115–17, 126; citizenship components 116–17
martyrs: *Riyad-us-Saliheyn* battalion 174, 183–8, 191–4; suicide attacks 170–95
Maskhadov, A. 26–7, 31–2, 175–84
Masood, S. 186
Mataradze, T. 120–1, 125
matrydom operations 170–95, *see also* suicide attacks
Medvedev, D. 5, 34, 40, 44, 47, 165; Federal Address (November 2009) 165; -Sarkozy ceasefire agreement 49
Mensheviks 103–4, 110
Merabishvili, V. 49
Mezhidov, A-M. 175–7
Middle East 4; train-and-equip militants 29; and War on Terror 29–30
migration 41, 131; Caucasian 139; and discrimination 156–66; ethnic 140; forced 117; insecurity 120; labour 117, 120; legacy 160–1; out 118–22, 125; and post-Soviet ethnic relations 153–6; Stavropol as destination 149; theory 131
military *jama'ats*: Chechnya 183–94
Minorities at Risk (MAR) database 7
*Mkhedrioni* 24
mobilisation 35; Georgian 20; justification 18–19
mobility: restrictions (Georgia) 119–20, 126; and Tushetians 119–20
*modus vivendi* 101
Moldova 7
Moore, C. 12, 170–97
Moran, D.: *et al* 165
Moscow: Centre for Ethnopolitical Studies 158; metro attack (2010) 16, 32, 190–2

Movement Against Illegal Immigration 153
movement restrictions 159–60, *see also* mobility
Mühlfried, F. 119, 123
*mujahedeen* volunteers 176–7
Musavatists 104
Muslims 101, 104; Sunni 2
MVD units 181

Nagorno-Karabakh: Autonomous *Oblast* 23, 31; Azerbaijan campaign/defeat 23–5, 51, 110; ceding 36; conflict 2–11, 16–27, 31, 36, 51–4, 110; conflict origins 8; status 17; young soldiers 57–73
Namitok, A. 101–2
nationalism 18–19, 27, 62, 103; Azerbaijan 21, 36, 103; border 122–4; Chechnya 27; ethno- 114, 150; exclusivist 23; Georgian 108; growth 142; particularist 145; Russian neo- 153–4; Turkish-Georgian-Armenian 122–3
neo-Nazi attacks 154–7, *155–7*
Nesterov, V. 148
Network of Ethnological Monitoring and Early Warning for Prevention of Conflicts (EAWARN) 151–2
*Nezavisimaya Gazeta* (newspaper) 45–6
Nikitin, V. 142
*nomenklatura* (Soviet) 17–19, 23, 34; Georgian 24
non-democracies 75–8
non-governmental organisations (NGOs) 11, 36; accountability 77; and democracies 74–95; functions 76–80; funding 74–5, 83; Georgia 80–95; and Georgian state officials 86; Government-Organised (GONGO) 88; hybrids 90–2; politics and civil society 75–8; pro-democracy fate 74–98; relationship forging 78–80, 84–7; service providers 88–90; transition to state 78–80; watchdogs 87–8
North Atlantic Treaty Organisation (NATO) 2–3, 30, 40, 46, 52–5, 109; Bucharest summit (2008) 43; enlargement 2, 54; Georgia's application 52–4; Strategic Concept 53–4
North Caucasus Federal District 11–12, 150; and Military District (NCMD) 44
North Ossetia 6

Obama, B. 33
Ochamchire naval base 46, 54
oil fields *see* gas/oil fields
O'Loughlin, J.: and Wittmer, F. 163
Open Society Georgia Foundation 83, 89
Operation Boomerang 172–4, 185–95

# INDEX

Organisation for Security and Cooperation in Europe (OSCE) 26, 49, 152; Istanbul summit (2000) 31; Minsk Group 26, 34
Orjonikidze, G. 104–5
Ottoman invasions 103; Third Army 103, 109
out-migration 118–22, 152; from Georgia 120–2, 125
Ozgen, N. 122

Palestine 71
Pallot, J. 151
Panorama research centre 152
Papava, V.: and Ismailov, E. 101
Pape, R. 172
Pasha, E. 103, 109
passport checks 159–60
Peoples Commissariat for Internal Affairs (NKVD) 106
*perestroika* 154
Peter the Great 100
petty traders 115, 124–5; and citizenship 115, 124–5
pile-sorting 119
pipelines 28, 111; Baku-Tbilisi-Ceyhan 7, 31, 122; gas/oil 28, 102, 107; kerosene 102
Polish Workers' Defence Committee 76
Political Science and International Studies (POLSIS) Department 1
politics: young soldiers 66–70
Popov, A. 11–12, 129–47; and Kuznetsov, I. 166
poverty 110, 115; chronic 111; reduction programme 121
Powell, C. 26
power centralisation 2–5
Pulitzer Centre on Crisis Reporting 152
purchasing power parity (PPP) 109
Putin, V. 5, 27, 45, 190

racist and neo-Nazi attacks 154–7, *155–7*
Raduyev, S. 176–7
railways 111
Rajbaddinov, J. 178
Ramishvili, L. 88–9
rank-and-file participants 9
rebels: Chechnya 9, 25–7, 31
refugees 115–19; displacement trauma 119; integration in Armenia 118–19
regional integration 11
Rehabilitation of Oppressed Peoples and Cossacks Bill (Russia 1992) 134
Reuter, J. 173, 181
revenues: gas/oil 29–31
rights: human 87–9, 93–4, 110, 148, 165; land 122
*Risk Society* (Beck) 71

*Riyad-us-Saliheyn* martyr battalion 174, 183–8, 191–4
Rogozin, D. 53
Rose Revolution (Georgia 2003) 11, 16, 24, 28–30, 74, 85, 94
Russia 2, 21–2, 102; Army 106, 109; Black Sea Fleet (BSF) 46, 55; Border Guard Service (FSB) 46, 52; -Chechnya conflict 2, 9, 12, 16, 22–7, 24–7, 170–95; Constitution 148; divide and rule policy 21; *Duma* 48; Federal Security Service (FSB) 186, 190; Federation (KPRF) 6, 41–2, 46, 119, 135, 153, 165; Foreign Policy Concept 42; -Georgia war (Aug 2008) 2, 7, 11, 15–21, 27–8, 32–4, 107–10, 135; Imperialism 7; internal abroad 163; Liberal Democratic Party (LDPR) 153; *lingua franca* 101, 106, 109; National Security Strategy (NSS) 41, 51; Near Abroad 16, 35, 40; neo-nationalism 153–4; policy 10–11, 40–56; Rehabilitation of Oppressed Peoples and Cossacks Bill (1992) 134; sanctions against Georgia 107; security forces 15; southern underbelly 50–1; state border strengthening 46–50; strategic backyard 42; winners and losers 51–4
Russian Academy of Sciences (RAS) 152
Russian military: Abkhazia 31, 35; Armenia (Gumri) base 25; Georgia bases 40–6; levers 42–6; presence 31; South Caucasus bases 40–6, *43*
Russian Military Doctrine 42
Russian National Unity 153–4
Russo-Chechen 2
Rustambeili, S. 106
Rustavi-2 television station 5, 82

Saakashvili, M. 30, 33–4, 37, 43, 83–4, 89–90, 108; government and Ergneti market 111; New National Movement 74, 82
Salafi: Dagestan community 177; and IIPB 175–9, 182–4, 191; *jihadism* 27, 32, 175
sanctions: Russian against Georgia 107
Saparov, A. 104–5
Sardarapat, Battle (1918) 103
Sargasyan, Pres S. 26, 51
Sargsyan, V. 26
Saudi Arabia community 182
Saudi *mujahed* (Khattab) 27, 176–9, 184
Sayat Nova 101
Sayfullah, A. 184–5
Sayyaf, A. 176
separatism 22
Serbia 110
service providers: NGOs 88–90
Shahnazarian, N.: and Ziemer, U. 11, 57–73
Shamba, S. 48

# INDEX

Shamil Abu Idris, Amir 185
Sharipova, M. 16
Shevardnadze, E. 24, 29–30, 33, 74, 80–8, 93–4; basic service provision failure 81–2; corruption charges 81–4, 90; democratic reform dedication 81; resignation 74
Shnukov, V. 150
Singer, J.D. 7
Skrylov, A.: and Gubarev, G. 131
Smith, J. 104
Sochi 135; Winter Olympics (2014) 52
socialism 121
soldiers *see* young soldiers
Somers, M.: and Gibson, G. 60
Soros, G. 83
South Caucasus republics 11, 40–2; and citizenship 114–26; Russian military bases 40–6, *43*; Russian policy 41–2
South Ossetia 2, 6–11, 17–18, 21–5, 35, 40–1; Autonomous Republic status 20, 105; border guards 47; -Georgia conflict 7–9, 23–4, 43–4; military bases 40, 44–50; motor-rifle 693rd brigade 45; Russian military 31; sovereignty recognition 33–4, 44, 48
SOVA Center for Information and Analysis 152, 166
sovereignty 32, 115; Abkhazia 33–4, 44, 48; Armenia 22, 34; South Ossetia 33–4, 44, 48
Soviet Union 2, 8, 135; central system collapse 2–3, 8, 34; Georgian constitution (1925) 20; Great Patriotic War 132; integration projects 104–6; intelligentsia 17–18; political/military control 3; top-down integration 109; Transcaucasian Federative Republic (ZSFSR) 99, 104–8; troop withdrawal 21
Special Purpose Islamic Regiment (SPIR) 171–82
Stalin, Joseph 105
Starr, F.: and Cornell, S. 150–1
state: democracy transition to 78–80
state-building: and conflicts 23–8
Stavropol 11–12, 148–69; bomb attacks 148; demography and geography 152–3; education quota system 164–5; ethnic relations 148–66; landlords and housing attitudes 158–61, *159–60*; migration destination 149; National and Cossack Affairs Committee 150; passport origin checks 159–60; racist and neo-Nazi attacks 154–7, *155–7*; study methodological issues 151–2; Union of Slavic Communities 148, 154
Strabo 100
Sufi brotherhoods 179–80

suicide attacks 12, 162; adaptation and innovation 186–9; analysis 172–5; Chechen-related 12, 162, 170–95; failed 186–90; female 181, 190; insurgency and adoption of operations 179–83; Islhan-Yurt festival 186; and martyrdom 170–95; and military *jama'ats* 183–94; Moscow metro (2010) 16, 32, 190–2; Operation Boomerang 172–4, 185–95; *shaheeds* (bombers) 12, 162, 185; waves 174, *see also* terrorism
Sunni Muslims 2
Suny, R. 23; and Laitin, D. 8
Swizerland 112

Tajfel, H.: and Turner, J. 59
Tajikistan 7, 176
Taliban 30
Targamadze, G. 89
Tazabayev, K. 185
Taziev, A. 184
Ter-Petrossian, L. 18, 24–6; resignation 26
Terek 154
territorial claim validity 8
terrorism 6, 29; Aldy (Feb 2000) revenge 192–3; Beslan siege school 1, 32, 171, 191–3; Dubrovka House 171; hostage-taking 171; and *jama'ats* 183–94; Moscow 171, 189–91, 194; Mozdok 188; Nazran 188; Nord Ost siege 171, 174, 182–7, 191; truck-bombs 180–1, 185–8; Victory Day Parade (Grozny) 190; war on 29–30; Yessentuki train 188–9, 192; Znamenskoye 186, *see also* suicide attacks
Theology Department 1
Tikhomirov, A. 15–16
Tishkov, V. 9, 104–5, 150–2
Tokluoglu, C. 36
traders *see* petty traders
train-and-equip militants 29
Transcaucasian Democratic Federative Republic (ZSFSR) 99, 102–3, 104–8, 112; collapse 107
Transnistria 7, 106
Transparency International 85, 92
triangular conflicts 10, 17–23
Trufanov, V. 52
Tsagarayev, M. 181–2
Turkey 35, 50, 101–2, 108, 112, 122; AKP Justice and Development Party 110; Meskhetian 110
Turkish-Georgian-Armenian nationalism 122–3
Turner, B. 116
Turner, J.: and Tajfel, H. 59
Tushetians 119; and mobility 119–20

# INDEX

Udugov, M. 175–9, 182
Ukraine 53–5
United Arab Emirates (UAE) 112
United Nations (UN) 26; Association of Georgia 85, 88; High Commissioner for Refugees 118; mission to Abkhazia (UNOMIG) 28, 49; Secretary General 26
unmanned aerial vehicles (UAV) 32
upstreaming 132–3; ethnic 132, 145
US Agency for International Development (USAID) 89, 110
Uzbec-Kyrgyz conflict 7

Vansittart, R. 108–9
Vendina, O.: *et al* 150
Verkhovskii, A. 166
violent crimes with hate motive 156, *158*
*Voennaya Mysl'* (military journal) 50
volunteers: Arab 173, 184; Islamic 3, 173, 184; *jihadi* 176; *mujahedeen* 176–7

War on Terror 29–30
Wardrop, O. 4
Washington Treaty 53
White Cossacks 131, 134
White Legion 27
White, R. 132–3, 136
Wilson, Pres Woodrow 103
Wittmer, F.: and O'Loughlin, J. 163

Woodiwiss, A. 125

xenophobia 15; and Cossack peoples 138–40

Yalcin-Heckermann, L. 11, 114–28
Yamskov, A. 104–5
Yandarbiyev, Z. 175–9, 182
Yannakakis, E.: and Mackridge, P. 135
Yeltsin, B. 24–7, 41, 179
young soldiers 57–73; being a patriot 66–7; child statistics 57–8; conflict impact 57–71; coping and revenge 68–70; food rationing 64; and honour 67–8; identity and belonging 59–60, 66–70; killer justification 69; masculinity 68; Nagorno-Karabakh 57–73; politics 66–70; post guarding 65; recruitment 60–3; war narratives 63–6; weapons training 67–8

al-Zarqi, A. 178
Zhordania, N. 103
Zhvania, Z. 74; United Democrats 82
Ziemer, U.: and Shahnazarian, N. 11, 57–73
Zoroastrianism 2
Zürcher, C. 8–9, 12

www.routledge.com/9780415825719

*Related titles from Routledge*

## New Perspectives on Turkey-EU Relations

Edited by Chris Rumford

This book makes the case for looking afresh at Turkey-EU relations in order to appreciate the richness and complexity of a relationship which is now more than 50 years old and is still not close to reaching fulfilment. The contributors challenge imbalances in conventional attempts to understand Turkey-EU relations by offering both a global context and new perspectives on the drivers of domestic politics. It represents a shift from a narrow EU integration/enlargement agenda. The contributions, collected here, offer an interpretation of Turkey-EU relations from a novel perspective, utilize a new framework of theory, and draw upon insights and perspectives from disciplines underrepresented in mainstream study of Turkey-EU relations.

This book was published as a special issue of the *Journal of Contemporary European Studies*.

**Chris Rumford** is Professor of Political Sociology and Global Politics at Royal Holloway, University of London.

May 2013: 246 x 174: 104pp
Hb: 978-0-415-82571-9
£85 / $145

For more information and to order a copy visit
www.routledge.com/9780415825719

Available from all good bookshops